Language learning disabilities

# LANGUAGE LEARNING DISABILITIES

## Diagnosis and Remediation

# Contributors

Gail P. Harris-Schmidt

Barbara B. Hoskins

Suzanne Timble Major

Elizabeth A. Noell

Nancy J. Spekman

# LANGUAGE LEARNING DISABILITIES

## Diagnosis and Remediation

### Carol T. Wren
DePaul University
Evanston, Illinois

AN ASPEN PUBLICATION®
Aspen Systems Corporation
Rockville, Maryland
London
1983

Library of Congress Cataloging in Publication Data

Main entry under title:

Language learning disabilities.

Includes bibliographies and index.
1. Language disorders in children.
2. Learning disabilities. I. Wren, Carol T.
RJ496.L35L37  1983  618.92'855  83-2544
ISBN: 0-89443-935-9

Publisher: John Marozsan
Editorial Director: R. Curtis Whitesel
Executive Managing Editor: Margot Raphael
Editorial Services: Eileen Higgins, Martha Sasser
Printing and Manufacturing: Debbie Collins

Library of Congress Catalog Card Number: 83-2544
ISBN: 0-89443-935-9

*Printed in the United States of America*

1  2  3  4  5

To Doris J. Johnson

# Table of Contents

Preface . . . . . . . . . . . . . . . . . . . . . . . . . . . . . . . . . . . . . . . . . . . . . . . . . . .  ix

Chapter 1—Language and Language Disabilities . . . . . . . . . . . . . . . . . .  1
    *Carol T. Wren*

    Introduction . . . . . . . . . . . . . . . . . . . . . . . . . . . . . . . . . . . . . . . . . .  1
    Part I. Normal Language and Its Development  . . . . . . . . . . .  6
    Part II. Language Disorders . . . . . . . . . . . . . . . . . . . . . . . . . . . .  10
    Part III. Synthesis . . . . . . . . . . . . . . . . . . . . . . . . . . . . . . . . . . . .  25

Chapter 2—Phonology . . . . . . . . . . . . . . . . . . . . . . . . . . . . . . . . . . . . . . .  39
    *Gail P. Harris-Schmidt and Elizabeth A. Noell*

    Part I. Phonology and Learning Disabilities . . . . . . . . . . . . .  39
    Part II. Diagnosis . . . . . . . . . . . . . . . . . . . . . . . . . . . . . . . . . . . .  55
    Part III. Remediation . . . . . . . . . . . . . . . . . . . . . . . . . . . . . . . . .  71

Chapter 3—Semantics . . . . . . . . . . . . . . . . . . . . . . . . . . . . . . . . . . . . . . .  85
    *Barbara B. Hoskins*

    Part I. Semantics and Learning Disabilities . . . . . . . . . . . . . .  85
    Part II. Diagnosis . . . . . . . . . . . . . . . . . . . . . . . . . . . . . . . . . . . .  96
    Part III. Remediation . . . . . . . . . . . . . . . . . . . . . . . . . . . . . . . . .  103

Chapter 4—Morphology and Syntax . . . . . . . . . . . . . . . . . . . . . . . . . . . 113
    *Carol T. Wren*

    Part I. Syntax and Learning Disabilities . . . . . . . . . . . . . . . . . 113
    Part II. Diagnosis . . . . . . . . . . . . . . . . . . . . . . . . . . . . . . . . . . . . 136
    Part III. Remediation . . . . . . . . . . . . . . . . . . . . . . . . . . . . . . . . . 144

**Chapter 5—Discourse and Pragmatics** .......................... **157**
Nancy J. Spekman

    Part I. Pragmatics and Learning Disabilities .............. 158
    Part II. Diagnosis ................................. 184
    Part III. Remediation .............................. 200

**Chapter 6—Conceptualization** ............................... **217**
Gail P. Harris-Schmidt

    Part I. Conceptualization and Learning Disabilities ........ 217
    Part II. Diagnosis ................................. 229
    Part III. Remediation .............................. 235

**Chapter 7—Reading** ........................................ **243**
Elizabeth A. Noell

    Part I. Reading and Learning Disabilities ............... 243
    Part II. Diagnosis ................................. 267
    Part III. Remediation .............................. 279

**Chapter 8—Written Language** ............................... **297**
Suzanne Timble Major

    Part I. Written Language and Learning Disabilities ........ 297
    Part II. Diagnosis ................................. 308
    Part III. Remediation .............................. 318

**Index** ....................................................... **327**

# Preface

Since the late 1970s, educators and clinicians have displayed a dramatic increase in interest in language problems of children. Unfortunately, there is little literature available to help them translate this interest into sound diagnostic and remedial practices. Although it generally is recognized now that auditory verbal disorders can affect children's performances in virtually every area of achievement—especially in oral language, reading, spelling, and written language—little has been written that the professional or advanced graduate student can use to understand current research and to formulate a framework upon which to base diagnostic and remedial strategies. It is with this in mind that this book was written.

The notion of a language disability makes sense only if the separate terms of the phrase are properly understood. First of all, it is necessary to know something about the nature of language and its normal development. Then one must discover what is involved in the concept of a learning disability, which is understood here as a disturbance in the psychological processing of information. Finally, because the two concepts of oral language development and auditory processing disorder overlap, there emerges the concept of a language learning disability. This concept, namely, a disturbance in processing oral language, is the specific theme of this book.

Although this book concerns itself with a large subset of learning disabled children, namely, those whose processing deficit(s) interfere with spoken or written language performance, the authors do not wish to convey the impression that all learning disabilities result from a language disorder or subsequently interfere with language performance. For example, visual nonverbal or visual-motor deficits, attention disorders, and hyperactivity may not interfere with language development. Although the focus of the field of learning disabilities has shifted generally toward the long overdue recognition of the important place of language disorders, the problems of children with other sorts of deficits also need to be recognized so that appropriate remedial services can be provided.

The focus of the book is also, to some extent, upon language disorders in younger children—because the majority of research on language development and disorders investigates this age group. But because the authors wish to emphasize that subtle language problems often persist in learning disabled individuals into adulthood, examples and suggestions have been included where appropriate for working with older children.

The first chapter opens with a look at the field of language and its normal development in children in the areas of phonology, semantics, and syntax, as well as the joint areas of discourse and pragmatics. It then turns to a general explanation of learning disabilities, providing a model of information processing that highlights specific levels of deficits likely to interfere with learning. By weaving this model into the traditional language divisions just mentioned, the concept of oral language disability is developed. In other words, Chapter 1 describes the general relationships between processing information and oral language disabilities in phonology and the other language domains.

Specific interrelationships between learning disabilities and the oral language domains are the topics of the next four chapters: phonology (Chapter 2), semantics (Chapter 3), syntax (Chapter 4), and discourse and pragmatics (Chapter 5). Each analyzes approaches to the language area in question and applies current knowledge and research to discussions of diagnostic and remedial planning.

The final three chapters cover the relationship of oral language disabilities to children's higher level thinking skills (Chapter 6), to reading (Chapter 7), and to spelling and writing (Chapter 8). Given the notion of the printed word as a visual symbol system superimposed on an auditory language base, it is only to be expected that problems in either understanding or using spoken language would interfere with children's ability to read (understand printed symbols) or write (use printed symbols). It is for this reason that the final chapters are devoted to the interrelationships of oral language disabilities and thinking, reading, and writing.

Although the chapters are written by different authors, this book is no mere collection of essays. The authors share a common theoretical position regarding learning disabilities, and after the first one, all of the chapters have a common general format. Each chapter is designed to integrate current knowledge from the fields of child language development and psycholinguistics in an understandable fashion with a workable and comprehensive model of learning disabilities.

Each chapter opens by focusing on the information processing model introduced in the first chapter (Part I), then proceeds to its implications for diagnosis of both receptive and expressive problems in oral or written language (Part II). In each case this includes evaluations of available tests, both informal and formal, as to how they specifically provide information relevant to the model of learning disabilities. The chapters then shift to remediation (Part III), providing specific strategies for planning appropriate individualized corrective programs for problems in oral language as well as in higher level thinking skills, reading, or written language.

The three parts of each chapter thus are tied together in the form of practical suggestions for intervention that are based on diagnostic material as well as on observed interrelationships between language and information processing abilities.

The general structure of this book, as well as much of its substantive content, has been inspired by the work of Helmer R. Myklebust and, even more directly, by that of Doris J. Johnson. Since all the authors have had the privilege of working with her at one time or another, our debts to her are various and profound. Hence this book is dedicated to her.

We also would like to thank her, as well as Jim Flege, Joan Kardatzke, Reid Lyon, Bonnie Litowitz, and Thomas Wren for reading part or all of the manuscript and for their helpful suggestions. Of course, we must add the usual note that they should not be held responsible for what we have ventured to say in these pages. Finally, each of us has been supported by family, colleagues, and friends too numerous to mention but without whom this book could not have been written.

*Carol T. Wren, Ph.D.*
June, 1983

# Chapter 1

# Language and Language Disabilities

*Carol T. Wren*

## INTRODUCTION

Children with language learning disabilities exhibit a wide variety of oral language problems. Some have difficulty in language comprehension—typically, in understanding the specific meaning of words or the form of the sentences used. For example, the responses of Billy (age 4½) indicate lack of comprehension of the clinician's questions:

> Clinician: What swims in water?
> Billy: Beach.
> Clinician: What should you do when you cut your finger?
> Billy: With scissors.
> Clinician: Why do you need to wash your face and hands?
> Billy: With soap.
> Clinician: We eat at _____.
> Billy: Fish.
> Clinician: You drink out of a glass and you also drink out of a
>
> _____.
> Billy: Some milk.
> Clinician: You walk with your legs and throw with your _____.
> Billy: Ball.

Comprehension problems are not limited to preschoolers, however. Todd (8½) has difficulty understanding the clinician's question in this discussion of making chocolate milk:

> Todd: And then we poured it.
> Clinician: OK.

> Todd: And then we stirred and then . . .
> Clinician: What did we stir?
> Todd: We stir wif a spoon.

Comprehension problems frequently persist in older children, interfering with language in social as well as academic situations. This same child, Todd (now 14 in these next examples), still has difficulty carrying on conversations because of failure to comprehend.

> Clinician: Do you have any plans for the summer?
> Todd: Get a job.
> Clinician: What kind of a job?
> Todd: A busboy or do dishes.
> Clinician: Do you know where yet?
> Todd: Well, I forgot, some places. But it's kinda hard.
> Clinician: Are you going to be working near home?
> Todd: Oh, I'll be playing outside.

In the next example, language comprehension, discrimination, and thinking problems interact as Todd has difficulty identifying the verbal absurdity.

> Clinician (reading): It was a beautiful summer day and George decided to go swimming. He put on his bathing suit and dove into the warm water. After half an hour of swimming, he dried himself off on the shore and lay in the hot summer sun. Then he looked at the water and said, "Gee, I think I'll go ice skating."
> Todd: You can't drove into the warm water. You walk to it, you swim in warm water.

Older children with comprehension problems frequently have particular difficulty understanding the meaning of abstract words, a difficulty that is compounded when they are expected to learn the meaning of new ones through reading. Thus, children with oral language comprehension problems like Todd's have extreme difficulty learning word meanings while reading, as well as comprehending what they read.

> Todd has just read several paragraphs discussing the concept of "immigrant."
>
> Clinician: So how would you define "immigrant?"
> Todd: Well, like he's from a different side, right, of a country.
> Clinician: He came from another country.

Todd: Country, but he was born in this country.
Clinician: He was born in another country.
Todd: His family was born . . . his family was born, uh, from another country but he was born in this country.
Clinician: That's true of Henry. Right. But Henry isn't an immigrant. His parents are immigrants.
Todd: . . . grants.
Clinician: Why were they immigrants? What makes them immigrants?
Todd: Uh, well, because they live in Mexico.

Language disorders also frequently manifest themselves as a variety of expressive problems. Tim (5), for instance, has difficulty pronouncing the sounds that make up words:

Clinician: Tim, tell me a story.
Tim: I 'got no-er part. (I forgot another part.)
Clinician: Can you tell me another story?
Tim: I do' know no-er part.
Clinician: Just make one up.
Tim: 'my hou' Mike was puttin' crash-up derbies wif dese two goff balls and wif tennis balls too. An' we ro dem, and we we bomb! An' I optin (opened) my drawer and I saw a . . . saw a wa-i-pop. And Mike said, "Let's bof share it." An' I said "How we a share it?" "We'll ta a wick one a time." An' I said "Could haf a whole fing, Mike." And he doesn' wan it.

Some children have difficulty selecting words with the correct meaning. For example, one girl excitedly told the clinician, "Lots of kids in our class received chicken pox!" Joanne (6) gave the following account of a picture of a mother and daughter mixing a cake in a large bowl:

First you get the um, powder and see, they're putting it in the dish. Then they are stirring it up and pretty soon they'll mix it up. Then it, see they goofed. They . . . it poured all out. And then they put it in the pan, and put it in the stove, and pretty soon it'll get a cake.

Some children have no difficulty with articulation or word meanings but like Suzanne (7) have considerable difficulty putting words together to form correct English sentences.

The Three Bears and Goldilocks. Once upon a time, Red Riding . . . no, Goldilocks was walking through the path. Then she saw beautiful house. And they was sweeping up, then they taked a little walk. Then she went had some . . . tasted the father bowl. Then she taste the mother bowl. Then the baby was just right so eat it all gone.

Other children with oral language problems have difficulty formulating their ideas into coherent verbal descriptions or relating the events of a story in correct order. Fred's (11) explanation of anthropology and David's (10) narration of a television program are good examples.

Anthropologists studies different cultures. Um, they, they uh, they uh, classify people how they look and where they live. Um, Japan . . . wait American people, . . . Japanese, wait . . . American and Japanese are two cultures from many different cultures. They uh, like uh, American people shake hands to greet people and meet them. Um, people move one place to . . . place to place to look for a job. They don't not, they do not uh, stay close to home. Japanese bow to greet people. Uh, parents parents wait . . . OK . . . parents live with the oldest son . . . they . . . uh Japanese . . . does stay close to home.

There was two guys and they were planning a robbery and uh and they done . . . done the robbery. They broke into this hotel and they uh, brought all these uh . . . money and this guy who was a detective . . . he was uh, checking out the glass . . . and he found out who done it and the guy went to the . . . into the court and . . . but first thing um . . . the uh . . . he had to go to the apartment and then his house . . . And he's going to the jail and now he's in the courtroom. And he said he did it and so he had ten years in jail.

Some learning disabled children have difficulty not with word meanings or grammar but with the broader, communicative function of language. They may be able to formulate adequate sentences but are unaware of the information needed by the listener. In the following example involving two 13-year-old boys, John is trying to explain to Mike how to make a simple glider. There is a screen between them to prevent them from seeing each other.

John:  OK. I want you get one those blue strips.
Mike:  OK. What uh what uh size?
John:  Are there two sizes? Hmmm? You should have two the same size.
Mike:  Well I got news for you. I don't have a small one.
John:  Oh, come on!
Mike:  What?
John:  Get the biggest one. Now. Fold . . . make a little circle with it.

Mike: What?
John: OK. Take . . . you take your thumb.
Mike: What thumb?
John: Oh, both thumbs.
Mike: Both thumbs.
John: You stick 'em out like a Fonzie. Hey! ya know!
Mike: (laughs)
John: OK. Now stick out your two second fingers.
Mike: Two fingers.
John: OK. OK. You got it?

Reading is integrally related to oral language and is more complex than a simple visual-to-auditory transfer. Knowledge of language at many interrelated levels is fundamental for efficient reading. As noted earlier in the case of Todd, problems with oral receptive language can interfere with reading comprehension; those with oral expressive language problems also frequently have difficulty with reading. For example, Steve is a child with oral syntax problems and significant difficulty with oral reading. The following reading errors reflect his expressive syntactic difficulties:

He clan over at the horse's course. He wish he had a horse! He wish he could be riding with the cowboy! He . . . what if he was only 5 years old? Had he grew up right here in the ranch? Had he rides old Lumby all around the wheat field? Where was old Lummox now, over the south. He was a big worker horse. What I want have a cow pony, with. . . . Why sure everyone thinks I'm just a baby.

(Compare to original text:) He glanced over at the horse corrals. He wished he had a horse! He wished he could be riding out with the cowboys! What if he was only 5 years old? Hadn't he grown up right here on the ranch? Hadn't he ridden old Lummox all around the wheat fields? There was old Lummox now, over to the south. He was a big work horse. What I want is a cow pony, thought Willie. Why should everyone think I'm just a baby?

Writing, too, is an integral part of language ability, involving more than just knowing where to put capitals and periods. The written language of 12-year-old Chris also reflects problems in oral syntax (not to mention spelling).

There I was in a raft going dome a river. I was ome of eath peple in the raft. Ther was mo way owt. I had to go 121 miles of water to get to end and I was vere sea sick all redde. I could tell it was going to be rwm. then

I look dome the river and all I cood see is withe water amd the raft was get cuser amd I was shank from fevr amd then we hit the water and we up and down. the water hit me a I fall owt the boat and the water was push all then owt of nower sane ome grade me and pull me in the boat. then some ome sead are you have fum and then I fanted.

It is children such as Chris and the others that this book is about. It is important to realize that children with language disabilities, both spoken and written, have difficulty in both academic and nonacademic social situations, as well as in later occupational endeavors. Language is an extremely complex human behavior but one that is essential to intellectual development as well as to interpersonal relationships. Language also is a developmental phenomenon. Consequently, before looking specifically at children with such disabilities, it is necessary to take a closer look at what language is and at the sequences of its normal development.

## PART I. NORMAL LANGUAGE AND ITS DEVELOPMENT

### Section 1. A Definition

One of the primary functions of oral language is interpersonal communication, although it also may be used for intrapersonal functions such as reasoning (Bloom & Lahey, 1978). As a major means of interpersonal communication (individuals also communicate nonverbally by gestures, facial expression, posture, and so on) language may be defined by a set of characteristic features (Bloom & Lahey, 1978):

1. Language is symbolic. Words arbitrarily represent real objects and experiences.
2. Language is shared. Words have meaning because speakers agree that certain groups of sounds represent experience.
3. Language is rule governed. It is a system of symbols that may be combined according to rules that also are arbitrarily agreed upon by speakers.
4. Language is generative. A rule-governed system allows speakers to produce correct novel utterances simply by adhering to the rules.

Such a definition contains a number of important assumptions. First, language is part of a complex cognitive system and is learned by means of cognitive processes. The relationship of language to cognition has been a source of interest and controversy among philosophers, psychologists, linguists, and educators for many years. Some consider language to be essential for thought; that is, cognition proceeds by way of language. Others maintain that language and thought are separate systems and that their development is relatively independent. Still others hold that cognition is essential for language; that is, language development is dependent upon prior cognitive development (Rice, 1980).

These positions are considered in more detail in Chapter 6 where the relationships between language and thought are discussed more fully. It is important here to indicate that there is an extremely important and complex relationship between language and cognition that is highlighted throughout the book.

A fair amount of confusion results from different uses of the term "cognitive." In one sense cognition or cognitive psychology is used broadly in contrast to behaviorism or other mechanistic views of learning. From the cognitive viewpoint in the broad sense, learning takes place in the mind and proceeds by way of complex constructive processes that encompass both perceptual and conceptual learning. There also is a narrower sense of cognition that is reserved for such processes as conceptualization, generalization, and problem solving, and is contrasted to other psychological processes such as language, memory, and perception. For purposes of this book, the term is used most frequently in the first sense while the terms "conceptualization" or "thinking skills" refer to the narrower sense. However, here and in Chapter 6, where the specific topic is the relationship of language to cognition, the term is used in the narrow sense.

The second assumption in that four-point definition is that language exists not just within a cognitive context but in a social context as well. Linguistic knowledge is acquired through interaction with the social environment (Lewis & Cherry, 1977). Language develops in an environment of communicative exchange with children's caretakers, and disruptions of this early communicative interaction have been shown to have a detrimental effect on language learning (Brown, 1958; Curtiss, Fromkin, Krashen, Rigler, & Rigler, 1974). Further, the social environment plays a major role in every communicative interaction. These topics are discussed in more detail in Chapter 5. It is important here to highlight the interrelationships between language and social development.

The third assumption involves the interrelationships between language performance and linguistic knowledge per se. Linguistic knowledge is thought to consist of not one, but a number of rule systems. Traditionally, researchers have studied those rule systems separately; much progress has been made in describing children's developmental course in learning each. Language performance, i.e., understanding and speaking, is a complex integration of those rule systems.

Historically, linguistic knowledge was divided into phonology, syntax, and semantics. Interest centered first on phonology or production of speech sounds. However, as it became clear that some speech sound production was dependent on certain aspects of grammar, interest focused on morphology and syntax. A similar recognition that certain aspects of grammar depend on word meaning (semantics) led psycholinguists to focus on semantic aspects of language. Most recently researchers have recognized that meaning often is dependent on communicative context; hence, the domain of pragmatics has been added to the study of child language.

These domains, or rule systems, are the topics of Chapters 2, 3, 4, and 5. These are somewhat arbitrary divisions, however, and it is important to emphasize at the outset the interrelationships among them.

### Section 2. Language Development

Based on this definition of language and its assumptions, it then may be asked, "What is it that children must learn?" It appears that children learning language should first learn that words represent experience, and then learn the various rule systems that govern their use in a variety of communicative contexts. Children's language is recognized to contain at least four interrelated rule systems in which they must be able to (1) communicate a message using (2) adequate grammatical rules and (3) appropriate words that are (4) pronounced correctly.

Tremendous strides have been made by researchers over the last two decades in documenting the course of child language development in phonology, semantics, syntax, and pragmatics. To teachers of children with language disabilities, information on normal development is vitally important to recognize when a problem exists and to answer the question, "What do I teach next?" (Crystal, Fletcher, & Garman, 1976).

Content planning in remedial work usually is based on the assumption that the normal order of acquisition within each of the domains is the most reasonable sequence for remedial teaching. This assumption has been challenged by Rees (1971), who finds no conclusive evidence that normal developmental order is appropriate for children with language problems. Dukes (1981) still discerns no conclusive evidence ten years later. Nevertheless, until more definite information can be produced either supporting or disproving this assumption, remediation generally is ordered on the basis of normal sequences of acquisition.

Teachers might be cautioned, however, that following normal development in some cases may not be advisable; for example, learning disabled children should not be taught to overgeneralize the regular past tense ending "-ed" to irregular verbs ("goed," "gived"). Although this is a stage in normal development, these children would be spending time on forms that they eventually would have to "unlearn."

It is beyond the scope of this chapter to present all the developmental information available in each of the major areas of language. Perhaps the greatest difficulty in assembling normative data in one easy reference form is the multiplicity of levels of analysis. In syntax, for example, development has been analyzed and charted at fairly gross levels such as the development of different sentence types or sentence transformations (Crystal, Fletcher, & Garman, 1976; Leonard, 1972; Menyuk, 1964; Morehead & Ingram, 1973). Other researchers have selected minute aspects of grammar and produced lengthy analyses of negation (Lee, 1974) or verb phrase development (Fletcher, 1979). Although some developmental information is summarized in each of the next four chapters, a list of readings is provided at the end of this chapter for those who wish further information about norms in a particular developmental area.

## Section 3. Models of Normal Language Development

A rationale for intervention requires not only knowledge of normal development but also some sense of what is involved in language learning. Once educators have an idea of what is learned, they then may ask, *"How* do children learn language?" Numerous models have been developed that are useful in understanding normal language learning; however, these typically direct attention back to the content of the language system, to *what* is learned. In general, these can be classified into two groups: broad models that analyze language as a whole and more specific ones that attempt to explain a single aspect of language such as phonology or syntax.

Broad models such as Bloom and Lahey's (1978) represent language as the "knowledge of the integration of content/form/use" (p. 22). Development does not proceed within isolated domains. Instead, meaning influences development of form; form influences the development of use, and so on. This model helps clinicians recognize the interdependence of language domains and plan a comprehensive remedial strategy for each child. Bloom and Lahey also suggest that language difficulties may be conceived of as disorders of content (semantics), form (phonology and syntax), or use (pragmatics). However, a crucial question is not addressed by such a model, namely, how children learn. With normal language learners such a question is less pressing since children learn so effortlessly. With disordered children, however, the problem is more acute, and the focus must be on the cognitive dimension of language in addition to the rule systems that are learned.

To begin to answer the question of how language is learned, theorists turn to psychological or cognitive processes. Stark (1981), for example, offers a model in which phonology, semantics, syntax, and pragmatics are arranged hierarchically, beginning with the smallest unit of meaning (phonemes) that are prerequisite to larger units (words, sentences, and conversations). It is important to note that Stark proposes that processing of larger language units (sentences and conversations) may affect development of smaller ones (words and sounds) and vice versa. Stark also proposes that the processes of attention and memory interact with each of these language domains to help explain how the system operates.

These processes of memory and attention clearly are important in understanding and speaking. Over the years various authors have cited the importance of a variety of other cognitive skills, such as perception (Menyuk & Menn, 1979), decentration (Gerber & Bryen, 1981), interpretation and evaluation of the message (Wiig & Semel, 1976), and feedback (Wiig & Semel, 1976). At this point, however, although researchers in normal child language do speculate as to the related processes that are necessary for language acquisition and use, they do not offer comprehensive models that systematically describe the necessary processes or the interrelationships among them. The chief, and very important, contribution of the field of normal development is a model of the language itself along with a developmental description of verbal products (Wing, 1982), or *what* is learned, i.e., what the child knows and can do as language skills develop over time.

In addition to broad models such as Bloom and Lahey's, theorists have provided detailed models that are appropriate to specific areas of phonology, syntax, and so on. These are presented in the next four chapters in more detail.

## PART II. LANGUAGE DISORDERS

### Section 1. Speech and Language Pathology

Traditionally, the field of speech and language pathology has been divided into speech disorders and language disorders. Language disorders then were further divided into the aphasias (based on known brain damage) and developmental disorders. These historical beginnings have had several important outcomes:

- The traditional focus on aphasic individuals with brain damage put language pathology more directly in the area of medical interest and rehabilitative therapy rather than in education. The net result, however, was that language therapy tended to remain somewhat isolated from developments in education. Children's language disorders were diagnosed and treated apart from the rest of their education. It is only since the late 1970s that a clear revolution has been taking place, with speech and language pathologists beginning to look more and more to their role in education.

- Speech and language theorists have made major contributions toward describing language disorders (Ingram, 1979; Lee, 1974) and toward developing excellent remedial programs (Lee, Koenigsknecht, & Mulhern, 1975).

- In contrast to the research on normal language, the field of speech and language pathology—which focuses on disorders of language learning—has supplied some insights into psychological processes that are related to adequate and inadequate language learning. The study of aphasics has provided fairly clear evidence that certain psychological processes such as memory, perception, and so on are closely related to language learning and use. So, for example, memory deficits affect children's ability to retrieve specific words they wish to say. Deficits in auditory perception affect their ability to understand spoken language.

Carrow-Woolfolk and Lynch (1982) have developed a very useful four-dimensional model of language learning and language disorders that attempts to integrate this research on disorders of psychological processing with the body of linguistic knowledge (rule systems) necessary for adequate language comprehension and production (Figure 1-1). They also highlight in their model the importance of the environmental and social context for language learning. The four dimensions involve (1) the linguistic code, (2) cognitive processes, (3) language performance, and (4) the communication environment.

---

**Figure 1-1** Four-Dimensional Model of Language Learning

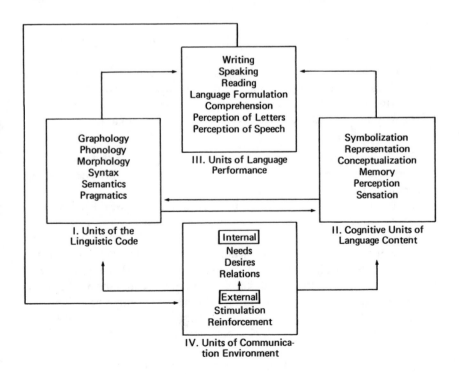

*Source:* Reprinted from *An Integrative Approach to Language Disorders in Children,* by Elizabeth Carrow-Woolfolk and Joan Lynch, by permission of Grune & Stratton, Inc., © 1982.

This model is helpful in illuminating the multidimensional nature of language performance that involves the integration of cognitive, linguistic, and social domains. It also is useful in understanding language disorders and how deficits in one dimension may interfere with development of others in many and complex ways.

Two important points should be made here with respect to the nature of these interactions between dimensions in the model.

First, as discussed, the linguistic rule systems of phonology, semantics, etc. (box I), actually are the content of language learning, or what is learned, while the cognitive processes such as attention and perception (box II) are related to how language is learned. Disorders in any particular process therefore may interfere with knowledge of one or more linguistic rules systems (semantics, syntax, etc.). Wing (1982) suggests that the interrelationship between linguistic rule systems and cognitive processes may be conceived as a matrix of possible interactions, and that a child ". . . may have a phonological disorder that does not involve all processes or a memory disorder that does not involve all linguistic levels'' (p. 3). Wing makes the important point that:

> books, articles, and clinical tests are still being published in which linguistic levels and language processes are listed as if they were parallel. For example, Wiig and Semel (1980) classified language problems as morphology, syntax, semantics, memory, and retrieval. Clearly, the first three items on this list are linguistic levels, whereas memory and retrieval are processes that impinge on all linguistic levels, as do other processes (p. 3).

This sort of parallel classification system is a major source of misunderstanding and confusion for teachers and diagnosticians.

Second, interactions between deficits in cognitive processes and language performance (box III) are often explained in terms of one-to-one cause/effect relationships between a single process (e.g. perception) and a certain symptom or type of language disorder (e.g. articulation). However, such explanations have been shown to be simplistic and inadequate in many cases (Hammill & Larsen, 1974; Rees, 1973). Nevertheless, this does not mean that educators must discard models that explain language disabilities in terms of cognitive processes and processing deficits. Instead, models, particularly of the cognitive element and its interrelationships with the other dimensions, must reflect the complexity of the human mind.

The exact nature of the interrelationships between processes and language comprehension or production still is a matter for discussion and continuing research. It is neither as simple nor as direct as it once was conceived. For example, Carrow-Woolfolk and Lynch (1982) suggest that the elements in their model may be related in four ways:

- Dependent. One element requires input from another element; thus if the first fails to develop so also will the second; for example, semantic development requires appropriate cognitive development.
- Cumulative. Dysfunctions in two or more dependent elements may combine to affect development in a third area; for example, hearing loss combines with perceptual deficit to affect language comprehension.
- Reciprocal. Interaction between two elements has a mutually enhancing or mutually constraining effect; for example, between perception and categorization.
- Relation by common source. Two elements may be related to a third element but not directly to each other. "For example, articulation and language comprehension may both relate to auditory memory but not necessarily to one another." (p. 206-207)

The complexity of the cognitive dimension still is not described adequately by the units in box II of this model however, especially when clinicians wish to understand disorders of learning. It is necessary to probe still further and explore in more detail the dimension of cognitive processes in order to avoid oversimplification of this element, and it is here that the field of learning disabilities makes a major contribution.

### Section 2.  Learning Disabilities

Learning disabilities cover a much broader spectrum of disorders than just language disabilities. Indeed, the term learning disabilities seeks to make sense of a number of seemingly disparate learning problems, including language acquisition. By adapting certain concepts from the field of cognitive psychology, experts in such disabilities have attempted to construct broad models that can account for processes and disorders, including those of learning language.

Before discussing the various models in this field, it is necessary to wade briefly into the troubled waters of the definition of a learning disability, particularly as to whether underachievement is a sufficient or merely necessary condition for qualifying.

"Specific learning disability" means a disorder in one or more of the basic psychological processes involved in understanding or in using language, spoken or written, which may manifest itself in an imperfect ability to listen, think, speak, read, write, spell, or to do mathematical calculations. The term includes such conditions as perceptual handicaps, brain injury, minimal brain dysfunction, dyslexia, and developmental aphasia. The term does not include children who have learning problems which are primarily the result of visual, hearing, or motor handicaps, of mental retardation, or of environmental, cultural, or economic disadvantages. (*Federal Register,* Vol. 42 (163), August 23, 1977)

This book accepts the definition of learning disabilities in the *Federal Register* (1977), but adheres to a fairly strict interpretation that excludes many underachieving children currently considered learning disabled by many educators. Three specific points must be made:

First, children may have difficulty with understanding, speaking, reading, writing, and arithmetic or mathematics for many reasons, many of which do not constitute reasons for labeling those individuals as learning disabled. The first group of reasons concern the integrities that must be present for normal learning (Johnson & Myklebust, 1967). At least average intelligence, stable emotional adjustment, adequate vision and hearing, and adequate health are all necessary for normal learning. Most scholars in the field agree that children with primary handicaps in these areas are not learning disabled. (This is not to say that retarded or emotionally disturbed children cannot have learning disabilities as well, but in such cases they would have multiple problems.) Nevertheless, in spite of general agreement in principle, practical problems arise. For example, as the definition of mental retardation changes, pressures increase to label children with IQs in the 70-to-85 range as learning disabled. The other group of reasons for underachievement focuses on conditions in the environment, rather than in the child. To learn normally, children must be at least minimally motivated and must have an adequate home environment and developmental background so that essential skills and knowledge necessary for more complex learning are present. They also must have had adequate instruction and opportunity to learn. Most of those who are underachievers are so because of one or more of these reasons. However, while the federal definition has excluded children with what might be called "environmentally caused" problems of underachievement, the trend in the field is to include them. (See Bateman, 1979, who specifically cites poor teaching as the major cause of learning disabilities.)

The second specific point revolves around the emphasis to be given to processing deficits in the learning disabilities definition. While the trend in the field is to assign less weight to processing deficits as the primary "cause," the consequences of such a move must be considered. When these two trends (i.e., including environmentally caused cases of underachievement and deemphasizing processing deficits) are taken together, it is clear that the floodgates have been opened and the nature of children labeled learning disabled is radically altered.

That is, virtually any children who are underachieving, except those with well-defined physical or mental handicaps, would qualify as learning disabled. (Incidentally, this trend may be responsible for estimates that approximately 40 percent of the school population is learning disabled.)

The trend's consequences are positive in some respects. Perhaps it has awakened practitioners to the fact that regular education is not succeeding in educating nonhandicapped children (Lieberman, 1980). Underachievers of all sorts obviously need special help. However, it is not at all clear that they need the same kind of help as do children who "truly" are learning disabled.

In other respects, the consequences are negative. It is highly questionable whether the trend has benefitted those children (estimated to be only 3 to 5 percent of the population) who are truly learning disabled. Those who are underachieving because of deficits in processing information, i.e., those who could indeed benefit from specific learning techniques, are being lost in the attempt to provide special education for masses of underachievers. If the label "learning disabled" continues to be applied to this much larger group of children, although it is difficult to take this suggestion seriously, perhaps a new category should be established for the subgroup with processing deficits.

The third specific point is that there also is a trend toward defining learning disability as a strictly school-related problem. While many disabilities typically show up in school settings, definitions that focus on "environmental causes" (including poor teaching) consequently also concentrate exclusively on academic problems such as reading and math. However, when considered from the perspective of processing deficits, learning disabilities are not exclusively school-related problems. Difficulties in processing nonverbal information may result in problems of a social nature that may interfere with adequate learning of self-help, adaptive skills, and interpersonal relations.

For example, visual-motor processing deficits may affect areas such as acquiring many occupational skills, driving, cooking, and participating in sports, as well as academic areas such as handwriting. Thus, in one sense, the interpretation of the definition should be narrowed to exclude those who are underachieving for reasons not related to processing disorders and should be broadened in another sense to include children whose processing disorders may interfere with nonacademic as well as academic tasks.

Admittedly, direct one-to-one cause/effect relationships between process and achievement have not been established conclusively. Correlational data cannot be used to establish direct causal relationships, but interpretations other than direct cause are possible. There probably is at least a reciprocal relationship between process and achievement as well as numerous indirect ones not yet identified.

How, then, can learning disabilities be regarded as deficits in psychological processing? Historically, this field grew out of research on a number of separate handicapped groups:

- Strauss and Werner (1942) at the Wayne County (Detroit) Training Institute found children labeled mentally retarded who did not fit the typical pattern of retardation. They appeared to exhibit a syndrome of characteristics (later called the Strauss Syndrome) of hyperactivity, poor visual perceptual, and visual-motor abilities. They generally had nonverbal deficits that affected academic and nonacademic behavior.
- Samuel Orton (1937), on the other hand, became interested in children with verbal visual problems that mainly affected reading ability. He found his population to have what he termed strephosymbolia (letter reversal) or verbal visual perceptual problems.
- Helmer Myklebust (1954) approached learning disabilities from a background in hearing impairment. His interest was in children with auditory verbal processing disorders or problems with spoken language. Myklebust also recognized that some of these exhibited behaviors indicated processing problems beyond the language disorder, such as visual perceptual and nonverbal deficits.

Thus the field began with the identification of rather disparate groups of children who had in common their inability to process certain types of information: auditory, visual or kinesthetic, verbal or nonverbal.

This common thread has been analyzed systematically by imposing upon it a framework adapted from information processing theory. Information theory provides a model for conceptualizing what happens in a learning task by describing hypothetical steps along a continuous path as bits of information or sensory data are processed in the mind. It is important to note at the outset that since learning presumably is a continuous process, divisions in that continuum such as perception or memory are essentially hypothetical constructs; that is, researchers have somewhat arbitrarily divided the learning process into steps or stages for the sake of convenience.

Although such divisions are necessary to help educators understand and talk about the very complex process of learning, such an approach runs the risk of compartmentalizing their thinking or leading them to assume that these steps or stages are real and separate entities. It is not necessary to fall into this trap, however, if clinicians keep in mind that learning is a continuous, integrated process, with multiple complex interrelationships between these constructs.

A learning disability or processing disorder thus may be conceived as a dysfunction in one or more of these various processes that may interfere with other psychological processes and also with learning outcomes such as reading or math. Although some researchers (Hammill & Larsen, 1974; Rees, 1973; Rosenthal, 1974) conclude that no consistent relationships exist between processes and final products (for example, between auditory perception and understanding spoken language), it would be premature to conclude that processes have nothing to do with learning disabilities.

It might more profitably be concluded that the relationship is perhaps not as direct or simplistic as once conceived. (Recall Carrow-Woolfolk and Lynch, who suggest at least four ways in which processes are related to language behavior; they may be: dependent, cumulative, reciprocal, or related indirectly by a common source.) In some children, clinical evidence is quite clear that a direct relationship does exist, for example between syntax problems in spoken language and difficulties in oral reading. In other children, more generalized disorders may account for several specific problems. For example, a disorder in rule generalization may surface in a number of areas as problems in oral language, reading, and spelling.

## Section 3. Models of Language Learning Disabilities

Various authors interested in learning disabled children have adapted information processing theory in somewhat different ways. Wiig and Semel (1976) present a hierarchically ordered model of processing auditory verbal information. They recognize two major areas of language processing: understanding and speaking (input and output), each of which utilizes a unique set of sequentially ordered, hierarchical processes. They hold that spoken language, to be understood, must be (1) registered by the ear, (2) perceived, (3) decoded linguistically, and (4) interpreted cognitively; expressively, information must be (5) conceptualized, (6) encoded linguistically, and (7) encoded motorically. Wiig and Semel also recognize the role of memory for storage and retrieval of information.

Gerber and Bryen (1981), who reflect a more recent trend, present the opposite viewpoint, emphasizing the detrimental effects that generalized or higher level cognitive deficits can have on language comprehension and production. They argue that all language learning disabled children have underlying subtle cognitive problems that account for their language disorders. These analysts suggest that such generalized cognitive processes as representational ability may be underdeveloped both verbally and nonverbally and thereby reflect "a quantitative developmental lag" (p. 58) that in turn affects language learning.

Two problems arise with these models, however. First, both present only one-way analyses of the continuous, integrated learning process and prevent practitioners from recognizing that important interrelationships exist in both directions along the continuum of learning. Both positions clearly offer valuable insights into psychological processing and processing disorders that need to be combined to illustrate the complex way in which cognitive processes interact. Particularly with older children in whom thinking skills are more developed, it may be necessary to examine multiple ways in which higher and lower level processes interact.

The second problem in these models, particularly in Wiig and Semel's, is that the focus is almost exclusively on auditory verbal processes. A more comprehensive model is needed to help bring together the disparate set of problems called learning disabilities and to help describe the relationship between spoken and written language as well as the variety of both verbal and nonverbal skills needed for effective communication. As noted earlier, language does not exist in isolation from its physical and social context, from other psychological functions, or from areas of academic and nonacademic achievement.

Johnson and Myklebust (1967) provide such a comprehensive model that encompasses spoken and written language as well as verbal and nonverbal areas of processing. It contains a number of frames of reference that, when taken together, form a multidimensional model of learning disabilities. These frames of reference may be used to analyze characteristics of information to be processed. Children may have difficulty processing information with certain characteristics, and tasks with certain requirements. By understanding the types of information that children can and cannot process, clinicians can then make inferences about the processing strengths and weaknesses of the children—and describe or classify the nature of the learning disability. These frames of reference also serve as a basis for modifying information presented in remediation.

Their first frame of reference introduces the distinction between verbal and nonverbal learning; that is, information may be either verbal (words) or nonverbal (objects, pictures, gestures). It is necessary to highlight the importance of both verbal and nonverbal processing. Not all experience can be classified as verbal. Indeed, much of children's interaction with the physical environment as well as their social interaction with others is nonverbal. Therefore, much of language's content, as well as its social context, requires nonverbal processing abilities; deficits in either verbal or nonverbal processes can interfere with adequate communication.

The author's clinical experience, specifically with learning disabled children, suggests that disorders may occur in processing one type of information but not the other. However, it is necessary to emphasize that although deficits may occur in verbal or nonverbal processes, this does not imply any specific theory of hemispheric functioning; it also cannot be presumed that all nonverbal processes occur in the right hemisphere and verbal processes in the left. Interrelationships between hemispheric functions appear to be more complex than was once supposed (Day, 1977).

The second frame of reference emphasizes that while understanding and expressing information are strongly related, they require different sets of processes. It also recognizes that reception precedes expression. Learning disabled children may exhibit different patterns of receptive and expressive language problems. Some appear to comprehend adequately but have difficulty producing appropriate language. Others have problems understanding what is said, with expression also usually disturbed.

Some authors have questioned the position that comprehension precedes expression. Bloom (1974), for example, suggests that production may precede comprehension. This discussion has highlighted the need for clarification of what is meant by the term comprehension. Does it mean a minimal pairing of a word with its referent, or does it mean a more complete acquisition of a concept, including multiple and figurative meanings and its relationship to other concepts? (See Carey, 1978; Carrow-Woolfolk & Lynch, 1982.) With this distinction in mind, it is possible to agree with Ingram's (1974) response to Bloom's position that some comprehension (of the first type) precedes production. While this assertion reaffirms the common sense of the traditional position, it also highlights the need for a position that can accommodate the idea of a developmental interaction between comprehension and production, gradually leading to a fully developed adult concept.

The third frame of reference indicates that stimuli are presented and processed through one of five sensory modalities. With the exceptions of taste and smell, which are exclusively nonverbal, both verbal and nonverbal stimuli may be processed by the other sensory pathways, although some combinations, such as auditory verbal information, are more common than others. Braille is an example of verbal tactile information while facial expressions represent visual nonverbal stimuli. Some learning disabled children appear to have difficulty processing information through one or more sensory systems simultaneously.

The fourth of these frames of reference is referred to by Johnson and Myklebust as the hierarchy of experience. The hierarchy suggests what may happen as pieces of sensory data are processed:

- Conceptualization
- Symbolization
- Short-term memory
- Perception
- Attention
- Sensation

For learning to take place, sense data first must activate the neural receptors: eyes, ears, skin. While problems at this level (blindness, deafness) do not constitute a learning disability (see definition), sensation is the first step in the processing of information.

Subsequently, attention mechanisms must allow the stimulus to be processed further. Some learning disabled children tend to be distractible, perseverative, or disinhibited (Johnson, 1981). They have difficulty maintaining or shifting attention. Others have difficulty with selective attention (Ross, 1976).

Perception is cited as the next level of stimulus processing. Chalfant and Scheffelin (1969) list several components of perception, among them differentiation of stimulus from no stimulus, stimulus localization, discrimination of different stimuli, discrimination of sequence, and figure-ground discrimination. Some learning disabled children appear to have difficulty with perceptual processes (Atchison & Canter, 1979; Kavale, 1981).

After a stimulus is perceived, it is recorded in short-term memory so it can be processed further. Some learning disabled children appear to have difficulty retaining images in short-term memory for further processing; although stimuli are attended to and perceived, they are not retained long enough for more complex cognitive processing to occur.

The next level of processing is that of symbolization, or attaching meaning to perceptions. A broad range of both verbal and nonverbal symbolic or representational behaviors occurs at this level. Experience can be symbolized in many different ways: as a spoken word, written word, numerical symbol, pictorial representation, and so on. Symbolic processes consist of both encoding and decoding these representations. Some learning disabled children have difficulty with one or more of these symbolic processes, such as comprehension of language, pictures, gestures, or facial expressions.

Conceptualization, the next level of the hierarchy, may be described as the process of classifying or categorizing individual bits of processed information into abstract groupings. As Johnson and Myklebust (1967) point out, although most categorization takes place with verbal concepts (cats, dogs, and mice all are animals), it is possible to imagine conceptualization without verbal symbols. For example, it is possible to classify rulers, compasses, protractors, and the like together without ever knowing the name for the items or the words ''school supplies'' as a label for the category, although the task obviously is easier with the verbal labels. The hallmark of conceptualization, then, is not simply a process of superordinate verbal labeling but rather one that allows grouping similar bits of experience together into meaningful categories. Some learning disabled children have difficulty seeing relationships at this level of processing.

To summarize, for learning to take place, a new piece of information must be attended to, adequately perceived, and held in memory at least briefly. At that point processing may stop, although what has been retained may not be very useful. For example, if children hear a group of sounds such as ''pferd'' frequently enough and if they attend, perceive, and remember it, they will have learned something new and probably will be able to reproduce it. However, if they are able to attach some meaning to this group of sounds (''horse'' in German), they will have learned a more useful piece of information. Integration of this newly learned word into total knowledge by classifying it with other similar experiences makes it available for a wide range of cognitive activities such as hypothesizing, problem solving, and so on.

This hierarchy, then, is the fourth of the frames of reference introduced by Johnson and Myklebust. Before proceeding, it may be helpful to expand the model by introducing additional features at the conceptualization level and by adding another, higher level, yielding the following:

- Metacognition
- Conceptualization
- Symbolization
- Short-term memory
- Perception
- Attention
- Sensation

Beginning with the expansion of the level of conceptualization, it may be noted that cognitive psychology has illuminated a number of higher level skills such as hypothesizing, generalizing, seeing cause/effect relationships, and so on. (A complete inventory is unavailable since much work is still going on in this area.) However, these cognitive skills, like categorization, all reflect the central concept of organizational thought.

Most important to language learning among higher level cognitive skills is rule generalization. While rules are mainly features of the language system itself, they also appear to have some psychological reality. That is, most children easily apprehend the regularities of content, form, and use in language and make generalizations so that they form novel utterances based on these regularities (rules). Rule learning is not limited to auditory verbal information. Nonverbal aspects of communication (prosody, gesture, body posture) all may be organized as rules that in turn can be used to generate and regulate behavior. Similarly, visual symbol systems (spelling, for example) may be seen as rule governed. Some learning disabled children appear to be unable to organize the regularities of language and to use these rules to generate behavior.

Rule learning generally is considered an implicit form of cognitive behavior. That is, rules can be generalized and applied later to regulate behavior without conscious awareness on the part of the learners. On certain occasions, however, explicit knowledge and use of rules (such as spelling rules) is very useful. This conscious awareness and manipulation of rules falls in the next level of the hierarchy.

This additional level is suggested in order to include in the model what with respect to language psychologists call metalinguistic skills: language about language, or the ability to reflect on language or take it as an object of knowledge. Explicit awareness of rules is one aspect of metalinguistic skill. Phonological, semantic, syntactic, and pragmatic rules become objects of knowledge that can be expressed linguistically and communicated.

For example, recognizing and analyzing sounds in words (Kinsbourne & Caplan, 1979; Shankweiler & Liberman, 1972) or analyzing and labeling a sentence as containing nouns, verbs, adjectives, etc., are metalinguistic skills. Other authors consider the ability to play with or manipulate the language as a metalinguistic skill. Hook (1976) finds that children able to learn a language similar to pig Latin are better able to analyze and manipulate letter sounds when reading.

Metalinguistic skills go beyond awareness of the language and its rules, however; a second aspect is the ability to apply the rules to specific situations consciously or explicitly. Some learning disabled children have difficulty with metalinguistic skills such as analyzing sounds in words or mental manipulation of the language (Hook, 1976; Vogel, 1974). Others have difficulty in applying rules in specific problem-solving situations. Selection and application of learning strategies are extremely difficult for these children, who are unable to make use of whatever explicit knowledge they have in learning tasks. It should be noted that deficits at the level of metacognition frequently are not limited to verbal or linguistic skills. Children who have difficulty with metalinguistic tasks often have more generalized deficits that make a wide range of problem-solving situations difficult. (At this point the larger question of interrelationship between language and thought becomes crucial; it is discussed in more detail in Chapter 6.)

As this fourth frame of reference was presented by Johnson and Myklebust (1967), it was hierarchically ordered beginning with attention and perception, and as such did not emphasize the importance of interrelationships between processes in both directions along the hierarchy of experience. More recently, however, Johnson (1981) has discussed the close interrelationships of processes within the information processing model and has suggested the need to emphasize effects in both directions in the continuum of learning (Johnson, 1982).

To illustrate: the interrelationships between perception and conceptualization should be considered. On the one hand, conceptualization cannot take place adequately if words are not perceived or discriminated correctly. If ''pen'' and ''pin'' are not discriminated, they will be categorized incorrectly as belonging to the same class. On the other hand, every act of discrimination appears to be an act of categorization (Eisenson, 1972). That is, words are discriminated on the basis of categories of sound, and discrimination proceeds by recognizing a member of a class of sounds. Thus the relationship between perception and conceptualization appears to be reciprocal; however, additional influences from third factors (e.g., attention or memory) also must be considered.

This is just one example of the complex relationships that may obtain between cognitive processes. All the processes mentioned are part of a complex whole.

This, then, is a multidimensional framework that is extremely useful in conceptualizing the learning process and its concomitant disorders.

- Verbal
  Nonverbal
- Receptive
  Expressive
- Auditory
  Visual
  Tactile/Kinesthetic
- Metacognition
  Conceptualization
  Symbolization
  Short-term memory
  Perception
  Attention

These frames of reference provide an extremely useful structure for understanding learning disabilities, bringing together such disparate problems as visual distractibility, auditory comprehension, reading, social perception, and so on as deficits in this multidimensional system of cognitive processing. Each may be thought of as a dysfunction in receiving or expressing specific types of verbal and nonverbal information, at one or more levels of the hierarchy, and in one or more sensory modalities.

It is important to point out an implication of this multidimensional view of cognitive processing for theories of learning disabilities. There is a tendency in the field to isolate one of these frames of reference as the only explanation or "cause" of learning disabilities. However, such attempts have not been successful because they adopt too simplistic a view of the learning process. Modality is one good example. The explanation of learning disabilities solely as deficits in processing auditory or visual information and the resulting division of learning disabled children into auditory learners and visual learners have come under considerable justifiable criticism. However, the notion of modality processing as one dimension of an integrated system still retains a good deal of validity in both remediation and research. (See Lyon & Watson, 1981.)

Similarly, many theories have isolated the dimension that includes the related processes of attention, perception, memory, symbolization, conceptualization, and metacognitive skills. Once again, a focus only on this dimension (see, for example, box II in the Carrow-Woolfolk and Lynch model) cannot account for the variety of learning problems found among these individuals nor can it serve alone as an adequate framework for diagnosis or remediation. Nevertheless, this does not mean that these processes should be rejected as unimportant; rather, their importance is enhanced in combination with the other frames of reference discussed. While it is tempting to search for a single explanation of language learning disabilities, it undoubtedly is more fruitful to consider models that allow for multiple explanations.

In sum, this model offers a broad framework for conceptualizing learning disabilities, including language dysfunctions. It is possible to view the Gerber and Bryen (1981) and Wiig and Semel (1976) models discussed earlier, when incorporated into this broader model, as two among many possibilities. That is, some children may exhibit dysfunctional learning styles for which the best explanation appears to be a deficit in processing of auditory information that may distort linguistic and higher level cognitive processes (Wiig & Semel). Others may have generalized cognitive deficits in thinking skills or organizational abilities (Gerber & Bryen; see also Reid & Hresko, 1981) that interfere with language performance and also may affect lower level processes such as attention or memory.

Although the many current theories of language development and disorders (Flood & Salus, 1982; Vetter, 1982; Wallach & Butler, in press) favor this second view and hold metacognition and strategy deployment to be of prime importance in explanations of language learning (and learning disabilities), a balanced view is more desirable. These theories have expanded educators' understanding of the wide variety of processes involved in the language learning task, but to suggest that metacognition or executive processes are the major explanation of language disorders is as narrow as holding a similar position with regard to auditory perception or memory. This author concurs with Carrow-Woolfolk and Lynch (1982) that the:

> wealth of past knowledge is essential to the preservation of a stable framework for understanding language and interpreting its disorders. New ideas are not seen as replacements for the old but as supplements, clarifications, and expansions of theories that may stimulate new ideas and insights. The necessity of holding onto the old while examining the new is of particular importance to the individual concerned with language disorders. Unless a broad historic base is used, there is a danger of following changes in the focus of language theory with changes in the assessment and intervention of language-disordered children. If this happens, children are taught according to the current views on language regardless of needs and abilities and regardless of the validity of the current theory. This can result in confusion on the part of the clinicians and failure to effect language change in children. (p. 4)

## PART III. SYNTHESIS

### Section 1. A Revised Model

Learning disabilities, then, may be understood as receptive or expressive dysfunctions at one or more levels of the hierarchy in processing auditory, visual, or tactile/kinesthetic information, both verbal and nonverbal, that results in poor learning. Learning in a number of areas may be affected: academic ones such as reading and math as well as nonacademic ones such as self-help skills and social development. Language, the basis of much interpersonal communication, is crucial to both academic and nonacademic growth. The areas of processing that may affect language learning, and the areas of development that are affected in turn by a language disorder are numerous and complex as well as potentially devastating to children.

While language is basically a verbal symbolic process, the larger area of interpersonal communication is both verbal and nonverbal. Thus a dysfunction involving any of the described frames of reference (receptive/expressive, verbal/nonverbal, auditory/visual/kinesthetic) and at any level of processing (attention, perception, memory, symbolization, conceptualization, metacognition) may affect the entire system and interrupt normal interpersonal communication.

However, to fully describe the impact that a learning disability may have on language learning in all its forms, and to focus more specifically on such dysfunctions, it is necessary to consider, in addition to the cognitive dimension, the social and linguistic dimensions already discussed. For example, Johnson (1981) suggests that "the rules for language be studied *in relation to* several psychological processes such as perception, memory and conceptualization" (p. 25, emphasis added). To do so, it is helpful to synthesize models from the fields of speech and language pathology as well as from learning disabilities.

The starting points are the four dimensions of the Carrow-Woolfolk and Lynch model (see Figure 1-1 above), but it is necessary to refine the box labeled cognitive units by superimposing upon it the model of learning disabilities just discussed, itself a multidimensional framework. That is, the cognitive dimension is itself an integrated system of processes that can be described within the several frames of reference. This interrelated system of cognitive dimensions must be studied as it relates to linguistic knowledge and environmental influences as well as to language performance itself.

With language learning disabled children, the source of the problem is within the dimension of cognitive processing, typically in spite of normal intelligence. Such children have difficulty processing various aspects of linguistic information and hence usually have problems in understanding or producing language. (The word "usually" is an important qualifier, however, since in some cases *strengths* in other areas of cognitive processing, environmental influences, or linguistic knowledge may enable children to overcome or compensate for the deficit and thus the problem is minimized or never identified.)

The rest of the book demonstrates how teachers can use knowledge from the perspectives of cognitive processing (and disorders of processing) and linguistic rule systems to assess and teach children with problems in comprehension and production of spoken and written language. The social perspective is considered, particularly as it relates to pragmatic knowledge and communicative competence; however, this dimension, specifically as it involves early language development, is not treated fully here. It also is clear that in many cases the learning (school) environment is a critical factor in exacerbating or minimizing a disability and that social and environmental factors such as those in language teaching should be recognized in remedial planning.

However, undue focus on instructional or environmental variables encourages professionals to define any child who is underachieving as learning disabled (see the above discussion of the definition of learning disabilities). Hence, this book retains a focus on the intrapersonal aspects of these dysfunctions while maintaining a balanced view of important factors in the learning environment.

The following chapters are organized along the lines of this synthesized model of language disabilities. However, their sequential order is not meant to imply only a one-way model. For example, pragmatic disorders may affect semantic development to the same degree that semantic disorders interfere with communicative ability. Similarly, each chapter's discussion of processing deficits is not meant to imply a one-way relationship involving attention, perception, memory, symbolization, conceptualization, and metacognitive strategies. Conceptualization and higher level thinking skills are shown to be as important as lower level processes such as perception and memory in language learning as well as in reading and writing. The uniqueness of each of these children requires a balanced assessment, i.e., one that recognizes that deficits in perception and memory as well as in conceptualization and thinking skills can interfere with their language learning, both spoken and written.

Two remaining points need to be made about this synthesized model: (1) the notion of language performance and specifically the relationship between spoken and written language, and (2) the implication for the relationship between the fields of speech and language pathology and of learning disabilities.

While the first point is implicit in the model as it stands, highlighting it here may be useful. Much has been written in the literature on both learning disabilities and on reading disorders about the importance of good oral language for reading (Gerber & Bryen, 1981; Goodman, 1973; Johnson & Myklebust, 1967; Wiig & Semel, 1976). Clearly also, oral language is related to spelling (Shankweiler & Liberman, 1972) and written language (Myklebust, 1973). While the model suggests that the auditory and visual processing of verbal information is interrelated, it is important to emphasize these links more specifically.

The acquisition of spoken and written language is developmentally a hierarchical one. While spoken words are arbitrary symbols imposed on experience, written words are visual symbols imposed not directly on experience but rather on the spoken representation (Johnson & Myklebust, 1967; Myklebust, 1973). Oral comprehension and spoken expression developmentally precede reading (written receptive language), and each precedes written expression (Johnson & Myklebust, 1967; Stark, 1981; Swisher & Aten, 1981; Wiig & Semel, 1976).

However, once the written forms begin to be acquired, the interrelationship becomes to some degree reciprocal. For example, reading becomes a major means of acquiring new concepts and word meanings that are used subsequently in oral language. Reading also affects development in other language domains. The derivational (morphological) structure of words often becomes clear for the first time when a child sees them in print (e.g., "nation," "national"). Similarly, the phonological structure of giant words such as "wunationindivisible" or "wunsapawnatime" emerges for many children only as the words are read.

By the same token, disorders of oral and written language also are reciprocally related (see the examples of Todd, Steve, and Chris at the beginning of this chapter). Hence, language disabilities are not one sort of disorder and reading disabilities another separate problem. Oral language problems frequently interfere with reading and spelling as children develop and the demands of the curriculum change. Similarly, those with primary problems in reading or spelling may have difficulty with the more advanced levels of oral language development.

The second consideration that arises from the adoption of this model is its implication for the relationship between the fields of speech and language pathology and of learning disabilities. In spite of the above considerations, children with language problems such as aphasia and apraxia often are viewed as separate from children with spelling, writing, or reading disabilities (dyslexia). This need not, indeed, should not be the case, however, if clinicians accept the position that language disorders do not exist as isolated phenomena.

To clarify this assertion, it first should be noted that, traditionally, language disorders have been associated with a number of handicapping conditions. The specific characteristics of the deaf, the severely emotionally disturbed, and the mentally retarded interfere in unique ways with their normal language acquisition. Speech and language therapists have worked with these populations for many years. They also work with another group of children sometimes labeled aphasic. A distinction often is made between children with known brain damage (aphasia) and those with no known brain damage. The latter group has been variously termed developmentally aphasic, language delayed, language disabled, clinically language disordered, and so on, and includes such problems as articulation deficits, syntax disorders, etc.

In direct contrast to these problems in the deaf, retarded, or disturbed, clinical language disorders generally are not associated with any handicapping condition or related syndrome of behavior but exist strangely alone. The lack of an explanation for these disorders has been buried in a prevailing attitude that ignores etiology and focuses on improving language performance.

Although, admittedly, undue emphasis on etiology is undesirable, there is an explanation for clinical language disorders, namely, that they are part of a syndrome of behaviors associated with the handicapping condition termed a learning disability—that is, a deficit in the cognitive processing of information that interferes with adequate language comprehension or production. These "clinical disorders" are rarely limited to oral language but typically are manifested in other language areas such as reading, writing, and spelling. Thus, while children with speech or language problems have been described as having isolated disorders, they are better viewed as having a learning disability. For example, many of those with articulation dysfunctions do not have isolated problems; rather, they have difficulty learning the phonological rules of the language. The author's clinical experience suggests that disorders that interfere with phonological rule learning sometimes start out at the oral expressive level but appear by school age as problems in decoding printed words or manipulating sounds for reading.

Put simply, language disorders are not one sort of problem and learning disabilities another. Thus, for purposes here, terms such as language disorder, developmental aphasia, and so on, are collapsed into one: language learning disability. While this approach may be politically problematic to many professionals, it is conceptually compelling. The rest of the book suggests how specific disorders of language processing in phonology, semantics, syntax, and pragmatics are better conceived of as learning disabilities.

This is not to say that the question of jurisdiction must necessarily arise in clinics or schools. Instead, it is a strong plea that professionals in both fields recognize the interdisciplinary nature of children's problems. Many learning disabilities teachers have little or no training in language remediation (one impetus for the writing of this book). Many language therapists also have little or no training in relating language disorders to other deficit areas or in developing integrated remediation programs. Of course there will be children with, for example, isolated articulation disorders that do not interfere with other areas, where less thought need be given to integrating various facets of remediation. However, the majority of those with language problems exhibit continuing difficulties in oral language, reading, spelling, and writing that must be understood and anticipated in order to provide adequate instruction.

### Section 2. General Implications for Diagnosis

Models are of little value if they do not guide the practical endeavor of helping language disabled children learn. With respect to diagnosis, the model may best be used to construct, through testing and observation, a descriptive, diagnostic profile of the needs and abilities, strengths and weaknesses of each individual learner. How, then, might the diagnostic process be organized to arrive at a useful profile? Clearly it is not a project that has a quick and easy, one-test solution. A series of questions may be developed that corresponds to the dimensions of the model:

- What is the relationship between comprehension and expression of language? Does a receptive deficit interfere with oral expression?
- What is the relationship between spoken and written forms of language? Do problems in oral language also manifest themselves in reading, spelling, and writing?
- What is the relationship between verbal and nonverbal aspects of language? Do nonverbal problems affect verbal areas?
- What is the relationship between auditory and visual processes? Is the problem entirely auditory, or do visual deficits interfere?
- What level of processing produces the problem? How do problems affect each other?
- Is the problem in phonology, semantics, syntax, pragmatics, or some combination of these?

From these questions, educators can assemble a comprehensive diagnostic battery of both formal and informal measures that is designed specifically to answer the series of questions.

To determine the exact nature of the language problem, the domain(s) affected must be studied in considerably more depth. The next four chapters, using normal language development categories, analyze each of the domains, suggesting appropriate formal and informal diagnostic measures that may be used.

In addition to structuring a set of questions around which a diagnostic battery may be devised, two general implications with respect to testing emerge from the model.

First, the model suggests that children with language problems may do poorly on assessment instruments for more than one reason. They may fail because they lack the language skill being tested but, depending on the nature of the materials and the task, also may be unable to process the test information itself. Problems of attention, discrimination, memory, or higher level thinking skills may interfere with a linguistic response. Problems of reception (comprehension) or expression (retrieval, formulation, or motor production) may prevent children from expressing what they know. Each test task must be analyzed to determine specifically what the children are being asked to do. If they are unsuccessful, then alternative hypotheses as to why they failed must be pursued as part of the diagnostic process.

Clinicians cannot simply assume that the children did not know the content of the test item.

The second consideration is a caution about testing language comprehension and expression. Comprehension of language can occur yet children still may lack the ability to express what they have understood (Johnson & Myklebust, 1967). Apraxic children may not be able to utter more than a few sounds but can be quite competent in understanding the language spoken to them. Similarly, those with memory and retrieval problems may not be able to recall material that they understood quite well. It follows, then, when assessing comprehension in some children, that deficits in expressive processes may interfere with adequate evaluation of reception.

Means must be devised to evaluate comprehension without requiring a spoken response. Recognition responses (pointing, multiple choice, yes/no, and manipulation of objects) are examples of formats that do not require expressive responses and that avoid potential interference from expressive deficits. Carol Chomsky (1969), for example, instructed children to manipulate doll figures to demonstrate the meaning of sentences.

However, many reading and listening comprehension tests use expressive responses to assess comprehension, thereby potentially confounding the data. Tests of oral reading comprehension, for example, often ask children to read a passage and answer questions orally after the passage has been removed. If they succeed, it can be assumed that comprehension is adequate; however, expressive problems may prevent them from indicating what they understood. If they fail to answer a comprehension question correctly, at least five possibilities arise:

1. they comprehended the information but never stored it;
2. they stored the information but could not retrieve it;
3. they could not formulate the answer appropriately into adequate spoken language;
4. they could not activate the motor patterns necessary to express what was comprehended;
5. they did not comprehend the information when read.

By eliminating an expressive response and relying on a recognition response (finding the correct answer in the text, multiple choice, yes/no), the examiner can be more sure that failure indicates lack of comprehension, the fifth possibility in that list. Thus, so-called comprehension measures must be analyzed carefully to determine the exact nature of the response required (Geffner, 1981).

The opposite problem also exists, as is made clear in Chapter 8. Recognition responses are inappropriate when the test specifically seeks to evaluate children's ability to express themselves. Recognizing the correct spelling of a word or correct punctuation of a written sentence is not equivalent to spontaneous production, so teachers must determine exactly what abilities (receptive or expressive) they wish to assess and what information they need to collect. It is valuable to structure testing batteries to include both recognition and production responses in order to determine whether discrepancies exist. Then hypotheses as to reasons for such discrepancies may be investigated further.

## Section 3. General Implications for Remediation

Because of the lack of knowledge about the validity and efficacy of virtually any intervention programs, remedial plans are based on a priori theories and principles (Panagos & Griffith, 1981) that may be more or less logical, more or less comprehensive. The individualized nature of learning profiles, the multiple possibilities for combinations of processing deficits, and their effects on specific children make creation of validity studies of specific remedial programs on large groups a forbidding task indeed. The theoretical model of learning disabilities that a teacher adopts thus assumes paramount importance in formulating a rationale for any remedial program. In addition, certain aspects of the theory of language are of crucial importance.

With respect to the theory of language, two features are especially important: (1) the relation of cognition to language development and (2) the relative autonomy of each of the domains of language: phonology, semantics, syntax, and pragmatics. Chapter 6 discusses the language and cognition issue.

The issue of linguistic context or the relationships among those language domains also is crucially important for developing objectives and teaching strategies for learning disabled children. Although historically remedial attention has focused on single domains (problems of articulation, syntax, communication), Panagos and Griffith argue that professionals now recognize the inseparability of these domains and feel that "the components of language and learning are too interrelated for anything but artificial separation by program developers" (p. 79).

However, while probably no one would argue for a view that these domains are entirely separable, evidence from learning disabled children supports a middle position. Certain such children appear to have deficits in only one language area (pragmatics, for example), a fact that argues for the view that these domains are semiautonomous (Johnson & Myklebust, 1967). While problems with phonology, semantics, or syntax generally interfere with communicative effectiveness, these systems appear to operate semi-independently of each other. Spekman (1978), for example, finds learning disabled children who have adequate skills in phonology, semantics, and syntax but who nevertheless have difficulty communicating messages efficiently to others in an experimental task. Here again clinicians must be alert to individual profiles of learning disabled children with respect to the effect of one language problem on other rule systems.

These aspects of language theory must be taken into account in remedial planning. Unfortunately, opinions change and it is difficult to know whether one year's views on such crucial questions as the relationship of cognition to language and the interrelationship among the various domains hold seeds of truth or will be replaced the next year with a different view.

However, while these language theory considerations are undeniably important, they focus on characteristics of the language system itself. It is important to also consider both the theory of learning disabilities and the characteristics of the children. Children may have purely expressive problems or receptive difficulties as well. The problem may exist mainly at the level of attention, perception, memory, symbolization, or of higher cognitive or motor skills. Even within a single domain, different profiles of disorder may exist and the pattern of language problems is not unrelated to the children's processing deficits.

For example, when investigating syntactic disorders, Wren (1980) finds that children who have problems discriminating, comprehending, sequencing, and remembering language also have difficulty formulating basic, simple sentence structures while those with deficits in only memory and sequencing do not. Thus any program designed for remediation must specifically take into account the processing profile of the individual child since each one learns differently (or may fail to learn for different reasons).

To summarize, learning disabled children who have difficulty with language are not like other groups, such as those with retardation or cultural disadvantage, who may also need language intervention. In the latter cases it may be enough to concentrate on language and curriculum variables when planning intervention. With language disabled children, learner variables—specifically, processing profiles—also must be taken into account to determine how they learn (or fail to learn) and how the cognitive dimension interacts with the language variables described earlier. To emphasize the need to consider these children from the perspective of interactions between language and such cognitive processes as attention, perception, and memory, Gerber and Bryen (1981) state, "language acquisition and use are inextricably related to these cognitive mechanisms . . . " (p. 83).

Thus, while the gap between diagnosis and remediation often has been lamented, it need not be if teachers take care to (1) be aware of the theories, models, or assumptions behind diagnostic evaluation and (2) make use of the same theoretical tools when designing intervention.

*Goals of Intervention*

A learning disability (and specifically a language dysfunction) may have far-reaching consequences in both academic and nonacademic areas. Language forms the basis for most academic subjects, particularly reading, spelling, and written formulation. Language problems may severely affect children's nonacademic development, e.g., overall social maturity and independent functioning. With this in mind, it is instructive to review typical goals of remedial language intervention.

Any element of language development generally has been limited to two objectives: (1) to fill in any gaps in the specific area (phonology, syntax, and so on), and (2) to assist the children in making steady developmental progress in learning more complex features of the system in question. It should be noted that these goals focus only on language-related aspects of intervention. While they may form a beginning for remedial planning, others must be added systematically.

Five interrelated goals need attention in remedial planning: (1) specific language objectives, (2) integration with other domains (semantics, syntax, etc.), (3) integration with other learning contexts (both academic and nonacademic), (4) related processing problems, and (5) cognitive strategies and other variables of learning style. Although the amount of emphasis given to each of these will depend on the individual child, each area should at least receive consideration as part of the goals for intervention. Planning may begin with a specific objective, but clinicians must also consider other language-related objectives (goals 2 and 3) and learner-related objectives (goals 4 and 5).

For example, a specific language objective such as discrimination or articulation of final "s" will have an impact on children's learning of plurals (semantic and syntactic domains). Thus remediation must be planned so that the targets are not taught in isolation but are integrated with other wider language objectives. Articulation of final "s" (and subsequent pronunciation of plurals) may have an impact on children's ability to read orally and spell a variety of words. Perhaps other learning contexts must be integrated as well. Thus, one group of goals for the learning disabled consists of larger and larger interrelated language contexts that must be taken into account in remedial planning.

In addition, there may be a reciprocal relationship between a variety of processing areas and specific language objectives that must be taken into account. Auditory discrimination of final "s," for example, should not be taught in isolation, but rather in meaningful relationship to plurals and possessives. Beyond processing deficits are a broader range of less direct but nevertheless important learner variables such as cognitive strategies, learning style, and personality factors:

- problem solving ability, including problem detection and comprehension of the task (Johnson, 1981)
- monitoring and use of feedback (Johnson, 1981; Wiig & Semel, 1976)
- memory strategies, including verbal rehearsal (Johnson, 1981)
- rule generalization and application (Johnson, 1981; Torgesen, 1975; Reid & Hresko, 1981)

- cognitive style (impulsive/reflective, field dependence) (Gerber & Bryen, 1981).

These must be taken into account in remedial planning.

In sum, the several dimensions of the model presented must be considered when planning intervention, both language related and learner related. Hence:

> The multidimensional approach to the learning disability is essential in order that the educational plan be sufficiently broad in scope. A uni-dimensional approach leads to a restricted educational plan; if the emphasis is on a specific disturbance without consideration for broader areas of function, the instruction concerns only the development of skills. On the other hand, an approach that considers only generalized deficits in reading or arithmetic is not sufficient to meet the child's needs. A remedial plan which includes both specific and generalized objectives permits the teacher to work on the deficits and to relate her efforts to all of the areas involved. (Johnson & Myklebust, 1967, p. 52)

*Teaching Strategies*

General teaching strategies, as well as remedial goals, may be derived from the model. Each learning disabled child has a learning style that is entirely individual. The remedial plan must be designed to meet those individualized needs. A diagnostic profile of the child (developed from the questions considered in the previous section ) serves as a guide to modify planning and teaching.

The job of teaching language learning disabled children is made more challenging by the existence of two bodies of strategies:

1. Techniques developed mainly by specialists and researchers in psycholinguistics and speech and language therapy based mainly on normal language development.
2. Techniques, developed by learning disabilities specialists for a range of problems broader than just specific language problems.

Traditionally, the former strategies have focused on language content and presentation of targets in small, logically sequenced steps, while the latter have focused on auditory and cognitive processes that, in some cases, may not have been directly related to substantial learning in the identified language area. However, when teaching language learning disabled children, it is necessary to distill the positive elements from both of these approaches.

This combined approach consists of teaching the children to ''listen, identify, discriminate, represent, retrieve, organize, produce, and correctly structure information'' (Panagos & Griffith, 1981, p. 71), using a variety of appropriate strategies developed from both learning disabilities and psycholinguistics. Information presented to the children must be modified to meet their individual needs, as determined in diagnostic testing.

Suggestions for teaching strategies and modifications for each language domain are presented in the following chapters.

---

**SELECTED READINGS IN LANGUAGE DEVELOPMENT**

*Phonology*

deVilliers, J., & deVilliers, P. *Language acquisition*. Cambridge, Mass.: Harvard University Press, 1978.

Olmsted, D. *Out of the mouths of babes*. The Hague: Mouton Publishers, 1971.

Poole, I. Genetic development of articulation of consonant sounds in speech. *Elementary English Review*, 1934, *11*, 159-161.

Shriberg, L., & Kwiatkowski, J. *Natural process analysis (NPA): A procedure for phonological analysis of continuous speech samples*. New York: John Wiley & Sons, Inc., 1980.

Templin, M. *Certain language skills in children: Their development and interrelationships*. Minneapolis: University of Minnesota Press, 1957.

*Semantics*

Anglin, J.M. *Word, object and conceptual development*. New York: W.W. Norton & Company, Inc., 1977.

Clark, E.V. What's in a word? On a child's acquisition of semantics in his first language. In T.E. Moore (Ed.), *Cognitive development and the acquisition of language*. New York: Academic Press, 1973.

Litowitz, B. Learning to make definitions. *Journal of Child Language*, 1977, *4*, 289-304.

Nelson, K. Concept, word and sentence: Interrelationships in acquisition and development. *Psychological Review*, 1974, *81*, 267-285.

Nelson, K. Semantic development and the development of semantic memory. In K.E. Nelson (Ed.), *Children's language* (Vol. 1). New York: Gardner Press, 1978.

*Syntax and Morphology*

Bowerman, M. The acquisition of complex sentences. In P. Fletcher & M. Garman (Eds.), *Language acquisition*. Cambridge: Cambridge University Press, 1979.

Crystal, D., Fletcher, P., & Garman, M. *The grammatical analysis of language disability*. London: Edward Arnold, Ltd., 1976.

Fletcher, P. The development of the verb phrase. In P. Fletcher & M. Garman (Eds.), *Language acquisition*. Cambridge: Cambridge University Press, 1979.

Garman, M. Early grammatical development. In P. Fletcher & M. Garman (Eds.), *Language acquisition*. Cambridge: Cambridge University Press, 1979.

Lee, L. *Developmental sentence analysis: A grammatical assessment procedure for speech and language disorders*. Evanston, Ill.: Northwestern University Press, 1974.

*Pragmatics*

Bloom, L., & Lahey, M. *Language development and language disorders*. New York: John Wiley & Sons, Inc., 1978.

Hopper, R., & Naremore, R. *Children's speech: A practical introduction to communication development* (2nd ed.). New York: Harper & Row Publishers, Inc., 1978.

Prutting, C. Process: The action of moving forward progressively from one point to another on the way to completion. *Journal of Speech and Hearing Disorders*, 1979, *44*, 3-30.

Rees, N. Pragmatics of language: Applications to normal and disordered language development. In R. Schiefelbusch (Ed.), *Bases of language intervention*. Baltimore: University Park Press, 1978.

Weeks, T. *Born to talk*. Rowley, Mass.: Newbury House Publishers, 1979.

---

## REFERENCES

Atchison, M., & Canter, G. Variables influencing phonemic discrimination performance in normal and learning disabled children. *Journal of Speech and Hearing Disorders*, 1979, *44*, 543-553.

Bateman, B. Teaching reading to learning disabled and other hard-to-teach children. In L. Resnick & P. Weaver (Eds.), *Theory and practice of early reading* (Vol. 1). Hillsdale, N.J.: Lawrence Erlbaum Associates, Publishers, 1979.

Bloom, L. Talking, understanding and thinking. In R. Schiefelbusch & L. Lloyd (Eds.), *Language perspectives: Acquisition, retardation, and intervention*. Baltimore: University Park Press, 1974.

Bloom, L., & Lahey, M. *Language development and language disorders*. New York: John Wiley & Sons, Inc., 1978.

Brown, R. *Words and things*. New York: The Free Press, 1958.

Carey, S. The child as word learner. In M. Halle, J. Bresnan, & G. Miller (Eds.), *Linguistic theory and psychological reality*. Cambridge, Mass.: The MIT Press, 1978.

Carrow-Woolfolk, E., & Lynch, J. *An integrative approach to language disorders in children*. New York: Grune & Stratton, Inc., 1982.

Chalfant, J., & Scheffelin, M. *Central processing dysfunction in children: A review of research*. NINDS Monograph No. 9. Bethesda, Md.: Dept. of Health, Education, and Welfare, 1969.

Chomsky, C. *The acquisition of syntax in children from 5 to 10*. Cambridge, Mass.: The MIT Press, 1969.

Crystal, D., Fletcher, P., & Garman, M. *The grammatical analysis of language disability*. London: Edward Arnold, Ltd., 1976.

Curtiss, S., Fromkin, V., Krashen, S., Rigler, D., & Rigler, M. The linguistic development of Genie. *Language*, 1974, *50*, 528-554.

Day, J. Right hemisphere language processing in normal right handers. *Journal of Experimental Psychology: Human Perception and Performance*, 1977, *3*, 518-528.

Dukes, P. Developing social prerequisites to oral communication. *Topics in Learning and Learning Disabilities*, 1981, *1*, 47-58.

Eisenson, J. *Aphasia in children*. New York: Harper & Row Publishers, Inc., 1972.

*Federal Register*, Vol. 42 (163), August 23, 1977.

Fletcher, P. The development of the verb phrase. In P. Fletcher & M. Garman (Eds.), *Language acquisition*. Cambridge: Cambridge University Press, 1979.

Flood, J., & Salus, M. Metalinguistic awareness: Its role in language development and its assessment. *Topics in Language Disorders*, 1982, *2*, 56-64.

Geffner, D. Assessment of language disorders: Linguistic and cognitive functions. *Topics in Language Disorders, 1981, 1,* 1-10.

Gerber, A., & Bryen, D. *Language and learning disabilities.* Baltimore: University Park Press, 1981.

Goodman, K. Psycholinguistic universals in the reading process. In F. Smith (Ed.), *Psycholinguistics and reading.* New York: Holt, Rinehart & Winston, Inc., 1973.

Hammill, D., & Larsen, S. The relationship of selected auditory perceptual skills and reading ability. *Journal of Learning Disabilities.* 1974, *7,* 429-435.

Hook, P. *A study of metalinguistic awareness and reading strategies in proficient and learning disabled readers.* Unpublished doctoral dissertation, Northwestern University, 1976.

Ingram, D. The relationship between comprehension and production. In R. Schiefelbusch & L. Lloyd, *Language perspectives: Acquisition, retardation, and intervention.* Baltimore: University Park Press, 1974.

Ingram, D. Phonological patterns in the speech of young children. In P. Fletcher & M. Garman (Eds.), *Language acquisition.* Cambridge: Cambridge University Press, 1979.

Johnson, D.J. Factors to consider in programming for children with language disorders. *Topics in Learning and Learning Disabilities, 1981, 1,* 13-28.

Johnson, D.J. Programming for dyslexia: The need for interaction analyses. *Annals of Dyslexia,* 1982, *32,* 61-70.

Johnson, D.J., & Myklebust, H.R. *Learning disabilities: Educational principles and practices.* New York: Grune & Stratton, Inc., 1967.

Kavale, K. The relationship between auditory perceptual skills and reading ability: A meta-analysis. *Journal of Learning Disabilities, 1981, 14,* 539-546.

Kinsbourne, M., & Caplan, P. *Children's learning and attention problems.* Boston: Little, Brown & Co., 1979.

Lee, L. *Developmental sentence analysis: A grammatical assessment procedure for speech and language disorders.* Evanston, Ill.: Northwestern University Press, 1974.

Lee, L., Koenigsknecht, R., & Mulhern, S. *Interactive language development teaching.* Evanston, Ill.: Northwestern University Press, 1975.

Leonard, L. What is deviant language? *Journal of Speech and Hearing Disorders, 1972, 37,* 427-446.

Lewis, M., & Cherry, L. Social behavior and language acquisition. In M. Lewis & L. Rosenblum (Eds.), *Interaction, conversation, and the development of language.* New York: John Wiley & Sons, Inc., 1977.

Lieberman, L. The implications of noncategorical special education. *Journal of Learning Disabilities,* 1980, *13*(2), 14-17.

Lyon, R. & Watson, B. Empirically derived subgroups of learning disabled readers: Diagnostic characteristics. *Journal of Learning Disabilities, 1981, 14,* 256-261.

Menyuk, P. Comparison of grammar of children with functionally deviant and normal speech. *Journal of Speech and Hearing Research, 1964, 7,* 109-121.

Menyuk, P., & Menn, L. Early strategies for the perception and production of words and sounds. In P. Fletcher & M. Garman (Eds.), *Language acquisition.* Cambridge: Cambridge University Press, 1979.

Morehead, D.M., & Ingram, D. The development of base syntax in normal and linguistically deviant children. *Journal of Speech and Hearing Research, 1973, 16,* 330-352.

Myklebust, H.R. *Auditory disorders in children.* New York: Grune & Stratton, Inc., 1954.

Myklebust, H.R. Learning disabilities: Psychoneurological disorders in childhood. *Rehabilitation Literature, 1964, 25,* 354-360.

Myklebust, H.R. *Development and disorders of written language* (Vol. 2). New York: Grune & Stratton, Inc., 1973.

Orton, S. *Reading, writing, and speech problems in children.* New York: W.W. Norton & Company, Inc., 1937.

Panagos, J., & Griffith, P. Okay, what do educators know about language intervention? *Topics in Learning and Learning Disabilities,* 1981, *1,* 69-82.

Rees, N. Bases of decision in language training. *Journal of Speech and Hearing Disorders,* 1971, *36,* 283-304.

Rees, N. Auditory processing factors in language disorders: The view from Procrustes' bed. *Journal of Speech and Hearing Disorders,* 1973, *43,* 208-219.

Reid, K., & Hresko, W. *A cognitive approach to learning disabilities.* New York: McGraw Hill Book Company, 1981.

Rice, M. *Cognition to language: Categories, word meanings, and training.* Baltimore: University Park Press, 1980.

Rosenthal, W.S. *The role of perception in child language disorders: A theory based on faulty signal detection strategies.* Paper presented at the American Speech and Hearing Association convention, Las Vegas, 1974.

Ross, A. *Psychological aspects of learning disabilities and reading disorders.* New York: McGraw-Hill Book Company, 1976.

Shankweiler, D., & Liberman, I. Misreading: A search for causes. In J. Kavanaugh & I. Mattingly (Eds.), *Language by ear and by eye.* Cambridge, Mass.: The MIT Press, 1972.

Spekman, N.J. *An investigation of the dyadic, verbal, problem-solving communication abilities of learning disabled and normal children.* Unpublished doctoral dissertation, Northwestern University, 1978.

Stark, J. Reading: What needs to be assessed? *Topics in Language Disorders,* 1981, *1,* 87-94.

Strauss, A., & Werner, H. Disorders of conceptualization in the brain-injured child. *Journal of Nervous and Mental Disease,* 1942, *96,* 153-172.

Swisher, L., & Aten, J. Assessing comprehension of spoken language: A multifaceted task. *Topics in Language Disorders,* 1981, *1,* 75-86.

Torgesen, J. Why do some learning disabled children have problems remembering? Does it make a difference? *Topics in Learning & Learning Disabilities,* 1982, *2,* 54-61.

Vetter, D.K. Language disorders and schooling. *Topics in Language Disorders,* 1982, *2,* 13-19.

Vogel, S. Syntactic abilities in normal and dyslexic children. *Journal of Learning Disabilities,* 1974, *7,* 103-109.

Wallach, G., & Butler, K. (Eds.). *Language learning disabilities in school age children.* Baltimore: The Williams and Wilkins Co., in press.

Wiig, E., & Semel, E. *Language disabilities in children and adolescents.* Columbus, Ohio: The Charles E. Merrill Publishing Co., Inc., 1976.

Wiig, E., & Semel, E. *Language intervention and assessment for the learning disabled.* Columbus, Ohio: The Charles E. Merrill Publishing Co., Inc., 1980.

Wing, C. Language processes and linguistic levels: A matrix. *Language, Speech, and Hearing Services in Schools,* 1982, *13*(2), 2-10.

Wren, C.T. *The relationship of auditory and cognitive processes to syntactic patterns in learning disabled and normal children.* Unpublished doctoral dissertation, Northwestern University, 1980.

Chapter 2

# Phonology

*Gail P. Harris-Schmidt and Elizabeth A. Noell*

## PART I. PHONOLOGY AND LEARNING DISABILITIES

In this and the next three chapters, the relationships between the specific domains of linguistic knowledge, cognitive processes, and language performance are examined in more detail, beginning with the smallest unit of language, i.e., speech sounds, and the domain of phonology.

Phonology is the study of the sound system of the language. This simple statement belies a change in thinking about the relationship of speech to language. Traditionally, articulation (speech) has been viewed as separate from knowledge of language. However, theories in the early 1980s view articulation as more than producing sounds correctly: apprehension and production of speech sounds are integrally related to knowledge of the other linguistic domains, particularly word meaning and grammatical structure. Phonological development requires many of the same cognitive processes (for example, "rule" generalization) as does maturation in syntax, semantics, or pragmatics. Thus, perception and articulation of speech sounds become an integral part of language development.

To the extent that disorders of phonological development are related to deficits in cognitive processes, they are best viewed, along with other dysfunctions, as learning disabilities. This is the case not only because phonological ability is closely related to cognitive processes but also because phonology's links to other aspects of language extend beyond spoken communication. Disorders in phonological development are not limited to oral language but frequently interfere with written language as well. For example, a phonological disorder that manifests itself in the preschooler as an articulation problem may appear later as a difficulty with phonic analysis in reading and/or difficulty with spelling.

Before examining approaches to the study of phonology, a review of some basic terms (Exhibit 2-1) is useful (deVilliers & deVilliers, 1978; Van Riper & Smith,

**Exhibit 2-1** Glossary of Major Terms in Phonology

---

**Allophone:** Phonetically different variants of a phoneme.

**Consonants:** Speech sounds of a language produced by the impeding or cutting off of air expelled from the lungs; usually categorized by manner and place of articulation and vibration of vocal cords.

**Distinctive Features:** Abstract articulatory or acoustic proper ties serving to distinguish among different phonemes.

**Intonation:** Changes in stress and pitch throughout a sentence that signal differences in meaning.

**Manner:** The nature of the interference with the stream of air; English classifies these as stops, plosives, fricatives, sibilants, affricates, laterals, nasals, and semivowels.

**Phone:** A physical manifestation of a speech sound.

**Phoneme:** An abstract group of allophones, meaningfully different from any other sounds.

**Phonemics:** The study of meaningfully distinctive (linguistically relevant) speech sounds in a particular language.

**Phonetics:** The study of the perception and production of all perceptibly different speech sounds used for communication in human languages.

**Phonological Rules:** Rules by which sounds are combined into words and that "account for" systematic variations in the form of words in different phonetic contexts.

---

1979). A brief study of these concepts helps in understanding the complexity children face in segmenting sounds, attaching sound to meaning, and understanding what is meant when one sound is contrasted with another.

## Section 1. Studying Phonology in Normal Children

*Speech Sound Perception*

Two major approaches to studying speech perception are apparent in the literature. Traditionally, it has been studied from the perspective of phonemic contrasts that affect meaning, typically by using a same/different judgment about minimally contrasted pairs of words (i.e., "cup," "cub"). This approach was primarily quantitative and developmental and it generally was found that the number of perceptual errors decreased as children matured.

More recently, efforts have been made to find a one-to-one correspondence between phonemes and the acoustic speech signal and to explain speech perception in terms of the way speech sounds are produced acoustically. Sophisticated laboratory equipment, including speech synthesizers, has been used to produce graphic representations of human speech and synthesized speech with extremely small acoustic variations between phonemes. Unfortunately, the original goal of finding a clear correspondence between articulated sounds and perceived phonemes proved rather elusive since the relationship of speech to phonemic perception is extremely complex and direct correspondence is infrequent. However, experimental work in this approach has revealed the importance to perception of relative cues and context and of both linguistic and articulatory knowledge (Borden & Harris, 1980).

While these general findings from the acoustic approach have significantly influenced attitudes toward the development and pathology of speech perception, most acoustic research uses either adults or infants as subjects and very few of the actual results have been applied to perception in normal children and even fewer to populations with perceptual or articulatory deficits (see, however, Koury-Parker, 1983; Tallal, 1980a, 1980b). Thus, on the whole, in the absence of an easily applicable, explanatory, acoustic model, the approach to studying speech perceptual disorders remains primarily descriptive and developmental. A refined version of this approach is presented in the next major part of this chapter.

## Speech Sound Production

For years speech pathologists treated expression of speech sounds as entities in isolation and attempted to teach them that way. The /k/ sounds (phones) in "keel" and "cool," for example, were not recognized as very different in their manner of articulation. Similarly, the fact that a child could pronounce /st/ in one context and not another was seen as an inconsistency and little else. As a result, /k/ and /st/ were taught with little regard for the way in which children used such sounds in context. Today, the teaching of sounds with no regard for the context into which they are placed has declined and more practitioners are aware of the theoretical reasons for their plans, turning to a number of newer approaches with children who have articulation disorders.

Jakobson (1968) and Jakobson, Fant, and Halle (1972) provide both a theoretical breakthrough and a model to which others could react in their description of distinctive features. Jakobson describes changes in word meaning resulting from the substitution of one sound for another. Sound changes may be based on minimal differences, such as in the move from "*bill*" to "*pill*" with a removal of voicing from the /b/. He outlines a number of characteristics that sounds can have and regards phonemes as characterized by a set of distinctive features that are specified in terms of articulatory and acoustic properties. Each phoneme is made up of a bundle of these features, with the presence ( + ) or absence ( − ) of each feature specified. Thus, phonemes can be ± voicing, ± continuant, ± vocalic, etc. Jakobson argues that children first learn sounds with the greatest contrast in terms of distinctive features, with more closely related sounds entering later.

His descriptions of development include the ideas that babbling is unrestricted and has no relation to children's later acquisition of adult phonology; that phonological development is the same as mastery of distinctive features; that children develop their own series of phoneme contrasts; and that their patterns of phonological development are systematic and universal (1968). deVilliers and deVilliers (1978) and Ingram (1976a, 1979) make two objections: (1) they state that there is much more individual variation than his universality theory would suggest and (2) they believe that language development based on distinctive features is probably a better description of children age 2 and above and therefore a valid way for looking at phonemic problems in older children.

A second widely mentioned theory is that of Stampe (1972), whose Natural Phonology posits an innate set of hierarchically structured processes that simplify adult words. Here, processes mean consistent patterns by which children simplify sounds or groups of sounds. In such a theory, all children would be expected to simplify adult words in the same ways. This universal pattern of development often is contradicted by actual speech samples but the concept of process analysis is a valuable contribution.

A third theory, generative phonology, examines speech sounds in the context of each other. Rather than looking at universals in the development of isolated sounds, this theory examines how sound segments combine with each other in regular patterns and the way they are pronounced in different phonetic contexts. Underlying phonemic classifications are studied in relation to the surface or spoken phonetic realization of those segments. Distinctive features are seen as multivalued, not just binary. Thus, the degree of stridency is examined, not just the presence or absence of a feature (Chomsky & Halle, 1968; deVilliers & deVilliers, 1978).

A fourth approach devised by Ingram (1976b, 1979) offers a model of phonological development that synthesizes Stampe's work on process analysis and distinctive feature theory and that parallels cognitive development. Ingram (1976b) also recognizes forces in addition to phonological ones that bear on the development of speech sounds. For example, he discusses the complex morphophonemic rules that govern vowel shifts in such words as "divine-divinity" and says children must understand the morpheme in order to isolate the sound change. Contrasts in stress (nonverbal prosodic features) also are related to meaning changes: e.g., "green house" vs. "greenhouse." It may be that some of these contrasts enter the vocabulary core as very separate entries, not as recognitions of morphophonemic changes (similar to irregular past tense morphemes that enter as separate forms before the regular past tense is learned and overused: e.g., "I broke" before "I breaked").

Ingram's model of process analysis (1976b), which allows for children's individual variation, provides both a method for studying development and a diagnostic method, discussed later in this chapter. Ingram's and others' theories of early normal phonological development are examined in the following discussion of the development of articulation.

According to Ingram, early phonological development can be divided into several periods:

- reflexive crying and vegetative sounds (0 to 8 weeks)
- cooing and laughter (8 to 20 weeks)
- vocal play (16 to 30 weeks)
- reduplicated babbling (25 to 50 weeks)
- nonreduplicated babbling and expressive jargon (9 to 18 months).

More sophisticated analyses of early utterances, including spectrographic studies and detailed scrutiny of distinctive features, have aided in the study of the move from one stage to the next. Difficulties remain in phonetic transcription, however, as some infants' sounds are not like adults' and can be accounted for by phonetic transcription only with difficulty.

Theories about early expressive development have varied greatly. For many years, a generally accepted behavioral theory (Morley, 1972) regarded the sounds of all languages as present very early. Then those appropriate to the language the children are learning are selectively reinforced by adults and develop while those of other languages drop out (Stark, 1979). Even the rate of vocal output is seen as influenced by appropriate rewards. However, this theory came under criticism as experiments showed that new vocal behavior was not influenced by experimental conditions and not predictable by reinforcement (Stark, 1979).

Ingram's (1979) research with expressive phonological development indicates that process analysis along with recognition of individual variation can be used to explain the period of development from 18 months to 4 years. During this time children go through considerable development in phonological ability, moving from single words with simple forms toward multiple word utterances that are high in intelligibility. Ingram maintains that children basically observe "sound laws" during this stage; that is, if they move back consonants to front and say "tat" for "cat," they are most likely also to say "do" for "go."

Ingram (1979) describes several normal processes that go on during this period. Substitution processes describe ways by which children change adult words. The most common of these are:

- **Stopping:** Fricatives are replaced with stops as in "tea/sea."
- **Fronting:** Velar and palatal consonants are replaced with alveolar ones as in "ta/call."
- **Gliding:** /w/ or /j/ often is substituted for the liquids /y/ and /r/ as in "weo/yellow."
- **Vocalization:** A vowel replaces a syllabic consonant, as in "apo/apple."

- **Vowel Neutralization:** Vowels change into oral and often centralized vowels, "buh/beet."

Ingram (1979) calls a second group assimilation processes. In these, children assimilate one segment in a word to another. Common processes include:

- **Voicing:** Consonants tend to be voiced when preceding a vowel and devoiced at the end of a syllable, as in "bik/pig."
- **Consonant Harmony:**

    1. **Velar Assimilation:** This occurs when the apical consonants tend to assimilate to neighboring velar consonants, as in "guk/duk."
    2. **Labial Assimilation:** This occurs when apical consonants tend to assimilate to neighboring labials, as in "bub/tub."
    3. **Denasalization:** Nasal consonants tend to denasalize in the neighborhood of nonnasal consonants as in "Bichelle/Michelle."

- **Progressive Vowel Assimilation:** Unstressed syllables assimilate to the preceding or following stressed vowels, as in "booidoo/bacon" (Ingram, 1979).

Ingram regards syllables as especially important in phonological analysis. This recognition of the "environment" of the sound is what therapists are being called on to recognize as more valid than separate sound treatment (Lorentz, 1976). Ingram (1979) and Menyuk and Menn (1979) recognize that sound substitutions vary according to the place of the sound in the syllable. Syllable structure processes include:

- cluster reduction, as in "pay/play"
- deletion of final consonant as in "bi/bib"
- weak syllable deletion, in which the unstressed syllable is omitted, as in "nana/banana"
- reduplication, in which the child repeats one syllable, as in "wawa/water."

In her review of 16 major phonological processes, Khan (1982) reports additional ones that are not mentioned as frequently in descriptions of development, including:

- **Affrication:** An affricate is used to replace a fricative, as /tʃʌvəl/ for "shovel."

- **Coalescence:** Words are produced with fewer syllables than their corresponding adult form, as in /mɛn/ for "melon." This phonological process differs from weak syllable deletion in that all the elements of all syllables are preserved.
- **Glottal Replacement:** This uses a glottal stop /ʔ/ to replace a consonant.
- **Metathesis:** This is an unusual phonological process described by Ingram (1976b) in which the sequence of two phonemes in a word is altered, e.g., /pɛsniə/ for "pencil" where the /n/ and /s/ are transposed (Khan, 1982).

Different children, rather than uniformly following universal principles, say the same word in a variety of ways. The complexity and novelty of a word may make it especially difficult for an individual child. Several authors mention the existence of "frozen forms," those that remain immature compared to other words in the vocabulary (deVilliers & deVilliers, 1979; Ingram, 1979). At the other end of the spectrum, children may use some unusually advanced words compared to their normally progressing development. Ingram recognizes both individual variation and some lack of correspondence between adult and child forms.

Related to individual simplification or idiosyncratic processes is the concept of phonological preferences for or avoidance of particular articulation patterns. The developmental literature suggests that children selectively attend to certain aspects of the phonological system during the acquisition process (Dunn & Barron, 1982). Dunn and Barron report that this attention becomes apparent when children, as they acquire their first words, avoid saying those containing a certain sound or class of sounds. On the other hand, some children do show a preference for a certain sound or sound class. Dunn and Barron reason that this behavior may be a means of simplifying the task of mastering the phonological system. When examining children with disordered phonology and planning for their remediation, it is useful to identify the characteristics in their speech that are individual ways of processing and producing phonological information. Moreover, it is equally important to recognize phonological processes that are typical of young children (Dunn & Barron, 1982).

Thus, it can be seen that simplifying processes and dynamic organization of children's own systems must be taken into account (Ingram, 1979) in developmental descriptions. From this discussion of approaches to articulation, the influence of the field of linguistics should be evident. Articulation errors no longer are described or treated as isolated entities. Rather, phonology is viewed as a rule-governed system; that is, it is an integral part of language. Further, the rule systems of the various domains of language, including phonology, are interrelated, and it is in this context that children with both speech disorders in both perception and production are seen as learning disabled—a view that of course is not the traditional one. The field of speech pathology has developed its own set of approaches for looking at articulation problems, discussed in the next section.

### Section 2. Studying Disorders of Phonology

Traditionally, phonological disorders have been in the realm of speech pathologists who have diagnosed and provided therapy for children with auditory discrimination and articulation problems. More recently, however, both psycholinguists and special educators have exhibited a renewed interest in atypical phonological development—the former group because these children provide interesting patterns for study and the latter because of the realization that phonological errors often affect oral language, reading, and written language.

Along with this renewed interest have come investigations into models or frameworks from speech and language pathology. The field has not produced broad models explaining phonological disorders; however, it has used a number of individual dichotomies that have been useful in describing several kinds of disorders. Crystal (1980) summarizes these classification devices as follows:

- receptive vs. productive
- organic vs. functional
- speech vs. language
- deviant vs. delayed
- normal vs. abnormal
- phonetic vs. phonemic.

Receptive vs. expressive (or productive) disorders is a dichotomy used both theoretically and clinically and in the design of many tests. Johnson and Myklebust (1967) argue that receptive processes must precede expressive ones and that, with the exception of pure expressive (motor planning) disorders or dysarthrias (muscle paralyses), receptive problems frequently underlie expressive disorders. However, there are few "pure" disorders of either kind; rather, there are many interactions, so the distinction may be helpful but incomplete.

Organic vs. functional disorders is a dichotomy that distinguishes disorders with known medical or anatomical causes (such as dysarthria in association with cerebral palsy) from those with no known cause. This may be a helpful distinction for clinical purposes because therapeutic intervention may be vastly different for the child who cannot move the tongue easily (dysarthric), the child who cannot do so voluntarily (apraxic), and the child who does so inconsistently in substitution patterns (called the "functional articulation" case, for lack of a better term). The distinction, however, may not be clearcut, the causes may be mixed, and the "functional" label is neither very helpful nor informative.

Speech vs. language disorders constitute a traditional distinction used to separate speech sound discrimination and articulation problems from those of syntax and semantics. This distinction grew from a "symbolic"-"nonsymbolic" distinction, according to Crystal (1980), as phonetic characteristics of speech were not considered to be symbolic, as were grammar and vocabulary. As noted, however, this distinction is being questioned by the newer studies in linguistics such as the work in process analysis (Ingram, 1976a). The symbolic-nonsymbolic distinction now is less than clearcut since many linguists contend that spoken language is being affected by some speech sound production difficulties, i.e., phonemic disorders. Nonsymbolic speech disorders, then, are only those where communicative intent is not lost (e.g., a frontal lisp, making "sun" sound like "thun").

Language deviance vs. language delay is a distinction that may have considerable impact on remediation. Children exhibiting language delay in phonology are said to be following the development of normal peers in sound acquisition but simply at a slower pace. Intervention would be directed at the developmental level at which the children are speaking and move upward chronologically, based on a developmental model. The use of such a model is not appropriate for many children, however, as patterns are not so clearcut for most of them. There may be a combination of deviance and delay patterns, so remediation may need to be more individualized than simply an attempt to move children along from one developmental level to the next. The related issue of language difference, which recognizes a dialectal or stylistic basis for variations, also must be considered.

The normal vs. abnormal distinction may be an attempt to force an artificial dichotomy onto a continuum that is not so easily specified. Crystal (1980) stresses the need to recognize dialects, expectations of listeners, familial speech patterns, etc., before one child's language is compared to another's or is labelled "abnormal."

Phonetic vs. phonemic disorders describe the differences in expressive speech based on the effect on meaning. This often may be a difficult or arbitrary decision based on listeners' perceptions and comprehension of children's utterances. However, the distinction does have utility for the study of rule acquisition in phonological development.

In sum, all of these frameworks can have value in descriptions of children's deviant phonology. Each of them has problems when utilized alone.

## Section 3. Phonological Disorders in Learning Disabled Children

Next is what is specifically known about the characteristics of learning disabled children with disorders in phonology. This section uses some of the categories described in the previous section, i.e., receptive vs. expressive problems, phonemic vs. phonetic, and organic vs. functional. Research is discussed in terms of the approaches presented in the first section. This section initially describes characteristics of receptive problems (speech sound discrimination deficits), then several types of expressive (articulation) problems: phonemic (linguistic) and phonetic (motor or organic), specifically apraxia and dysarthria.

*Speech Sound Discrimination Problems*

Auditory perception or, more specifically, speech sound discrimination, constitutes the major receptive process in phonology. Research using a quantitative approach and the traditional same/different task has shown that many language learning disabled children have impaired capacity to discriminate auditorily between consonants when they are embedded in minimally paired syllables, words, or sentences (Haggarty & Stamm, 1978; Hook, 1976; McReynolds, 1966; Weiner, 1969; Wren, 1980).

In contrast to the quantitative approach, Wiig and Semel (1976) apply a distinctive feature model. They report that these children confuse words containing sounds that differ by one feature more frequently than those that differ by two or more.

In these as well as other studies, auditory discrimination has been investigated using naturally spoken words, syllables, or sounds as stimuli (Atchison, 1975; Atchison & Canter, 1979; Flynn & Byrne, 1970; McReynolds, 1966; Weiner, 1969). However, Lubert (1981) suggests that auditory perceptual deficits could result from an impairment of the ability to detect features that respond to specific acoustic characteristics (as opposed to articulatory characteristics) of the speech wave that cue the perception of phonemes. In investigating this hypothesis, researchers have used synthesized speech or nonspeech signals as stimuli and tasks that do not require a verbal response. Fairly consistent results have been obtained among studies examining the abilities of language disordered children to recognize the order in which two perceptually different sounds occur. In general, it has been found that these children have more difficulty than normal counterparts discriminating rapid sound sequences as well as judging the order of sound sequences when the interstimulus intervals are brief (Lowe & Campbell, 1965; Tallal & Piercy, 1973, 1974, 1975; Tallal & Stark, 1980; Tallal, Stark, Kallman, & Mellitis, 1981). These data confirm clinical impressions that many language learning disabled children have difficulty processing auditory language presented at a normal speaking rate, which often is too fast for them.

The research on the relationship between articulation deficiency and auditory discrimination is conflicting and inconclusive. Poor auditory discrimination has been found to correlate with articulation disorders (Wepman, 1960), and some researchers suggest that individuals who have poor articulation also have poor auditory discrimination (Powers, 1971; Weiss, Lillywhite, & Gordon, 1980; Wepman, 1960; Winitz, 1969). The relationship of perception to articulation in children specifically labelled learning disabled was the subject of a study by Matthews and Seymour (1981). They compare children with articulation defects only to those who have learning disabilities in addition to articulation defects. Their results show that poor speech perception is strongly related to articulation defects in both groups and that the specifically learning disabled children are poorest on a measure of discrimination of their own articulation errors.

Additional questions arise, however, when the problem of children's perception of their own errors is considered. Some studies find that children are unable to detect their own articulation errors (e.g., "I said 'fis' not 'fis'.") but can discern mistakes by others. Other studies find that children detect their own errors when they hear a recording of them later (Borden & Harris, 1980). Thus, the relationship of perception of others' speech to production, as well as of one's own, still needs further research.

In contrast to the typical view that perception may interfere with articulation, Winitz (1969) suggests that poor auditory discrimination could result from articulation disorders rather than being the cause of them. Thus, although it seems logical that poor auditory discrimination could result in articulation deficiencies, this hypothesis has not been conclusively supported by research. Nevertheless, clinical experience suggests that auditory discrimination problems frequently affect meaning and are reflected in the articulation of words.

For example, one learning disabled adult said, "We're going to have an *academic* of mosquitoes" instead of *"epidemic."* Another time, the same adult said, "There are a lot of *verbals* to consider" instead of *"variables."* One learning disabled child said, "Miss Her gave me a nail box" instead of "Miss Herd gave me a mailbox" and that a "foreign person" is one who speaks like us but with an *"accident"* instead of an *"accent."* It is very likely that these errors occurred because they were misperceived originally.

*Phonemic Production Disorders*

Recent approaches to phonology have provided significant data on articulation problems in learning disabled children. Singh, Hayden, and Toombs (1981) use distinctive feature theory to predict subgroups of children with speech and language disorders. They analyzed articulation errors for subgroups of children with (1) articulation disorders, (2) language disorders, and (3) other speech disorders (including cleft palate, hearing impaired, mentally retarded, and stutterers). The results reveal that the feature systems used by each group are sensitive to differences in basic maturational, linguistic, and etiological factors.

To illustrate, the articulation disordered group shows an effect of age across all features: voicing, nasality, continuancy, sibilancy, front, sonorancy, and labiality. Further, 3-year-olds and 4-year-olds perform significantly lower across all features than all other age groups, and 5-year-olds significantly lower than those 6, 7, and 8 years old. Thus, there is a systematic increase in performance as a function of age.

Similar results are found for the language disordered group. However, age differences in feature processing are more pronounced in the articulation disordered group than in the language one. Singh and his colleagues reason that this suggests that the performance of the articulation disordered is more age dependent than that of the language disordered. They add that articulation disorders without concomitant language delay represent an inability to manipulate distinctive features accurately. Distinctive feature errors for the language disordered group, on the other hand, may represent a more general linguistic delay. Statistical data for children having other speech disorders were not available because of the small number of subjects in the sample.

An analysis of the feature system of the articulation disordered group suggests that its feature system is more consistent with normal acquisition than that of the language disordered. That is, this group tends to follow the phonological rules of English. For instance, the often-substituted phonemes also are those that occur most frequently in the language. Thus, the feature system of the articulation disordered group is more consistent with normal acquisition than that of the language disordered.

Ingram (1978, 1979), using process analysis, reaches the following conclusions regarding children with deviant phonological development:

1. Deviant children have systematic phonological systems.
2. Most of the phonological processes found in deviant speech also exist in normal children's speech.
3. Deviant children occasionally use phonological processes that are not found in normal children or that occur in them with much less frequency.
4. Certain phonological processes persist in the speech of deviant children.
5. Deviant children's phonology is more than just delayed because of the factors cited in items 3 and 4.
6. Deviant children use a large number of homonyms and have difficulty using speech sounds contrastively.
7. Deviant children use more simplifying processes than normal children at a comparable level of development.

However, findings using these more recent theories still are tentative. McReynolds and Elbert (1981) criticize Ingram's work and maintain that few quantitative criteria have been applied to determine how often certain processes or patterns appear regularly in normal children. In a preliminary study, they report fewer instances of process "errors" (cluster reductions, deletions, etc.) than would be expected. They raise the point that the traditional articulation evaluation by type of error and place in word (e.g., omission of final /t/; substitution of medial d/b) is not necessarily faulty and may be a more accurate description of phonological disorders. Nevertheless, process analysis as a diagnostic tool has gained some acceptance (see the section on diagnosis) and seems to be compatible with the way specialists study other areas of language learning disabilities.

To summarize, phonemic disorders are considered to be a linguistic problem, a deviancy in the acquisition of the phonological rules. In taking a linguistic approach to the study of this type of articulation disorder, it is assumed that there are certain phonological processes that apply to classes of sounds, not just to individual sounds, that children use when organizing the sound system of the language, and that deficits in a number of cognitive processes (e.g., abstraction of distinctive features, rule generalization) may interfere with phonological development.

*Phonetic Production Disorders (Apraxia and Dysarthria)*

Apraxia, in contrast to phonemic disorders, is the inability to form the volitional motor movements for speech. Apraxia has been studied extensively in adults and also has been observed in children. To describe this behavior in children, terms such as developmental apraxia (Rosenbek & Wertz, 1972), verbal apraxia (Chappell, 1973; Johnson & Myklebust, 1967) or articulatory apraxia (Eisenson, 1972) have been used. In children, the nature of the apraxia and its severity vary from individual to individual. Neurological data also suggest the involvement of cortical areas from both hemispheres (Rosenbek & Wertz, 1972). In contrast, in apraxic adults, specific areas of the brain seem to be involved.

With apraxia of speech, individuals may show impaired positioning of the speech musculature and faulty sequencing of muscle movements for the volitional production of phonemes with little or no impairment of linguistic knowledge. That is, children with apraxia know what they want to say but are unable to program the speech musculature appropriately. This sort of expressive disorder in the auditory system may be compared to the visual-motor disorder of dysgraphia. In the latter problem, children are unable to program fine muscle movement in the hands and fingers for writing. Again, they know what they want to write but cannot coordinate their movements, resulting in jerky, imprecise, often unrecognizable letter formation. The analog in the auditory modality is jerky, imprecise articulation with accompanying alterations in prosodic features (rate, rhythm, and juncture) (Darley, Aronson, & Brown, 1975). Hence apraxia, like dysgraphia, may be considered to be a learning disability involving the motor programming component of expressive acts.

Not all production disorders are learning disabilities, however. To illustrate the limits of the concept, apraxia may be distinguished from dysarthria, a different sort of phonetic disorder, in that the latter involves actual paralysis of the speech musculature and thus is not a learning disability since a psychological processing disorder is not involved. Dysarthric patients know where and how to move their articulators but cannot because of paralysis. Apraxia patients, on the other hand, have difficulty knowing how to program these motor speech movements in spite of adequate muscle strength.

In dysarthria, there is evidence of slowness, weakness, or change of tone of the actual speech musculature (Darley, Brown, & Aronson, 1975). The deviant articulation is consistent and predictable and is a direct result of muscle weakness. All the basic motor processes such as respiration, phonation, resonance, articulation, and prosody often are involved. There are various types of dysarthria: flaccid, spastic, ataxic, hypokinetic, hyperkinetic, and mixed dysarthrias. (For an in-depth discussion of these types, see Darley et al., 1975, and Luchsinger & Arnold, 1965.)

Dysarthric patients typically demonstrate imprecise articulation of consonants through distortions rather than substitutions. In general, the accuracy of their articulation does not vary from one occasion or context to the next (e.g., imitation vs. conversation vs. reading). As the rate of speech increases, intelligibility decreases. Consonants such as /s/ and /l/ are the most difficult to produce (Johns & Darley, 1970).

Clinical experience suggests that some learning disabled children with apraxia may have accompanying dysarthric conditions. Usually, the dysarthria is mild in comparison to cerebral palsy children and other neurologically involved youngsters with dysarthria.

*Subtle Problems*

Many learning disabled children and adults do not misarticulate any sounds as evidenced on formal articulation tests and do not show signs of apraxia or dysarthria. Their conversational speech generally is intelligible, and to the casual listener no articulation problems are noticeable. However, they may have subtle problems pronouncing polysyllabic words. They tend to make numerous errors on the Echolalia Subtest of the *Slingerland Screening Tests for Identifying Children with Specific Language Disability* (Slingerland, 1970). This test requires the individual to say multisyllabic words (e.g., "curiosity, spaghetti") and phrases ("sheets and pillow cases") at least three times in succession. Learning disabled children and adults often omit or substitute sounds or missequence sounds and words. For example, one learning disabled individual said "curiojedy" for "curiosity" and "donimoes" for "dominoes." Another said "eating sagetti and vegebles." Children with minor functional articulation problems, apraxia, dysarthria, and phonemic disorders, also may have difficulty on the Echolalia Subtest.

In sum, learning disabled children have been found to have both receptive and expressive problems in phonology. Receptively, they have difficulty with auditory discrimination. Expressively, they have (1) difficulty learning patterns of sound articulation that signal changes in meaning, (2) difficulty learning the volitional motor patterns for speech sounds, or (3) subtle problems with the sounds in multisyllabic words.

## Section 4. Phonology and Processing Disorders

In working with children with either receptive or expressive problems of phonology, it is vital to know whether and how phonological disorders affect their other areas of learning. Is meaning affected by the speech sound disorder and, if so, do the children realize it? Do the speech sound problems affect other areas of receptive and expressive language such as language comprehension, oral reading, or spelling? How do psychological processes such as attention or conceptualization interact with the phonological disorder? Levels of processing are discussed in relation to phonological disorders.

*Attention*

Attention disorders underlie the learning and academic problems of many learning disabled children. Kneedler and Hallahan (1981) suggest that selective attention is related to short-term memory and metacognitive abilities. In contrast to earlier descriptions of learning disabled children as distractible and in need of medication or behavior modification to control their wandering attention, a newer image has begun to emerge of learners who fail to attend because they have deficient strategies for encoding and organizing information (Torgesen, 1981). This view of attention has implications for children with phonological disorders in terms of spontaneous learning as well as diagnosis and remediation. Not only must clinicians call attention to the task, they also must ensure that the children become active participants, teaching them to bring strategies to bear on learning sound differences and patterns.

*Discrimination*

Underlying perceptual disorders have surely been the most researched area of those seen as contributing to expressive phonological abilities. Receptively, auditory discrimination has been studied with the traditional tests (Goldman, Fristoe, & Woodcock, 1970, 1974; Wepman, 1973) and more recently with spectrographic instruments (Eimas, 1974) so that perception may be studied with well-controlled artificial speech. Although it has been observed clinically that children make production errors that appear to be perceptually based, controversies remain regarding the influence of underlying perceptual problems on articulation. (See the previous discussion in Section 3.)

The relationship of perception to written language ability also is a matter of debate. Kavale (1981) has examined more than 100 studies of perceptual abilities in reading disordered individuals and concludes that when the studies are taken together, a definite relationship can be documented. Other studies (Koury-Parker,

1983; Tallal, 1980a, 1980b; Tallal & Piercy, 1973, 1974; Wepman, 1960) also suggest a relationship between auditory perception and reading although its nature needs further investigation.

In recent years, it has been suggested that certain subgroups of reading disabled children have specific deficits in auditory perception that interfere with their ability to acquire phonics skills. Tallal (1980a, 1980b) reports that some children with reading disabilities have difficulty in the discrimination of rapidly presented information. Tallal hypothesizes that this deficit, in turn, can lead to difficulty in analyzing the speech code at a phonemic level. These deficits are felt to affect phoneme discrimination and sound-symbol correspondences at the phonics skills level of reading.

Shankweiler, Liberman, Mark, Fowler, and Fischer (1979) suggest that poor readers may have subtle deficits in their perception of the acoustic cues for speech. In a speech perception study, Koury-Parker (1982) finds differences between two groups of normal children with high (good) and low (poor) phonics skills. Those with high phonics skills are found to be superior to those with low phonics skills. Clinical experience also suggests a strong relationship between auditory discrimination (particularly of multisyllabic words) and spelling.

Auditory training in speech sound discrimination was traditionally a prerequisite to articulation therapy (Van Riper, 1962). Then, with harsh attacks on the efficacy of such training (Rees, 1973), training in discrimination was discounted as often irrelevant to speech and language development. Now, however, numerous researchers recognize the importance of children's mismatches between sounds produced and their perceptions of them (Berry, 1980; Johnson & Myklebust, 1967; Winitz, 1969).

*Memory*

Torgesen (1981) declares that memory problems are universal to learning disabled children. Failure of long-term retention, he believes, is perhaps the only characteristic that all learning disabled children have in common. He attributes much of this problem to failure to actively attend to, plan, and code tasks for memory. This may be especially true of phonology tasks or articulation exercises that are presented in a rote, rather meaningless manner. Teaching children new sounds through categorizing them into meaningful groups or patterns may be a strategic device that could utilize a conceptual means to aid attention and memory.

*Symbolization*

More than perception, levels of meaning (symbolization) are being examined now as the basis for phonological disorders. The meanings of words, of morphological endings, and of phrases and sentences in language and oral reading all may contribute to and influence speech sound perception and production. Frequently children misperceive unfamiliar words by "hearing" a word already known to them. For example, one little boy misperceived the word "cupboard" as "cover" (cupboard doors do cover) and also misarticulated the word as "cover" and later as "covered." In diagnosing phonemic problems it is important to note that a mistake such as omission of a final /s/ could be a phonemic, a morphological (grammatical), or in some cases an oral reading error.

*Conceptualization*

Conceptualization disorders can affect the ability to detect regularities or "rules" by which phonemes are simplified and later learned in adult patterns. Teaching phonemes through the use of categories of sounds and emphasis on the changes in meaning they affect may be a useful strategy that can influence not only the conceptual level of learning but also active attention and memory.

*Metalinguistic Ability*

The relationship of metalinguistic abilities and phonology is of some interest. In perception of speech sounds, traditional tests require a degree of metalinguistic awareness that is not necessary in everyday speech. Same/different judgments require children to compare two words consciously and make a metalinguistic judgment as to their similarity. Some may fail this sort of discrimination task because of their inability to apply the criterion of sameness consciously, not because they do not hear the two as different words.

Other authors stress the importance of metalinguistic skills at the phonology level as they relate to reading. Gibson and Levin (1975), and Liberman, Shank-weiler, Liberman, Fowler, and Fischer (1977) stress the importance of phoneme segmentation as a process related to reading acquisition. Many language learning disabled individuals with deficient reading skills are unable to analyze or segment sentences into words or words into syllables and sounds.

Auditory synthesis, or blending, also is crucial for phonetic decoding of words. This process may be defined as the ability to bring together individual sounds or syllables to form a word. Children with apraxia or those having subtle problems with multisyllabic words (e.g., "ecomony" for "economy," "Alaksa" for "Alaska," "prititive" for "primitive") may have particular difficulty with tasks requiring blending skills. Seemingly isolated articulation problems thus may be related to a variety of underlying difficulties and in turn have significant effects on many areas of oral or written language.

## PART II. DIAGNOSIS

This section discusses the clinical procedures used in the diagnosis of receptive and expressive phonological disorders as they relate to learning disabled children.

Various diagnostic tools are reviewed and categorized according to which of those two processes they test. This distinction is important in diagnosis and remedial planning for the learning disabled since both receptive and expressive processes develop interdependently and interact in varying degrees. It is not a simple case in which children with an articulation disorder merely substitute one sound for another (Ingram, 1976b).

## Section 1. Assessment of Speech Sound Discrimination

### A Framework for Assessment

As was discussed in the first section in this chapter, an approach to assessment that focuses on the articulatory (as opposed to acoustic) characteristics of speech sounds and words is the most applicable to the task. However, this approach must be refined. It is not enough to look only at the distinctive features of the misperceived sounds, although this is an important element in assessment; clinicians also must consider a number of different but interrelated factors.

First, clinicians must distinguish between phonetic and phonemic perception. That is, although some children may be able to actually perceive differences between words, they may not realize that the sound variances signal differences in meaning. Other children may recognize sound changes only in meaningful contexts but not in nonsense words. Testing therefore must provide an opportunity for clinicians to evaluate the children's ability to recognize (1) sound differences per se and (2) changes in meaning as a result of the sound change.

Second, practitioners must consider whether the measure assesses the children's ability to perceive their own or someone else's speech. Unfortunately, as Weiss et al. (1980) have pointed out, there are no adequate formal measures for assessing such self-discrimination abilities. Most studies have used tests that assess the children's abilities to discriminate someone else's speech and not their own misarticulated sounds. Nevertheless, clinicians must informally assess both types of perception.

Other factors that must be considered include the modality of input stimuli, familiarity of the words used, the length of the words, and whether or not they are embedded in context.

As to the third factor, input stimuli, educators first must consider whether the test uses only an auditory stimulus or a combination of auditory and visual stimuli (pictures). Some tests (*Auditory Discrimination Test*) (Wepman, 1973) use only spoken input. Other tests contain pictures (*Goldman-Fristoe-Woodcock Test of Auditory Discrimination*). With a picture identification task, the client typically is shown two, three, or four pictures with a label or descriptive term that varies in a minimal way phonemically (Locke, 1980a) such as "shack-sack-tack-back." The child then points to the correct picture upon hearing the examiner (or taped form) say its label. Some learning disabled individuals perform better on tests that provide an external referent such as pictures than on those that do not (*Auditory Discrimination Test*) because the pictures serve as visual cues. Once they know what their choices are, they can discriminate more accurately. Clinical experience with children who have had a history of otitis media indicates they do better on tasks when given this kind of preset.

Both formats have some methodological problems that clinicians need to consider. With respect to the traditional auditory same/different format, Locke (1980a) suggests that cognitive processing can place some constraints on the decision-making processes during discrimination testing. Specifically, after perceiving the two stimuli in a same/different task, the children have to make some decision regarding whether they are the same. They may judge that two words such as "lath-lash" are the same because (1) although they perceive both stimuli correctly, they do not understand what the examiner means by "same" or "different," or (2) they perceive both words correctly but do not comprehend that the differentiating feature is important to the examiner. Since the children do not consider it important, they do not report it.

Locke (1980b) also questions the validity of using the picture identification paradigm since the client never is asked to judge whether one phoneme is different from another. The examiner determines discrimination ability on the basis of a series of differential identifications of the phonemes. Given the set of "line-sign-vine-shine," Locke hypothesizes that it is possible that a person could point to a given picture, "vine" for example, and still not have discriminated /v/ from /s/, /l/, and /sh/. The individual could conduct a self-terminating search, finding the picture "vine" on display, without fully taking into consideration the other pictures and determining the contrasting phoneme of their names.

The fourth factor, word familiarity, demonstrates that changes in performance can occur depending upon whether the words are real or nonsense. (Unfamiliar words may function as nonsense words, e.g., "vie/thigh.") Learning disabled individuals often do poorly on tasks containing nonsense words as compared to real ones. As Hook and Johnson (1978) indicate, the ability to perform these types of metalinguistic tasks is more difficult than those containing real words. In general, they find that the ability to deal with such tasks is the last type of auditory discrimination to be acquired, perhaps because they require a greater ability to apply rules and analyze sound differences. Others perform poorly on picture tests not because of an auditory discrimination problem but because of a vocabulary deficiency. For example, given the pictures "lake" and "rake," the clinician may say, "Point to the lake." Children with poor receptive vocabulary may fail because they do not know what a lake is or are not familiar with the term "lake." This still may be the case even though they eventually pass all the training items. In this case, higher level symbolic processes (i.e., vocabulary) influence lower level processes (i.e., perception).

Moreover, lower level processes can affect higher level functions, i.e., auditory discrimination problems can interfere with vocabulary development. Some children misperceive words and as a result confuse their meanings. For example, one learning disabled boy could not hear the difference between "toad" and "tote" and labelled or pointed to a "toad" as "tote" and vice versa.

Word length is the fifth variable affecting auditory discrimination. It has been the authors' clinical experience that older individuals (both adolescents and adults) may discriminate monosyllabic words adequately but not multisyllabic ones, especially when unaccented syllables are varied (e.g., "pin-pen" vs. "hesitation-hestation").

A sixth factor, context, gives some learning disabled individuals auditory discrimination difficulties. That is, problems arise only when the words are presented in context or when the persons listen to sentences. For example, a learning disabled boy who could correctly discriminate isolated word pairs was asked, "How many children are sick?" The boy replied, "Six?" because he was not sure what the clinician asked. Another boy was asked, "What growls?" and he replied, "Peas and beans." Apparently, he perceived the word "growls" as "grows." When it was pointed out that the clinician did not say "grows" but "growls," he responded appropriately. In contrast, other children have difficulty with isolated word pairs but can discriminate words in a context that provides additional cues to meaning.

Finally, it is useful to assess the metalinguistic perceptual skills of analysis and synthesis of speech sounds, particularly if the children's major problem is in reading. Some children may be able to perceive words correctly and even judge whether two words sound the same or different but not be able to analyze them into their individual sounds. While this advanced level of analysis is not necessary for everyday speech, research has suggested that it is an important ability in learning phonics (Shankweiler et al., 1979). Clinical experience suggests that children who have difficulty at lower levels of perceiving differences in words also will have problems analyzing words into component sounds.

In sum, assessment of perception of speech sounds must include information about the children's ability to discriminate words in a variety of contexts to determine exactly where perceptual problems occur and under what conditions. It is rarely enough to say that the children simply have perceptual problems. Pinpointing the nature of the difficulty is extremely important in planning appropriate remediation. Clinicians must select a battery of diagnostic tests that systematically vary the nature of the input and of the response. By observing discrepancies in performance under such varying conditions, it is possible to identify the problem more exactly and to suggest hypotheses as to why the children behave as they do. Variables that must be included in a systematic analysis are:

- phonemic vs. phonetic discriminations
- others' speech vs. self-speech
- pictures vs. no pictures
- familiar words vs. unfamiliar words
- meaningful words vs. nonsense words
- single syllable words vs. multisyllable words
- single words vs. words in context
- linguistic vs. metalinguistic skills.

*Formal Tests*

In general, formal tests do not systematically incorporate these variables nor do they even include all of those distinctions. This is not to say, however, that clinicians should not use these tests. A thorough assessment of perceptual abilities must include a variety of tests, and diagnosticians must analyze each one to determine the nature of both the stimulus input and the response required. An appropriate battery that provides information about speech perception in many contexts may then be constructed.

The *Auditory Discrimination Test,* for example, contains single-syllable words using a same/different judgment. Some words are meaningful to most children but others are not. Thus, an analysis of the errors might reveal inability to discriminate nonmeaningful pairs, i.e., children report that nonmeaningful pairs sound the same.

The *Goldman-Fristoe-Woodcock Test of Auditory Discrimination* (GFW), in contrast, uses an identification format with pictures (point to "rake"). The cognitive level of this task more closely resembles what occurs in normal language processing (meaningful recognition of a verbal label) and is less demanding than a metalinguistic same/different judgment. Again, the task uses single-syllable words in isolation, and although the training items try to ensure meaningful stimuli, children may learn to associate a label with a picture without really acquiring the meaning of the stimulus word.

Other measures, such as the *Sound Discrimination Test* (in Templin, 1957), use nonsense words in contrast to meaningful words. Comparison of performance on this measure and the GFW, for example, may indicate a discrepancy in the children's ability to use meaning as an aid to discrimination. Many of the sophisticated laboratory studies that include synthesized speech use syllables as the unit of perception. These also are essentially nonmeaningful stimuli, a factor that may influence results.

The following list identifies some available standardized auditory discrimination tests; Darley (1979) provides a complete review.

- *Auditory Discrimination Test* (Wepman, 1973)
- *The Boston University Speech Sound Discrimination Test* (Pronovost, 1953)
- *Goldman-Fristoe-Woodcock Test of Auditory Discrimination* (Goldman, Fristoe, & Woodcock, 1970)
- *Goldman-Fristoe-Woodcock Diagnostic Auditory Discrimination Test* (Goldman, Fristoe, & Woodcock, 1974)
- *Screening Test for Auditory Perception* (Kimmell & Wahl, 1969)
- *Sound Discrimination Test* (in Templin, 1957)
- *A Test of Sound Discrimination* (Irwin, 1972b)
- *Washington Speech Sound Discrimination Test* (Prather, Miner, Addicott, & Sunderland, 1971)

Formal tests that assess auditory analysis and synthesis include the

- *Lindamood Auditory Conceptualization Test* (Lindamood & Lindamood, 1971, analysis)
- *Illinois Test of Psycholinguistic Abilities* (Kirk, McCarthy, & Kirk, 1968, synthesis).

*Informal Tests*

Clinicians generally need to supplement formal tests with informal ones to systematically vary the content of the discrimination tasks according to the framework presented earlier. Tasks may be devised to incorporate contrasts of single-syllable with multisyllable words and isolated words from those in context. Wren (1980), for example, embeds target words in short three-, four-, and five-word sentence pairs ("He is sleepy/He is sleeping"). By using phonological contrasts in sentences, it also is possible to observe whether syntactic or semantic constraints can aid perception. For example, children may be able to perceive the final *s* in "The cups are white"/"The cup are white," but not in "He is sick"/"He is six."

Finally, in assessment of metalinguistic analysis and synthesis, it often is beneficial to follow up formal tests with informal measures to evaluate the ability to analyze words into sounds and syllables. This procedure may help diagnosticians to probe further and pinpoint where the auditory perception problem lies. It also helps confirm or refute hypotheses regarding the nature of the disability. For a given individual, the diagnostician will be able to control more systematically variables such as word or sentence length, syllable length, and meaningfulness of the stimuli.

## Section 2. Assessment of Phonemic Production Disorders

Several systematic frameworks exist for the assessment of phonemic articulation disorders. The most traditional analysis of such dysfunctions is entirely descriptive and focuses on isolated sounds and types of errors: omission, substitution, distortion, and addition. Within that descriptive framework, individuals may exhibit any combination of those errors.

An omission is a misarticulation in which a phoneme is not produced in the place where it should occur. For example, an individual may say /da/ for "dog." Final consonants in words are omitted more commonly than are initial or medial consonants. In consonant clusters, one sound usually is omitted (e.g., /bu/ for /blu/, /top/ for /stop/).

A substitution is an articulation error in which an improper phoneme is produced in place of the correct one. For example, the individual may say /bwu/ for /blu/. In general, substitutions occur more often in the medial and final positions of words than in the initial one. Common substitutions include /w/ for /r/ and /l/ and /θ/ for /s/. Most substitutions differ from the target phoneme by one distinctive feature. (As is discussed later, this is not the case with apraxia of speech.) Winitz (1975) indicates that phoneme substitutions differ in terms of place of articulation (where the sound is produced in the same mouth) rather than in features such as manner (how the sound is produced) or voicing (whether or not the voice is used in sound production).

A distortion is a misarticulation in which the target phoneme is modified or approximated, resulting in an incorrect production. The incorrect approximations do not differ from the target sound to the extent that they become another standard sound, so they still are not substitution errors. Distortions typically are similar visually or acoustically to the target phoneme.

An addition is an articulation error in which a phoneme is inserted unnecessarily in a word (e.g., /pigə/ for /pig/). It is common to see a schwa sound inserted in a consonant cluster or at the end of a word (e.g., /bəlaek/ for /blaek/).

Another traditional classification scheme for diagnosing and treating articulation errors takes into account the position of sounds within the word or syllable. For diagnosis, errors are described according to the initial, medial, or final position of words (e.g., /m/ as in "*m*et," "ha*mm*er," and "ha*m*") or in terms of how the consonant sounds relate to the syllable, as noted by the terms "prevocalic," "intervocalic," and "postvocalic."

By contrast, Chomsky and Halle (1968) offer a system of distinctive features. They, along with others (Fisher & Logemann, 1971; Jakobson, Fant, & Halle, 1952; McReynolds & Huston, 1971; Singh, 1976), describe features of phonemes in terms of various categories. Although there is disagreement over the best set of features, researchers commonly cite Chomsky and Halle's five major categories:

(1) major class features, (2) cavity features, (3) secondary aperture features, (4) manner of articulation features, and (5) source of features (Weiss et al., 1980).

The important point underlying distinctive feature analysis is that phonological disorders are best diagnosed and treated according to the type of feature(s) involved rather than as isolated sounds. Distinctive feature analysis is based on the assumption that children learn classes of sounds based on distinctive features, not individual sounds.

An additional framework, phonological process analysis, was discussed earlier and is considered in depth in the next section.

*Articulation Testing*

Articulation tests are used by speech and language pathologists to identify individuals with phonological disorders, to produce error analyses, to provide an index to intelligibility, and to determine the degree of variability in the individuals' articulation (Newman, 1979).

These tests are designed to assess systematically each speech sound in an individual's articulation repertoire, typically through picture naming tasks. The rationale is that this approach is less time consuming than testing for articulation in conversation.

The following is a list of tests of articulation that classify errors, in the traditional manner, as additions, omissions, distortions, and substitutions. They are reviewed elsewhere by Darley (1979) and Weiss et al. (1980):

- *Arizona Articulation Proficiency Scale* (Fudala, 1961)
- *Austin Spanish Articulation Test (ASAT)* (Carrow, 1974)
- *A Deep Test of Articulation* (McDonald, 1964)
- *The Denver Articulation Screening Examination (DASE)* (Drumwright, 1971)
- *Developmental Articulation Test* (Henja, 1963)
- *Goldman-Fristoe Test of Articulation (GFTA)* (Goldman & Fristoe, 1969)
- *Integrated Articulation Test* (Irwin, 1972a)
- *Photo Articulation Test (PAT)* (Pendergast, Dickey, Selmar, & Soder, 1969)
- *Predictive Screening Test of Articulation* (Van Riper & Erickson, 1968)
- *The Templin-Darley Tests of Articulation* (2nd ed.) (Templin & Darley, 1969)
- *Weiss Comprehensive Articulation Test (WCAT)* (Weiss, 1978).

Of more interest here are tests designed to provide a method for phonemic analysis, i.e., a linguistic approach to analyzing child phonology, since it is believed that the phonological disorders of many of the learning disabled result from a basic problem in language. This section does not focus on isolated sounds such as /r/, /s/, or /l/, although there are some individuals with these types of problems.

The distinctive feature theory approach to phonological development (Jakobson, Fant, & Halle, 1952; Chomsky & Halle, 1968) is being used increasingly by speech pathologists. It provides a comprehensive framework for analyzing and predicting articulatory performance. However, for the most part, frameworks rather than standardized tests have been developed for describing abnormal phonological development in terms of distinctive features (Compton, 1970; Costello & Onstine, 1976; Leonard, 1973; McReynolds & Huston, 1971; Oller, 1973; Pollack & Rees, 1972; Singh, Hayden, & Toombs, 1981; Singh & Singh, 1976; Weiner & Bernthal, 1978).

The *Fisher-Logemann Test of Articulation Competence* (Fisher & Logemann, 1971) is one formal measure that provides a distinctive feature analysis of the child's phonological system. Sounds are tested in isolated words on the basis of syllabic function. The distinctive feature system, which is not compatible with many others (Singh, 1976) includes: (1) voicing (voiced and voiceless), (2) place of articulation (bilabial, labiodental, tip-dental, tip-alveolar, blade alveolar, blade-prepalatal, front-palatal, central palatal, back-velar, and glottal), and (3) manner of articulation (stop, fricative, affricate, glide, lateral, and nasal). Vowel phonemes are analyzed according to a four-feature system: tongue height (high, mid, and low), place of articulation (front, central, and back), degree of tension (tense, lax), and lip rounding (rounded, unrounded).

McReynolds and Engmann (1975) have developed an informal procedure for analyzing children's articulatory competence based on Chomsky and Halle's (1968) distinctive feature system. Their method does not include a formal articulation test. They recommend that the clinician obtain a reliable and representative profile of the children's articulation through spontaneous speech or from responses to items on any articulation test. Their feature system includes the following: vocalic, consonantal, high, back, low, anterior, coronal, round, tense, voice, continuant, nasal, and strident. This system does not coincide with that of Fisher and Logemann, although data from either approach could be converted easily for analysis.

Process analysis theory also has yielded some diagnostic measures, two of which are discussed: *Procedures for the Phonological Analysis of Children's Language* (Ingram, 1981) and the *Natural Process Analysis* (Shriberg and Kwiatkowski, 1980). These differ from traditional articulation tests in that they are not sound specific. They emphasize how the sounds within a language can function for a given individual to signify meaning, that is, the person's language sound pattern. They allow for the analysis of phonological rules the children acquire. Phonological rules describe the regularity of the sound pattern observed in an individual's language. These tests also are concerned with phonological processes that describe the kinds of changes that apply to classes of sounds, not just individual sounds, that the individual uses to simplify adult speech (Ingram, 1981). For example, if a child replaces an adult /k/ with a /t/, it also is possible that other back consonants may be changed into corresponding front consonants (for example, /d/ for /g/). These changes can be categorized as fronting. Thus, the advantage of this system over the more traditional one of describing individual substitutions is that it relates changes that at first may seem unrelated. Moreover, this system provides a more explanatory description of development (Ingram, 1981).

These procedures also take into account that speech sounds are produced differently in different contexts. Even though in traditional articulation tests sounds may be tested in different positions in as many as three words, the validity of using only this elicitation technique has been questioned by Newman (1979) and Ingram (1981). They maintain that sounds must be assessed in a much wider variety of contexts, which is best achieved by eliciting a sample of spontaneous language.

The *Natural Process Analysis* (NPA) involves sound patterns obtained from continuous speech. It is designed specifically for remediation purposes for those with delayed speech development. The NPA includes eight processes: (1) final consonant deletion, (2) velar fronting, (3) stopping, (4) palatal fronting, (5) liquid simplification, (6) regressive and progressive assimilation, (7) cluster reduction, and (8) unstressed syllable deletion. These processes have been defined earlier.

The NPA has two coding procedures: (1) entering selected words on transcription sheets in their appropriate coding boxes, and (2) assigning a code to each consonant, consonant cluster, and polysyllabic word (e.g., CV, VC, CVC, CCVC, CCVCC, CVCCVC). The second coding procedure is designed to take into account the variability of sound production, depending upon the contextual constraints. The NPA also has a summary sheet that includes: (1) a phonetic inventory of correctly and incorrectly produced sounds, (2) the eight natural processes, and (3) notes that discuss any particular concerns or observations made by the clinician.

To obtain an in-depth and accurate assessment of children's phonological system, the clinician using this technique should expect to spend considerable time gathering and scoring the speech sample. Time needed to obtain a speech sample may vary across children. For the less verbal, recording may take longer in order to get a representative sample. For the clinician who is experienced in phonetic transcription and who is familiar with NPA procedures, it takes approximately an hour to an hour and a half to score (Shriberg & Kwiatkowski, 1980).

Ingram (1981) offers an alternative approach to phonological analysis. Although his method may be used for children with delayed speech, Ingram contends that it has a broader range of use. He discusses five major goals for the program:

1. It must be complete, covering different aspects of phonological development. It allows the clinician not only to compare the child's language to the adult's but also to examine the speech sounds independent of the adult language. Speech errors also are analyzed in terms of general patterns or phonological processes that occur.
2. It must be a flexible approach in that it can use any data (spontaneous speech samples, picture elicitation), sample size, and variant pronunciations.
3. It must be adaptive, that is, be adjusted for analysis of particular features of various individuals. In other words, the clinician should be able to select a particular aspect of the analysis that is most relevant to an individual's need. It should not be necessary to perform the whole analysis from beginning to end regardless of the child's needs.
4. It must be designed to be cumulative in that it provides sets of analyses that offer new information about the child at each step. The practitioner should not have to proceed laboriously through all the steps before obtaining a meaningful profile.
5. It must be normative, providing explicit measures so that the data can be collected and analyzed with some consistency across clinicians as well as by the same clinician.

Ingram's approach includes four kinds of phonological analyses: phonetic, homonyms, substitution, and phonological process. The phonetic analysis examines the production of speech sounds, disregarding the adult model, providing information on what sounds the children can and cannot articulate. It also includes information on articulation of sounds in the initial, medial, and final positions of words as well as the frequency of the preferred sounds. Ingram reasons that frequent sounds should receive special status since some children prefer to say certain sounds as opposed to others.

The analysis of homonymy is included because it is considered to be a characteristic of delayed language in children. This occurs "when the child produces the same phonetic form for two or more adults words that normally are not homonymous" (Ingram, 1981, p. 45), for example, /ba/ for "ball" and "balloon." Provisions are made to determine the extent of homonymy not only among words but also among phonetic forms. For instance, children may have a large number of homonymous words but few phonetic forms in their repertoires; on the other hand, they may have a large repertoire of phonetic forms that may represent homonymous words. In general, as the number of homonymous words increases, the more unintelligible the speech becomes.

The substitution analysis is used to determine the sound replacement in (1) the initial and final position of syllables, (2) consonant or consonant clusters occurring between two vowels, and (3) consonant or consonant clusters occurring between two consonants or syllabic segments (e.g., "pa*p*er," "can*d*le"). It also measures the frequency of substitutions. This aspect is taken into account since some children have widespread sound substitutions and others only infrequent mispronunciations. Moreover, as Ingram indicates, differences may arise depending upon where the sound occurs in the word.

The phonological analysis describes sound substitutions by a finite set of phonological processes and determines the extent to which they occur. This analysis is designed to provide an explanation for the occurrence of the substitution errors. Although there have been questions regarding (1) how a process is defined (Ingram, 1981), (2) how many processes there are (Khan, 1982), and (3) how a process is measured (Ingram, 1981), this approach still offers a viable method for examining the linguistic aspect of phonological disorders.

*Assessment of Stimulability and Intelligibility*

It also is useful to obtain an estimate of stimulability of the misarticulated sounds. To test for stimulability, the diagnostician usually models the sounds both in isolation and in words and asks the child to repeat them correctly. Visual cues and/or instructions regarding the phonetic placement also may be provided. Usually the child is given several trials to articulate the sound(s) correctly. In general, it is believed that the more stimulable an individual is, the better the prognosis. However, as Turton and Clark (1971) and Weiss et al. (1980) indicate, some individuals can imitate well but do poorly in therapy because of basic problems in language and cognition. These persons may have a linguistic deficiency hindering them from acquiring the phonological rules.

A measure of intelligibility is used as an indicator of the severity of the articulation disorder. In the *Weiss Comprehensive Articulation Test* (Weiss, 1978), intelligibility is calculated by counting the number of intelligible words in a sample of 100 consecutive words selected at random from a larger corpus. This number then is subtracted from 100, which yields the intelligibility score. Weiss (1978) believes that it is preferable that a panel of three persons, rather than only the diagnostician, listen to tape-recorded samples to obtain a reliable intelligibility score.

*Elicitation Procedures*

Several formal elicitation techniques are used in standardized tests: picture naming, imitation of words or sentences, and spontaneous speech samples. There are advantages and disadvantages with each. Picture naming can provide a quick, easy assessment of articulation. It also has an advantage over imitation in that the results are not contaminated by a model of sound production. However, it also poses problems. For example, it is difficult to create a set of pictures that can reliably elicit the target word, and the authors' clinical experience suggests that some pictures on some tests are unclear and often do not produce the desired results without prompting from the clinician.

In contrast, imitation tests such as portions of *The Templin-Darley Tests of Articulation* (1969) can provide auditory or visual cues to produce the sound(s) correctly and can yield useful information as to stimulability for remediation purposes. Sentence repetition tasks provide an index of articulation in connected language. This has an advantage over assessing words in isolation since it places demands on the children that are similar to a spontaneous conversation situation (see the *Goldman-Fristoe Test of Articulation*).

An elicited or spontaneous speech sample is included in some tests (Goldman & Fristoe, 1969; Shriberg & Kwiatkowski, 1980; Weiss, 1978). These procedures are useful for individuals who are willing or capable of producing running speech. It is very difficult to get those who are less verbal to tell or retell a story or carry on a conversation. This may not be the best method for children with unintelligible speech since it is difficult to ascertain what they are referring to or wanting to say. Accurate coding of their misarticulations is extremely difficult.

Informal means of elicitation of articulation samples typically consist of one or more of the following tasks: (1) conversation, (2) elicited statements or answers to questions, (3) naming, (4) imitation, and (5) serial verbalizations (Weiss et al., 1980). These informal measures often are used as supplements to formal articulation testing. Perhaps the best measure of articulation proficiency is engaging the individual in conversation. As long as the child is capable of carrying on a conversation, this technique can provide a good estimate of intelligibility and the nature of the misarticulations under normal circumstances. Topics discussed should relate to the person's interests.

Related to this conversational technique are elicited language samples in which the children tell a story, one that is either familiar or that they have made up. Elicited statements are useful since target sounds can be produced in relatively spontaneous language situations. Naming and imitation are useful screening devices, especially when a quick measure of articulation proficiency is necessary. These measures entail having the children name objects in the room, body parts, colors, animals, etc. Clinicians also may ask them to repeat words and sentences containing the target phonemes. Serial verbalizations include counting, reciting the alphabet, naming the days of the week and months of the year, etc.

A combination of both standardized and informal elicitation procedures, using picture naming, imitation, and sentence repetition, is necessary to determine proficiency in a wide variety of contexts. Discrepancies among different types of tests provide clues as to the strengths and weaknesses of each child. For example, some children may perform adequately on repetition tests where a model is provided but poorly on spontaneous tests, whether of single words or connected language. Remediation for such children proceeds differently from that for those whose performance is adequate on all measures of single words but who have difficulty articulating certain sounds in both imitated and spontaneous contexts.

A number of other factors must be considered when selecting a battery of articulation tests. The number and types of words are important in determining whether or not a given phoneme is mastered. Conventionally, most articulation tests assess a phoneme three times, once each in the initial, medial, and final positions. For an analysis of articulation competence and/or distinctive feature analysis, this number is not enough (Ingram, 1976b; McReynolds & Engmann, 1975) since an individual may pronounce a word correctly in one context but not in another. Taking this notion into consideration, McDonald (1964) developed a test in which each phoneme is sampled in approximately 30 different contexts.

Articulation also can vary according to the types of words used as stimulus items. Factors such as the number of syllables and parts of speech have been shown to influence articulation (Ingram, 1976b; Shriberg & Kwiatkowski, 1980). Most of the standardized tests assess phonemes in monosyllabic words, but with language impaired children, sound production often breaks down in multisyllabic words. Shriberg and Kwiatkowski also indicate that the structural complexity (canonical forms) of words is not consistent across all phonemes in most standardized tests. There are simple (e.g., CVC) and complex (e.g., CVCCVC) canonical forms. Those analysts observe that fricatives, affricates, liquids, and glides are tested less often in simple canonical forms than are stops. Canonical forms containing more complex syllable shapes and more syllables per word (e.g., CVC vs. CCVC, CVCVC) may elicit more simplification processes.

Syntactic, morphological, and morphophonemic constraints also influence phonology. Most of the articulation tests primarily assess nouns since they are easily pictured and can be used with children and nonreaders, but as Shriberg and Kwiatkowski (1980) point out, nouns comprise only 24 percent of the speech used by normal 5-year-olds. Misarticulations can differ across parts of speech (Templin, 1957). Shriberg and Kwiatkowski (1980) indicate that final clusters in nouns are reduced more often than are initial clusters, while just the opposite is true for verbs.

Some test items assess phonemes in words containing morphological endings (e.g., /z/ in "toes," /z/ in "matches," /ŋ/ in "swinging"). Some children may omit or substitute these sounds because of problems in morphology, not phonology. Plural inflections, for example, make the target item more complex and therefore confound the test by adding a morpheme and a word-final cluster or syllable to the canonical form (Shriberg & Kwiatkowski, 1980).

There are a few informal tasks that may be used to differentiate between morphological and phonological errors. One is to compare the children's ability to say the sound in words in which they function as a morphological ending and in words in which they do not (e.g., "sw*ing*" vs. "jump*ing*"; "dea*d*" vs. "lande*d*"; "toe*s*" vs. "fuz*z*"). If the children cannot produce the sound only when it functions as a morpheme, then it could be hypothesized that the problem lies at the level of morphology, not phonology. Another task could assess the children's comprehension of morphology to determine whether or not there is a consistent pattern of errors in understanding past tense, comparatives, or plurals.

Morphophonemic changes also can affect articulation. Morphophonemics refers to phonemic changes that result when a morpheme is added to a word (Ingram, 1981) such as nation/national or refer/reference.

In sum, several factors have influenced the construction of articulation tests that clinicians must keep in mind when selecting tests to assess learning disabled children: the number and type of words or contexts in which the phonemes are tested, the type of elicitation procedure, and the type of analysis of the speech sounds (i.e., traditional, distinctive feature, process analysis).

Practitioners need to use a variety of tests to produce a comprehensive profile of disordered children. By systematically analyzing the format of each test, they can build a battery of tests that provide detailed information about the articulation of each child. Discrepancies in performance on different tests generally yield critical information for diagnosis and remediation. For example, children who do well on tests that use only uninflected nouns, but poorly on tests that use words with morphological endings, may have a syntactic disorder that interferes with phonological production. Such hypotheses as to the nature of the problem may then be investigated informally. Clinicians must be aware of the advantages and disadvantages of the traditional descriptive model of speech sound analysis as well as distinctive feature analysis and process models since pertinent information may be gathered from each.

### Section 3. Assessment of Phonetic Disorders—Apraxia

Assessment of apraxia usually includes use of an oral mechanism exam as well as standardized articulation tests, but diagnosis typically is based on clinical observation of behavior. The following are characteristics of apraxia taken from the works of Chappell (1973); Johnson and Myklebust (1967); Rosenbek, Hansen, Baughman, and Lemme (1974); Rosenbek and Wertz (1972); and Yoss and Darley (1974):

1. Apraxic children show less than the normal ability to imitate a speech signal (sounds, syllables, and words). Their spontaneous production and imitative speech are evidence of inaccurate articulation, labored speech, and difficulty sequencing sounds and syllables in words. Imitation or volitional speech often is more difficult than involuntary speech. For instance, apraxic children may produce automatic or reflexive movements or gestures adequately but have serious difficulty if they have to imitate them on command.

2. Examination of their oral mechanism reveals a lack of facility for forming volitional jaw-lip-tongue patterns, positions, and movements for articulation of sounds and syllables such as biting the lower lip or puckering the lips. However, it is important to note that apraxic children do not display facial and lingual paralysis.
3. The learning rate for sound production is slow even with intense stimulation.
4. Receptive abilities invariably are superior to expressive ones. However, this does not imply that receptive abilities are always intact. The authors' clinical experience suggests that these children often exhibit below-average comprehension abilities. Before assuming adequate auditory comprehension, clinicians should make certain they have tested auditory receptive vocabulary for all classes of words, not just nouns, as well as auditory comprehension for connected language, including sentences and stories. Even the most receptively "intact" child may exhibit subtle receptive processing problems that are not always picked up by standardized tests.
5. The subject children have adequate intelligence.
6. Phonemic errors consist of omissions, substitutions, distortions, additions, repetitions, and prolongations. However, omissions of sounds and syllables occur more often than do substitutions of sounds and syllables.
7. Phonemic errors increase as the length of the words or number of syllables becomes longer. These errors vary according to the complexity of articulatory movements. Apraxic children have the most difficulty with fricatives (/s/, /z/, /θ/, /ð/, /f/, /v/, /ʃ/, /h/,), affricates (/dʒ/, /tʃ/), and consonant clusters (/bl/, /st/). Errors often are highly inconsistent.
8. Connected speech tends to be less intelligible than would be expected given the child's performance on an articulation test of single words.
9. Deviant prosody is evidenced by slowed rate, even stress, and spacing. Rosenbek and Wertz (1972) suggest that these characteristics may result from attempts to compensate for the problem.

Yoss and Darley (1974) identify several predictors that significantly differentiate children with developmental apraxia of speech from those with other articulation disorders. The main predictors:

1. Neurological findings, such as difficulty in fine motor coordination, gait, and alternating motion rates of the tongue and extremities (often manifested as a generalized dyspraxia);
2. Two- and three-feature articulation errors (for example, /p/ for a /ð/, an error in place, voicing, and continuancy), prolongations and repetitions of sounds and syllables, distortions and additions in repeated speech tasks;

3. Distortions, omissions, additions, and one-place errors in spontaneous speech;
4. Slower-than-normal rate on measurement of oral diadochokinesis [diadochokinesis pertains to the rate and accuracy with which an individual can repeat sounds in sequence, as in /p-p-p-/ for /puh tuh kuh/; /buh duh guh/];
5. Poor maintenance of syllable sequences and shapes; polysyllabic words altered by addition, omission, or revision of syllables (p. 23-24).

## PART III. REMEDIATION

### Section 1. Phonemic Disorders

*Goals and Issues*

Traditionally, the approach to the remediation of phonological disorders proceeded on a sound-by-sound basis. One classic approach used extensively by many speech pathologists is Van Riper's (1962) stimulus method. His approach begins with articulatory discrimination training, followed by teaching individual sounds in isolation, then in syllables or words, and finally in sentences and conversation. This method has proved quite effective for remediating children with functional articulation problems, i.e., those who mispronounce isolated sounds such as /r/, /s/, etc. Other similar approaches that teach isolated sounds include programmed instruction (Mowrer, 1977), a multiple phonemic effort (McCabe & Bradley, 1975), and paired-stimuli (Weston & Irwin, 1971).

However, approaches to articulation therapy have shifted to focus on remediation of the processes that are assumed to underlie the phonological disorder. Two approaches—distinctive feature theory and phonological analysis—are discussed since they consider the linguistic rules underlying phonological acquisition.

Two issues must be noted briefly first: (1) the desirability of remediating receptive (auditory discrimination) deficits and (2) the still tentative nature of the concept of a linguistic approach to articulation therapy.

The relationship of speech sound perception problems to articulation deficits still is a matter of some debate. On a clinical level, some children exhibit fairly clear perceptual problems that then appear in distorted articulation. However, many others tend to perform poorly on auditory discrimination tests but the relationship is not clear since perceptual errors do not match articulation errors.

Research has provided little information to illuminate the problem since approaches to studying speech sound discrimination and articulation differ considerably and little effort has been made to investigate directly the relationship between perception and production. Further, most research on perception in the last decade or so has been carried out on adults or infants. Thus the debate as to the need to include work on auditory perception as part of articulation therapy continues (Berry, 1980; Rees, 1973).

From the point of view of the field of learning disabilities, it should be noted that while auditory perceptual deficits (verbal as well as nonverbal) may be related to a number of receptive and expressive functions (e.g., comprehension, articulation, reading, and spelling), the nature and direction of those linkages are complex. However, two points may be made clearly: (1) it generally has been found that remediation of perceptual deficits should not be carried out in isolation since such work appears to have little carryover to other areas, and (2) verbal perceptual deficits are not improved by working on nonverbal perception areas such as discriminating environmental sounds, sequences of tones or claps, and the like. Clinicians should be cautious of commercial materials that focus on nonspeech perception. It is useful to combine work on discrimination with other areas of deficit where it appears that problems with phoneme discrimination may interfere with language comprehension or speech sound production (see Chapter 1 for general guidelines).

The second major issue is the still theoretical nature of the linguistic approach to remediation of articulation problems. As pointed out in Chapter 1, approaches to remediation are based on *a priori* theories and principles, and the theory of language a clinician holds determines the direction remediation will take. Although opinion is strong in favor of viewing many articulation problems as those of rule learning, there still is considerable debate as to the correctness of a language approach to therapy.

In favor of the language approach, Lorentz (1976) criticizes speech pathologists for treating each sound separately in their analyses of children's output. He believes that speech pathologists have provided an analysis of substitutions, omissions, and distortions without looking at the environmental conditions accompanying the sound (e.g., what sounds surround the targeted one and what is its position in a word). He asserts that traditional speech therapy ignores the systematic simplifying processes and "environmental" effects adjacent sounds have on each other.

Berry (1980) speaks strongly against teaching isolated phonemes since children neither perceive nor produce phonological units by isolating one phoneme at a time. She describes phonological development as dependent on a matrix of other linguistic systems—prosody, syntax, vocabulary, and coarticulation—all of which act on phonological production and, in turn, must be acted upon. In fact, Berry takes up the notion of the "syntagma" (Kozhevnikova & Chistovich, 1965) as the unit of communication and perception; a unit usually made up of six or seven syllables held by rhythmic constraints that constitutes the basic unit of communication and governs phonological development. Deviant rules then cause poor production and may be connected to imperceptions or integrative problems with other areas of oral language. Berry discounts many ''simple articulation problems,'' considering deviant phonology to be a language deficit.

Winitz (1969) agrees and discounts simple ''phonetic production learning'' since phonology is being learned as one subsystem of the language. Children are not just acquiring sounds in isolation, although phonetic production, i.e., working with meaningless sounds, may developmentally precede learning the phoneme system of English.

Compton (1970), too, prefers a systematic look at the principles that give rise to misarticulations. He says the patterns of children's productions form an organized collection of phonological principles—a generative phonology—and that therapy can be accomplished best by working with the youngsters' rules.

Diagnostic and remedial plans based on these conclusions remain controversial, however. While the above theorists, as well as Ingram (1976a, 1978), argue against traditional practices in phonological therapy, McReynolds and Elbert (1981) caution against assuming that children have a systematic rule-based pattern to their phonology. They maintain that the existence of processes has not been documented well enough in normal children, and suggest that the traditional classification scheme of omissions and substitutions may be more appropriate for children with articulation disorders.

In spite of these criticisms, some empirical support for the validity of a linguistic approach exists (Ruder & Bunce, 1981; Weiner & Bankson, 1978). Weiner (1981) finds that an approach based on minimal contrasts or a lexical framework is effective. In this technique, pairs of words are presented, one of which the child typically mispronounces, thereby making it identical to the other. When confronted with the homonymous words, the child must change pronunciation in order to be intelligible. Weiner reports that this approach, based on concepts and word meanings, is more viable than a phonetic placement method. He also contends that the need for separate auditory discrimination training and production practice of isolated sounds and syllables has been eliminated since the word pairs themselves contain minimal contrasts.

Even among proponents of language-based therapy, opinion as to the method of choice is not uniform. Distinctive feature therapy (McReynolds & Huston, 1971; Ruder & Bunce, 1981) may be contrasted with process analysis and training. In distinctive feature diagnosis and treatment, verbal output is analyzed according to the features present or absent in production: voicing, continuance, stridency, etc. Therapy then focuses on certain distinctive feature oppositions. A phoneme might be chosen for emphasis because of the bundle of features of which it is made.

For example, Ruder and Bunce (1981) choose to teach /t/ to a child who already could use /s/ and /k/ because of the features the three sounds share. They do not discount phonological processes and agree that those, rather than unrelated sounds, should be the target of therapy. However, they see their clients as having phonetic, not phonemic, disorders that result in misarticulations of almost all consonants, rather than systematic clusters of errors.

In sum, although the still theoretical nature of the proposition is recognized, most children with phonemic disorders may best be viewed as not having "simple" articulation problems but rather as belonging within a framework of processing problems for all areas of language. Disorders of phonology rarely exist in isolation; instead, they are closely related to other aspects of information processing.

### Distinctive Feature Approach

According to distinctive feature theory, children's aberrant articulation productions are rule governed and therefore it should be possible to teach the underlying rules to effect articulation change. It is assumed that several sounds can be corrected by teaching the correct use of one feature. Specifically, children who learn the rule that governs one feature should be able to learn all phonemes containing that feature (Costello, 1975). Treatment techniques based on distinctive feature theory involve teaching two sounds that differ by one feature (Costello, 1975; McReynolds & Bennett, 1972; McReynolds & Engmann, 1975).

There are several basic instructional principles:

- Distinctive features are taught in the context of phonemes. They are not overt entities but are elements of a phoneme that do not occur alone. Typically, several phonemes are used to teach a feature.
- Minimally contrasting pairs of sounds (such as k/g) are used to teach ( − ) and ( + ) aspects of the nontarget feature.
- Some procedure that measures the improvement of nontarget phonemes is implemented.

The goal of distinctive feature therapy differs from traditional articulation therapy in that it is geared to teach not a phoneme but a feature through using contrasting phonemes that differ with respect to the presence or absence of the target feature.

The McReynolds and Engmann (1975) method utilizes a programmed instructional approach to teach distinctive features. The first procedure involves the selection of a feature to train. They say that if for any feature the error rate is 25 percent or less, then the feature is considered established in the child's speech. Error rates in the 40 to 50 percent range indicate inconsistent production, usually depending on the phoneme or word position. When the error rate approaches the 65 percent level, the child evidences a rather inconsistent production of the feature in phonemes and it should be considered for training. An error rate of 80 percent or more indicates that the child has not acquired the feature and should receive high priority for teaching.

After the feature has been selected, a phoneme pair is chosen for training because, according to distinctive feature theory, the child must learn the ( + ) and ( − ) contrast. Two kinds of stimuli are used: a pair of nonsense pictures and a pair of verbal nonsense syllables (e.g., CV or VC syllables). Four vowels are used in the syllables: /a/, /i/, /ae/, and /u/. The responses are imitative, then spontaneous. For instance, when presenting a nonsense picture, the examiner may say "Say _____" or "What is this?" Schedules and criteria levels are specified to determine the mastery of each phase.

Variations of this distinctive feature theory approach have been implemented. Weiner and Bankson (1978) report some success in teaching a feature not in the context of a single sound but in a variety of sounds containing the feature. Thus, emphasis is placed on the identification and production of features in a variety of appropriate sounds. Costello and Onstine (1976) also implement a programmed instruction approach that incorporates simultaneous instruction on multiple phonemes. Their program includes the following steps: (1) isolation, (2) CV and VC syllables, (3) words, (4) sentences, (5) stories, and (6) conversation. Their data also show feature generalization to untreated deviant phonemes. Other researchers (Ruder & Bunce, 1981; Weiner & Bankson, 1978) provide data to support this hypothesis that distinctive feature analysis allows for a theory-based methodology for structuring articulation.

Blache, Parsons, and Humphreys (1981) find that distinctive features can be taught through using lexical contrasts or minimal word pairings (as opposed to nonsense syllables). The children are taught to discriminate and produce sounds and words using pairs of words that differ by a single distinctive feature. For example, the teacher says the words and the child points to them. Weiner (1981) also reports that teaching features at a lexical level is effective. This information may be important to keep in mind since some learning disabled children may respond better to real words than to nonsense stimuli.

*Phonological Process Approach*

The phonological process approach has remediation potential because of its specification of the rules that underlie articulation problems. The methodologies giving rise to this approach have evolved from psycholinguistic research (Compton, 1970; Ingram, 1976a). This method uses distinctive features to describe articulation errors as well as to make explicit statements regarding changes in a phonological process. Moreover, they are used as a predictive device to show how processes can be changed through therapy (Ingram, 1976b).

In remediation of phonological processes, Ingram suggests that the clinician should eliminate the child's tendency to simplify adult speech and at the same time should teach the client to produce more sounds contrastively, that is, to mark one word as different from another. To accomplish higher degrees of intelligibility, the goals of therapy are to (1) eliminate or reduce phonetic variation or instability, (2) eliminate homonyms, and (3) establish phoneme contrasts within the children's system. The first two goals work on a word-to-word basis while the third takes into account children's entire phonological system.

Processes that are producing the greatest phonetic variation and homonymy are selected as the major target of therapy. The selection of contrasts is based on the work of Jakobson (1968). For example, stop consonants develop from a /p/-/t/ contrast to a /p/, /t/, /k/ one. Ingram (1976b) indicates that "establishing the contrast with /k/ involves the elimination of fronting, showing the interaction between processes and contrasts" (p. 45). To teach contrasts, he specifies two guidelines: (1) establish contrasts that result in a system used by younger children and (2) proceed in the direction in which contrasts are established by elimination of simplification processes.

It is important to reiterate here the point made in Chapter 1 that in planning, teachers must look beyond specific phonemic targets to interrelated content areas (semantics, syntax, and pragmatics, as well as reading, spelling, and written language) and also to possible areas of processing deficit (perception, selective attention, and memory as well as higher level problems with meaning and rule generalization).

### Section 2. Phonetic Disorders—Apraxia

*Goals*

Treatment for apraxia involves clinical procedures that differ from those used to remediate articulation problems arising from aberrant phonological rules. Apraxia is not a linguistic disorder but rather a phonetic dysfunction resulting from an inability to program volitional auditory-motor movements; it is similar to dysgraphia, which is the inability to program visual-motor movements. Although Ruder and Bunce (1981) report using distinctive feature theory to remediate phonetic problems, the central core of the program for apraxia generally is considered to be to establish auditory-motor integration and memory for articulation behavior (Chappell, 1973). The children must learn to internalize tactile-kinesthetic-proprioceptive information that relates the speech sounds to their motor events. Images of sounds and sound combinations of words must be assigned motor components (Chappell, 1973).

In several cases the initial objective of beginning therapy is to assist the children in establishing volitional control over tongue and lip movements. After some gross control over the speech apparatus has been acquired, the children are taught to imitate sustained vowels followed by consonants that have highly differing contact and articulatory movements. Highly visible consonants such as /p/, /t/, /f/, and /k/ often are introduced early. It is important to try to move to meaningful words as quickly as possible. Drill on nonsense syllables may not be as effective as work with real words.

*Procedures*

For any given child, the specific sounds and their sequence should build on what can be articulated readily or easily. A thorough phonetic inventory can yield this information. For example, it has been the authors' clinical experience that some children find imitating less visible consonants such as /ʃ/ easier than highly visible ones such as /b/, or voiceless consonants easier than voiced ones. Other children find VC syllables easier to produce than CV. Treatment in this case would begin with the former syllable type. The clinician should determine which long or short vowels are easy to articulate and begin therapy with them. In sum, treatment should begin with helping children combine the easiest sounds with vowels to produce meaningful words such as "she, see, he, tea, pea, key."

After they can produce CV and VC syllables, CVC syllables usually are introduced. Rhyming words are effective. As they progress, carrier phrases can be introduced using the words they can articulate (e.g., "my hat, my cat, my bat," etc.). To stabilize the auditory-motor image of the sounds, the clinician must plan for frequent review periods and practice throughout the day. Numerous opportunities for producing newly learned sounds or words must be provided.

Chappell (1973) indicates that backward chaining may be a useful technique for those who lose the motor image of the final consonant sound in CVC words such as "meat." For example, the children may produce /mi/ but forget how to articulate /t/ when it is added to the word. The youngsters may be asked first to articulate /t/, then /it/, and finally /mit/. Yoss and Darley (1974) suggest that stress and intonational patterns may be improved through the pairing of diphthongs with consonants accompanied by visible movements of some kind to accentuate the change of phonetic placement.

Several teaching strategies can be implemented selectively, depending upon which one(s) work best for various children. It is important to use only those that are facilitative (Johnson & Myklebust, 1967). For example, some learn best by watching the clinician's mouth movements and listening to the sound(s), others when the printed letter or word is shown along with the auditory-visual stimulation. It has been the authors' clinical experience that written language or reading instruction (when it is tailored specifically to a child's needs) can facilitate and reinforce articulation therapy (see the case study in Chapter 7). Other learning disabled children benefit from verbal instructions (e.g., "lift your tongue"). For still others, a motorkinesthetic approach may be necessary (Chappell, 1973) in which the clinician stimulates or assists motor movements by actually manipulating the child's articulators (see Young & Hawk, 1938). Sometimes children perform better if they proceed from producing sounds first without the voice and then with the voice.

In summary, the effective therapy program should focus on: (1) establishing volitional control over the speech apparatus, (2) mastering the motor movements of sounds and syllables through repeated drills, and (3) providing a meaningful speaking vocabulary as rapidly as possible (Chappell, 1973).

**REFERENCES**

Atchison, M. *Variables influencing phonemic discrimination performance in normal and learning disabled first-grade-age children.* Unpublished doctoral dissertation, Northwestern University, 1975.

Atchison, M., & Canter, G. Variables influencing phonemic discrimination performance in normal and learning disabled children. *Journal of Speech and Hearing Disorders, 1979, 44,* 543-556.

Berry, M. *Teaching linguistically handicapped children.* Englewood Cliffs, N.J.: Prentice-Hall, Inc., 1980.

Blache, S., Parsons, C., & Humphreys. J. A minimal-word-pair model for teaching the linguistic significance of distinctive feature properties. *Journal of Speech and Hearing Disorders, 1981, 46,* 291-295.

Borden, G., & Harris, K. *Speech science primer: Physiology, acoustics and perception of speech.* Baltimore: The Williams and Wilkins Co., 1980.

Carrow, E. *Austin Spanish articulation test (ASAT).* Hingham, Mass.: Teaching Resources Corporation, 1974.

Chappell, G. Childhood verbal apraxia and its treatment. *Journal of Speech and Hearing Disorders, 1973, 3,* 362-368.

Chomsky, N., & Halle, M. *The sound pattern of English.* New York: Harper & Row, 1968.

Compton, A. Generative studies of children's phonological disorders. *Journal of Speech and Hearing Disorders, 1970, 35,* 315-339.

Costello, J. Articulation instruction based on distinctive feature theory. *Language, Speech, and Hearing Services in Schools, 1975, 6,* 61-71.

Costello, J., & Onstine, J. The modification of multiple articulation errors based on distinctive feature theory. *Journal of Speech and Hearing Disorders, 1976, 41,* 199-215.

Crystal, D. *Introduction to language pathology.* Baltimore: University Park Press, 1980.

Darley, F. (Ed.) *Evaluation of appraisal techniques in speech and language pathology.* Reading, Mass.: Addison-Wesley Publishing Company, Inc., 1979.

Darley, F., Aronson, A., & Brown, J. *Motor speech disorders.* Philadelphia: W.B. Saunders Company, 1975.

deVilliers, J., & deVilliers, P. *Language acquisition.* Cambridge, Mass.: Harvard University Press, 1978.

Drumwright, A. *The Denver articulation screening examination (DASE).* Denver: Ladoca Project and Publishing Foundation, Inc., 1971.

Dunn, C., & Barron, C. A treatment program for disordered phonology: Phonetic and linguistic considerations. *Language, Speech, and Hearing Services in Schools, 1982, 13,* 100-109.

Eimas, P. Linguistic processing of speech in young infants. In R. Schiefelbusch & L. Lloyd (Eds.), *Language perspectives: Retardation and intervention*. Baltimore: University Park Press, 1974.

Eisenson, J. *Aphasia in children*. New York: Harper & Row Publishers, Inc., 1972.

Fisher, H., & Logemann, J. *The Fisher-Logemann test of articulation competence*. Boston: Houghton Mifflin Company, 1971.

Flynn P., & Byrne, M. Relationship between reading and selected auditory abilities of third grade children. *Journal of Speech and Hearing Research*, 1970, *13*, 731-740.

Fudala, J. *Arizona articulation proficiency scale*. Los Angeles: Western Psychological Services, 1961.

Gibson, E., & Levin, H. *The psychology of reading*. Cambridge, Mass.: The MIT Press, 1975.

Goldman, R., & Fristoe, M. *Goldman-Fristoe test of articulation*. Circle Pines, Minn.: American Guidance Service, Inc., 1969.

Goldman, R., Fristoe, M., & Woodcock, R. *Goldman-Fristoe-Woodcock test of auditory discrimination*. Circle Pines, Minn.: American Guidance Service, Inc., 1970.

Goldman, R., Fristoe, M., & Woodcock, R. *Goldman-Fristoe-Woodcock diagnostic auditory discrimination test*. Circle Pines, Minn.: American Guidance Service, 1974.

Haggarty, R., & Stamm, J. Dichotic auditory fusion levels in children with learning disabilities. *Neuropsychologia*, 1978, *16*, 349-360.

Herja, R. *Developmental articulation test*. Ann Arbor, Mich.: Speech Materials, 1963.

Hook, P. *A study of metalinguistic awareness and reading strategies in proficient and learning disabled readers*. Unpublished doctoral dissertation, Northwestern University, 1976.

Hook, P., & Johnson, D.J. Metalinguistic awareness and reading strategies. *Bulletin of the Orton Society*, 1978, *28*, 62-78.

Ingram, D.M. Current issues in child phonology. In D.M. Morehead & A.E. Morehead (Eds.), *Normal and deficient child language*. Baltimore: University Park Press, 1976.(a)

Ingram, D. *Phonological disability in children*. London: Edward Arnold Ltd., 1976. (b)

Ingram, D. The production of word-initial fricatives and affricates by normal and linguistically deviant children. In A. Caramazza & E. Zurif (Eds.), *Language acquisition and language breakdown: Parallels and divergencies*. Baltimore: The Johns Hopkins University Press, 1978.

Ingram, D. Phonological patterns in the speech of young children. In P. Fletcher & M. Garman (Eds.), *Language acquisition*. Cambridge, England: Cambridge University Press, 1979.

Ingram, D. *Procedures for the phonological analysis of children's language*. Baltimore: University Park Press, 1981.

Irwin, O. Integrated articulation test. In O. Irwin (Ed.), *Communication variables of cerebral palsied and mentally retarded children*. Springfield: Charles C Thomas, Publisher, 1972. (a)

Irwin, O. A test of sound discrimination. In O. Irwin (Ed.), *Communication variables of cerebral palsied and mentally retarded children*. Springfield, Ill.: Charles C. Thomas, Publisher, 1972. (b)

Jakobson, R. *Child language, aphasia and phonological universals*. The Hague: Mouton Publishers, 1968.

Jakobson, R., Fant, C., & Halle, M. *Preliminaries to speech analysis: The distinctive features and their correlates*. Cambridge, Mass.: The MIT Press, 1952.

Johns, D., & Darley, F. Phoneme variability in apraxia of speech. *Journal of Speech and Hearing Research*, 1970, *13*, 556-583.

Johnson, D.J., & Myklebust, H.R. *Learning disabilities: Educational principles and practices*. New York: Grune & Stratton, Inc., 1967.

Kavale, K. The relationship between auditory perceptual skills and reading ability: A meta-analysis. *Journal of Learning Disabilities,* 1981, *14,* 539-546.

Khan, L.M. A review of 16 major phonological processes. *Language, Speech, and Hearing Services in Schools,* 1982, *13,* 77-85.

Kimmell, G., & Wahl, J. *Screening test for auditory perception.* Novato, Calif.: Academic Therapy Publications, 1969.

Kirk, S., McCarthy, J., & Kirk, W. *Illinois test of psycholinguistic abilities.* Chicago: University of Illinois Press, 1968.

Kneedler, R., & Hallahan, D. Self-monitoring of on-task behavior with learning disabled children: Current studies and directions. *Exceptional Education Quarterly,* 1981, *2,* 73-82.

Koury-Parker, D.I. *Identification and discrimination of synthetic speech sounds by children with varying phonics skills.* Unpublished doctoral dissertation, Northwestern University, 1983.

Kozhevnikova, V.A., & Chistovich, L.A. *[Speech: Articulation and perception]:* (National Technical Information Service, trans.). Springfield, Va.: U.S. Department of Commerce, 1965.

Leonard, L. Teaching by the rules. *Journal of Speech and Hearing Disorders,* 1973, *38,* 174-183.

Liberman, I., Shankweiler, D., Liberman, A., Fowler, C., & Fischer, F. Phonetic segmentation and recoding in the beginning reader. In A. Reber & D. Scarborough (Eds.), *Towards a psychology of reading: The proceedings of the City University of New York Conference.* Hillsdale, N.J.: Lawrence Erlbaum Associates, Publishers, 1977.

Lindamood, C., & Lindamood, P. *Lindamood auditory conceptualization test (LAC).* Boston: Resources Corporation, 1971.

Locke, J. The inference of speech perception in the phonologically disordered child, Part 1: A rationale, some criteria, the conventional tests. *Journal of Speech and Hearing Disorders,* 1980, *45,* 431-444.(a)

Locke, J. The inference of speech perception in the phonologically disordered child, Part 2: Some clinically novel procedures, their use, some findings. *Journal of Speech and Hearing Disorders,* 1980, *45,* 445-468.(b)

Lorentz, J. An analysis of some deviant phonological rules of English. In D.M. Morehead & A.E. Morehead (Eds.), *Normal and deficient child language.* Baltimore: University Park Press, 1976.

Lowe, A., & Campbell, R. Temporal discrimination in aphasoid and normal children. *Journal of Speech and Hearing Research,* 1965, *8,* 313-314.

Lubert, N. Auditory perceptual impairments in children with specific language disorders: A review of the literature. *Journal of Speech and Hearing Disorders,* 1981, *46,* 3-9.

Luchsinger, R., & Arnold, G. *Voice-speech-language clinical communicology: Its physiology and pathology.* Belmont, Calif.: Wadsworth Publishing Co., Inc. 1965.

Matthews, D.A. & Seymour, C.M. The performance of learning disabled children on tests of auditory discrimination. *Journal of Learning Disabilities,* 1981, *14,* 9-11.

McCabe, R., & Bradley, D. Systematic multiple phonemic approach to articulation therapy. *Acta Symbolica,* 1975, *6,* 1-18.

McDonald, E. *A deep test of articulation.* Pittsburgh: Stanwix House, 1964.

McReynolds, L. Operant conditioning for investigating speech sound discrimination in aphasic children. *Journal of Speech and Hearing Research,* 1966, *9,* 519-528.

McReynolds, L., & Bennett, S. Distinctive feature generalization in articulation training. *Journal of Speech and Hearing Disorders,* 1972, *37,* 462-470.

McReynolds, L., & Elbert, M. Criteria for phonological process analysis. *Journal of Speech and Hearing Disorders,* 1981, *46,* 197-203.

McReynolds, L., & Engmann, D. *Distinctive feature analysis of misarticulations.* Baltimore: University Park Press, 1975.

McReynolds, L., & Huston, K. A distinctive feature analysis of children's misarticulations. *Journal of Speech and Hearing Disorders,* 1971, *36,* 155-166.

Menyuk, P., & Menn, L. Early strategies for the perception and production of words and sounds. In P. Fletcher & M. Garman (Eds), *Language acquisition.* Cambridge, England: Cambridge University Press, 1979.

Morley, M. *The development and disorders of speech in childhood.* Edinburgh, Scotland: Churchill Livingstone, 1972.

Mowrer, D. *Methods of modifying speech behaviors.* Columbus, Ohio: The Charles E. Merrill Publishing Co., Inc., 1977.

Newman, P. Appraisal of articulation. In F. Darley (Ed.), *Evaluation of appraisal techniques in speech and language pathology.* Reading, Mass.: Addison-Wesley Publishing Company, Inc., 1979.

Oller, D. Regularities in abnormal child phonology. *Journal of Speech and Hearing Disorders,* 1973, *38,* 36-47.

Pendergast, D., Dickey, S., Selmar, J., & Soder, A. *Photo articulation test.* Danville, Ill.: The Interstate Printers & Publishers, Inc., 1969.

Pollack, E., & Rees, N. Disorders of articulation: Some clinical applications of distinctive feature theory. *Journal of Speech and Hearing Disorders,* 1972, *37,* 451-461.

Powers, M. Functional disorders of articulation: Symptomatology and etiology. In L. Travis (Ed.), *Handbook of speech pathology and audiology.* New York: Appleton-Century-Crofts, Inc., 1971.

Prather, E., Miner, A., Addicott, M., & Sunderland, L. *Washington speech sound discrimination test.* Danville, Ill.: The Interstate Printers & Publishers, Inc., 1971.

Pronovost, W. *The Boston University speech sound discrimination test.* Boston: Go-Mo Products, 1953.

Rees, N. Auditory processing factors in language disorders: The view from Procrustes' bed. *Journal of Speech and Hearing Disorders,* 1973, *38,* 304-315.

Rosenbek, J., Hansen, R., Baughman, G., & Lemme M. Treatment of developmental apraxia of speech: A case study. *Language, Speech, and Hearing Services in the Schools,* 1974, *5,* 13-22.

Rosenbek, J., & Wertz, R. A review of fifty cases of developmental apraxia of speech. *Language, Speech, and Hearing Services in the Schools,* 1972, *3,* 23-33.

Ruder, K., & Bunce, B. Articulation therapy using distinctive feature analysis to structure the training program: Two case studies. *Journal of Speech and Hearing Disorders,* 1981, *46,* 59-65.

Salus, P., & Salus, M. Developmental neurophysiology and phonological acquisition order. *Language,* 1974, *50,* 151-160.

Shankweiler, D., Liberman, I., Mark, L., Fowler, C., & Fischer, F. The speech code and learning to read. *Journal of Experimental Psychology: Human Learning and Memory,* 1979, *5,* 531-545.

Shriberg, L., & Kwiatkowski, J. *Natural process analysis (NPA): A procedure for phonological analyses of continuous speech samples.* New York: John Wiley & Sons, Inc., 1980.

Singh, S. *Distinctive features: Theory and validation.* Baltimore: University Park Press, 1976.

Singh, S., & Singh, K. *Distinctive features: Principles and practices.* Baltimore: University Park Press, 1976.

Singh, S., Hayden, M., & Toombs, M. The role of distinctive features in articulation errors. *Journal of Speech and Hearing Disorders,* 1981, *46,* 174-183.

Slingerland, B. *Slingerland screening tests for identifying children with specific language disability.* Cambridge, Mass.: Educators Publishing Service, Inc., 1970.

Stampe, D. *A dissertation on natural phonology*. Unpublished doctoral dissertation, University of Chicago, 1972.

Stark, R. Prespeech segmental feature development. In P. Fletcher & M. Garman (Eds.), *Language acquisition*. Cambridge, England: Cambridge University Press, 1979.

Tallal, P. Auditory temporal perception, phonics and reading disabilities in children. *Brain and Language*, 1980, *9*, 182-198. (a)

Tallal, P. Language and reading: Some perceptual prerequisites. *Bulletin of the Orton Society*, 1980, *30*, 170-178. (b)

Tallal, P., & Piercy, M. Developmental dysphasia: Impaired rate of nonverbal processing as a function of sensory modality. *Neuropsychologia*, 1973, *11*, 389-398.

Tallal, P., & Piercy, M. Developmental aphasia: Rate of auditory processing and selective impairment of consonant perception. *Neuropsychologia*, 1974, *12*, 83-93.

Tallal, P., & Piercy, M. Developmental aphasia: The perception of brief vowels and extended consonants. *Neuropsychologia*, 1975, *13*, 69-74.

Tallal, P., & Stark, R. Speech perception of language-delayed children. In G. Yenikomshiam, C. Ferguson, & J. Kavanaugh (Eds.), *Child phonology: Perception* (Vol. 2). New York: Academic Press, 1980.

Tallal, P., Stark, R., Kallman, C., & Mellitis, D. A reexamination of some nonverbal perceptual abilities of language impaired and normal children as a function of age and sensory modality. *Journal of Speech and Hearing Research*, 1981, *24*, 351-357.

Templin, M. *Certain language skills in children*. Minneapolis: University of Minnesota Press, 1957.

Templin, M., & Darley, F. *The Templin-Darley tests of articulation*. (2nd Ed.) Iowa City, Iowa: Bureau of Educational Research and Service, 1969.

Torgesen, J. The relationship between memory and attention in learning disabilities. *Exceptional Education Quarterly*, 1981, *2*, 51-60.

Turton, L., & Clark, M. Linguistic theory and the child. *Acta Symbolica*, 1971, *2*, 42-47.

Van Riper, C. *Speech correction principles and methods*. Englewood Cliffs, N.J.: Prentice-Hall, Inc., 1962.

Van Riper, C., & Erickson, R. *Predictive screening test of articulation*. Kalamazoo, Mich.: Western Michigan University, Continuing Education Office, 1968.

Van Riper, C., & Smith, D. *An introduction to general American phonics*. New York: Harper & Row Publishers, Inc., 1979.

Weiner, F. The perceptual level of functioning of aphasic children. *Cortex*, 1969, *5*, 440-457.

Weiner, F. Treatment of phonological disability using the method of meaningful minimal contrast: Two case studies. *Journal of Speech and Hearing Disorders*, 1981, *46*, 97-103.

Weiner, F., & Bankson, N. Teaching features. *Language, Speech, and Hearing Services in the Schools*, 1978, *9*, 29-34.

Weiner, F., & Bernthal, J. Articulation feature assessment. In S. Singh & J. Lynch (Eds.), *Diagnostic procedures in hearing, speech and language*. Baltimore: University Park Press, 1978.

Weiss, C. *Weiss comprehensive articulation test (WCAT)*. Hingham, Mass.: Teaching Resources, 1978.

Weiss, C., Lillywhite, H., & Gordon M. *Clinical management of articulation disorders*. St. Louis: The C.V. Mosby Company, 1980.

Wepman, J. Auditory discrmination, speech and reading. *Elementary School Journal*, 1960, *9*, 325-333.

Wepman, J. *Auditory discrimination test*. Chicago: Language Research Associates, 1973.

Weston, A., & Irwin, J. The use of paired stimuli in the modification of articulation. *Journal of Perceptual Motor Skills*, 1971, *32*, 947-957.

Wiig, E., & Semel, E. *Learning disabilities in children and adolescents*. Columbus, Ohio: The Charles E. Merrill Publishing Co., Inc., 1976.

Winitz, H. *Articulatory acquisition and behavior*. New York: Appleton-Century-Crofts, Inc., 1969.

Winitz, H. *From syllable to conversation*. Baltimore: University Park Press, 1975.

Wren, C.T. *The relationship of auditory and cognitive processes to syntactic patterns in learning disabled and normal children*. Unpublished doctoral dissertation, Northwestern University, 1980.

Yoss, K., & Darley, F. Therapy in developmental apraxia of speech. *Language, Speech, and Hearing Services in the Schools*, 1974, *5*, 23-31.

Young, E., & Hawk, S. *Motorkinesthetic speech training*. Stanford, Calif.: Stanford University Press, 1938.

# Chapter 3

# Semantics

*Barbara B. Hoskins*

## PART I. SEMANTICS AND LEARNING DISABILITIES

Following the domain of speech sounds is the next larger unit of language: words. The interrelationships between sounds and words are complex not only because sounds always are produced in the context of words but also because meaning plays a crucial role at this level of language.

The study of the development of word meaning in children has burgeoned since about 1970. The richness of this theoretical and empirical harvest has yielded valuable information to direct educators' work with language learning disordered children. This provides a perspective from which to more clearly examine and then facilitate the continuing process of learning word meaning. This newer perspective encompasses aspects of word meaning not previously within practitioners' scope of study. In fact, the widely accepted theoretical view has shifted from a fairly unidimensional quantitative approach to the study of semantic development to a broader, more qualitative view of what it is to know the meaning of a word.

This chapter examines several of the major issues addressed in the literature on the development of word meaning and suggests how these theoretical views can contribute to the diagnosis and remediation of children with language learning difficulties. Although the term "semantics" has been used to refer to various aspects of meaning in language theory, for purposes here, it is defined as the study of word meaning. Acquisition is examined in terms of development of the lexicon. Historical trends are reviewed that track the move from a view of semantic acquisition that focused on the number of words used by a child at any time (or vocabulary counts) to the new interest in various dimensions of the development of word meaning such as:

- what is included in the category of items named by a particular word
- how the internal structure of the category of named items is organized and how this organization develops

- what relationship exists between various words or concepts stored in knowledge structure.

## Section 1. Approaches to Studying Semantics

During the 1960s, an overriding interest in children's syntactic or grammatical development left semantic/conceptual learning relatively unstudied. The major concept used to explain the development of meaning in children was referential theory (see Alston, 1964). That is, words were seen as symbols that stood for something in the world. From this view, the development of word meaning was seen as a fairly unitary all-or-nothing phenomenon of labeling objects or events. "Dog" referred to a particular type of animal and "cookie" to a specific kind of food.

Vocabulary growth thus could be accounted for by counting the number of words used at any particular point along the developmental sequence. Children's rapid, in fact geometric, growth in the number of words in their vocabularies has been documented in word counts of the sort reviewed by McCarthy (1954). It could be observed that, although children typically knew only a few words at the age of 1, by 2 they usually demonstrated knowledge of many more than 200. By examining the number and kinds of words they knew at various ages, the progression of vocabulary development was charted but was largely unexplained.

A closer inspection of referential theory reveals the limitations of this view. First, several words or lexical items may be used to name any individual referent. The family pet may be called "doggie," "Spot," or a "cocker spaniel." Second, individual vocabulary items often are used to refer to widely varying kinds of objects and events in the world. "Plate" might mean something to place food on, or a metal piece inserted into some kind of machinery. Third, it also is evident that many words do not seem to have any particular referent—"and," "the," "is," and "or" do not refer to any particular item or event and yet are meaningful. "Love," "hate," and "courage" are equally difficult to categorize. Thus, even though referential theory seemed to account for "what it is to know a word" in a fairly straightforward manner, it left many questions regarding meaning unanswered.

Early work by Brown (1958) raised questions as to whether children first learned abstract category names or specific concrete labels. He suggests that children do not learn words in either an abstract-to-concrete or concrete-to-abstract progression but rather that they are guided in the types of words they acquire by the naming practices of adults. He suggests that the meaning of a word refers to a class of events rather than to a simple referential link. Word meaning is linked, then, to knowing a concept. The development of concepts and meaning is seen to be an evolving process (Vygotsky, 1962) that is based on categorization and organization of various items and events in the children's world.

The seeds of these notions thus were emplanted in the late 1950s and early 1960s but were not explored in any depth until later because of the intense interest in syntactic development. However, as questions on the limitations of a structural approach to language learning were raised, there emerged a renewed interest in how children's conceptual processes provided a basis for language learning in general and semantic development in specific.

Anglin's (1970) work, summarized in his book, *The Growth of Word Meaning*, signals an important move away from a unitary view of vocabulary development. He explores the questions that had been raised as to the direction of lexical acquisition but also further investigates the notion that word meanings develop along various dimensions during the acquisition process. He uses a variety of experimental tasks to examine different dimensions of word meaning: (1) sorting to observe the kinds of hierarchical relationships that children use to organize meaning and (2) free recall and word association tasks to reveal how words are clustered. His results chart a gradual growth between the ages of 3 and adulthood in the ability to see relationships within and among concepts or words. This early study laid the groundwork for examining the various dimensions or the "architecture" of developing word meaning.

Clark's (1973) research marks another milestone in the move toward a more in-depth exploration of semantic development. Her model of semantic acquisition addresses the concept that what a word means to a child is not necessarily the same as it does to an adult. She uses data from early diary studies to demonstrate that the meaning of a word evolves for children and that errors in labeling items reveal this evolution.

Her *Semantic Feature Hypothesis* was proposed to explain children's overgeneralization errors in early naming, i.e., overuse of a term to refer to instances that are not, in adult usage, instances of that term. For example, one child uses the word "moon" to refer to a lemon wedge, a crescent-shaped cookie, and the eyes on a toy dog. According to Clark's formulation, word meaning can be represented by a set of semantic features. Features are seen to be basic attributes or perceptual characteristics that determine what items are to be called by a certain name.

Children are regarded as basing early meanings on a few features and therefore include a large number of items in each category. Initial use of the word "dog" may be based on the features: + animal, + furry. Later, as more features are added to this set, word meaning becomes narrower or more specific: "dog" may then be + animal, + furry, + four-legged, further defining the category of items to which that name can apply. By adding features, the internal structure of the category of items can be seen to develop over time.

It should be noted that Clark's data come from children's errors in word usage or extension to various instances of those words in their worlds. Her formulation emphasizes how children use perceptual attributes to apply words to objects and then modify their criteria until they approximate adult usage.

In contrast to Clark's emphasis on the primacy of perception in early word use, Nelson (1978) offers a theoretical framework that emphasizes the role of function in semantic/conceptual development. She suggests that concept learning is the foundation for word meaning. Thus, she begins by evaluating the nature of early concepts and then suggests how words are "attached" to these concepts.

According to Nelson (1974, 1977), a concept is based on a functional core, derived from children's experience with objects in an action-oriented instance. For example, the concept "ball" may be based on an experience of rolling or bouncing a ball with the mother. She suggests that, following several experiences with the item, e.g., "ball," children begin to recognize relations between the object and the actions or individuals acting on it. These may include relationships such as location action, actor, or possessor. Next, she theorizes children begin to abstract out descriptive features of the item, such as round, large, or red. Based on these features, the children may select other instances of the concept and, finally, in some cases, attach a label or name to the item. She points out that the children initially may just recognize the name of the item, then use the name later.

Nelson (1974), therefore, describes word meaning as based on personal action-based experiences, although later naming may be guided by perceptual attributes. Word meaning thus may involve various stages of learning, not the least complex of which may be the development of a concept.

Experimental and theoretical work on adult word meaning also offers some useful notions regarding the structure of concepts and meaning. A study by Lakoff (1973) suggests that concepts and word meanings are not clearly defined entities. Lakoff notes that adult usage of terms such as "sort of" and "kind of" may indicate that words or concepts have "fuzzy edges." That is, it is not always clear whether an instance is to be included in one category of meaning (e.g., fruits) or another (e.g., vegetables). This idea may have interesting implications for language learning disordered children in that they typically have considerable difficulty with ambiguity, a component that seems to be inherent in the language system.

Rosch (1976, 1978) further suggests that conceptual/semantic categories have internal structure that should be considered in a developmental model. As she notes, some instances of the category "bird," for example, are considered more birdlike than others. That is, a robin might be considered a central instance of the category "bird" and an ostrich a peripheral member. Central instances may be expected in children's early developing lexical categories while peripheral items may not be included initially.

An apparent example of this was seen when a boy 2½ years old was visiting the zoo. He was willing to accept the label "bird" when applied to parrots, ducks, and even wild turkeys but when faced with an ostrich and told to "Look at the big bird," he replied, "No! Hossie." It does appear that, during development of word meaning, the children's categorical groupings may exclude some of those that are in adults' and, in particular, may omit peripheral members of the set from their early lexicon.

Anglin's (1977) work further contributes to an understanding of the multifaceted nature of semantic learning. He also uses a variety of experimental tasks to examine semantic/conceptual development. These include various kinds of sorting and categorizing tasks designed to observe how children decide which object to include in a given term or label. Some of these tasks probe for the children's use of superordinate and subordinate terms to organize classes or groups. Anglin also examines diary data on children's naming, or extension, of terms, as well as definitional tasks to observe the intention or the properties that youngsters refer to as critical for word meaning.

Findings on children's early use of terms reveal that there is neither a unidirectional specific-to-general nor general-to-specific progression in vocabulary development. Rather, children learn common nouns at an intermediate level of generality that is functionally salient in their lives. Anglin terms this "behavioral equivalence," a level at which children and their elders can use terms to group items of everyday use or those that the youngsters may behave toward in a similar way. This is akin to what Rosch (1973, 1978) refers to as the basic object level.

In studying extension or use of a term to apply to various instances of a concept, Anglin reports that children make responses that are overgeneralized (including instances that adults might not include) or undergeneralized (omitting instances that adults might include) depending upon the particular individual's experiences, the concept being investigated, and the nature of the instances presented.

This extension of terms to various instances, therefore, reflects the fact that children do not see categories as having well-defined boundaries (Lakoff, 1973). Instead, a given concept has "internal structure," which means that it is composed of a core meaning (including the clearest examples of the category) surrounded by members of decreasing similarity to the core. Rosch (1976, 1978) also supports this notion that children respond differentially to central, as compared to peripheral, members of a category and do not seem to include the latter elements until later in their development of word meaning.

Anglin makes an important distinction between the extension of word meaning to various instances that might be labeled by a word and the intension of that word. Intension involves the properties that individuals see as defining for a word, or the basis on which they might explain its meaning. Findings from explanations and definitions across various ages demonstrate that there is not a direct correspondence between children's intensional and extensional meaning. Young children do not know what properties are defining and do not express knowledge of category structure and hierarchical relationships among words.

It also is clear that whether errors of overextension or underextension occur depends on the nature of the task. Overgeneralization errors are more obvious in production and undergeneralization most apparent in comprehension tasks. That is, when a child names items incorrectly, such instances are obvious while items that are not named, of course, are not noted. Conversely, when asked to "find all the birds," the child's undergeneralizations or omissions are more evident. This discrepancy is interesting in that it demonstrates that word meaning involves various aspects of conceptual development and that any individual task may tap into a different aspect of meaning.

One aspect of the semantic conceptual system under scrutiny is how that semantic/conceptual knowledge is stored in the memory structure. With the advent of computer technology as applied to psychological and linguistic issues, some fairly sophisticated models of semantic memory have been developed. The work of Collins and Quillian (1972) and Rummelhart, Lindsay, and Norman (1972) suggests that semantic/conceptual knowledge can be described in terms of a network of information. They define this network as a complex array of "nodes" that may stand for words, concepts, events, episodes, or propositions, connected to one another by various labeled arcs or relations. This model provides a view not only of what knowledge an individual holds in storage but also of how it is related to other known information by means of categorical or logical links. These links are organizational devices by which individuals retain, relate, and retrieve meaningful information. In this way, knowledge of words is depicted as having a complex, interacting structure that develops in intricacy as new relations are added, labels are learned, and events and episodes are experienced. From this view, the study of memory is not regarded as separate from the organization of the lexicon. How semantic information is related is inextricably tied to how it is stored and retrieved.

Although most of the research has been directed toward explaining the adult semantic/conceptual system, some application to children's acquisition of word meanings has been offered from a semantic network model. Riegel (1970) proposes a developmental model that separates types of relations into (1) the infralogical, based on the physical relationships between objects or events, and (2) the logical that link words to one another in knowledge structure.

Examples of logical relations are antonymy or contrast and superordination or categorization. Infralogical relations include parts and locations. Riegel reports that as children develop cognitively, they use a wider range of these relations to form definitions and explanations. Norlin (1976), in evaluating children's developmental progression, suggests that they use infralogical rather than logical relations early and that they use an additional infralogical relation—function—most frequently to define terms and retrieve items at all age levels.

Litowitz (1977) demonstrates the application of a semantic network or relations framework to the evaluation of early definitions in children (ages 4½ to 7½). She says definitional tasks can shed light on what information is considered basic to word meaning—that is, the intension of a word. Litowitz reports that although adults use taxonomy or superordinate structure to describe words (e.g., a dog is an animal . . .) as well as an attribute . . . (that barks) to develop formal definitions, children's early definitions are not structured using semantic relations in the same way. She suggests that those definitions are word associations and examples of actual experiences and that they often include function.

A range of definitional forms can be observed before formal adult definitions are seen. In response to the question "What does _____ mean?" children may provide:

- a nonverbal or semantically empty statement such as for "snap"—"like that"
- word associations such as for "bicycle"—"the man"
- a concrete example of actual experience, as in "knife"—"when you're cutting carrots"
- an awareness of a definitional form or general social information such as "knife"——"a knife is when you cut with it"
- a formal definition of the form A ____ is a ____ that ____, for example "a castle is something that a king lives in."

This latter definitional form requires that children use lexical relations such as superordination and attribution to supply salient information to the expression of meaning. Litowitz suggests that the scoring of definitional tasks in many formal tests overlooks these qualitative differences that should be analyzed more sensitively in terms of the kinds of relations children use to express intension.

In summary, the developmental literature has begun to reveal the complexity of issues involved in the study of semantic/conceptual development. It has been well documented that what a word means to a child is not necessarily the same as what an adult assumes. Learning word meaning is an evolving process. Clark (1973) describes this as learning features or components of meaning. Others, such as Nelson (1974), define the process as beginning with an action-based functional core, later moving to the abstraction of attributes, and then applying words meaningfully. Anglin (1977) and others show that children learn terms that are not necessarily either concrete or abstract but that they do acquire terms that adults present as functional or "behaviorally equivalent."

Word meaning reflects concept learning and therefore involves learning categorical structures. These categories of meaning have internal structure. Rosch (1976) and Anglin (1977) demonstrate that some instances of a category of items such as "bird" clearly are central members and that others are more peripheral ones that are invoked less commonly. Natural categories thus are seen to have internal structure and fuzzy edges.

It also has become clear from Anglin's (1977) work that there are many dimensions of meaning that are tapped by various experimental tasks. For example, observation of children's word use or production may reveal many overgeneralizations while comprehension or category inclusion may show under-generalization in that many peripheral items may be left out. The way in which children select instances to which a word may apply (extension) may be quite different from the intension, or the information they see as defining a particular category.

The lexicon is arranged within a hierarchical system of relationships that children learn in a gradual manner between the ages of 3 and adulthood. These relations include superordination, subordination, attribution, and a complex set of infralogical and logical relations (Riegel, 1970). These kinds of relations can structure how individuals comprehend, store, retrieve, and define meaningful information.

This multidimensional view of semantic development presents a challenge to those interested in the growth of meaning in children. It is clear that a simplistic, all-or-nothing approach to assessing and teaching vocabulary will not provide the answers needed to develop appropriate diagnostic and remedial methods for work with language learning disordered children. Rather, the task must be approached with a willingness to include various dimensions of the process of learning and an interest in using the tools available in a discriminating, conscious manner.

### Section 2. Semantic Disorders in Learning Disabled Children

The new view of meaning holds interesting implications for educators' work with language learning disordered children. Various aspects of meaning have been defined so that it now is possible to observe more clearly what it is that disordered individuals understand about the meaning of words. Clinicians' questions may include:

- What items or instances are recognized or labeled correctly?
- What is the basis on which items are included in a named category?
- Are peripheral, as well as central, instances recognized or named appropriately?
- Where do children set the boundaries for what is included in a category?
- How do children understand that a particular word or concept relates to other pieces of known information?
- How do they understand the superordinate category to which this item belongs?
- How do they recognize other similar terms and opposite terms?
- How do they use this information in formulating definitions and explanations?

Consideration of these aspects of meaning provides a framework from which to examine the kinds of semantic errors found in the language learning disordered. Although few empirical studies exist that illuminate the nature of these semantic disorders, the author's clinical experience suggests that semantic difficulties may be subtle, yet pervasive. Many language disordered children and adults use fairly adequate vocabulary in their explanations or descriptions. Although they may use a large number of "fillers," e.g., "stuff" and "sort of," they often can find lexical items to meet their general conversational needs. Similarly, in specific test situations they may be able to identify a certain pictured object or event.

However, these behaviors give only a glimpse of what a word means to that individual. Using a word in a self-generated context may indicate only that the person has learned that particular referential link between word and situation. Some authors (Wiig & Semel, 1976) suggest that language learning disordered individuals may in fact use a large number of vocabulary items to compensate for their inability to use words flexibly in a variety of relations.

Words may not mean the same thing for disordered individuals as they do for normal learners. The former may understand some familiar or concrete usages of a term but not a great many other less central usages. They may not hold the same characteristics as criterial as others do. One child describes "strong," for example, as "big" and "heavy," while this is not necessarily true.

Harris (1979) finds that learning disordered children do not include the same kinds of items in their category construction as do normal students. When she provided common items to be sorted—foods, toys, school supplies, and cooking utensils—the 7-year-old learning disabled children often produced disorganized heaps of items and gave contradictory reasons for forming categories. Others generated groups that were figurative or graphic representations. Some learning disordered 9-year-olds based groupings on pretend or perceptual reasons while their normally achieving age mates did not. The learning disordered also gave more semantically empty reasons ("they're all things"), reflecting less well-developed category structures than did normal youngsters.

These kinds of findings support the notion that learning disordered individuals often do not organize word categories and concepts as effectively as do normal persons. The author's clinical experience also suggests that even though the disordered individuals may use a term to name or recognize an item that usually is agreed upon as a common example of a concept, they also may include many others that are not usually considered correct (overgeneralizing) or may omit items that usually are included (undergeneralizing). These may be noted in errors of comprehension or word use or in formulation of explanations or definitions.

Comprehension and word use errors may suggest that the learning disordered individuals have acquired the rudiments of meaning for a particular item but have not fully developed the concept. One very bright language disordered adult who was receiving assistance reading a banking textbook read the passage, "The nature of the banking industry. . . ." When questioned as to the meaning of the term "nature," she said she had been wondering why the author referred to flowers and trees in a banking text. Such errors suggest a limited range of meaning that does not yet include abstract or ambiguous usage of a term.

Learning disabled children and adults often are considered to be concrete or literal in their interpretations. They misinterpret directions and do not understand humor that involves word play or multiple word meanings. A 10-year-old boy, given the directions: "Make an X above the line, now make one below the line," drew an X above the designated line and then a numeral 1 below that line. This misinterpretation of the use of the term "one" suggests a literal or rigid pattern of comprehension that also was seen in many of the tasks with which this child had difficulty.

In social situations, comprehension of abstract or perhaps unusual meanings of a word may be required to interpret metaphors and idioms. One particularly sophisticated learning disordered adult could not understand why someone told her she was "barking up the wrong tree." She came close when she decided that the metaphor had to do with having bark grow on the wrong tree so she changed the direction of her fund-raising project. Other examples include comprehension of phrases such as "eats like a bird," which requires that the user abstract out the quality (or quantity) being described and apply this idea to a new situation. This kind of relational thinking makes many social situations uncomfortable for the language learning disordered.

Blue (1981), underlining this point, suggests several kinds of utterances that are to be avoided in conversation with language disordered individuals: sarcasm, idiomatic expressions, ambiguous statements, indirect requests, and words with multiple meanings. He explains that these kinds of expressions require a degree of language proficiency that the language disordered usually have not acquired. Interpretation of these messages involves comprehension of abstract word meanings and recognizing underlying relations between lexical items.

Some word comprehension errors seem to be related to individuals' difficulty recognizing relationships between categories of events. For example, where learning disabled children are asked to group items and then provide a category label (taxonomy), they may not recognize that the couch, chair, and table they have grouped may be labeled with a general term "furniture." The word furniture, in fact, may be used correctly in certain situations, e.g., "What are these things in your living room?" but may not be applied as a label for a set of named objects. Similarly, more advanced students may not be able to abstract out the relationship of two items in the initial portion of an analogy, e.g., "Glove is to hands as . . ." in order to apply that relation to the second part of the analogy, ". . . sock is to _____."

Difficulty recognizing the organization inherent in systems of meaning may result in a range of language difficulties. When information is not stored in an organized fashion, retrieval difficulties are common and memory strategies may be poor.

In addition, it is difficult for language learning disabled individuals to organize definitions and explanations along logical, hierarchical lines. Definitions give splinters of facts with no reference to a general category name or a criterial piece of information. For example, rather than a response such as "a bicycle is a vehicle with two wheels," a learning disabled 14-year-old responded, "I got a green one." Similarly, explanations may begin with a detail rather than a general introduction, e.g., "E.: Tell me about your family. C.: We go horseback riding." Not knowing how information is organized thus results in fragmented communication.

It is evident that no simple, quantitative approach to examining word meaning is adequate in determining the nature of these comprehension deficits. Rather than solely accounting for the number of words recognized, it is important to determine what is included in the meaning of a word or phrase and under what circumstances the individuals will comprehend or utilize certain semantic units. Language learning disordered youngsters may not (1) include peripheral items in a semantic category, (2) recognize a word's ambiguous contexts, and (3) recognize relationships between the meaning of one word and other related items.

### Section 3. Processing and Semantic Disorders

Difficulties in comprehending or using words meaningfully can be the result of processing difficulties at any of several points along a continuum. As might be expected, if hearing acuity or speech perception is not accurate, words may be misperceived and meaning misinterpreted. For example, persons often are described as having very concrete vocabularies and as having difficulty with interpretations of idioms, word play, and general verbal humor. Similarly, if memory functions of the learning disabled are poor, the ability to retain and recall information related to a particular semantic item will be limited.

Memory functions appear in many ways to be inseparable from semantics; that is, knowledge stored in memory is in some way labeled as semantic. Thus, a network of semantic information provides an organizational structure for remembering and retrieving knowledge. If the organizational system is poor, information is likely to be remembered poorly and retrieved ineffectively. Along the same lines, if semantic organization is better developed, more organized memory strategies may be available to the learning disabled individuals.

Conceptualization also is linked inextricably to semantic development. As noted, to know the meaning of a word is to know a concept. Word meaning refers to labeling a class or category of events. If conceptual structure is poor, i.e., categorization skills are weak, comprehension and word usage reflect this disorder. Words may be attached to a concept (Nelson, 1974) or, on the other hand, may be an "invitation" to form a concept (Clark, 1973). In either case, the disordered children must learn to organize and classify information in order to develop word meaning.

Difficulties in learning word meanings may be reflected in other areas. As has been widely recognized (Johnson & Myklebust, 1967), disorders in comprehension of oral language can affect reading, writing, and mathematical learning:

- When language learning disabled individuals do not understand the meaning of the words they read, the reading tasks may become purposeless.
- Various combinations of word meaning must be understood in order to write effectively.
- Most mathematical learning is based on verbal concepts of size, shape, and quantity; if these concepts are not understood, arithmetical operations can become meaningless rituals.

A thorough analysis of the structure and content of word meaning for the language learning disordered can provide an important basis for remedial programming. This should include an assessment not only of what vocabulary items are meaningful but also of what is included in known semantic categories and under what circumstances the individuals can comprehend or use semantic information.

## PART II. DIAGNOSIS

### Section 1. Rationale for Assessment Battery

Although the theoretical literature on semantics presents a multidimensional view of word meaning, a diagnostic rationale for evaluating the development of meaning in language learning disordered children lags far behind. In most diagnostic evaluations, a vocabulary test—or, at the most, a test of concepts—is the sole probe used. The vocabulary test, moreover, generally is used only to test for the quantity or number of words known rather than to examine the nature of the meaning the children apply to particular lexical items. Thus, the rationale for diagnosis still is based on referential theory and not on a multidimensional model of word meaning.

In spite of the fact that most diagnostic assessments thus are still based on a unidimensional model, a wide range of diagnostic tools is available to examine various dimensions of word meaning. It must be recognized, however, that a quantitative approach to the use of these tools does not provide a full picture. In one receptive vocabulary test (Dunn, 1981), the children are presented with a series of words and asked to point to pictures that might represent the meaning of each word. In other tasks, words are presented and the children are asked to retrieve an opposite or otherwise related term. On still others, they are asked to défine words and the responses are scored as either correct or incorrect.

Use of any of these tasks in isolation or a simple all-or-nothing scoring without further item analysis provides only a general account of one dimension of semantic development. On the other hand, a range of both formal and informal tasks based on the multidimensional model described can provide a fuller analysis of the depth and breadth of semantic development.

**Section 2. Areas to Assess**

*Receptive Skills*

**Basic Vocabulary:** Testing for knowledge of basic vocabulary may be performed using a recognition task that requires a minimum of verbal output on the part of the child. For instance, the *Peabody Picture Vocabulary Test* (PPVT) (Dunn & Dunn, 1981) may be used to assess word meaning in isolation or the *Boehm Test of Basic Concepts* (Boehm, 1971) to evaluate comprehension of word meaning in the context of a sentence. Care should be taken to include not only recognition of basic nouns but also of verbs, prepositions, adjectives, and adverbs as well as terms of time, space, and quantity.

**Category Structure:** The items included in a category, "bird" for example, may differ from individual to individual. Therefore, to determine the boundaries or extent of inclusion in a particular category of word meaning, both central or common instances may be included, as well as peripheral or more unusual instances of that set. Sorting or categorization tasks using a variety of objects and/or pictures may provide a fuller idea of the extent to which children can apply a particular label or term. In addition, some determination can be made as to the bases on which a particular individual seems to identify items in a named category. For instance, "ball" may seem to be determined on the basis of all round objects or on the basis of function, i.e., something that can be rolled or tossed. This can add useful information to an assessment of the various dimensions of meaning available to the children.

**Abstract Language:** Examination of receptive skills also may include testing for recognition of ambiguous terms or abstract language such as idioms or terms that have double word meanings. These are tasks on which language learning disordered individuals often have particular difficulty. The *Dictionary of Idioms* (Boatner & Gates, 1966) is an excellent source for assessment items.

**Lexical Relations:** Analysis of knowledge or relationships between word meanings may provide insight into individuals' organization of semantic comprehension. Testing for superordinate category terms, opposites, synonyms, modifiers, and parts in relation to wholes may reveal particular deficits in the ability to structure semantic knowledge. Tests of analogies on devices such as the *Illinois Test of Psycholinguistic Abilities* (Kirk, McCarthy, & Kirk, 1968) and the *Detroit Tests of Learning Aptitude* (Baker & Leland, 1959) provide some of these probes.

*Expressive Skills*

**Retrieval:** Evaluation of individuals' ability to use particular lexical terms also should involve testing for retrieval skills. Items known to be held in their receptive vocabulary can be presented nonverbally (e.g., in picture or object form) and the reaction time the children take to name them can be determined. Difficulty retrieving particular lexical items may be indicative of poor semantic organization and may be a reason for limited vocabulary usage.

**Spontaneous Language in Context:** Children's spontaneous errors in word usage can be an important source of information regarding the structure of meaning. As has been pointed out in many diary studies, children's errors in word usage often reflect their overgeneralization of meaning to incorrect instances. It is valuable to note whether these errors are based on specific attributes that an item may have in common with the named concept. An emphasis on perceptual as compared to functional attributes may indicate what children see as important and, thus, indicate their learning style. In addition, error patterns can indicate how they include or exclude peripheral members of a category and thus the extent of their concept development.

**Definitions:** Definitional tasks often are included in tests for expressive vocabulary. However, scoring of performance usually is (1) an all-or-nothing process, (2) having correct or incorrect information, or at most (3) range of completeness: 0, 1, 2. A more qualitative analysis of the ability to define may include an examination of the competence in using categorical labels and appropriate modifying information to formulate complete definitions of the Aristotelian type: "An X is a (category name) that (description)" (Litowitz, 1977).

A range of more to less mature forms may be observed and analyzed with an eye to the type of semantic information used to formulate the definition. Young children often use gestures to define terms. Although this would be incorrect on most scoring guides, it does reveal some basic knowledge regarding words. Children also may make word associations that reveal aspects of the semantic network they are developing.

In addition, immature definitions often include personal experiences, again revealing a component of knowledge or representation. Mature definitions, on the other hand, use semantic relations such as taxonomy or superordinate structure to define words, then add criterial modifier or functional information. Looking for this qualitative information in examining performance on definitional tasks may yield valuable insights as to the development of the children's semantic system.

**Sequencing and Organization:**  The ability to organize informational units into well-formulated explanations is an extension of the use of semantic knowledge. If children understand how a concept is organized and its relationship to other information in a network of knowledge, they will have the foundation for organized expression of these concepts. If they do not recognize what is essential and what is not, and if hierarchical and interactive relationships among and between concepts are disordered, oral formulation of semantic notions will be fragmented. Therefore, a complete assessment of knowledge and use of semantic/conceptual information should include an examination of the ability to sequence and organize explanations and to engage in discourse.

## Section 3. Testing Procedures

In assessing this range of semantic skills, several test procedures were mentioned. When using a specific procedure with a particular individual, it is important to select and analyze results carefully with an eye to the nature of the task (Johnson & Myklebust, 1967) and the aspect of semantic/conceptual knowledge under examination. A sample analysis of some commonly used tests follows.

*The Peabody Picture Vocabulary Test (PPVT)* (Dunn, 1965; Dunn & Dunn, 1981) is probably the most frequently used tool for assessing vocabulary skills. It tests knowledge of single words using a picture selection format. These items are single words presented orally, with four pictorial choices. As the examiner says each word, the child is asked to point to the one picture that best represents the meaning of the word. As noted by Wiig and Semel (1980), the vocabulary includes predominantly nouns, with some present progressive verbs, and a few adjectives. The task requirements are fairly simple: that the child process the auditory-verbal information in the form of one word presented by the examiner, visually attend to and interpret the pictorial stimuli, and respond with a pointing response.

In terms of the aspect of semantic knowledge under examination, this test assesses whether one specific pictured item is recognized as an instance of a particular labeled category. The task uses very specific probes to test for recognition of particular pictured instances across a limited range of vocabulary items. It does not claim to yield information on the other instances that a child may recognize or name with a given word. Some children may have a great deal of information regarding a vocabulary item but the pictured stimuli may not represent instances that are particularly meaningful to them.

Although the PPVT is fairly easy to administer and is used widely, some limitation on its application to language learning disordered children should be noted. It is important to analyze whether task demands interfere with performance and thus confound the results. Although confounding variables are fairly minimal on this test because of its simple format, some aspects of the procedure are worth consideration. These include noting whether the children are able to process the auditory signal correctly or whether there is interference because of poor auditory acuity or perception. It is important to observe whether the children scan the visual stimuli completely or interpret the pictures correctly. Some have particular difficulty interpreting the line drawings that are presented and perform poorly because of this factor rather than because they lack semantic knowledge. The kinds of errors or comments the children make should be included in an interpretation of results.

The PPVT therefore may be chosen as a screening instrument to provide a general guide to children's recognition of named items. Further informal assessment can follow to determine what the children know about items that they did not recognize correctly on the test so as to decide whether they identify other picture instances as belonging to that class. These informal tasks could include: recognizing and naming instances that may be more central or more peripheral members of a category; sorting and categorization tasks; and performing word association, sentence completion, and definitional tasks. These would allow the clinician to see what the children include in a particular concept, the limits of their knowledge, and how they define the key aspects of meaning for a particular word.

The *Boehm Test of Basic Concepts* (Boehm, 1971) is designed to evaluate concepts of quantity, number, space, and time. It contains 50 items selected from curriculum materials for grades K-1. The items are presented in the form of an oral direction associated with three pictorial choices or a composite line drawing.

It requires the children to process the auditorily presented direction (this may be in the form of several sentences), visually attend to and interpret the line drawings, and respond by marking the correct pictured item.

This instrument, much like the PPVT, also tests for recognition of a particular pictured instance that may belong to a set of information regarding a specific word. The items on the Boehm are of interest in that they are primarily adjectives and adverbs—terms not usually examined on other vocabulary tests, which present primarily nouns and verbs. It also should be noted that this test requires that the children comprehend the particular semantic element (e.g., more, some, before, last) within a sample of connected language.

For some children this may be less difficult in that there may be some information in the context of the direction that prompts recognition. For others, problems attending to, comprehending, and retaining the information in the directions may interfere with performance on the conceptual task. In addition, as noted earlier, some may have some knowledge of the tested concept but may not recognize the particular pictured item as an instance of that concept.

Again, further informal testing may reveal what other kinds of semantic information the children may be able to comprehend or produce regarding the concepts in question. The Boehm is an excellent screening instrument to assess whether children have some knowledge of basic vocabulary used at the kindergarten level. However, for a thorough analysis, additional formal and informal tasks are needed, as was suggested for the PPVT.

The *Auditory Association Subtest* of the *Illinois Test of Psycholinguistic Abilities* (Kirk et al., 1968) evaluates children's ability to recognize meaning relations by completing verbal analogies. It is a sentence completion instrument in which the children process a sentence presented orally and then respond with a word to complete the analogy, e.g., "Grass is green, sugar is _____."

Semantic requirements are that the children comprehend the lexical items and the semantic relation described in the first sentence; then understand the term used in the second incomplete utterance; and finally, be able to retrieve a term that will complete the second sentence, using the same association as in the first sentence. Associations that are tapped include relationships such as antonymy, attribution, part-whole, and function.

This test allows the examiner to survey whether the children can use an associational network with facility. An item analysis of error patterns is necessary, however, in order to reveal what particular kinds of relations cause difficulties for particular individuals. Informal testing in areas of strength and/or weakness can then be designed to further investigate the ability to see relationships between named categories.

The *Vocabulary Subtest* of the *Wechsler Intelligence Scale for Children—Revised* (WISC-R) (Wechsler, 1974) involves definitional tasks to assess expressive vocabulary skills. In this task, the children are presented with a word orally and are asked to explain or define the term orally. They not only must abstract out the basis on which they define the term but also must demonstrate some ability to construct a definition using relations such as taxonomy, synonymy, and attribution (Litowitz, 1977). The scoring guide on the WISC-R has a three-level range: a score of 2 is earned if the children use synonyms, major functions, primary attributes, taxonomy, or appropriate causal relationships; a score of 1 for responses that are incomplete; 0 for empty or irrelevant answers. As Litowitz points out, these tests "measure breadth of vocabulary rather than the depth of knowledge" (p. 301). Further analysis of the kinds of relations used to form definitions can provide more insight into the structure of meaning.

These descriptions provide just a sampling of the tests available to probe various aspects of semantic learning. (An additional array of tests is reviewed by Wiig and Semel [1980].) The purpose of the analysis here is to provide a perspective from which to examine task components and the aspects of semantic learning that are tapped. By considering these factors, the clinician can choose test instruments carefully with an eye toward examining specific components of the multidimensional process of learning word meaning.

## Section 4. Relation to Other Areas of Learning

An examination of deficits in semantics also should include an assessment of the effects of this disorder on memory skills, reading comprehension, written language, and mathematics.

*Memory*

Storage of information in memory appears to be determined by the meaning relations by which the material is organized; hence, semantic development and memory skills are virtually inseparable. An assessment of semantic memory can include an analysis of how information is categorized and retrieved. It has been demonstrated that when information is chunked or grouped according to superordinate categories, learning disabled children seem to recall a larger number of items than when information is random (Newman, 1979). An assessment of memory for information that is grouped semantically, in contrast to unrelated items, can provide evidence as to whether semantic organization categories are, or could be, used by a particular individual. Remediation in semantic organization then could be directed toward development of memory skills.

*Reading*

Comprehension of word meaning provides an important basis for reading comprehension. Difficulties with the ability to make inferences thus reduce reading comprehension skills (Johnson & Myklebust, 1967). Assessment of problems in reading comprehension should begin with an analysis of the individuals' ability to understand conceptual/semantic material at the oral language level. Testing materials such as the *Durrell Listening-Reading Series* (Durrell & Hays, 1970) are useful tools for such analysis. (See Chapter 7 for a fuller review of reading assessment.)

*Written Language*

Similarly, Johnson & Myklebust (1967) demonstrate that use of meaningful oral language usually is basic to production of meaningful written language. Therefore, if visual-motor skills do not seem to interfere significantly with writing skill, evaluation of the ability to utilize an adequate vocabulary in oral language may provide a starting place from which to examine whether individuals can write conceptually well-developed material.

*Mathematics*

Further, in that understanding of verbal concepts of time, space, and quantity is basic to mathematical processes, difficulties in word meaning may be reflected in poor abilities in that field. An assessment of both verbal and nonverbal mathematical concepts may reflect a need to direct remedial efforts toward developing a conceptual/semantic basis on which to build the desired knowledge.

In summary, a thorough examination of the nature and extent of semantic knowledge may require the use of a range of formal and informal testing probes. A careful analysis of the circumstances under which individuals are able to respond appropriately should be performed to determine what information is available, how it is organized, and what teaching strategies would be most fruitful in developing a rich verbal repertoire.

## PART III. REMEDIATION

### Section 1. Goals of Remediation

The purpose of remediation is not to teach all possible language forms or all available lexical items. Rather, it is more feasible to teach language learning disordered individuals how the language system is organized and to present some workable strategies by which they can understand and learn to use it to generate an appropriate vocabulary and to communicate effectively. Part I of this chapter has described some of the dimensions along which word meaning develops. These dimensions can be incorporated in a framework for teaching. Since language disordered individuals may be restricted to concrete interpretation and literal use of words, well-planned remedial programming can offer a guide to expand and develop a flexible system of semantic knowledge.

For children with severe problems or for those at early language developmental stages, Holland (1975) suggests that teaching a lexicon should take the form of presenting a limited selection of terms that can be used as a microcosm for language learning: ". . . language therapy should provide a model of the language world to the child and should present him or her with opportunities to participate fully in using that model" (p. 519). She makes some useful suggestions for the choice of items to include in this core lexicon:

- Learning Childrenese: It is important to consider the function of words children speak. Their words not only are referential but also should include items such as "all gone," "more," and "go." It is not enough to teach "go" in relation merely to naming the behavior of running or labeling a picture of a moving object. "Go" also must be taught as an action of the child's body, as an act of leaving the room, and so on.
- Organicity: Children should learn words that are important to them. These may include emotionally laden terms such as "kiss" and "frightened" and others immediate to the child, such as "me," "mommy," and "daddy," rather than "blue" and "cup."

- Here and Now: Comprehension of what children are saying requires that the environment in which they are saying it be understood. Children primarily talk about the present and the physical environment, including emotional features and continuing needs. In a clinical-educational setting, it is useful to focus on immediate, continuing activities and events, using these as opportunities to teach word meaning.

- Communication and Relevant Language: Language is not labeling or matching but instead is an active, dynamic process of interpersonal interchange. Consequences of communicating are the natural rewards of being understood or getting what was requested. Language disordered children should have the opportunity to see themselves as senders and receivers of information rather than simply rehearsing words or sentences.

- Language Therapy as a Communication Microcosm: The core lexicon should be "maximally exploitable" and maximally usable. This means choosing words that can demonstrate various aspects of the language system.

Holland offers a list of 35 different lexical items that can meet this set of guidelines. She suggests pronouns, names of individuals in the child's life, some salient verbs and descriptors, and relational terms as well as clinically useful words such as ball, block, and car.

Lahey and Bloom (1977) also make valuable suggestions regarding the choice of items for a core lexicon. They add to Holland's contribution a reference to the importance of carefully considering the "nonlinguistic context," or the means by which various word meanings can be demonstrated. They point out that items that are very difficult to demonstrate should be omitted from an early lexicon. They also underline the need to teach "relational" words such as verbs, adjectives, and prepositions as well as "substantive" ones such as names of persons and places. In general, they support Holland's suggestions and include an emphasis on teaching words that can be used later to demonstrate various aspects of the form and content of language (see also Lucas, 1980; Wiig & Semel, 1980).

A lexicon for older children with limited verbal skills also can be chosen with these guidelines in mind. Vocabulary items should be functional; that is, they should be words that are potentially useful to these individuals to meet communication needs across various situations. In addition, they should be terms that express experiences and concepts familiar and basic to those persons' world. Giraffe and tiger, for example, may not be real or functional items for an individual with a limited expressive language repertoire. Finally, as Holland (1975) and Lahey and Bloom (1977) suggest, initial lexical targets should be items that can be combined in various syntactic relations and can be used to demonstrate different aspects of semantic/conceptual organization.

Once a core lexicon is selected, a remedial program should be designed to highlight the various aspects of learning word meaning discussed above. This should include dimensions such as:

- instances or items that may be encompassed under the particular labeled category
- instances that demonstrate the internal structure of the category (i.e., central and more peripheral instances)
- the borders or limits of the category
- relationships that exist between that particular word or concept and other related concepts.

If the various aspects or dimensions of word meaning are taught in an organized manner, the disordered individual may develop a more complete framework for what it means to "know a word."

### Section 2. Remedial Strategies

To teach word meaning is to develop multidimensional concepts that can be labeled and used within the language system. It does not entail simply teaching a referential link between word and object or event. Rather, the teaching process must be directed toward not only introducing a word or concept but also developing the dimensions of the category to which the word refers and, finally, placing that learned information within a network of organized knowledge.

As pointed out in the section on diagnosis, remedial techniques used to teach vocabulary do not reflect a view of word meaning as a multidimensional, enduring process. Programs and materials often are designed to introduce a vocabulary item, develop a link between a label and a pictured instance of the object or event, and move on to another, all the while building, word by word, a long list of "new vocabulary items." The task of developing word meaning beyond this initial introduction is left to children's ability to "generalize." "Generalizing" a concept is the process of building a category of events to which a word applies and constructing a set of relations between the newly learned item and other information.

If individuals' language learning systems are normal, the development of this structure of semantic/conceptual knowledge takes place in a natural progression. If the individuals' language learning systems are disordered, however, the process is not so simple. They often do not generalize or develop information beyond simple referential links. Language remediation should be directed toward teaching them how to develop a category structure and to place new information within an organizational system.

The following framework offers seven sequential steps to facilitate the development of word meaning in language learning disordered individuals.

### Teaching What Is Included in a Semantic/Conceptual Unit

Since learning word meaning is more than acquiring a simple referential link between word and item, it is clear that teaching the meaning of a word involves a category of items or events. Tasks such as presenting a particular picture or object to elicit a name are insufficient. Instead, various central instances of the word in question must be put forward in a range of contexts. The items chosen should be common objects and activities and should be the most easily recognized instances available. Real objects and realistic pictures are most appropriate. When various instances are presented in natural contexts, children gain the opportunity to recognize items in their various forms.

Presenting items in varying contexts allows children to develop what Nelson (1974) refers to as a functional core. Play situations can be set up so that they may begin to engage in the active, dynamic process of learning word meaning. In addition, by beginning to recognize various instances of a concept, they can start the process of sorting out which properties or attributes of the item are critical or important and which are optional.

Color or size may be optional characteristics for an item such as a ball while shape and function may be critical to the meaning of the word. In this way, the children can begin to comprehend the basic elements of word meaning. Word use or naming may become a part of these activities using common names or what Rosch (1976) calls those at the "basic object level."

### Teaching Categorical Structure

Once the children have had the opportunity to experience various instances of an object or event, category structure may be developed by various sorting and categorization tasks. At this point, instances of two different conceptual groups may be presented and the children encouraged to sort these. These groups may be labeled, "Find all the _____," sorted, and categorized in various ways in order to stabilize the children's developing notions of the nature of the type of items included in a particular labeled concept. At this level, items still should be commonly recognized, central instances of the concept.

### Teaching the Peripheral Instances of a Category

Once children recognize and begin to label commonly recognized instances of a concept, more peripheral or unusual instances may be introduced. The new items need not have all the common characteristics of the category. When teaching "bird," for example, clinician and children already may have explored robins, canaries, and blackbirds as belonging to the category; now, hawks and egrets and ostriches may be added. In this manner the internal structure of the category is developed.

## Teaching the Borders of a Word or Concept

The next step is to present both instances and noninstances of the category. Johnson and Myklebust (1967) refer to this as teaching positive and negative instances of a concept. Teaching at this level clarifies for the children what is important to a specific concept and thus what delineates it. The practioner may be teaching "tree" and the children may recognize many instances of "tree" but now they also must recognize which items are not included in the concept. Although this process may have begun during earlier categorization tasks, now more closely related items may be identified and typed.

## Teaching Superordinate Structure

Once children have developed a set of concepts, work on hierarchical category structure can commence. If they are cognitively ready, they can learn to categorize several known concepts under a superordinate type name. This level of activity can begin at the receptive level by teaching the children to recognize items by their category name, grouping similar items by superordinate title, and abstracting out appropriate ones when presented with a group of named items.

## Teaching Relations to Other Words and Concepts

Various other relationships between items can then be taught in order to build a logically organized semantic network. The children can be taught to recognize relationships between items, including synonymous terms, opposites or antonyms, attributes or modifiers, parts in relation to wholes, etc. The teaching of relations between known items can build a foundation for organized, connected language as well as provide an organizational basis for memory and retrieval.

## Choosing New Words and Concepts Based on an Available Network

New semantic elements can be taught now in relation to already known items. Words can be introduced in varying contexts, category structure can be developed, and semantic relations taught in line with the foundation laid previously. In this way, children can begin to learn that their world and their language systems are organized and predictable. They then can begin to acquire and use a semantic system in a generative manner.

Materials to teach semantics are, in fact, readily available. Objects and events in the child's world are the most productive stimulus items. Beyond these, assorted toys can be found. The items chosen should be as realistic as possible. Pictures can be used to demonstrate objects not readily available in a teaching setting. Caution should be exercised, however, regarding the overuse of picture files to represent exemplars. Pictured instances do not themselves offer the dimensions of experience through which the individuals can learn the attributes and functions that may be important to full development of a semantic unit.

Materials also must be presented in a manner that takes into account the language learning disordered individuals' strengths and weaknesses. The number of items presented for categorization will be limited by the children's attentional skills. Similarly, memory factors will limit the number of items and relations that can be presented. Cognitive disabilities also may limit the individuals' ability to comprehend abstract concepts and relations.

## Section 3.  Summary

Semantic development now is being viewed as an evolving, dynamic process. Knowing the meaning of a word is not an all-or-nothing phenomenon but rather something that develops over time along various dimensions. Researchers have shown that the meaning of a word is tied inextricably to learning a concept—that is, a category of events can be labeled using a particular word. These categories are structured and organized in ways that make learning their meaning a geometric and generative developmental process.

This perspective on the nature of word meaning provides a framework from which to assess and plan remedial programs for language learning disordered individuals. Error patterns in comprehension or use of words can be analyzed and interpreted more carefully. Educators can observe what instances are included in a conceptual/semantic unit, what is central and peripheral to a category, and what the limits of word meaning may be. They also can observe the relationships between word meanings that individuals comprehend and how those persons use the logical relationships between words to organize knowledge.

A set of assessment areas has been presented that can serve as a guide to evaluate various dimensions of word meaning. It has been pointed out that in exploring what it means to know a word, careful selection and interpretation of testing materials is critical. It is important to select tests with the intention of tapping into a particular aspect of word meaning. For each test, clinicians must recognize not only the aspects of meaning that are brought into play but also the components of the task that may influence performance. That is, the nature of the stimuli and of the response required may affect performance in such a way that children may actually have the semantic knowledge that is being tapped but be unable to demonstrate it because of interfering task variables. Thus, in probing semantic knowledge, it becomes important to be conscious not only of what aspects of meaning are under examination but also the nature of the instrument being used for the analysis.

In that learning word meaning is a dynamic, evolving, multidimensional process, teaching also must be an active process that takes the various dimensions of meaning into account. As noted earlier, the purpose of a remedial program cannot and should not be to teach all possible words and meanings but to teach how word meaning is structured and organized so that disordered individuals can begin to recognize the "order" in the semantic system and, thus, learn to learn.

This means carefully selecting a lexicon to teach that not only is potentially meaningful to the children but also can be used to demonstrate various aspects of meaning and word use. Following this, a remedial program can be developed that can demonstrate: (1) what is included in a named category, (2) what the structure of that group is, (3) what the limits are for use of a particular word, and (4) how a word or concept is related to others in a network of knowledge. In this way, the disordered individuals have the opportunity to experience what it is to know the meaning of a word and can continue to build an organized, self-generating system of semantic information.

The semantic system, then, is an evolving network of knowledge that has various dimensions and aspects. Research will continue to reveal this complexity. It is important, however, that educators continuously translate and absorb this theoretical knowledge into teaching and clinical work with language learning disordered individuals. The raw materials are available. It is the teachers who must weave them into a pattern that supports the disordered individuals in the act of learning to learn.

---

**REFERENCES**

Alston, W.P. *Philosophy of language*. Englewood Cliffs, N.J.: Prentice-Hall, Inc., 1964.

Anglin, J.M. *The growth of word meaning*. Cambridge, Mass.: The MIT Press, 1970.

Anglin, J.M. *Word, object and conceptual development*. New York: W.W. Norton & Company, Inc., 1977.

Baker, H.J., & Leland, B. *Detroit tests of learning aptitude*. Indianapolis: The Bobbs-Merrill Co. Inc., Test Division, 1959.

Blue, C.M. Types of utterances to avoid when speaking to language-delayed children. *Language, Speech, and Hearing Services in Schools,* 1981, *12*, 120-124.

Boatner, M., & Gates, J.A. *A dictionary of idioms*. West Hartford, Conn.: American School for the Deaf, 1966.

Boehm, A.E. *Boehm test of basic concepts*. New York: The Psychological Corporation, 1971.

Brown, R. How shall a thing be called? *Psychological Review,* 1958, *65*, 14-21.

Clark, E.V. What's in a word? On a child's acquisition of semantics in his first language. In T.E. Moore (Ed.), *Cognitive development and the acquisition of language*. New York: Academic Press, 1973.

Collins, A., & Quillian, M.R. How to make a language user. In E. Tulving & R. Donaldson (Eds.), *Organization of memory*. New York: Academic Press, 1972.

Dunn, L.M. *Peabody picture vocabulary test*. Circle Pines, Minn.: American Guidance Service, 1965.

Dunn, L.M., & Dunn, L.M. *Peabody picture vocabulary test–Revised.* Circle Pines, Minn.: American Guidance Service, 1981.

Durrell, D. & Hays, M. *Durrell listening-reading series.* New York: Harcourt, Brace, Jovanovitch, Inc., 1970.

Harris, G.P. *Classification skills in normally achieving and learning disabled seven- and nine-year-old boys.* Unpublished doctoral dissertation, Northwestern University, 1979.

Holland, A. Language therapy for children: Some thoughts on context and content. *Journal of Speech and Hearing Disorders,* 1975, *40,* 514-523.

Johnson, D.J., & Myklebust, H.R. *Learning disabilities: Educational principles and practices.* New York: Grune & Stratton, Inc., 1967.

Kirk, S.A., McCarthy, J.J., & Kirk, W.D. *Illinois test of psycholinguistic abilities* (Rev. ed.). Urbana, Ill.: University of Illinois Press, 1968.

Lahey, M., & Bloom, L. Planning a first lexicon: Which words to teach first. *Journal of Speech and Hearing Disorders,* 1977, *42,* 340-350.

Lakoff, G. Hedges and meaning criteria. In R. McDonald & A.R. Duckert (Eds.), *Lexicography in English.* New York: New York Academy of Sciences, 1973.

Litowitz, B. Learning to make definitions. *Journal of Child Language,* 1977, *4,* 289-304.

Lucas, E. *Semantic and pragmatic language disorders: Assessment and remediation.* Rockville, Md.: Aspen Systems Corporation, 1980.

McCarthy, D. Language development in children. In L. Carmichael (Ed.), *Manual of child psychology.* New York: John Wiley & Sons, Inc., 1954.

Nelson, K. Concept, word and sentence: Interrelationships in acquisition and development. *Psychological Review,* 1974, *81,* 267-285.

Nelson, K. Cognitive development and the acquisition of concepts. In R.C. Anderson, R.J. Spiro, & W.E. Montague (Eds.), *Schooling and the acquisition of knowledge.* Hillsdale, N.J.: Lawrence Erlbaum Associates, Publishers, 1977.

Nelson, K. Semantic development and the development of semantic memory. In K. Nelson (Ed.), *Children's language* (Vol. 1). New York: Gardner Press, Inc., 1978.

Newman, D. *An investigation of learning disabled children's utilization of taxonomic organization to facilitate memory performance.* Unpublished doctoral dissertation, Northwestern University, 1980.

Norlin, P. *A study in developmental lexical semantics: The use of intralinguistic relationships in the definition and retrieval of concrete nouns by young children.* Unpublished doctoral dissertation, Northwestern University, 1976.

Riegel, K.F. The language acquisition process: A reinterpretation of selected research findings. In L.R. Goulet & P.B. Baltis (Eds.), *Life-span developmental psychology, research and theory.* New York: Academic Press, 1970.

Rosch, E. On the internal structure of perceptual and semantic categories. In T.M. Moore (Ed.), *Cognitive development and the acquisition of language.* New York: Academic Press, 1973.

Rosch, E. Principles of categorization. In E. Rosch & L. Lloyd (Eds.), *Cognition and categorization.* Hillsdale, N.J.: Lawrence Erlbaum Associates, Publishers, 1978.

Rosch, E., Mervis, C., Gray, W., Johnson, D., & Boyes-Bream, P. Basic objects in natural categories. *Cognitive Psychology,* 1976, *8,* 387-439.

Rummelhart, D., Lindsay, P., & Norman, D. A process model for long-term memory. In E. Tulving & R. Donaldson (Eds.), *Organization of memory.* New York: Academic Press, 1972.

Vygotsky, L.S. *Thought and language.* Cambridge, Mass.: The MIT Press, 1962. (Originally published, 1934.)

Wechsler, D. *Manual for the Wechsler intelligence scale for children—Revised*. New York: The Psychological Corporation, 1974.

Wiig, E.H., & Semel, E.M. *Language disabilities in children and adolescents*. Columbus, Ohio: The Charles E. Merrill Publishing Co., Inc., 1976.

Wiig, E.H., & Semel, E.M. *Language assessment and intervention for the learning disabled*. Columbus, Ohio: The Charles E. Merrill Publishing Co., Inc., 1980.

# Chapter 4

# Morphology and Syntax

*Carol T. Wren*

## PART I. SYNTAX AND LEARNING DISABILITIES

Although thoughts may be uttered as single, isolated words ("Help!"), they are expressed more frequently in a larger grammatical context, either as modifications ("Don't") or combinations of words ("Look here!"). The topics of the previous chapters—sounds and meanings—are important aspects of word modifications and combinations (grammar). For example, in modifications, sounds are manipulated in such words as "walk," "walks," "walked," or "ball," "balls" in order to modify the meaning. Hence, deficits in knowledge of grammar, word meanings, or sounds may interact and interfere with adequate communication. This chapter involves grammar and its disorders. Grammar traditionally is divided into two parts: (1) morphology, or the addition and substitution of word parts that modify meaning ("cat/cats," "sit/sat") and (2) syntax, or the combining of words to form phrases and sentences.

## Section 1. Approaches to Studying Syntax

Of all the types of language disorders, morphology and syntax problems are perhaps the most widely recognized among language learning disabled children (Hallgren, 1950; Johnson & Myklebust, 1967; Rabinovitch, 1959; Wiig & Semel, 1976; Zangwill, 1960). More strongly, Wiig and Semel (1976, p. 194) note that "the consensus of the available data on morphological and syntactic abilities of learning disabled children and adolescents indicates that we can expect deficits in a large proportion of this population." In fact, they find that "between 75 percent and 85 percent of learning disabled youngsters may experience significant delays in the acquisition of syntax" (Wiig & Semel, 1975). Syntax problems range from very severe difficulties connecting words to form sentences (for example, "Then she go upstairs that door sleeping Goldilocks") to much more subtle factors such as the inability to inflect nonsense words with appropriate English endings. For example, some children are capable of completing the sentence, "Here is a cat; here are two _____," but cannot add a plural ending to a nonsense word in the same format, "Here is a wug; here are two ____" (Berko, 1958; Wiig & Semel, 1980).

It is helpful first to look closely at existing knowledge of morphology and syntax. Morphology can be defined as a body of rules used to inflect words appropriately. These inflections (or word endings) include tense markers on verbs ("ed, s, ing, en"), plural ("s") and possessive ("'s") on nouns, and others such as "er," "est," and "ly" on adjectives and adverbs. Some inflections vary depending on the phonological composition of the word it modifies. For example, the plural marker "s" can be pronounced "s" as in cats, "z" as in cans, or "ez" as in boxes. Researchers have uncovered a fairly consistent order of acquisition among normal children for inflections in general and for the variants of certain inflections such as the plural "s" (Derwing & Baker, 1979).

Although it has been clear to linguists that word inflections follow a body of clear-cut rules, only since the early 1970s has evidence been uncovered that children acquire morphological inflections not word by word but rather on the basis of these rules. It appears that children learn to inflect classes of words or, in the case of plural "s," for example, subclasses of words in a consistent order, indicating that they operate on the basis of a rule. That is, once a certain inflection (such as "ing") is learned, it appears at approximately the same time on many verbs that the children already have mastered (Derwing & Baker, 1979). The rules are not explicit, of course, and it is likely that order and ease of acquisition of these rules are influenced heavily by meaning (Brown, 1973) as well as by phonetic features (Derwing & Baker, 1979).

Exactly how young children learn English rules still is a matter for investigation. However, it seems that a process of meaningful abstraction must occur where they hear the regularities of the language spoken to them such as "Give me the ball," "Now give me the balls," and attach meaning from context to the contrasting feature "s." As children assemble successive meaningful examples of a contrast ("cup/cups," "doll/dolls," "car/cars"), they appear to understand that "s" signals a meaningful piece of information, i.e., "more than one." Eventually, this regularity, or implicit rule, can be used in their own production to signal the intended meaning.

Similarly, syntax can be defined as a body of rules for putting words together, with most of the rules dealing with the correct ordering of words within phrases or sentences. At the simplest level, syntactic rules govern the order of subjects, verbs, and objects in simple, declarative sentences, i.e., "John kicks the ball" (not "kicks the ball John"), or the order of adjectives in a noun phrase, i.e., "the big green ball" (not "the green big ball"). At a more complex level, syntactic rules govern transformations of basic sentences into questions, passives, negatives, etc. (Chomsky, 1957). Implicit rules also determine correct formation of both coordinate and subordinate complex sentences. Although psycholinguists do not agree on the exact rules that are needed to generate all the possible sentences of a language, the fact that children do construct correct, novel ones (i.e., ones they have never heard), argues strongly for the psychological reality of a system of implicit syntactic rules.

Once again, it is not clear just how children learn such a complex body of rules. Research suggests that meaning plays a large part (Bloom, 1970; Bloom & Lahey, 1978; Bowerman, 1976). As children hear language spoken, they begin to abstract categories of meaning from words with similar functions in a sentence. The most common functions are agents, actions, and objects. The children also appear to note that consistent relationships exist between the participants in an event in the real world and the way the event is described linguistically. For example, various family members throwing a ball in turn are always described in the relationship of agent-action-object. In traditional grammatical categories this relationship is denoted as subject, verb, and object or SVO (Crystal, Fletcher, & Garman, 1976), the most common syntactic rule in English.

Having described, in general terms, the aspects of language covered in this chapter, next are possible approaches to studying syntax in learning disabled children. Two major approaches can be identified (Aram & Nation, 1975):

1. Some investigators have classified children with language disabilities into subgroups based on etiology (Adler, 1964; McGinnis, 1963; McGrady, 1968; Myklebust, 1954; Wood, 1964). Research along these lines has attempted to identify language patterns that are characteristic of certain etiological groups, such as children with aphasia, deafness, etc. While this sort of classification is a useful first step in describing syntactic problems, the resulting categories are too broad and tend to obscure wide variations within each etiological group.
2. An alternative approach bypasses the question of the cause of the problem and classifies language disabled children on the basis of the language they actually present (Aram & Nation, 1975; Lee, 1974; Leonard, 1972). Research based on this performance approach attempts to identify subgroups of children who have similar patterns of language disorder and to refine the descriptions of those patterns. This method seems more useful for providing a clear description of those with syntactic problems.

In this performance approach to investigating syntax disorders it is helpful to use a distinction set forth in Chapter 1. Oral language may be divided into receptive understanding and expressive production (Johnson & Myklebust, 1967), and the realm of syntax is no exception. Children must comprehend a syntactic form or structure before they use it consistently. For example, although a young child may produce isolated words containing a plural "s" such as "peas," consistent productive use of the plural ending is preceded by an understanding or comprehension of the meaning of that inflection (Brown, 1973; Johnson & Myklebust, 1967). In other words, children's understanding of a morphological feature is conceptually separate from and usually precedes their expressive production of that feature. Similarly with syntactic structures: children will understand, for example, that inversion of the subject and verb signifies a question ("Is it red?") before they are able to ask questions correctly themselves.

As might be expected, most research into syntactic problems of the learning disabled has concentrated on expressive aspects (Lee, 1974; Leonard, 1972; Menyuk, 1964) because of the inherent difficulty in studying receptive processes, although some attention is being directed toward devising appropriate receptive language tasks (Chomsky, 1969; Clark, 1973; Miller, in preparation). To study comprehension adequately without the possible interfering effects of poor memory, formulation, or articulation, a format must be devised that requires no oral production. Carol Chomsky (1969), for example, asked children 5 to 10 years old to manipulate doll figures to illustrate their understanding of a given syntactic structure.

Keeping in mind that most studies of the performance approach have focused on expressive competence, this review now turns (following Crystal et. al., 1976) to ways in which syntactic problems have been described. These are discussed in approximately chronological order. It is important to note that, as with semantics, over time there has been a shift from quantitative to qualitative methods of descriptions, which has been very beneficial in terms of actually understanding the nature of syntactic disorders in learning disabled children.

*Parts of Speech*

Historically, the first method for investigating syntax deficits was that of classifying words into parts of speech, then studying the frequency and range of nouns, verbs, adjectives, and so on. Thus, McCarthy (1930) found young children to use predominantly nouns, but as they grew older, nouns decreased and verbs, adverbs, and pronouns increased proportionately. This approach also is used by Wepman in his work with adult aphasics (Jones, Goodman, & Wepman, 1963).

Major problems arise, however, because the context in which the language sample is collected critically influences the frequency and range of nouns, verbs, etc. Furthermore, many English words commonly are cross-classified as several parts of speech. For instance, children tend to use words such as "swing" as nouns in definitions but not necessarily in everyday speech. Most seriously, the quantity of nouns, verbs, etc., does not necessarily indicate presence or absence of a deficit, particularly because this approach leaves a good deal of syntactic development undescribed.

Syntax properly includes the ordering of words within phrases and clauses and construction of various types of sentences. These features, along with knowledge of morphological rules, are not described by this approach.

*Sentence Length*

A second method of analyzing syntax uses the criterion of length of response. It generally is accepted that syntax development correlates highly with increased mean length of response (MLR) during the preschool years (but cf., Scharf, 1972). Brown (1973) develops the notion of mean length of utterance (MLU), a more refined measure of length that calculates the average number of morphemes per utterance.

However, used as a method of describing syntactic disorders, MLR or MLU provide little information and are only very rough measures. They can, in fact, be quite misleading since a number of external variables influence utterance length, e.g., socio-economic status (SES), IQ, sex, nature of the stimulus, etc. (Cowan, Weber, Haddinott, & Klein, 1967; Minifie, Darley, & Sherman, 1963). Further, as mentioned, quantity does not necessarily indicate presence or absence of a deficit, particularly because the process of embedding clauses increases complexity but decreases length. And once again, what the children actually have acquired by way of syntactic knowledge is not described.

*Selective Commentary*

A third group of attempts to analyze syntactic disorders may be classed under what Crystal et al. call "selective commentary." Some authors have noted what changes occur as child language becomes more complex, then use these changes as part of a syntactic checklist (Carrow, 1973; Lee, 1974). This approach is an improvement on the earlier ones but still is not a complete description of children's language patterns because it charts only the milestones of language development. Occasionally authors (Lerea, 1958) select isolated aspects of syntax but do not answer the question of why certain items are chosen and not others. Studies using these methods provide considerably more syntactic information than the first two discussed but the information still is incomplete and not easily classified.

*Transformational Grammar*

Transformational grammar for years was the most widely used method of analyzing syntactic problems. In this method, researchers, using some adaptation of N. Chomsky's (1965) work, generally investigate the number or types of transformations present in the children's language. The focus here is on the rules the children must learn to transform a basic sentence into related forms and the manipulation of words and word order that the rules require.

Transformational grammar has been the most comprehensive and systematic approach used by researchers interested in describing children's syntactic disorders. Unfortunately, the results have not been promising since many studies have found no differences or only one of delay between normal and language disordered children (Johnston & Schery, 1976; Morehead & Ingram, 1973). Critics of this method such as Crystal et al. (1976) maintain that the lack of results stems from the fact that the transformational approach does not focus on, but rather presupposes, many of the syntactic structures needed to construct the simple, active, declarative sentence—the locus of major difficulties among many language disordered children.

## Case Grammar

This is a somewhat newer theory (Chafe, 1970; Fillmore, 1968) that incorporates deeper semantic relationships into surface syntax. This approach exchanges the traditional syntactic categories of subject, object, etc., for such categories as agent, instrument, etc. A declarative sentence is seen not as a statement composed of a noun phrase and verb phrase, each of which has equal importance, but as a statement composed of a verb that assumes primary importance and its phrases that stand in various relationships (cases) to the verb.

Some research has been done that applies case grammar to normal children (Bloom, Lightbown, & Hood, 1975; Bowerman, 1976; Cupples, 1978) but little to children with syntactic difficulties. The research using case grammar with the language disordered has investigated the presence and frequency of occurrence of the various case relations and has determined whether these children have at least the basic case relations (e.g., agent, patient, instrument) with which to begin learning the more formal rules of grammar in adult speech (Leonard, Bolders, & Miller, 1976).

The difficulty with the case grammar approach, which is used primarily by semanticists, is that it is not a complete syntactic theory. Although the above studies investigate case relations in very young children (at the one-word and two-word stages), nothing is known about how such case relations develop or how youngsters might learn formal adult rules of syntax. Thus, the usefulness of a case grammar approach is limited to analyzing specific aspects of the syntax of the very young.

## Structural Analysis

Structural analysis (or Immediate Constituent Analysis) denotes an approach to syntax that consists of a detailed study of the surface structures of sentences. That is, structural analysis focuses on breaking sentences down into their component grammatical parts or structures (parsing). For example, "The boy is going to the store" consists of a subject, verb, and adverbial element. These elements in turn are composed of phrases ("the boy," "is going," "to the store") that have their own internal structure and follow specified rules, and so on. By breaking down a sentence into its constituent parts, it is possible to make an inventory of the grammatical structures and the rules that govern them that children must know in order to construct a sentence.

This approach to studying syntax was developed in the years just before the advent of transformational grammar (N. Chomsky, 1957). However, it was all but forgotten for many years since transformational theory seemed to hold so much promise for explaining the problems of children with syntactic disabilities. That promise generally has not been fulfilled, since most studies using a transformational approach have failed to find differences (except of delay) between normal and language disabled children.

Crystal et al. (1976), advocating the use of the structural approach, point to similar conclusions among many researchers who have used transformational grammar. Menyuk (1964) finds that disabled children are unable "to determine the complete set of rules that are used to generate and differentiate structures at any level of the grammar" (p. 119). Leonard (1972) reports that of all the structures he studied, the two that best met his criteria for needing immediate clinical attention are noun phrases and verb phrase omissions, not problems with transformations. Morehead and Ingram (1973) write that the only measure that produces significant results in their study of syntactically disordered children is one that counts the number of major lexical items per construction type. Their conclusion (much like Menyuk's) is that the deviant children's difficulty lies in their inability to "develop and select grammatical and semantic features which allow existent and new major lexical categories to be assigned to larger sets of syntactic frames" (p. 343). Finally, Crystal et al. (1976) endorse the claim of Longhurst and Schrandt (1973) that "structural linguistic concepts could prove valuable to the assessment of language development in children" (p. 248).

It also is quite significant that several researchers and clinical teachers have developed methods of diagnostic analysis and remedial instruction based on this qualitatively rich and comprehensive method of syntax analysis (Dever, 1978; Engler, Hannah, & Longhurst, 1973; Tyack & Gottsleben, 1974).

The work of Crystal, Fletcher, and Garman (1976), also within this framework of structural linguistics, is particularly helpful. They begin by identifying three levels of syntactic structure: clause, phrase, and word (morphological) structures. They then trace the development of these structure types from the two-word combination stage through adult sentences. Each sentence in a child's language sample is analyzed to determine its clause, phrase, and word structures; the frequency of occurrence of each structure then is tabulated and entered on a developmental profile sheet.

In the *Language Assessment, Remediation, and Screening Procedure* (LARSP), (Crystal, et al., 1976), Crystal identifies five major elements of clause structure: subject (S), verb (V), object (O), complement (C), and adverbial (A). Noun phrase (NP) elements include: determiner (D), adjective (Adj), and noun (N). Verb phrase (VP) elements include: verb (V), particle (Part), copula (Cop), and auxiliary (Aux). Adverbial phrase elements include: prepositions (Pr), the above-mentioned noun phrase elements, and intensifiers (Int). Word structure elements include "ing," "plural," "ed," "en," "3rd singular," "genitive," "est," "er," "ly," and the contracted forms of the negative, auxiliary, and copula. A sentence is then described in terms of these three levels of structure. For example:

|  | *I* | *did have* | *a drink of lemon* | *at home.* |
|---|---|---|---|---|
| Clause: | S | V | O | A |
| Phrase: | Pron | Aux + V | NPrNP | PrN |
| Word: |  | ed |  |  |

Provision also is made for analyzing questions, commands, and complex sentences. The Crystal et al. method has several advantages over the others described here. It is both comprehensive in its analysis of syntactic structures and developmental in nature. The division of syntactic structures into clause, phrase, and word structures is particularly important since it focuses attention on the development of basic clause structures that are assumed to be adequate in many other accounts of language development. For example, Brown's (1973) stages (semantic relations, grammatical morphemes, modalities of sentences, sentence embedding, and coordination of sentences) assume adequate clause structure development and focus on phrasal and morphological elaborations of the basic sentence and subsequently on transformations. Although it takes some time to learn to use the Crystal et al. approach, the categories and explanations are much clearer, for example, than Engler et al. (1973). It also has the advantage of being based on *A University Grammar of Contemporary English* (Quirk, Greenbaum, Leech, & Svartvik, 1973), to which problems of analysis can be referred.

Most significantly, unlike earlier approaches that merely counted parts of speech or measured sentence length, this procedure seeks to identify patterns of strengths and weaknesses. It has the potential for providing a clear description of children's syntactic problems that can be useful for remedial planning. Crystal identifies 11 patterns of deviant syntactic usage, only 8 of which are applicable to children (the 3 others apply more to adult aphasics). They differ from patterns of normal development in that, in normal children, structures of clause, phrase, and word develop simultaneously and in a balanced manner. In disordered children, imbalances may be seen among and within clause, phrase, and word structures. Although the numbers Crystal et al. assign to each pattern are retained, they are listed here in order of importance.

**Pattern 2:** The children produce words and phrases but lack coherent sentence (clause) structure.

**Pattern 3:** The children have a reasonable clause structure but phrase structure is weak or absent, resulting in telegraphic speech.

**Pattern 4:** The children's clause and phrase structures are basically intact but there are very few word inflections.

**Pattern 5:** The children's word structure development is strong but clause and phrase structure are weak. (Crystal says this pattern also is found from time to time among retarded children, p. 115).

**Pattern 6:** The children have great difficulty moving from simple to complex sentence patterns. "The child may produce one-sentence utterances only, or may string a number of sentences together with little or no linguistic or logical connectivity between them" (p. 115).

**Pattern 8:** The children present unanalyzable, deviant, or "other" sentences in large numbers. "Other" is a category Crystal et al. use to classify the structures in a language sample that do not fall within the specific categories. However, the categories are quite comprehensive and a large number of "other" sentences is unlikely and therefore significant.

**Pattern 1:** The children's profile is of pure delay. The development of word, phrase, and clause structures are even and balanced but are characteristic of much younger children.

**Pattern 7:** The children have a balanced profile of syntactic structures but with few utterances during a half-hour sample and possibly an abnormally high frequency of repetitions. This situation may indicate a disorder or simply a sampling problem. Further investigation is necessary.

The structural approach, and in particular the work of Crystal and his colleagues, holds considerable promise for understanding the problems of children with syntactic disabilities. In addition to comprehensiveness, their notion of imbalance in development of clause, phrase, and word structures appears to be a very fruitful approach to describing syntax problems in learning disabled children. Their categories of word, phrase, and sentence structures are used throughout the rest of this chapter to analyze syntactic deficits.

## Section 2. Syntactic Disorders in Learning Disabled Children

With this background, the analysis turns to what is known specifically about the syntax of learning disabled children. Studies investigating their syntax generally have addressed two separate but related questions. The first is, "Do learning disabled children differ from normals in their receptive and expressive syntax?'' The second question, which presumes a positive answer to the first, is, "What are the characteristics of the deviant language?''

Little information is available on learning disabled children's receptive understanding of syntax but the studies that do exist indicate significant differences between some of those youngsters and those who are normal. Semel and Wiig (1975) find that learning disabled children are significantly lower than normals on *The Northwestern Syntax Screening Test* (NSST) (Rev. ed.) (Lee, 1971), a measure that asks them to point to a picture that best describes a sentence.

Wren (1980), using *The Miller-Yoder (M-Y) Test of Grammatical Comprehension,* (Miller & Yoder, 1975) a test that has a similar picture format, finds that 6-year-old children with expressive syntax problems also are significantly different from normals in their comprehension of syntactic structures and that those with the most serious expressive problems also have significantly lower comprehension of syntactic information.

Vogel's (1974) results also are significant. In testing a group of learning disabled dyslexic children, she also reports differences between the learning disabled and normal children on the receptive portion of the NSST. Another significant finding relates to ability to recognize the meaning of prosodic patterns. The learning disabled are less able than normals to identify prosodic melodies that differentiate questions (rising tone at end of sentence) and statements (falling tone) in sentences composed of nonsense words. Thus it appears that some of the learning disabled have difficulty comprehending both verbal and nonverbal aspects of grammatical information in English sentences.

More information is available on expressive syntax and morphology; however, the results are less clear, in part because a variety of approaches have been used to investigate this question and the method appears to influence the answer. This is analyzed now in terms of the six approaches delineated in the first section of this chapter.

*Parts of Speech*

No recent work is available that primarily uses this method. Its relevance in the present context is mainly that young children with syntactic deficits generally score lower on measures of the variety of parts of speech used. This sort of analysis is typically done in conjunction with other analyses.

*Sentence Length*

Here again, no recent research is available and the relevance of this method, like that of the preceding one, is that children with syntactic difficulties generally achieve lower scores on measures of sentence length than do normals.

*Selective Commentary*

The few available studies using some form of the selective commentary approach often find significant differences between syntactically disordered and normal children (Vogel, 1974; Wiig & Semel, 1975; Wiig, Semel, & Crouse, 1973). However, these studies analyze only isolated aspects of syntax.

*Transformational Grammar*

Transformational grammar for years was the most widely used method of analyzing syntactic problems. However, although initially it seemed like a promising line of investigation, the results have been equivocal.

Menyuk (1964) compares ten normal and ten linguistically deviant children matched for age. Studying 28 transformations and 38 restricted forms in their speech, she reports differences in the use of both. Her results are questionable, however, because she accepts any significance level above chance, i.e., .50. In fact, only one transformation reaches a significance of .05, and none of the restricted forms do.

Leonard (1972) tests two groups of nine children matched for age using a combination of categories from Lee and Canter (1971) and Menyuk (1964). He reports several significant differences between normal and language impaired children, including some basic clause structures as well as some transformations.

Morehead and Ingram (1973), in contrast, compare two groups of 15 normal and deviant children matched for language level and investigate several measures of syntactic development: phrase structure rules, transformations, inflections, and the mean number of major lexical categories per construction type. Only the last measure (not strictly a transformational one) and language level differentiates the two groups. Morehead and Ingram conclude that the major difference between the groups is one of language level; that is, deviant children learn syntax more slowly than do normals.

Although the evidence generally fails to differentiate the two types of children except in terms of delay of development, clinicians need not agree with the conclusion of Morehead and Ingram that normal and disordered children do not differ in the "organization or occurrence of specific subcomponents of their base syntax" (p. 340). The inconclusive nature of most of the studies cited may be caused by the use of the transformational grammar (TG) model. Crystal et al. (1976) make this point quite strongly.

> the results have been disappointing. The main reason is that the most
> important studies have shown that the salient differentiating features are
> precisely those not readily describable in terms of the TG model. The set
> of transformations, for example, as defined by Chomsky (1957 or 1965)
> have turned out to be singularly undiscriminating. The syntactic features

which most directly distinguish the various kinds of ability which we want to characterize emerge as being sentence construction types (i.e., patterns of Subject, Verb, Object, etc. . . .) which TG on the whole pays little attention to and which other models treat in a much more direct way. (p. 34)

## Case Grammar

Leonard, Bolders, and Miller (1976), in a thoughtful and complex study, investigate possible differences between normal and language disordered children using a modification of Fillmore's (1968) case grammar, that analyzes the relationship of noun phrases to the verb in sentences. They compare four groups of ten children each—two groups matched for chronological age and two for language level (MLU). However, they come to the same conclusion as Morehead and Ingram did for transformational grammar, namely, that there is no difference between normal and disordered children in their command of the rules for case relations, the latter just learn them more slowly.

Freedman and Carpenter (1976) also examine a group of normal and impaired children using a modified Schlesinger (1971) model. They examine children at Brown's (1973) Stage I (MLU 0-1.99) and again find no differences in the case relations present in two-word utterances. They conclude that disordered children have at least the basic semantic relations with which to begin but they may have difficulty learning the more formal syntactic rules found in adult speech.

It appears that the research using either transformational or case grammar has failed to provide a clear answer to the question of whether learning disabled children differ syntactically from normals. Some studies find differences but most do not. However, interpretation of negative findings is difficult; it is not clear whether there simply were no differences, or whether these specific approaches were not appropriate for uncovering existing differences.

## Structural Analysis

Although many clinical remedial approaches have been developed using this method, little research has been conducted to investigate differences between normal and learning disabled children.

Wren (1981), using the work of Crystal, Fletcher, and Garman (1976) and of Crystal (1979), finds significant differences between 6-year-olds with syntax problems and normal children. She identifies two subgroups of learning disabled children, each with an imbalanced profile of syntactic development and each differing significantly from the balanced developmental profiles of a control group of normal children. (These findings are described in more detail at the end of this section.)

In sum, research has not provided a definitive answer to this first question although most clinicians working with syntactically disordered children intuitively feel that differences do exist. However, it still is possible (even likely) that there are subtle differences between normal and language disabled children.

What, then, is known about the characteristics of the grammatical understanding and expressive abilities of learning disabled children? The distinctions of receptive and expressive language and of clause, phrase, and word structure provide a framework for discussion.

Experimental knowledge of characteristics of receptive language is extremely limited since the few studies that do investigate this aspect of syntax provide no item analysis of the data. However, clinical observations by the author as well as by Wiig and Semel (1976) provide some information. At the level of comprehension of word structures, certain morphological inflections such as "en" on verbs (indicating past perfect), "er" and "est" (indicating comparative and superlative relationships), as well as contracted word forms ("they're," "we're," etc.) appear to be difficult for some learning disabled children with receptive syntax problems. Comprehension of the specific grammatical functions of such words as "but," "or," "if," "then," "either," and "neither" also are problematic.

At the level of the phrase, comprehension of the verb phrase (particularly tense and mood) is difficult for some. Wiig and Semel (1976) observe that the zero reference point in the time domain is fluid for many learning disabled children and that they therefore do not distinguish a shift in meaning between past, present, and future verb forms. Similarly, comprehension of mood, which often is expressed by auxiliary verbs ("must," "should," "will," etc.) also is difficult to comprehend.

At the level of the clause, comprehension of complex structures can be problematic. If the clause structure deviates from normal SVO order (which most closely represents the logical order of real events), some learning disabled children begin to have difficulty. For example, sentences with word order inverted for emphasis prove confusing (Wiig & Semel, 1980) and some may not be able to follow directions such as "With your right hand, point to the letter A."

For some children, transformations such as passives, negatives, and questions also appear to cause problems (Wiig & Semel, 1976). Other children with more subtle problems find that only the more complex forms of such transformations are difficult. For example, the syntactic structures used to express a particular meaning may vary from simple to complex. "I can't go and Jane can't go either" also can be expressed as "Neither Jane nor I can go." Learning disabled children may be able to comprehend the first sentence but not the more complex structure of the second (which expresses the same meaning). Similarly with question forms: one learning disabled girl was able to comprehend, "Here are a cat and a kitten, which one is bigger?" However, she could not understand the question, "Which is bigger, a kitten or a cat?"

The process of embedding also increases the syntactic complexity of sentences and interferes with comprehension. For example, a learning disabled child may comprehend, "If you win, then you get the prize," but not "Whoever wins gets the prize." To summarize: comprehension problems appear to exist in some learning disabled children at the levels of word, phrase, and clause structures.

Educators' knowledge of the characteristics of the expressive syntax of learning disabled children is based on experimental as well as clinical information. At the level of word structures, Wiig, Semel, and Crouse (1973) find that the learning disabled have abnormal patterns of acquisition of morphological endings on the *Wug Test* (in Berko, 1958). They have particular difficulty with progressive ("ing"), third person singular ("s"), and past tense ("ed") verb forms, possessive ("'s"), and adjective endings. Leonard (1972) reports that these children also have difficulty with contractions.

Looking at phrase structure, Leonard (1972) finds that a group of language disordered children has difficulty with pronouns, articles, and adjectives in noun phrases and with auxiliaries in verb phrases. Johnston and Kahmi (1980) note significant difficulty with the verb phrase auxiliary system and infinitives. Wren (1981), as well as Johnston and Kahmi, reports that these children use fewer adverbial phrases than do normals. Two of the main functions of adverbial phrases are to provide (1) variety in sentence structure and (2) spatial and temporal information. It appears that learning disabled children avoid adverbial phrases and prefer to rely on the more basic, simple SVO structure.

Wren (1981) finds that some learning disabled children have problems mainly with Crystal's (1976) late-developing phrases such as verb phrases with two auxiliaries and with postmodifying noun phrases. Others have problems involving word order of even simpler phrases (e.g., "the big great chair"), errors of addition and omission of articles and adjectives in noun phrases, modals and auxiliaries in verb phrases, and prepositions and articles in adverbial phrases.

At the clause level, learning disabled children generally use less complex sentences (Johnston & Kahmi, 1980) and make more errors in them. The most important indicators of need for immediate clinical attention are omissions of noun and verb elements from clause structures (Leonard, 1972). Wiig and Semel (1975) discern that even learning disabled adolescents tend to have persistent syntactic problems at the clause level, producing many agrammatical and incomplete sentences when asked to make one up using a stimulus word.

In sum, then, learning disabled children with expressive problems again appear to have difficulties at the word, phrase, and clause levels. However, it would be incorrect to end this description of syntax here because that would leave the impression that all such youngsters exhibit all of the problems just described or that specific problems appear randomly in the language of any one of them.

Here Crystal's (1976) notion of patterns or profiles of disorders of syntax is extremely important and advances understanding substantially. Just as the description of subgroups of dyslexia (Johnson & Myklebust, 1967; Lyon & Watson, 1981), improves understanding of reading characteristics and remedial needs of these children, so also does the concept of subgroups or profiles enhance awareness of those with syntactic deficits. Indeed, the entire concept of defining a syntactic disorder as an imbalance among clause, phrase, and word structures is a significant contribution to resolving the question of whether the problem of language disordered children is one of deviance or delay. (For a discussion of the problems of deviance vs. delay see Johnston and Kahmi, 1980, and Johnston and Schery, 1976.)

Crystal's (1976) patterns suggest that not all learning disabled children have the same syntactic profile and hence need differential remedial content. Unfortunately, aside from that study, which originally identified the patterns, no research has been published that verifies these profiles. In a recent study, however, Wren (1981) finds two profiles or subgroups of syntactic disorder among learning disabled 6-year-olds. She compares 30 learning disabled children with syntax disorders to a normal group using a recorded language sample of 200 utterances per child upon which LARSP analyses are performed. To understand the profiles of the disordered children, it first is necessary to describe the syntax of normal 6-year-olds. (The transcripts in Exhibits 4-1, 4-2, and 4-3 are all of middle-class, Caucasian children.)

The normal children (Exhibit 4-1) display frequent use of all types of complex sentences. Their errors in clause structure are very infrequent and consist of omissions of conjunctions and occasional clause elements. As for phrase and word structures, they frequently use two auxiliaries in their verb phrases, more adjectives in noun and prepositional phrases, and more postmodifying noun phrases than do the deviant children, thus signifying more elaborate phrase structure overall. In addition, they are more likely to use appropriate word endings on adjectives and adverbs. When they make errors, these occur in phrase and word structures more commonly than in clauses, indicating that some development still is taking place in these forms. Although normals use more elaborate phrase structures than do the deviant children, they still have some difficulty with the verb auxiliary system and occasionally omit determiners from noun and prepositional phrases. Past tense verb endings also cause some problems.

The first of the disabled groups, the children with Profile A (Exhibit 4-2), resemble the normals in their use of more elaborate clause structures. Also like the normals, they can use and manipulate adverbial elements in sentences fairly easily. Errors in clause structures in simple sentences are infrequent but increase in complex ones. This suggests that these children are operating under certain processing constraints so that when they attempt complex sentences, mistakes are more frequent.

The phrase structure of children with Profile A reveals certain gaps such as infrequent use of verbs with two auxiliaries; errors in phrases and word structure

**Exhibit 4-1** Transcript of a Normal Child

Goldilocks and the three bears.
Once upon a time Goldilocks went for a walk and the three . . .
She found a house and they went out for a walk because their porridge was too hot.
So Goldilocks came in the door.
And she ate up the porridge and then she went to sleep.
That one . . . the father's is too hot.
The mother's is too cold.
And the baby's was just right.
She ate the baby's.
And then she sat down in the father's chair and it was too hard.
She sat down in the mother's chair, it was too soft.
She sat down in the baby's chair and it was just right and she broke it.
And then she went upstairs and she went to sleep in daddy's bed, and it was too hard.
She went to sleep in mother's bed and it was too soft.
And she went to sleep in baby's bed and it was just right.
And then the bears came in and said, "Somebody has been eating my porridge."
"Mine too."
And then . . . "somebody's been eating mine and they ate it all up."
"Somebody's been sitting in my chair."
"Somebody's been sitting in my chair."
"Somebody's been sitting in my chair and it's broke."
"Somebody's been sleeping in my bed."
"Mine too."
"Somebody's been sleeping in my bed and they're still there."
And then Goldilocks ran away.

are more frequent. Verb markers cause the most difficulty, with many noun and pronoun errors also evident. Thus, these children exhibit a pattern of advanced sentence structure containing numerous errors, in contrast to normals who also use elaborate structures but make few mistakes. Both of these profiles contrast vividly with Profile B (Exhibit 4-3).

The children exhibiting Profile B use fewer complex structures than do Profile A or normal children and make more errors in them. They use less elaborate clause structures and make considerably more errors in them, including more mistakes in word order and more incomplete and unanalyzable utterances. Their phrase structures are much less elaborate and contain more errors than the other groups. While the same types of problems arise, mainly with auxiliary verbs, determiners, and prepositions, more errors of order appear and these children tend to omit the noun from noun phrases and prepositional phrases. Word structure mistakes follow essentially the same pattern as the other groups but appear far more frequently. Verb endings cause the most difficulty, with many more errors in the

**Exhibit 4-2** Transcript of a Child with Profile A

The three bears were living in a small house.
And then they went somewhere.
She cooked some porridge.
And then the Goldilocks came and ate it . . . the little bowl.
And she ate the three bowls of . . . of the porridge.
The big bowl was for daddy.
And the middle one was for the mommy.
The little small one was for the baby.
She ate the little small one.
Now she sawed . . . sit in the bed . . .
Now she sit in the bed . . .
I mean, she sit in one of the chairs.
First, she tried the big one.
Then she tried the mama one.
Then she tries the little baby one and the little baby one she falled.
Now she went in the big daddy's bed.
And then he . . . then she wasn't comfortable.
And Goldilocks went to the mama's one.
And then she hopped in that one and that one was uncomfortable.
And then Goldilocks went in the small one and she liked that one.
That broke.
The porridges . . . the porridge was all gone.
Somebody was tasting my porridge.
Somebody ate my porridge.
Somebody ate her [for "his"] porridge.
He couldn't get up on his chair and get in.
Oh, and then they sat in the little . . . in the chairs.
And then the daddy bear liked the chair.
And the mommy one liked the chair.
But the little baby one it broke.
And somebody was in the little . . . in the little's . . . little baby's bed.
And then she got up and went away.

present and progressive forms. Pronoun errors indicate considerable difficulty with case markers but person and number errors also are evident. Omissions of plurals and genitives account for most of the noun errors.

Thus the children with Profile B exhibit a pattern of less elaborate syntactic structures and far more errors in each type of formation. Lack of control over the basic clause structures of simple sentences is an especially serious problem. These children clearly have much more serious deficits in syntactic production and language processing.

**Exhibit 4-3** Transcript of a Child with Profile B

Three bears.
This is Gloldilocks [sic] and the three bears.
Once upon a time, and three bears that go out in the forest for a walk.
And there's the mama bear, no, the papa bear, the mama bear, the little bab . . . the little . . .
little bear.
And Goldilocks is eating the big porridge.
That be too hot.
Eat the middlesize porridge.
That be too hot.
Eat the little tiny, that be the right.
Her try each bed.
That be the comfortable chair.
Her broke the chair.
He go in the mama's bed.
That be too hard.
And he go in the daddy's bed.
That be too hard.
Go in the baby bear's.
That be all right.
And "someone eating my porridge," says the daddy bears.
Why that two little bears? "Someone be eating my porridge," says the mama bear.
And "someone be eating my porridge," says the the little tiny bear.
Look at the chair, oh, oh.
"Someone be sitting in my chair," says the mama bear.
"Someone be sitting in my chair," says the papa bear.
"And my chair is broken," says the little bear.
Lookit, lookit, Goldilocks is little.
Oh, her eyes are open.
"And someone be sleeping in my bed," says the mama . . . no, says the daddy bear.
"Somebody sleeping in my bed," says the mama bear.
"Somebody sleeping in my bed," says the little bear.
Gloldlocks [sic] is in the bed.
Turn the page.
Why Goldilocks is running away?
Because . . . I don't know.
Because . . . he eat up all the porridge.
Because they be angry.
Yeah, from them bears.

Thus it can be seen that educators' and clinicians' knowledge of the nature of syntactic deficits and these experts' ability to describe qualitative differences in the syntax of learning disabled children has advanced significantly from initial quantitative tallies of nouns and verbs.

## Section 3.  Processing and Syntactic Disorders

In order to have a more complete understanding of syntactic disorders it is necessary to emphasize that among learning disabled children these problems generally do not exist in isolation but rather are tied intimately to other auditory, cognitive, and linguistic processes.

As the model of language learning disabilities in Chapter 1 as adapted from Johnson and Myklebust (1967) demonstrates, linguistic stimuli are processed after they are received by the ear and the learner must attend to the stimulus. A particular stimulus must be discriminated from similar stimuli and an auditory image must be created and stored in short-term memory for further processing. The stimulus must be associated with a meaning through the process of symbolization, which then may be combined with other symbols in higher level cognitive processes such as categorization, rule generalization, logical inferential thinking, and metalinguistic knowledge.

In learning disabled children, a disturbance at any level of this continuous process may interfere with linguistic functions, including comprehension and expression of syntax (Johnson & Myklebust, 1967). Within the process of symbolization, disturbances in other linguistic domains, e.g., phonology, semantics, or pragmatics, also may interfere with adequate acquisition of syntactic rules at both receptive and expressive levels (Johnson & Myklebust, 1967; Wiig & Semel, 1976; Wren, 1980).

### Attention

In receptive syntax, attention appears to be a prerequisite for all subsequent learning (Johnson & Myklebust, 1967; Ross, 1976). If children do not attend consistently, important information inevitably is missed. Thus, a disturbance at the level of attention would appear to affect their ability to retain and comprehend syntactic structures. Inconsistent attention might lead them to hear only segments of syntactic structures, thereby making it difficult to understand what was said or to abstract adequate syntactic rules.

### Discrimination

Deficits in auditory discrimination may affect comprehension of syntax indirectly through the close relationship of discrimination to phonology and semantics. For example, children who cannot distinguish between "in" and "on" have difficulty associating those symbols with their proper meaning, with the concomitant problem of using these prepositions to formulate correct syntactic structures. Discrimination may affect children's comprehension of inflectional endings more directly. Morphological inflections frequently are unstressed and may be difficult for learning disabled children to perceive. (Attention problems may exacerbate problems of discrimination of unstressed inflections.) Wren (1980) investigates the ability of syntactically disordered children to discriminate pairs of inflected and uninflected words. To make the task as close as possible to normal language learning, the target words are embedded in very short sentences. The children are asked to judge whether or not two sentences that differ by a single morpheme sound the same. For example, "The cups are white," "The cup are white," "He is sleeping," "He is sleepy." Children with Profile A do not differ significantly from normals on this task. However, those with Profile B score significantly lower on this measure (probability = .0000). Thus, for some language learning disabled children, discrimination of morphological endings in context may interfere significantly with comprehension (and subsequent production) of morphological inflections.

Changes in word stems such as in irregular plurals and past tense verbs also may cause difficulty for children with problems in auditory discrimination. "Mouse, mice"; "foot, feet"; "sit, sat"; and "get, got" all may be difficult for children who have difficulty discriminating vowel sounds.

*Memory*

Problems of auditory imagery or short-term memory also may impede comprehension of syntactic structures. Johnson and Myklebust (1967) find it useful to distinguish certain aspects of memory (span and sequence) from general, overall memory. Long or complex sentences, especially those with embedded clauses, may require linguistic processing that exceeds short-term memory capacity in some learning disabled children (Wiig & Semel, 1976). The ability to retain the sequence of words in short-term memory also is critical for adequate generalization of syntactic rules that deal specifically with word order. The interrelationship of attention and memory is important to keep in mind as well, since an attentional deficit can prevent adequate storing of verbal stimuli, and attention and memory problems are commonly found together (Johnson & Myklebust, 1967).

*Symbolization*

At the level of symbolization, clinicians must consider the effect that problems in the other domains of language may have on comprehension of morphology and syntax. The close relationship between semantic processes and syntax has been clearly recognized by psycholinguists (Bloom, 1970; Brown, 1973) as well as by those working with learning disabled children (Johnson & Myklebust, 1967; Johnston & Kahmi, 1980; Wiig & Semel, 1976).

The function of any syntactic form is to communicate meaning; thus, deficits in comprehension of semantic units interfere with comprehension of syntactic structures that incorporate those units. Abstract words, or those that express temporal and spatial relationships such as prepositions, are difficult for many learning disabled children to comprehend, which in turn affects their ability to comprehend and generalize rules for structures that contain those words. For example, one girl who did not understand that the concept of "alternative" was central to the meaning of the word "or" replied "yes" when asked if she wanted to use a crayon or a pencil.

Wiig and Semel also note the reciprocal relationships between semantics and syntax, where the latter also can make learning of word meanings more confusing. They cite, for example, the sentence, "He is at school" and "He went to school," which have the same meaning but the selection of different verbs governs the choice of different prepositions, thereby causing confusion in some learning disabled children as to the meaning of "to" and "at." Similarly, certain syntactic conventions such as inflected forms of pronouns ("she/her") mark distinctions in meaning that are not readily apparent to young normals and many learning disabled children who may view these forms as interchangeable.

So far the relationship of semantics and syntax at the level of single word meanings has been considered. It is equally important to highlight the relationships of syntactic structures to semantic propositions. Semantic propositions are thought to be related to syntactic structures by a body of regular rules (Chafe, 1970; Chomsky, 1965; Fillmore, 1968). Although psycholinguists do not agree as to the exact nature or number of rules, they do seem in accord that one semantic proposition often can be represented by more than one syntactic structure. For example, "He cut the bread with a knife"; "With a knife he cut the bread."

Furthermore, the logical complexity of the underlying proposition and the syntactic complexity of the sentence structure may vary independently of each other. That is, a cognitively complex proposition may be expressed in simple syntax and a simple proposition in complexly embedded syntax. For example, a complex familial relationship such as second cousins (the proposition) may be explained in very simple syntax, "He is my second cousin." But if the children do not grasp the meaning of the relationships involved, the lack of meaning interferes with comprehension of the syntactic structures. Reciprocally, however, it should be noted that complex syntax can interfere with comprehension of relatively simple propositions. For example, many learning disabled children have difficulty understanding "Neither Jane nor I can go," which embodies two extremely simple propositions, "Jane can't go," and "I can't go."

Wiig and Semel (1973) find that these children have difficulty comprehending sentences that encode five types of relational propositions. Listed in order of descending difficulty, these are: familial, spatial, temporal, passive, and comparative. Further research shows that these comprehension deficits persist into adolescence (Wiig & Semel, 1974).

Discourse and pragmatic features of language also may affect comprehension of syntax. The importance of top-down processes in comprehension is widely recognized both in active listening comprehension (Bransford & Franks, 1971) and reading comprehension (Smith, 1971). Most research has investigated how discourse features of language interact with comprehension of semantic features, i.e., comprehension of lexical items (single words) or propositions. For example the meaning of the word "score" in the sentence "Let's hear the score" (Anderson, Reynolds, Schallert, & Goetz, 1977) might refer to a baseball game or a musical composition, with comprehension depending on the context of surrounding discourse to resolve the ambiguity.

Similarly, however, surrounding context may permit comprehension of syntactically complex sentences. The previous example, "Neither Jane nor I could go," might be comprehended in the following context: "I asked my mother and Jane asked her mother if we could go to the movies. Unfortunately they both refused. Neither Jane nor I could go." It may even be hypothesized that complex syntactic structures are learned primarily by inference from context.

Language disordered children who have difficulty making linguistic inferences may not be able to make use of top-down strategies to aid in comprehending syntactic structures. However, lower level processes such as poor memory span also may significantly influence their ability to make use of contextual information. With this discussion of inference, the theme has modulated from purely linguistic or symbolic considerations to those of higher cognitive processes.

*Conceptualization*

In conceptualizing, higher level thinking skills of inference and generalization become central. Children who have difficulty generalizing and abstracting the regularities of linguistic experience may have specific problems with syntax and morphology. For example, irregular verbs, the plural allomorphs ("s," "z," "ez") etc., may be extremely confusing. These children may have problems understanding sentences that vary in meaning according to word order, "John pushes Mary, Mary pushes John," or transformations of sentences, "I am hungry, Am I hungry?" etc.

So far consideration has been given to how processing deficits may interfere with comprehension of syntax. Expressive syntax may be similarly affected by specific auditory and cognitive processes, including receptive problems. Any distortions or limitations of the children's data base caused by problems in comprehending syntactic forms will interfere as well with adequate rule generalization. Johnson and Myklebust (1967) state: "Ability to formulate sentences is a complex skill requiring many integrities, including ability to understand, to remember word sequences, to manipulate symbols and to generalize principles for sentence structure." Thus, any deficits in receptive processes (discrimination, memory span, comprehension, or rule generalization) can effect adequate expressive syntax.

Not all learning disabled children have syntactic difficulties at the receptive level. There also are those whose comprehension is intact but who nevertheless are unable to express themselves in adequate grammatical form. Still others, with purely expressive problems, can understand very well and can recognize their sentences as incorrect if they are read back to them but are unable to correct them (Johnson & Myklebust, 1967).

*Articulation*

A number of specific problems may affect expressive syntax. Some learning disabled children have difficulty learning to use the facial muscles appropriately for speech (apraxia). Apraxic conditions may interfere with syntactic production (Johnson & Myklebust, 1967) in that children may know what they want to say but omit or avoid specific structures because they contain  sounds they are unable to produce. Apraxic children generally have limited syntactic repertoires.

*Retrieval*

Other learning disabled children have difficulty with dysnomia—retrieving from memory the exact word they wish to say (Johnson & Myklebust, 1967; Wiig & Semel, 1976), which also can affect the quality of their syntax. They generally leave sentences unfinished, "Here's the umm . . ." "It's blue and umm . . ." In other cases, their circumlocutions affect the syntax of a sentence because the circumlocution does not fit the grammatical frame of the original sentence. For example, one child, unable to think of "dressing room," stated "There's a swimming pool and a . . . like that thing that dresses up to get in your bathing suit."

*Formulation*

Still other children have difficulty with expressive syntax because they cannot use or apply the grammatical rules they appear to have generalized implicitly. Many children with syntactic disability can recognize sentences as being correct or incorrect without being able to produce them correctly themselves (Johnson & Myklebust, 1967). Some of them thus appear to know the rules but not be able to use them to construct their own sentences. The quality and amount of language produced by children with expressive syntax problems varies widely and it is perhaps most helpful to distinguish these youngsters on the basis of the severity of the disorder.

Children with extremely severe expressive aphasia may not be able to inflect words or put them together at all and simply resort to use of single words and gestures (Johnson & Myklebust, 1967). Others may be able to string words together in lists or loose associations but without the cohesion of a well-formed sentence. For example, one 6-year-old boy with severe expressive aphasia, when trying to tell his clinician that his little cousin was visiting, said "Jimmy baby room."

Others are less severely involved. It is useful to refer to the earlier discussion of Crystal's (1976) analysis of expressive syntactic problems through observation of children with syntax problems who have difficulty constructing correct utterances at the levels of words, phrases, or clauses. Children who are less severely involved may have difficulty with morphology, "And Goldilock say somebody eat my porridge," or phrases "And she sat down on the big great chair;" "Somebody been eaten my porridge;" or clauses, "And they went that door sleeping Goldilocks." It is among children at this level of severity that Wren (1981) found the two subgroups with different patterns of imbalance among these structures discussed previously.

Finally, a group of learning disabled children who appear to be least severely involved grammatically can produce syntactically correct utterances in spontaneous conversation but cannot perform adequately on structured linguistic tasks such as sentence repetition, sentence building, sentence completion, or sentence transformations (Rosenthal, 1970; Vogel, 1974; Wiig & Semel, 1976; Wren, 1980). These children seem to be able to get by on limited syntactic ability by selecting simple, familiar forms for use in everyday conversation (which does not usually demand complex linguistic ability). However, on structured tasks where they must consciously manipulate more complex structures, their limited capacities become apparent.

In many cases, these children's oral language deficits are not identified until they are required to produce substantial samples of written language in the middle grades in school. Johnson and Myklebust (1967) caution that although direct parallels cannot be drawn between spoken and written language, nevertheless many problems in written syntax may be traced back to mild problems in oral expressive syntax.

## PART II. DIAGNOSIS

Fortunately, diagnostic instruments in syntax and morphology are numerous and in some cases have managed to keep pace with the evolution from quantitative to qualitative analysis. This section reviews and evaluates formal diagnostic tools available for assessing both morphology and syntax at the receptive and expressive levels and suggests informal measures that can supplement formal tools.

### Section 1. Measures of Receptive Morphology

It is important to recall the principle that it is best to assess receptive abilities with a response that does not rely heavily on memory or expressive capacities (see

Chapter 1). Three formal measures that assess receptive morphology all use a multiple-choice response where the children point to one of three or four pictures that illustrate the structure being assessed. It should be noted that they all assess morphology in a sentence context, which presumes some knowledge of syntax.

The *Northwestern Syntax Screening Test* (NSST) (Lee, 1971) (receptive portion) and Carrow's *Test for Auditory Comprehension of Language* (TACL) (Carrow, 1973) measure a variety of morphological forms. These tests can be used to obtain an overall age score or a developmental level of morphological acquisition. In addition, with language disordered children such measures may constitute the basis for an item analysis or inventory of comprehended forms.

The *Miller-Yoder (M-Y) Test of Grammatical Comprehension* (Miller & Yoder, 1975) assesses numerous morphological forms using a similar format. Although this test provides more tentative norms for computing developmental levels, it, too, can be used to construct an inventory of forms that the children do not yet comprehend.

Three limitations of these measures should be pointed out, however. The first, unfortunately common to most tests of syntax and morphology, is that they are normed only for young children, generally up to age 7, since grammatical development presumably is largely complete by then.

The second limitation, relevant more specifically to some learning disabled children, is the requirement that they select a picture (line drawing) that illustrates a particular form. Those with visual attention or perception deficits may not be able to select the correct picture but nevertheless may comprehend the form being assessed. It is advisable not to rely on a single measure to determine unacquired morphological forms. Rather, forms that are missed on the M-Y or NSST should be followed up with informal probes to determine whether the children do comprehend the meaning of missed forms.

For example, if the children fail to indicate the correct picture illustrating "She drank the milk," and point to "She will drink the milk," the clinician could informally ask the youngsters to pantomime the appropriate actions. A second alternative is to limit the number of pictures to one and then ask the children to select one of two sentences that describe it. With a picture of a girl having finished a glass of milk, the children are asked to choose the better sentence: "She drank the milk" or "She will drink the milk." In informal measures it also is possible to eliminate the sentence context and limit the stimulus to a single word to minimize problems of comprehension at the level of syntax, e.g., (show me) "drank," (show me) "drink."

The third limitation is the small number of items used to assess comprehension of a particular morphological ending. It is important to assess children's comprehension of a particular morphological form over a variety of words. Although children may confuse "shoe" and "shoes," for example, they may comprehend numerous other instances of plural words. Informal assessment using pictures or real objects, and requiring a multiple choice or manipulative response, can be designed to probe comprehension of morphological inflections missed on formal measures.

## Section 2. Measures of Receptive Syntax

Comprehension of syntax, as opposed to morphology, involves understanding of sentence-length utterances and how the various elements in phrases and clauses are related to each other. Comprehension at the syntax level assumes understanding of the meanings of individual words comprising the sentence. Although difficulties with semantics may interfere with syntactic understanding, the focus here is on comprehension either of the meaning conveyed by the form of the utterance or of the relationships among grammatical elements present.

Linguists distinguish between two levels of sentence structures. The first level is that of basic sentence structures involving subjects, verbs, objects, and adverbials (Crystal et al., 1976) that can occur in a small number of acceptable combinations: SVO, SVOA, SVAA, etc. The second level is that of transformations of these basic sentences (Chomsky, 1957). These include variations on basic sentences such as passives, negatives, and questions as well as those containing coordinate and subordinate clauses. Formal tests of comprehension of grammar generally focus on this second level, assuming that while problems may occur in complex transformations, children have no difficulty with basic sentence structures. Although this may be the case for young normals, some learning disabled children may have difficulty with simple sentence comprehension, depending on the severity of the syntactic disorder.

Perhaps the most useful formal test for basic simple sentence structures is the *Assessment of Children's Language Comprehension* (ACLC) (Foster, Giddan, & Stark, 1972). Here, as in most comprehension tests, children are asked to select an appropriate picture to correspond to the words spoken. The ACLC provides another useful feature in its vocabulary pretest. If children fail any item, the clinician must immediately ask why. Since the test here is for syntax, it is important that the clinician be certain that the error is caused by a lack of syntactic comprehension, not lack of understanding of any word(s) comprising that sentence.

In general, these assessments at the level of both morphology and syntax must either prescreen the vocabulary used in the test or be followed up by checking each word meaning in any missed sentences. Further, as Johnson and Myklebust (1967) point out, problems in comprehension should not be confused with disorders of attention, discrimination, or memory, since these may all interfere with understanding. Clinicians must be alert to other processing deficits that may interfere with adequate assessment of syntactic comprehension. The ACLC is limited by the silhouette picture stimulus. Some learning disabled children may have difficulty not with the syntactic form per se but rather with picture selection because of deficits in picture interpretation or attention.

Other tests of syntactic comprehension focus mainly on transformations or complex clause structures. The NSST, M-Y test, Carrow's TACL, the *Test of Language Development* (TOLD) (Newcomer & Hammill, 1977), and the *Clinical Evaluation of Language Functions* (CELF) (Semel & Wiig, 1980) all contain items that assess higher level syntactic structures such as negatives and passives. Wiig and Semel (1980) provide item analyses of many of these tests that may be useful to clinicians wishing to select a test containing a specific grammatical form. Unfortunately, none of the tests measure syntactic forms in a comprehensive and systematic manner and each leaves clinicians wondering why some specific forms were selected and not others (Crystal et al., 1976).

The available standardized tests thus may provide an overall score or language comprehension level for a particular child but are preliminary to more in-depth diagnostic evaluations of grammatical comprehension. Although combining several tests increases the comprehensiveness of knowledge about children's syntactic abilities, a framework is needed to organize the data. The *Language Assessment, Remediation, and Screening Procedure* (LARSP) (Crystal, Fletcher, & Garman, 1976) can be used as such an organizing framework. Crystal and his colleagues organize simple basic sentences, transformations, and complex structures into a clear developmental profile. The approximately 100 structures on the profile were selected on the basis of the frequency of use in normal children. The LARSP thus provides the most commonly used grammatic structures, ranging from morphological inflections through complex sentences in developmental order.

Although the LARSP is designed as a measure of expressive syntax, it is exceptionally useful informally as a comprehensive framework for assessing syntax comprehension. Clinicians may select items from specific formal tests corresponding to LARSP structures; for example, the item "boy riding the horse" from the ACLC is of the "SVO" structure in the LARSP terminology. Some clinicians may find it more useful to construct their own informal items for each LARSP structure. Although such a comprehensive assessment of syntax is time consuming (and, indeed, not necessary for every child), for those whose main problem is comprehension of syntax, a thorough systematic assessment is essential to eliminate the hit-or-miss character of so much assessment and remediation.

## Section 3. Measures of Expressive Morphology and Syntax

Most assessment of morphology and syntax occurs at the level of expressive production. While many learning disabled children have disorders at the expressive level, it is important to emphasize that if they fail to formulate correct grammatical sentences, the clinician again must ask why and determine whether the problem is really at the level of comprehension. Assuming, however, that problems with auditory attention, discrimination, and memory as well as with comprehension of word meanings, morphology, and syntax have been eliminated or recognized as possible contributing factors, expressive syntax then can be assessed.

A number of different types of tests have been used to formally assess children's expressive syntax that range along a continuum from highly structured to unstructured. The most highly structured type of test is sentence repetition. Sentence completion and sentence building—asking children to form a sentence using specific stimulus word(s)—fall in the middle range. Spontaneous language samples are the least structured.

The advantage of highly structured tests is their ability to elicit data on specific grammatical forms, while spontaneous language samples may not provide any examples of forms the clinician may want to evaluate. On the other hand, the more structured the task, the less realistic the testing situation becomes. In many cases children can produce forms spontaneously but make errors on those same forms on structured tests, indicating the artificiality of the testing situation. The additional task demand of explicit awareness of the form being tested also may produce questionable results. Thus, a combination of test formats is necessary to a comprehensive assessment.

Tests of morphology generally are designed with a sentence completion format. One test of morphology is in *The Illinois Test of Psycholinguistic Abilities* (ITPA) (Kirk, McCarthy, & Kirk, 1968) *Grammatic Closure* subtest. Here children must supply the correct inflection for real words and complete a sentence illustrated by an accompanying picture, e.g., "Here is a ball. Here are two _____." The *Berry-Talbott Test of Grammar* (Berry, 1966) and *Wug Test* (in Berko, 1958) use nonsense words in the same format. In these latter tests, use of nonsense words focuses more specifically on the children's knowledge of morphological rules by eliminating meaning as a cue. "Here is a Wug. Now there are two of them. There are two _____." However, these nonsense word tests also seem to require a level of explicitness or consciousness of knowledge that is not necessary in everyday language learning. That is, a 2½-year-old who can easily apply plural "s" to a variety of real nouns may not be aware enough of the process involved to be able to produce "Wugs" until age 4 or 5. Clinicians thus cannot assume that children who fail to supply a correct inflection to a nonsense word have not yet acquired the plural rule for real words (Derwing & Baker, 1979).

As for the assessment of syntax, all of the various formats have been used. Numerous tests with a sentence repetition format are available, among them the *Detroit Tests of Learning Aptitude* (DTLA) (Baker & Leland, 1967), *Carrow Elicited Language Inventory* (CELI) (Carrow, 1974), CELF, and TOLD. However, clinicians must be cautious in interpreting the results when testing learning disabled children. Miller (1981) states that the use of sentence repetition tasks is based on a number of assumptions:

1. Linguistic processing occurs in repetition tasks.
2. Repetition tasks involve short-term memory processes.
3. Sentence processing in short-term memory is dependent upon the linguistic knowledge available to the child.
4. If stimulus sentences exceed the child's short-term memory span, then the child must rely upon his or her linguistic knowledge to facilitate memory in order to correctly repeat the sentence.
5. Since the child's knowledge of the language provides an organizational strategy for short-term memory in processing incoming linguistic stimuli, his or her imitative responses should index his or her knowledge of the language, particularly the structural or grammatical components. (p. 153)

These assumptions are not always justified for normal children, and although it is "generally agreed that some processing takes place in elicited imitation procedures . . . it is not clear what is processed or whether this processing is related to comprehension processes or production processes" (Miller, 1981, p. 153). These assumptions are even less valid for some learning disabled children since deficits in both comprehension and short-term memory could seriously interfere with repetition and clinicians simply cannot be sure whether errors are the result of comprehension, memory, or production problems (see also Brinton, 1979). However, repetition exercises may be used with some learning disabled children as part of a larger battery of syntax tests if it is fairly certain that attention, comprehension, and memory are intact. Sentence repetition tasks thus have limited usefulness with these children.

The *Producing Formulated Sentences* subtest of the CELF (Semel & Wiig, 1980) uses a sentence building format. It asks children to construct sentences using words from grammatically important categories: nouns, verbs, adjectives, adverbs, pronouns, negatives, conjunctions, and prepositions. Although the CELF subtest contains only 12 items, it provides useful guidelines for designing supplementary informal tests. Additional stimulus words in each category can be added informally to ensure a more comprehensive picture of the children's abilities.

The spontaneous language sample format has been used to collect information about children's syntax for several decades. Historically, the first spontaneous samples took the form of diaries or journals meticulously kept by researchers (Leopold, 1939). Others, including Bloom (1970), Brown (1973), and Weir (1962), collected samples at regular weekly intervals to chart the grammatical development of normal children.

Collecting language samples of disabled children under clinical or classroom conditions presents special problems, however. Three such problems must be considered:

1. Time available in the classroom or clinic is limited so it is important to make sure that the sample is representative of the children's language.
2. Comparison of children's performance to others the same age, or of a single child's progress from lesson 1 to lesson 2, requires that the samples be similar in content. However, any attempt to control the structures produced by the children diminishes the representativeness of the sample; that is, the structures they typically use may not be produced simply because of controls established to ensure comparability.
3. A related consideration is whether to collect a sample of the children's maximum, or a typical, performance. This is particularly important with the learning disabled since there frequently is a wide gap between what they can do and their everyday language.

Although the conflicting needs of representativeness and comparability and of maximum and typical performance cannot each be met, care in the construction of elicitation tasks can do much to ensure the best possible language sample. Suggestions for elicitation techniques are provided by Bloom and Lahey, 1978; Miller, 1981; O'Donnell, 1978; and Wren, 1981.

Once an adequate language sample has been collected and transcribed accurately, numerous formal techniques are available to analyze the sample that correspond roughly to the approaches to syntax discussed in the first part of the chapter.

Techniques are available for computing sentence length or length-complexity values (McCarthy, 1954; Miner, 1969); however, they yield minimal information as to the grammatical rules the child possesses.

Other measures analyze selected parts of speech. *Developmental Sentence Scoring* (DSS) (Lee, 1974) and its complementary *Developmental Sentence Types* (DST) (Lee, 1966) choose specific structures (pronouns, verbs, negatives, conjunctions, and question forms) as benchmarks to measure the overall level of syntactic development. The DSS score indicates the developmental level of those specific structures. This measure is particularly useful in that it strikes a middle ground between comprehensiveness (which naturally is time consuming) and ease of scoring. It also yields an overall developmental score.

If a more comprehensive, systematic analysis is desired, a wide variety of additional measures have become available that have been reviewed and compared, most of which use the structural analysis approach:

- *Assigning Structural Stage* (ASS), in Miller, 1981
- *Case Relation Analysis* (CRA), in Scroggs, 1967
- *Co-occurring and Restricted Structure Procedure* (CORS), in Muma, 1973
- *Indiana Scale of Children's Clausal Development* (ISCCD), in Dever and Bauman, 1971
- *Language Assessment Remediation and Screening Procedure* (LARSP), in Crystal, Fletcher, and Garman, 1976
- *Language Sampling, Analysis, and Training* (LSAT), in Tyack and Gottsleben, 1974
- *Linguistic Analysis of Speech Samples* (LASS), in Engler, Hannah, and Longhurst, 1973

Crystal, Fletcher, and Garman (1976); Longhurst and Schrandt (1973); and Miller (1981) provide in-depth comparisons of many of these methods. Miller concludes that a method must be selected with a specific purpose and particular child in mind. The variety of instruments available provides flexibility for clinicians that is especially useful when dealing with learning disabled children.

It is unfortunate, however, that learning to use any grammatical analysis as a tool is relatively time consuming, making Miller's conclusion less than practical for most clinicians and learning disabilities specialists, so they must make some decision as to which one or two instruments are desirable and appropriate in a wide variety of situations.

Characteristics of the LARSP that favor its adoption by clinicians are its comprehensiveness, the specificity of the manual, and perhaps most important (features not considered by Miller) the developmental nature of the profile and its corresponding use as a comprehensive plan for remediation. The gap between assessment procedures and remedial planning has long been lamented. Crystal, Fletcher, and Garman provide a basic rationale for remedial planning through their identification of specific types or patterns of developmental dysfunctions and in their definition of syntactic disorders as imbalances in development of clause, phrase, and word structures.

Before turning to that important topic, however, consideration must be given to informal procedures that may be used to supplement standardized analyses of syntax. While informal procedures lack the organized comprehensiveness of standardized measures Gerber and Bryen (1981), Leonard, Perozzi, Prutting, and Berkley (1978), and Miller (1981) all argue strongly for informal measures to support the finding from syntactic analyses. Gerber and Bryen cite four uses of informal methods:

1. Clinicians may study language samples in greater detail. Fletcher (in Crystal, 1979) provides guidelines for greater detail in studying verb phrase

development. Similarly, although many syntactic procedures examine noun phrases, informal analyses would permit clinicians to study specific elements of the NP and determine whether, for example, the children have difficulty with mass vs. count nouns in relationship to use of determiners "a," "the," and "some."

2. Clinicians may assess features not included in formal tests.
3. Clinicians can use informal assessment to help determine why children are having difficulty with a particular syntactic feature. Analyses of the surrounding context may indicate constraints (either linguistic or auditory) that interfere with certain structures.
4. Clinicians may find informal analyses can help determine the strategies used by the child. Miller (1981) describes the use of informal distributional analysis procedures by which clinicians can reorganize a language sample according to "specific utterance characteristics" (p. 27). Although Miller specifically describes distributional analyses in terms of sentence length, sentences may be classified and arranged according to any semantic or syntactic feature to illuminate strategies individuals may use.

For example, Crystal (1980) cites one aphasic man who used more than one incorrect form of the present progressive. While the subject produced "man walking," "man smiling," "man eating," "man sitting," and "man running," he also used "man is fall down," "man is jump" and "man kick ball."

Although these may seem at first like random errors (it might simply be hypothesized that a production capacity deficit prevented this man from stringing all the elements together), further analysis indicates that an alternative and more likely explanation revolves around the semantic features of these verbs. While eating, sitting, and so on contain no specific duration or end point, kicking, falling down, and jumping do. Thus, the man's strategy appears to be to mark verbs of unspecified duration with the "ing" form and verbs of short duration with "is" or with no marker at all. Analyses such as these all are possible at the level of informal evaluation of language samples.

## PART III. REMEDIATION

### Section 1. Goals of Syntax Intervention

The goals of remedial efforts in syntax generally have been, first, to fill in any existing gaps in children's acquisition of syntactic rules and, second, to assist them in making steady developmental progress in learning new structures and rules (Crystal et al., 1976). However, as discussed in Chapter 1, with learning disabled children it is necessary to look beyond teaching syntactic structures in isolation.

Additional goals must be provided and, using diagnostic information, it is necessary to delineate both the language and learner variables that must be taken into account. By applying the general goals described in Chapter 1, five interrelated areas that need attention in remedial planning can be derived:

1. syntax targets
2. integration with other language domains
3. integration with other learning contexts (reading, written expression, learning in other content areas, i.e., math, science, social studies)
4. related processing problems
5. cognitive strategies for syntax learning and other related variables of learning style.

It is particularly important to plan appropriate goals for each area in order to ensure integrated learning and avoid simply teaching splinter skills.

## Section 2. Remedial Procedures

Although the emphasis given to each of these five objectives will depend on the individual child, teaching strategies may be derived from both content and learner variables. Formal programs and informal procedures for remediating syntax problems in learning disabled children are examined next, taking each area in turn.

### Syntactic Targets

Most formal commercially available materials for remediating syntax are aimed specifically at a few isolated structures such as present progressive and past tense in verbs and various inflectional endings and question forms. These include *Syntax One* and *Syntax Two* (Ausberger, 1976) and *TSA Syntax Program* (Test of Syntactic Abilities) (Quigley & Power, 1979). However, none of these materials can be relied on to provide a broad framework for an ongoing curriculum for a child with a syntactic disorder.

More comprehensive schemes are published by researchers and other professionals in the field: Crystal et al. (1976); Dever (1978); Miller and Yoder (1974); and Tyack and Gottsleben (1974). Their advantage is that they provide workable systems of language analysis, based on normal language development, that allow clinicians to locate children's weaknesses and determine what to teach (content). The Miller and Yoder and the Tyack and Gottsleben programs focus mainly on the younger stages of development while Dever's is more suitable for children who already have basic grammatical structures but who may need help with more advanced ones. The LARSP (Crystal et al., 1976) has managed to span the entire developmental range quite comprehensively. Its notion of balanced and imbalanced development provides a unique rationale for an overall framework for syntactic goals and knowing what to teach next.

### Integration with Other Language Domains

The interrelationships between syntax and other domains, particularly semantics, have been discussed earlier. Clinicians must go beyond teaching syntactic structures in isolation and instead must relate them to other facets of language. At the earliest stages of development, syntactic structures are almost entirely subsumed by aspects of meaning and semantic functions (Bloom, 1970; Brown, 1973; Miller & Yoder, 1974). However, as children develop, the relationship between syntax and semantics becomes somewhat more independent (Dever, 1978). Meaning generally is an aid to learning new grammatical forms. For example, inflectional endings regularly mark changes in meaning in the real world: "ball, balls." However, for some language disordered children, meaning can interfere with the abstraction of syntactic regularities. They may use incorrect structures because they are attempting to mark meanings that are not discriminated in English, such as in Crystal's example of the subject who used "man run" for verbs of indefinite duration and "man is fall" for verbs of fixed, short duration. Relating an arbitrary syntactic code to meaningful events can be difficult for some.

Clinicians must provide experiences that solidify semantic/syntactic relationships. Published materials offer some useful information for the earliest stages of language development (cf. especially Brown, 1973). Perhaps the best strategy teachers can use is that of logical groupings of syntactic structures and presentation of examples designed to demonstrate the semantic underpinnings of each. Principles for presentation of positive and negative instances of semantic/syntactic concepts (see Chapter 3) may be applied here as well. For example, with older learning disabled children, implicit negatives such as "unlikely," "prevent," or "neither/nor" may cause syntactic confusion (Wiig & Semel, 1976). However, by relating these forms to each other and to the simpler forms ("not likely," "does not let," "not x or y") the children may begin to gain control over them.

Clinicians also must be aware of potential interaction between syntactic disorders and communication ability (pragmatics). Spekman (1977) reports that in a dyadic communication task, learning disabled children provide less relevant information to solve a problem. Clinicians must present opportunities for children with syntax problems to engage in interactive language situations where they may learn appropriate syntactic forms to supply information or describe activities to others, or to solve problems in a group.

### Integration with Other Areas of Learning

Chapters 7 and 8 describe the effect that syntax deficits may have on reading and written language and provide remedial suggestions for those areas. Integration of oral syntax into the content areas (at school or at the preschool level) is a factor clinicians should be aware of not only for its importance in its own right but also because content areas provide rich sources of topical material around which to build integrated syntax lessons rather than teaching isolated structures. Gerber and Bryen (1981, Chapter 6) provide many worthwhile suggestions for using content area material with older school-age children. Similar ideas can be adapted for primary and preschool children, using appropriate math, science, and social studies concepts.

*Processing Deficits*

In the field of learning disabilities, the controversy over training processing deficits still rages and the evidence is far from conclusive about the efficacy of remediation, primarily because too many variables are as yet untested. In spite of research to date, the author's clinical experience has shown that some emphasis on deficit areas is helpful so that the children have the opportunity to become as independent learners as possible.

Regardless of whether processing deficits appear to be "causing" the syntax problem or whether a broader language or cognitive deficit is "causing" the auditory processing problem (and either is likely), it seems reasonable that work on specific deficits should be coordinated with syntactic goals. So, for example, if children are having difficulty with auditory sequencing that appears to affect syntactic ordering of words, then such training should be done with meaningful words, not tones, environmental sounds, digits, or nonsense words (Johnson & Myklebust, 1967). Published materials that purport to train processes must be viewed with extreme caution since they necessarily remove work on improving perception, memory, and so on from the relevant learning context of any particular child. It is suggested that discrimination, memory, or sequencing problems may be worked on using the same lesson content (perhaps a science experiment or a cooking project) as is involved in syntactic structures. Only the focus shifts: from learning a specific syntactic form to discriminating, sequencing, or remembering that and similar structures.

*Cognitive Strategies and Variables of Learning Style*

As described in Chapter 1, problems with cognitive strategies may interfere with learning syntax as well as other aspects of language. Selective attention, verbal rehearsal, problem solving, rule generalization and application, monitoring, and so on may affect adequate acquisition of grammatical rules. It is necessary, then, to consider problems with cognitive strategies both as they are related to children's motivation to learn in a remedial setting and as they affect their ability to learn the syntactic rules of English.

Again, little is to be gained from working on cognitive strategies in isolation. Cognitive variables may be incorporated logically into lesson plans at the beginning of a class if problems of attention, problem identification, etc., interfere with the learning set. They logically also may follow specific work on syntax to develop skills in problem solving or monitoring. Particularly with older children, once a structure has been learned and practiced, specific verbal problems may be set up in which the object of the lesson is not additional practice on the target structure but actually teaching the needed cognitive strategies. If, for example, children recently have learned to use "before" and "after" in adverbial clauses, an appropriate activity (science experiment, instructions for building or making something) may be constructed that contains such sentences as: "Before pouring the liquid, heat the flask to 200 degrees," or "After heating the flask to 200 degrees, pour the liquid." The lesson then may be structured to help the students identify the problem verbally, solve it, monitor for syntactic comprehension, or develop selective attention.

### Section 3. Teaching Methods and Strategies

The job of instructing language learning disabled children is made more challenging by the existence of two bodies of teaching strategies. The first is related to developmental language learning and has been devised mainly by specialists and researchers in psycholinguistics and speech and language therapy. The other is the body of knowledge developed by learning disabilities specialists for a range of problems broader than just syntax. The former traditionally have focused on language content and presentation of syntactic structures in small, logically sequenced steps while the latter have stressed auditory and cognitive processes that, in some cases, may not have been directly related to substantial learning in syntax. However, when teaching the language learning disabled, it is necessary to distill the positive elements from both of these approaches.

A number of useful formal and informal strategies are available from the first group of specialists. Lee, Koenigsknecht, and Mulhern (1975) present a format for language teaching in small groups, particularly of younger children. A unifying theme, story, or activity can frame a lesson that focuses on a few selected grammatical structures. The clinician directs the telling of a story that contains the selected structures, thereby modeling correct production. Individual children then are asked to repeat these modeled structures, incidentally providing peer modeling for others in the group.

Dever (1978) provides an alternative method involving choral speaking designed for small groups of somewhat older children. While this model supplies less of an overall context for language learning (it does not necessarily involve a story or activity), the lessons do involve day-to-day school and home situations and Dever clearly states that they must have relevance to the children's daily life.

This method focuses on teacher modeling and choral drill so that each child receives a maximum amount of practice. Most drills take the form of question-and-answer sessions; an aide helps the children respond together.

Both of these methods rely on a single strategy or technique: teacher-initiated modeling and child repetition. On the other hand, Muma (1971) suggests the opposite strategy and delineates ten techniques used primarily for individual, as opposed to small-group, remediation whereby the clinician responds to child-initiated utterances. These include expansions and corrections as well as more formal exercises where the clinician uses the children's own utterances and devises ways for them to complete, revise, or change them. Thus clinicians have a wide range of techniques for presenting target structures, both child- and clinician-initiated, and for group and individual remediation, a variety that is particularly important when working with learning disabled children, each with a unique syntactic profile.

Muma and Pierce (1981) also make an important distinction between direct facilitation (all of the techniques described above) and indirect facilitation (which can be accomplished through the use of parallel talking as the children engage in a continuing activity). The advantage of indirect facilitation techniques is that syntactic structures are taught in as natural a way as possible. The rationale for indirect facilitation originates in psycholinguistic theory that subordinates language structure to its function. Syntax thus is taught indirectly in a continuing meaningful context (Muma & Pierce, 1981).

The techniques presented thus far have varied from highly structured group drills to much less formal indirect facilitation, any of which may be selected when working with specific learning disabled children. However, those have been developed from the perspective of psycholinguists, and while they all are important for remedial intervention, they are insufficient in two ways:

1. Clinicians should not select these techniques randomly but must have some basis on which to choose the ones that will be most beneficial to each individual learning disabled child. Learning characteristics such as severity of the syntax problem, auditory and visual processing deficits, and cognitive strategies may be used as a basis for selecting specific techniques. While indirect, naturalistic intervention may be adequate for some children with mild problems, many do not learn well and indeed have not learned by indirect instruction prior to intervention. The remedial environment therefore may need to be different from the one in which the children have not learned.
2. Clinicians should note that all of these methods focus exclusively on production of syntax. Although some learning disabled children have only expressive deficits, others may have difficulty with other aspects of learning syntax. Discrimination, comprehension, and retention of syntactic patterns

as well as monitoring of those patterns must be the focus of remedial instruction for some children.

It is equally important to consider remedial techniques developed from the perspective of learning disabilities. It is unnecessary, however, to advocate a separate, entirely different set of teaching strategies or methods. Knowledge from the field of learning disabilities can be used most appropriately to adapt and modify the above methods for the specific needs of individual children. Techniques suggested by Dever (1978); Lee, Koenigsknecht, and Mulhern (1975); Muma (1971); and others can be modified to suit the learning profiles of particular children.

To close this chapter, two types of modification are described. The first focuses on ways of modifying strategies originally designed to teach production of syntax by including instruction in receptive aspects of syntax, the second on methods of modifying input and output demands of the learning task to accommodate individual pupils.

Since it is particularly important for some learning disabled children to begin syntactic intervention at the level of receptive processes, methods must be modified to meet those needs. Comprehension, for example, generally is taught by pairing an experience, either nonverbal (an action, picture, facial expression, etc.) or verbal (description, explanation), with the appropriate syntactic structure (Johnson & Myklebust, 1967). Those authorities suggest that the simultaneous timing of the presentation of experience and language structure is the critical element in teaching comprehension. Perhaps equally crucial is the arranging and highlighting of the experience (verbal or nonverbal) so that the children can abstract the critical features of the situation that are being labeled by the syntactic structure (see the discussion in Chapter 3 on semantic features).

For example, Dever's (1978) method, which focuses entirely on production of correct syntactic structures and assumes comprehension by the children, might be modified to enhance understanding by providing activities, pictures, or events simultaneously with target structures. On the other hand, if learning disabled children have difficulty comprehending question forms, the clinician might avoid both the Dever and the Lee approaches and select other methods such as some suggested by Muma.

It also is necessary in some cases to modify the input or output demands of a learning task. Consideration must be given to the nature of the stimulus materials, i.e., what they require in terms of auditory and visual processing? (Lerner, 1981; Johnson & Myklebust, 1967). Pictures often are used as stimuli for teaching syntactic structures. However, it must be asked whether problems in picture interpretation (visual comprehension) will interfere with children's ability to abstract the features of the experience that is to be paired with the language structure.

Some formal methods such as Dever's might be modified to incorporate more visual stimuli: objects, pictures, activities, or printed words. On the other hand, some children are distracted by visual stimuli so for them a technique such as Dever's may be well suited. To use another example, Lee's method, which usually incorporates a flannel board or other visual activity, could be modified to reduce such elements to a minimum for visually distractible children, thereby focusing mainly on auditory input.

It is important to recognize the wide variety of combinations of stimuli available and to determine what works best for each child. Stimuli range from entirely nonverbal experiences to highly verbal ones to combinations of auditory and visual input. Johnson (1981) suggests that in some cases, older children might benefit from presentation of syntactic structures through the printed word since some can comprehend a structure better visually than auditorily. The *Fokes Sentence Builder* (Fokes, 1976) as well as certain materials used to teach syntax to the deaf such as the *Fitzgerald Key* (Fitzgerald, 1963) may be useful for presenting grammatical structures in printed form. Informal written materials designed by the clinician also are appropriate. In some cases, such as with deaf children, teaching syntax must be accomplished entirely through reading, without any auditory processing.

Thus clinicians should be aware that it is not necessarily the case that auditory input (modeled utterance) and auditory output (repetition by children) constitute the only or even preferred method for teaching syntax to every learning disabled youngster.

---

**REFERENCES**

Adler, S. *The nonverbal child*. Springfield, Ill.: Charles C. Thomas, Publisher, 1964.

Anderson, R., Reynolds, R., Schallert, D., & Goetz, E. Frameworks for comprehending discourse. *American Educational Research Journal, 1977, 14*, 367-381.

Aram, D.M., & Nation, J.E. Patterns of language behavior in children with developmental language disorders. *Journal of Speech and Hearing Research, 1975, 18*, 229-241.

Ausberger, C. *Syntax one*. Tucson: Communication Skill Builders, Inc., 1976.

Ausberger, C. *Syntax two*. Tucson: Communication Skill Builders, Inc., 1976.

Baker, H., & Leland, B. *Detroit tests of learning aptitude*. Indianapolis: The Bobbs-Merrill Co., Inc., 1967.

Berko, J. The child's learning of English morphology. *Word, 1958, 14*, 150-177.

Berry, M. *Language disorders of children*. New York: Appleton-Century-Crofts, Inc., 1969.

Berry, M.F. *Berry-Talbott language test 1: Comprehension of grammar*. Rockford, Ill.: M.F. Berry, 1966.

Bloom, L. *Language development: Form and function in emerging grammars*. Cambridge, Mass.: The MIT Press, 1970.

Bloom, L., & Lahey, M. *Language development and language disorders*. New York: John Wiley & Sons, Inc., 1978.

Bloom, L., Lightbown, P., & Hood, L. Structure and variation in child language. *Monographs of the Society for Research in Child Language*, 1975, *40*, (Serial No. 160).

Bowerman, M. Semantic factors in the acquisition of rules for word use and sentence construction. In D.M. Morehead & A.E. Morehead (Eds.), *Normal and deficient child language*. Baltimore: University Park Press, 1976.

Bransford, J., & Franks, J. The abstraction of linguistic ideas. *Cognitive Psychology*, 1971, *2*, 331-350.

Brinton, J. Sentence-repetition tasks compared with expressive language performance. In D. Crystal (Ed.), *Working with LARSP*. New York: Elsevier-Dutton Publishing Co., Inc., 1979.

Brown, R. *A first language: The early stages*. Cambridge, Mass.: Harvard University Press, 1973.

Carrow, E. *Test for auditory comprehension of language*. Austin, Texas: Urban Research Group, 1973.

Carrow, E. *Carrow elicited language inventory*. Austin, Texas: Learning Concepts, 1974.

Chafe, W. *Meaning and the structure of language*. Chicago: The University of Chicago Press, 1970.

Chomsky, C. *The acquisition of syntax in children from 5 to 10*. Cambridge, Mass.: The MIT Press, 1969.

Chomsky, N. *Syntactic structures*. The Hague: Mouton Publishers, 1957.

Chomsky, N. *Aspects of a theory of syntax*. Cambridge, Mass.: The MIT Press, 1965.

Clark, E. What's in a word? On the child's acquisition of semantics in his first language. In T.E. Moore (Ed.), *Cognitive development and the acquisition of language*. New York: Academic Press, 1973.

Cowan, P.A., Weber, J., Haddinott, B.A., & Klein, J. Mean length of spoken responses as a function of stimulus, experimenter, and subject. *Child Development*, 1967, *38*, 191-302.

Crystal, D. (Ed.). *Working with LARSP*. New York: Elsevier-Dutton Publishing Co., Inc., 1979.

Crystal, D. *Research trends in the study of child language disability*. Keynote address, First Annual Symposium on Research in Child Language Disorders, Madison, Wis., 1980.

Crystal, D., Fletcher, P., & Garman, M. *The grammatical analysis of language disability*. London: Edward Arnold, Ltd., 1976.

Cupples, W. *Relational semantics in the language of young preschool children: Pronominal and nominal variation*. Unpublished doctoral dissertation, Northwestern University, 1978.

Derwing, B., & Baker, W. Recent research on the acquisition of English morphology. In P. Fletcher & M. Garman (Eds.), *Language acquisition*. Cambridge, England: Cambridge University Press, 1979.

Dever, R.B. *TALK: Teaching the American language to kids*. Columbus, Ohio: The Charles E. Merrill Publishing Co., Inc., 1978.

Dever, R.B., & Bauman, P.M. Indiana scale of children's clausal development. Mimeographed, 1971; reprinted in T. Longhurst (Ed.), *Linguistic analysis of children's speech: Readings*. New York: MSS Information Corporation, 1974.

Engler, L.F., Hannah, E.P., & Longhurst, T.M. Linguistic analysis of speech samples: A practical guide for clinicians. *Journal of Speech and Hearing Disorders*, 1973, *38*, 192-204.

Fillmore, C.J. The case for case. In E. Bach & R.T. Harms (Eds.), *Universals in linguistic theory*. New York: Holt, Rinehart & Winston, 1968.

Fitzgerald, E. *Straight language for the deaf*. Washington, D.C.: Volta Bureau, 1963.

Fokes, J. *Fokes sentence builder*. New York: Teaching Resources Corporation, 1976.

Foster, C.R., Giddan, J.J., & Stark, J. *ACLC: Assessment of children's language comprehension*. Palo Alto, Calif.: Consulting Psychologists Press, 1972.

Freedman, P., & Carpenter, R. Semantic relations used by normal and languaged impaired children at Stage I. *Journal of Speech and Hearing Research,* 1976, *19,* 784-796.

Gerber, A., & Bryen, D. *Language and learning disabilities.* Baltimore: University Park Press, 1981.

Hallgren, B. Specific dyslexia: A clinical and genetic study. *Acta Psychiatrica Neurologica* (Copenhagen), Supplement 65, 1950, 1-287.

Johnson, D.J. Factors to consider in programming for children with language disorders. *Topics in Learning and Learning Disabilities,* 1981, *1,* 13-28.

Johnson, D.J., & Myklebust, H.R. *Learning disabilities: Educational principles and practices.* New York: Grune & Stratton, Inc., 1967.

Johnston, J.R., & Kahmi, A. *The same can be less: Syntactic and semantic aspects of the utterances of language impaired children.* Paper presented at the First Annual Symposium on Research in Child Language Disorders, Madison, Wis., June, 1980,

Johnston, J.R., & Schery, T.K. The use of grammatical morphemes by children with communication disorders. In D.M. Morehead & A.E. Morehead (Eds.), *Normal and deficient child language.* Baltimore: University Park Press, 1976.

Jones, L.V., Goodman, M.F., & Wepman, J.M. The classification of parts of speech for the characterization of aphasia. *Language and Speech,* 1963, *6,* 94-108.

Kirk, S.A., McCarthy, J., & Kirk, W.D., *The Illinois test of psycholinguistic abilities.* Urbana, Ill.: University of Illinois, Institute for Research on Exceptional Children, 1968.

Lee, L. Developmental sentence types. *Journal of Speech and Hearing Disorders,* 1966, *31,* 311-330.

Lee, L. *The Northwestern syntax screening test* (Rev. ed.). Evanston, Ill.: Northwestern University Press, 1971.

Lee, L. *Developmental sentence analysis: A grammatical assessment procedure for speech and language disorders.* Evanston, Ill.: Northwestern University Press, 1974.

Lee, L., & Canter, S. Developmental sentence scoring: A clinical procedure for estimating syntactic development in children's spontaneous speech. *Journal of Speech and Hearing Disorders,* 1971, *36,* 315-340.

Lee, L., Koenigsknecht, R., & Mulhern, S. *Interactive language development teaching.* Evanston, Ill.: Northwestern University Press, 1975.

Leonard, L. What is deviant language? *Journal of Speech and Hearing Disorders,* 1972, *37,* 427-446.

Leonard, L., Bolders, J., & Miller, J. The examination of the semantic relations reflected in the language usage of normal and language disordered children. *Journal of Speech and Hearing Research,* 1976, *19,* 371-392.

Leonard, L., Perozzi, J., Prutting, C., & Berkley, R. Nonstandardized approaches to the assessment of language behaviors. *ASHA,* 1978, *20,* 371-379.

Leopold, W. *Speech development of a bilingual child* (4 vols.). Evanston, Ill.: Northerwestern University Press, 1939.

Lerea, L. Assessing language development. *Journal of Speech and Hearing Research,* 1958, *1,* 75-85.

Lerner, J. *Children with learning disabilities* (3rd ed.). Boston: Houghton Mifflin Company, 1981.

Longhurst, T., & Schrandt, T. Linguistic analysis of children's speech: A comparison of four procedures. *Journal of Speech and Hearing Disorders,* 1973, *38,* 240-249.

Lyon, R., & Watson, B. Empirically derived subgroups of learning disabled readers: Diagnostic characteristics. *Journal of Learning Disabilities,* 1981, *14,* 256-261.

McCarthy, D. *The language development of the preschool child.* Minneapolis: University of Minnesota Press, 1930.

McCarthy, D. Language development in children. In L. Carmichael (Ed.), *Manual of child psychology* (2nd ed.). New York: John Wiley & Sons, Inc., 1954.

McGinnis, M.A. *Aphasic children: Identification and education by the association method.* Washington, D.C.: Volta Bureau, 1963.

McGrady, H. Language pathology and learning disabilities. In H.R. Myklebust (Ed.), *Progress in learning disabilities* (Vol. 1) New York: Grune & Stratton, Inc., 1968.

Menyuk, P. Comparison of grammar of children with functionally deviant and normal speech. *Journal of Speech and Hearing Research,* 1964, *7,* 109-121.

Miller, J. *Assessing language production in children: Experimental procedures.* Baltimore: University Park Press, 1981.

Miller, J. *Assessing language comprehension in children: Experimental procedures.* Baltimore: University Park Press, book in preparation.

Miller, J., & Yoder, D., An ontogenic language teaching strategy for retarded children. In R. Schiefelbusch & L. Lloyd (Eds.), *Language perspectives: Acquisition, retardation, and intervention.* Baltimore: University Park Press, 1974.

Miller, J., & Yoder, D. *The Miller-Yoder test of grammatical comprehension.* Madison, Wis.: University of Wisconsin Experimental Materials, 1975.

Miner, L.E. Scoring procedures for the length-complexity index: A preliminary report. *Journal of Communication Disorders,* 1969, *2,* 224-240.

Minifie, F., Darley, F., & Sherman, D. Temporal reliability of seven language measures. *Journal of Speech and Hearing Research,* 1963, *6,* 139-148.

Morehead, D., & Ingram, D. The development of base syntax in normal and linguistically deviant children. *Journal of Speech and Hearing Research,* 1973, *16,* 330-352.

Muma, J.R. Language intervention: Ten techniques. *Language, Speech, and Hearing Services in the Schools,* 1971, *5,* 7-17.

Muma, J.R. Language assessment: The co-occurring and restricted structure procedure. *Acta Symbolica,* 1973, *4,* 12-29.

Muma, J.R., & Pierce, D. Language intervention: Data or evidence? *Topics in Learning and Learning Disabilities,* 1981, *1,* 1-11.

Myklebust, H.R. *Auditory disorders in children.* New York: Grune & Stratton, Inc., 1954.

Newcomer, P., & Hammill, D. *Test of language development.* Austin, Texas: Empiric Press, 1977.

O'Donnell, L. *Language sampling: Linguistic research applied to learning disabilities.* Paper presented at the Association for Children with Learning Disabilities, Kansas City, Mo., 1978.

Quigley, S., & Power, D. *TSA syntax program.* Beaverton, Ore.: Dormac Co., 1979.

Quirk, R., Greenbaum, S., Leech, G.N., and Svartvik, J. *A university grammar of contemporary English.* London: Longman, 1973.

Rabinovitch, R.D. Reading and learning disabilities. In S. Arieti (Ed.), *American handbook of psychiatry* (Vol. 2). New York: Basic Books, 1959.

Rosenthal, J. A preliminary psycholinguistic study of children with learning disabilities. *Journal of Learning Disabilities,* 1970, *3,* 391-395.

Ross, A. *Psychological aspects of learning disabilities and reading disorders.* New York: McGraw-Hill Book Company, 1976.

Scharf, D.J. Some relationships between measures of early language development. *Journal of Speech and Hearing Disorders,* 1972, *37,* 64-74.

Schlesinger, I. Production of utterances and language acquisition. In D. Slobin (Ed.), *The ontogenesis of grammar*. New York: Academic Press, 1971.

Scroggs, C. Analyzing the language of hearing impaired children with severe language acquisition problems. *American Annals of the Deaf*, 1977, *122*, 403-406.

Semel, E., & Wiig, E. Comprehension of syntactic structures and critical verbal elements by children with learning disabilities. *Journal of Learning Disabilities*, 1975, *8*, 53-58.

Semel, E., & Wiig, E. *Clinical evaluation of language functions*. Columbus, Ohio: The Charles E. Merrill Publishing Co., Inc., 1980.

Smith, F. *Understanding reading*. New York: Holt, Rinehart & Winston, Inc., 1971.

Spekman, N.J. *An investigation of the dyadic, verbal problem-solving communication abilities of learning disabled and normal children*. Unpublished doctoral dissertation, Northwestern University, 1977.

Tyack, D., & Gottsleben, R. *Language sampling, analysis, and training*. Palo Alto, Calif.: Consulting Psychologists Press, 1974.

Vogel, S. Syntactic abilities in normal and dyslexic children. *Journal of Learning Disabilities*, 1974, *7*, 103-109.

Weir, R. *Language in the crib*. The Hague: Mouton Publishers, 1962.

Wiig, E., & Semel, E. Comprehension of linguistic concepts requiring logical operations by learning disabled children. *Journal of Speech and Hearing Research*, 1973, *16*, 627-636.

Wiig, E., & Semel, E. Logico-grammatical sentence comprehension by learning disabled adolescents. *Perceptual and Motor Skills*, 1974, *38*, 1331-1334.

Wiig, E., & Semel, E. Productive language abilities in learning disabled adolescents. *Journal of Learning Disabilities*, 1975, *8*, 579-586.

Wiig, E., & Semel, E. *Language disabilities in children and adolescents*. Columbus, Ohio: The Charles E. Merrill Publishing Co., Inc., 1976.

Wiig, E., & Semel, E. *Language intervention and assessment for the learning disabled*. Columbus, Ohio: The Charles E. Merrill Publishing Co., Inc., 1980.

Wiig, E., Semel, E., & Crouse, M. The use of morphology in high risk and learning disabled children. *Journal of Learning Disabilities*, 1973, *6*, 457-465.

Wood, N.E. *Delayed speech and language development*. Englewood Cliffs, N.J.: Prentice-Hall, Inc., 1964.

Wren, C.T. *The relationship of auditory and cognitive processes to syntactic patterns in learning disabled and normal children*. Unpublished doctoral dissertation, Northwestern University, 1980.

Wren, C.T. Identifying patterns of syntactic disorder in 6-year-old children. *The British Journal of Disorders of Communication*, 1981, *16*, 101-109.

Zangwill, O. *Cerebral dominance and its relation to psychological function*. London: Henderson Trust, 1960.

# Chapter 5

# Discourse and Pragmatics

*Nancy J. Spekman*

Preceding chapters have focused on various aspects of the linguistic system, including phonology, syntax, and semantics. Research traditionally has focused on each area in isolation, frequently neglecting the interrelationships that exist among the various components. Clinicians also frequently have overlooked the fact that language is used by individuals, within a dynamic context, to communicate a variety of intentions and to accomplish different goals or objectives.

Linguistic competence alone, including mastery of the phonological, syntactic, and semantic rule systems of a language, does not guarantee that an individual will demonstrate appropriate language use. Blank, Gessner, and Esposito (1979), for example, report a case study of a child with well-developed syntactic and semantic systems but who experienced almost total failure to use language socially and appropriately.

Language research since about 1970 is perhaps most notable for the redirection of emphasis from the notion of linguistic competence to that of communicative competence (Launer & Lahey, 1981). Successful verbal communication requires that the speaker learn what to talk about and under what circumstances, as well as how to say it. It requires that the listener provide appropriate feedback and that both partners know the rules regarding cooperation, turn-taking, sequencing, violations and repairs, and other responsibilities (Garvey & Baldwin, 1970; Grice, 1975; Hymes, 1971; Schegloff, 1972; Schegloff, Jefferson, & Sacks, 1977). Performance must be adapted continuously and should reflect the ability to utilize these complex and diverse factors in the generation of messages. Thus, appropriate linguistic selections are made in light of individual and situational demands and are determined both socially and cognitively.

Clearly, children are not born with the ability to communicate successfully; even as adults, individuals continue to err with respect to what they say, to whom they say it, and how they say it. Like most forms of human knowledge, receptive and expressive communication skills develop gradually throughout childhood (Bruner, 1975; Halliday, 1973, 1975; Prutting, 1979; Rees, 1978).

157

## PART I. PRAGMATICS AND LEARNING DISABILITIES

### Section 1. A Conceptual Framework for Pragmatics

Pragmatics, as defined by Bates (1976b), refers to the rules governing the use of language in a social context. Mastery in this complex area requires the integration of linguistic, cognitive, and social abilities. While there is as yet no one agreed-upon theoretical approach to the study of pragmatics, the more immediate need in the field is the more practical one of providing an organizational overview of the very wide variety of component skills that are thought to constitute pragmatic competence. The taxonomy of abilities is by no means complete and various researchers are eclectically using a variety of existing theories (from philosophy, linguistics, and psychology, among others) to illuminate component skills.

In many cases, there is little obvious relationship among the works of various authors since they are constructing their own individual taxonomies of skills to investigate. In addition, little has been done to make sense of these disparate studies in a manner that is useful to clinicians in assessment and treatment of pragmatic disorders. The purpose of the first part of this chapter is to provide a broad framework for conceptualizing pragmatic competence and to describe what is thought to constitute that capability.

The confusing catalogue of component skills might be organized in several ways and it still is necessary to work at the level of constructs. That is, an organizational framework is selected based on theoretical good sense but little empirical proof. One logical way to proceed is to look at the possible progression of broader and broader contexts that influence communication success. Beginning from the point of view of the speaker, there are four major areas:

1. Communicative intentions has to do with the function or intent of messages and the form those intentions can take.
2. Presuppositions encompass content of messages and inclusion of appropriate information based on the needs of a listener. Here the context broadens to include the communicative partner to a greater degree since the speaker must know or infer what the listener needs to know.
3. Social organization of discourse involves maintaining a dialogue between partners over several conversational turns. This includes adequate functioning in terms of intentions and presuppositions as well as knowing how to sustain and repair conversations.
4. Environmental context overlaps the others and requires consideration of the impact of environmental factors (e.g., the availability of feedback, modalities available for communication, and physical setting) on communicative effectiveness.

This section examines each area in turn, suggesting important subskills and approaches that have been used to investigate them.

*Communicative Intentions*

Language may be used to serve a wide variety of functions, including among others commenting, requesting, protesting, greeting, promising, and directing (Austin, 1962; Searle, 1969). The function that a speaker expects a message to serve is known as the communicative intention. According to Labov (1972), it is the message's intention, rather than its superficial linguistic structure, that determines what will happen next in discourse.

Speech act theory provides the most commonly used framework for explaining and examining communicative intentions. The unit of analysis, the speech act, is not restricted or defined by traditional grammar. For example, it need not be a sentence. Austin (1962) suggests that each speech act contains three major components:

1. locutionary act: the actual verbal utterance and the proposition or content it contains
2. illocutionary act: the meaning intended by the speaker
3. perlocutionary act: the effect of the speech act on the listener.

Ideally, the illocutionary and perlocutionary acts are parallel, such as when a speaker's promise to arrive by noon serves to convince the hearer that a punctual arrival is assured. However, everyone is acutely aware that intentions frequently are misconstrued and result in unintended effects. For example, attempts at sarcasm or humor actually may be interpreted as insults.

Since Austin (1962), terminology has shifted somewhat. The term ''speech act'' has been narrowed to refer more exclusively to the illocutionary force or intention of an utterance. The word ''performative'' also has been used to refer to the underlying communicative intent (Parisi & Antinucci, 1973).

Developmentally, there is general agreement that children discover the idea of communication at some point during Piaget's Stage IV (coordination of secondary schemata) or V (tertiary circular reactions) of sensorimotor development (Bates, Camaioni, & Volterra, 1975; Escalona, 1973; Sugarman, 1973). It is at this stage, between 9 and 12 months of age, that children first demonstrate purposeful use of gestures and vocalizations that appear to serve as precursors to verbal communications and that also may be used later in conjunction with verbal messages (Bates et al., 1975; Carter, 1979; Dore, 1973). For example, infants may wave their arms to be picked up, react negatively to the removal of a desired object, wave bye-bye, point to and/or direct their visual gaze at a desired object, or tug at an adult to gain attention.

Diverse taxonomies have been proposed for classifying communicative intentions of infants (Bates et al., 1975; Bates, 1976a; Carter, 1974; Dore, 1975; Greenfield & Smith, 1976; Halliday, 1975). Despite some differences in available taxonomies, there is at least widespread agreement that very young children are successful in communicating a variety of intentions before they have any or much control over the linguistic system. Chapman (1981) notes also that despite different terminology, certain categories are common to most of the classification systems, including participation in routines, requests for objects or activity, rejection, comments, and later requests for information.

Beyond the sensorimotor stage, children's increasing linguistic sophistication is accompanied by an expansion of the range of intentions, an increase in the forms available for coding them, and a refinement in the utilization of these different forms. However, theorists have not been able to provide a complete list of intentions expressed and often do not agree on their possible range. There also has been no systematic delineation of the relationships among specific grammatical forms, other communicative behaviors, and particular intentions.

In the process of becoming competent communicators, children must learn to both comprehend and generate a variety of communicative intentions as well as the means by which they can be coded. More specifically, they must:

1. acquire knowledge of the range of communicative intentions that can be expressed;
2. gain linguistic sophistication so they can use a variety of syntactic forms and lexical items to convey intent, as well as master the gestural and paralinguistic conventions of the community;
3. learn the social conventions that govern the selection of a particular form to express an intention within a particular social situation or that affect the selection of a particular interpretation.

Each of these areas of competence is examined next in relation to communicative intent.

**Range of Intentions:** As noted, experts in this area have proposed diverse taxonomies to catalog the wide range of communicative intentions that may be expressed. The absence of consensus may be related to factors such as the use of different terminology as well as methodological considerations such as small sample sizes, varying developmental levels of children studied, and varying communicative contexts. Halliday (1973, 1975) suggests that the taxonomy probably changes developmentally, yet few researchers have attempted longitudinal studies.

Despite the diversity, however, consideration of the various systems together can provide some broad categories of communicative intentions that may be helpful to clinicians, including: labels; statements of facts, rules, attitudes, feelings, and beliefs; descriptions; acknowledgments; requests for attention, objects, actions, and information; greetings; protests, denials, and rejections; practicing; and responses to requests.

**Forms of Intentions:** Skilled communicators have numerous means available for accomplishing any particular intention. Communicative intentions can be conveyed gesturally, through a large variety of body movements; paralinguistically, through changes in stress patterns, duration, intonation, pitch, and intensity levels; and/or linguistically, through words, phrases, and sentences.

For example, a speaker wants to get someone to close a window. Gesturally, the speaker can assume a shivering posture with teeth chattering. Paralinguistically, emphatic stress, an annoyed tone, and/or increased volume might be used to highlight the intent. Linguistically, the speaker might use an explicit performative form such as "I command (order) you to close the window," a direct imperative such as "Close the window," a polite indirect form such as "Would you mind closing the window?" or an even less direct form or hint such as "I should have worn a sweater."

It thus should be evident that communicative intentions may be expressed either directly, in forms permitting easy recognition of the illocutionary force, or indirectly, in forms requiring some degree of inference to ascertain the intended meaning. The most widely examined communicative intention in this regard is the directive or the use of language to direct the behavior of another (Dore, 1974; Garvey, 1975; Mitchell-Kernan & Kernan, 1977; Read & Cherry, 1978; Shatz, 1978a, 1978b; Spekman & Roth, 1981).

Ervin-Tripp (1977) presents six types of directives ranging along a continuum from direct to less direct to illustrate different ways in which an individual might get someone to provide a cookie:

1. Direct imperative: "Give me a cookie."
2. Imbedded imperative: "Can you give me a cookie?"
3. Permission directive: "May I have a cookie?"
4. Personal need or desire statement: "I want (need) a cookie."
5. Question directive: "Are there any more cookies?"
6. Hint: "I haven't had a cookie in a long time," or "Those cookies sure smell yummy."

It should be noted, however, that the particular syntactic form or content of an utterance cannot always be equated with the user's intent. In other words, the same utterance can convey a variety of possible intentions. For example, "May I have some salt?" may be used to request permission or gain factual information (such as when addressed to a physician prescribing a diet) or to direct the behavior of another (such as when addressed to a dinner companion).

It also is important to recognize that any one message may contain gestural, paralinguistic, and linguistic information. Ideally, the intent expressed by each means is the same; however, there are instances in which the messages actually are contradictory (e.g., the use of sarcasm) and the listener must learn which one to attend to.

**Social Conventions Governing Forms of Intentions:**  The speaker's selection among alternative forms of a message, as well as the intent ascribed to each utterance by a listener, depend upon a wide variety of factors. For example, context plays a significant role. In the context of a very draughty room, the polite request "Would you mind closing the window?" is intended not as a request for affirmation but as a request for action. Similarly, different forms may be required to request information or permission in a classroom vs. at home. Other important social factors include the degree of familiarity and the status relations between the partners.

In sum, the ability to communicate intentions appropriately requires a variety of skills that include mastery of both linguistic and nonlinguistic means of communication as well as their integration with social and cognitive abilities.

*Presupposition*

Successful communication (both oral and written) is highly dependent on the inferential abilities of both partners. As noted, listeners often must infer the speaker's intent rather than rely exclusively on a literal interpretation of what is said. Speakers also must infer information about their partners and the context in order to determine the appropriate content and form of a message.

It is understood that within any interaction, there is some information that is "old" or taken for granted and some that is "new." Speaker and listener both must differentiate between the two, i.e., between what is presupposed and what is asserted. Presupposition, then, has to do with the assumptions regarding communicative context that are necessary to make an utterance verifiable and/or appropriate (Bates, 1976b).

Appropriate use and interpretation of presupposition is possible when the interlocutors have established what Rommetveit (1974) refers to as a "temporarily shared social reality." The establishment of this shared knowledge base makes it possible for the speaker to make appropriate selections of what to talk about (and what not to talk about) and how to say it.

On the one hand, competent communicators understand that there is no need to state explicitly what already is known. On the other hand, they must present information the listener is known not to possess. Thus, competent communicators know how to formulate messages differently to different audiences. Without this necessary shared reality, communication breakdowns occur. For example, the following dialogue (Spekman, 1982) occurred between two boys separated by a barrier:

It's a triangle.

> Huh?

It's a triangle.

> What is?

Oh . . . the whole thing . . . it's going to
look like a triangle.

> Okay.

In this example, communication failure was avoided because the listener indicated confusion and the speaker then was able to make what was previously presupposed more explicit.

Shared information of knowledge can be established between interlocutors in several ways: (1) by mutually monitoring some shared aspect of the physical setting, (2) by sharing some general knowledge of the speech situation itself or of the communicative partner (e.g., age, status, past experiences), and (3) by mutually monitoring the preceding discourse.

To make appropriate judgments regarding the amount or degree of shared knowledge, a speaker must develop a sense of audience. This ability to successfully assume more than one perspective, i.e., to assume a point of view other than one's own, is referred to as role-taking. According to Flavell (1974), successful interpersonal inference requires (1) the awareness that a particular situation requires inferential activity, (2) the inferential activity itself, and (3) its application in subsequent behavior. Thus, a speaker must assess the needs of the audience based on knowledge of the individual(s), the discourse, and the context, then utilize this information in the preparation of messages. The content and form of the language should reflect this process.

Role-taking skills have been shown to increase with age in a variety of contexts, including tasks of a perceptual, conceptual, and/or communicative (or social) nature (Feffer, 1970; Flavell, Botkin, Fry, Wright, & Jarvis, 1968; Garvey & Baldwin, 1971; Krauss & Glucksberg, 1969; Looft, 1972; Piaget, 1926; Rubin, 1973). Interestingly, preschool children have been found to demonstrate a considerably greater degree of role-taking ability than Piaget (1926) predicted.

Evidence of the development of presupposition and role-taking skills comes from examining different aspects of children's language during communication. For example, several investigations have focused on the nature of the information that children include in conversations and have concluded that even at the one-word stage they tend to comment on aspects of the environment that are maximally informative or communicative (Greenfield & Smith, 1976; Greenfield & Zukow, 1978; Snyder, 1978). Snyder (1981) states of children that

They commented on those objects, persons, states or events that were new, changing, or uncertain. Contextual information that was old or constant in the situation [and thus could be presupposed] did not receive comment. (p. 38)

A variety of referential communication studies also have demonstrated improvement with age in the ability of speakers to provide the information needed for task success (Dickson, 1974; Garvey & Baldwin, 1971; Glucksberg & Krauss, 1967; Glucksberg, Krauss, & Weisberg, 1966; Krauss & Glucksberg, 1969; Krauss & Rotter, 1968).

Developmental evidence is obtained from studies that demonstrate changes in the forms (as contrasted with content) of messages. A number of studies have investigated linguistic and pragmatic changes that appear to reflect the sensitivity of children to different attributes of their audiences, including:

- listener age (Camaioni, 1979; Gleason, 1973; Masur, 1978; Sachs & Devin, 1976; Shatz & Gelman, 1973)
- listener verbal ability (Marinkovitch, Newhoff, & MacKenzie, 1980; Masur, 1978)
- state of knowledge of listener (Maratsos, 1973; Menig-Peterson, 1975)
- cognitive level of listener (Guralnick & Paul-Brown, 1977, 1980).

While it is accepted that children are more egocentric than adults and that they frequently fail to adapt to a listener's perspective, it would appear to have been demonstrated overwhelmingly that young children have considerable control over their interaction strategies. They do talk differently to different people. Many of these studies also find that when talking to younger or otherwise less advanced partners, preschool children do not adopt the level of the listener but instead maintain a level slightly above or more advanced. It has been hypothesized that children, like adults, produce a level of language developmentally useful to their partners.

A successful communicator thus must be able to assess the shared reality that exists between partners, which assumes at least a minimum amount of role-taking ability. Children also must learn to control both the content of the message (old and new information, implicit and explicit information) as well as its form (length, complexity) in order to adapt it to the perceived needs of the audience. In addition to these rather broad requirements regarding appropriate use of presupposition, the competent communicator must control certain specific linguistic conventions (deictics and direct/indirect reference).

**Deictics:** These are linguistic elements that refer to, or stand for, people, things, places, and time: personal pronouns (''I, you''), demonstrative pronouns ("this, that"), adverbs of location ("here, there") and of time ("before, after, then, now"), and certain verbs ("come, go, bring, take"). Deictic terms of themselves are empty of meaning and can be interpreted only by knowing something about the communication act in which they play a role (Fillmore, 1975). In other words, their interpretation depends upon, or presupposes, the existence of another element either within the discourse itself or within its context. Their use thus represents an intersection of linguistic and social or pragmatic abilities.

The primary purpose of deictics in discourse is to code information that is assumed to be common knowledge between interlocutors. The correct/incorrect usage of deictics appears to reflect an individual's ability to establish this shared perspective. For example, it is easy to imagine a listener's confusion at the following (taken from Spekman, 1982) in which the thing(s) referred to are not identifiable:

. . . and *it*'s not exactly *it* . . . *it*'s when you put *it* beside *it* . . . *it*'s not *it*
. . . you put *it* under *that*.

Developmentally, deictic terms appear very early but their syntactic use may be mastered well before their pragmatic use. Deictics frequently are contrastive so correct use requires mastery of the "speaker principle," which has to do with the shifting nature of reference (e.g., "I" and "you"), and the "distance principle," which requires understanding of a proximal/nonproximal distinction (e.g., "here" and "there," "this" and "that") (Clark, 1978; Clark & Sengul, 1978). Developmental studies have focused on individual deictic contrasts involving

- personal pronouns (Bloom, Lightbown, & Hood, 1975; Chipman & deDardel, 1974; Huxley, 1970)
- demonstrative pronouns (deVilliers & deVilliers, 1974; Webb & Abrahamson, 1976)
- terms of locations (Bloom, Rocissano, & Hood, 1976; Charney, 1979)
- deictic verbs (Clark & Garnica, 1974; Richards, 1976).

However, there is need for a system for evaluating deictic usage from a communicative perspective that can be utilized across age ranges and across communication situations and that is not limited to only one or two deictic terms. Spekman (1978, 1982) recommends use of the Fillmore (1975) framework (described briefly below) for such an analysis because it permits simultaneous analysis of deictic type and function, or the way they are used to establish shared knowledge.

In his framework, Fillmore (1975) identifies five types of deictics, defined according to the nature of what is being referenced:

1. Person/thing deictics refer to the individuals involved in the communication act ("you, me"), other persons ("he, she, they"), or to physical objects within or external to the communication setting ("it, that, this").
2. Spatial deictics include the location(s) in which individuals or objects are positioned ("here, there, top").
3. Time deictics cover times and locate events in time relative to the time of interaction ("then, now, before").
4. Discourse deictics involve the matrix of the discourse itself within which the utterance has a role ("in the above paragraph," "discussed below").
5. Social deictics are the social relationships of the participants that determine the choice of intimate, honorific, polite, or insulting speech levels (e.g., Rob, Robert, Mr. Spekman, Professor Spekman).

Fillmore also identifies three functions that specify the different ways in which deictics are used to establish shared knowledge—gestural, symbolic, and anaphoric. These form a continuum reflecting the degree to which correct interpretation is dependent upon the physical setting of the speech situation as opposed to the language used.

The gestural function refers to the situation in which the interlocutors must monitor some shared aspect of the physical setting. For example, in

Put *this there.*

the listener must identify the what and the where by monitoring the speaker's pointing gesture, eye movements, or the like.

Symbolic deictics are those whose interpretation involves a shared knowledge of certain aspects of the speech situation, regardless of how this information is obtained (direct perception, previous experience, and so on). For example, in

When will you be *here?*

the listener identifies the location as the place at which the speaker is located.

Anaphoric deictics, in contrast, involve shared information that was established previously in spoken (or written) discourse. For example,

John went to the store. *There he* bought some milk.

**Direct/Indirect Reference:** A competent speaker who wishes to comment on a particular referent that is not contextually present, has not been mentioned previously, and about which the listener cannot be assumed to know, typically will use a form of indefinite reference as an introduction. Once introduced, the referent can be presupposed or assumed to be shared by the interlocutors and then may be referred to with a more definite form, such as the definite article ("the") or a pronoun. For example:

> *A gang* of teens was reported to have looted several stores. *They* did several thousand dollars' worth of damage. *The gang* has been in trouble before.

Hickman (1980) states that the function of indefinite forms ("*a* gang") in such instances is to "create" referents linguistically; subsequent coreferential phrases rest on relations within the text rather than on those between text and context as in most instances of deixis. Hickman suggests that mastery of such definite/indefinite forms evolves from earlier deictic uses of speech.

In mastering the use of definite/indefinite reference forms, two distinctions are necessary: (1) between specific ("the dog") and nonspecific ("a dog") reference; and (2) between speaker and listener and their different perspectives. Thus, while a referent may be concrete or known to the speaker, it may not be so established in the listener.

In experimental tasks, adults always have been found to use an indefinite article to introduce a referent for the first time and the definite article subsequently. Young children, in contrast, tend to overuse the definite article as if falsely assuming greater shared knowledge than had been established already. Age of mastery of direct/indirect reference has yet to be established; experimental results indicate a range of mastery from ages 3 to 10 (Brown, 1973; Hickman, 1980; Karmiloff-Smith, 1977, 1979; Keenan & Klein, 1975; Maratsos, 1976; Warden, 1976). These contradictory results result at least in part from the nature of the experimental tasks used.

In summary, deictics and definite/indefinite reference are common, frequently occurring linguistic terms whose correct use ultimately represents the integration of syntactic, semantic, and pragmatic knowledge. They may be used as measures of the speaker's ability to assume the listener's point of view, to provide the listener with appropriate information, and to avoid what is redundant.

## Social Organization of Discourse

The preceding two sections discuss pragmatic abilities within the fairly narrow context of individual speakers and listeners and how they code and interpret intentions and information in individual utterances. However, conversations and a variety of other discourse situations involve a dynamic interchange between interlocutors, a process necessitating a sense of cooperative effort and shared purpose during which each partner is expected to demonstrate appropriate turn-taking behaviors and skill in both speaker and listener roles.

Chapman (1981) identifies three levels of analysis beyond the individual utterance level that may tap various aspects of the social organization of conversation or discourse:

1. Messages can be viewed with respect to immediately preceding and following utterances so they may be categorized as to whether they acknowledge preceding information, answer a question, comment on something, and so on.
2. Utterances may be examined within a still larger framework that may consist of such functions as topic initiation, maintenance, and termination, turn allocation, and repair of communication breakdowns.
3. Discourse may be analyzed as to the relationships established between the interlocutors such as the degree of politeness or formality and of dominance and control.

The discussion next focuses mainly on the second level of analysis.

As with other skills, children must learn to participate appropriately in discourse situations. The earliest social interactions, such as those between mothers and infants, have been studied for evidence of developmental antecedents or skills precursory to later communicative competence. Early interactions involving neonates and infants are characterized by regularity and repetition, symmetry and turn-taking, mother sensitivity to infant responsiveness and movements, and infant sensitivity to adult speech and timing (Bruner, 1975, 1977; Kaye, 1977; Lewis & Freedle, 1973; Sander, 1977).

Counter to Piaget's (1926) notion that preschool children are egocentric and therefore almost exclusively engage in collective monologues, it has been demonstrated overwhelmingly that they do contribute to conversations with both adults and peers (Bates, 1975; Camaioni, 1979; Donahue, 1977; Garvey, 1975; Keenan, 1974; Keenan & Schieffelin, 1976; Mueller, 1972; Sachs, 1977; Shatz & Gelman, 1973). This involves both reciprocity, i.e., the interchanging of roles (speaker, listener), and of intentionality (Shaffer, 1977). Bloom et al. (1976) and Keenan and Schieffelin (1976) find young children extremely variable in the number of turns over which they can maintain a topic. Their data suggest that adult-child conversations tend to be maintained over a larger number of turns when the youngster initiates the topic and when the focus is an object present in the environment.

While some researchers have determined that adults generally maintain and structure their dialogue with children (Bloom et al., 1976; Gleason, 1973), others have examined child-child interactions and have found that true exchanges do occur in the absence of a structuring adult (Garvey & Hogan, 1973; Mueller, 1972). Bates (1976a), suggests that adults and clinicians actually may be too helpful in conversations by not requiring children to face their communicative inefficiencies. She notes that peers may pressure each other toward greater conversational skill by failing to respond to utterances that are important to the speaker.

There are a variety of mechanisms available to conversational partners to facilitate and maintain successful exchanges. Following rules such as staying on topic and being truthful, relevant, and brief (Grice, 1975) is of course helpful. Mueller (1972) reports that obtaining a child's attention is the best predictor of success in receiving a reply in dyads of preschoolers. Donahue (1977) and Keenan and Schieffelin (1976) cite examples of children as young as 2 using verbal and nonverbal attention-getting devices in their interactions with adults and who do not proceed with their messages until they have won the listener's attention.

In addition, partners typically provide each other with continual feedback that may influence the direction of the conversation. Major feedback devices are questions used to indicate confusion ("huh?") or the need for previous messages to be elaborated, clarified, or repeated. Garvey (1977) refers to questions serving this purpose as contingent queries. Other forms of feedback include head nods, a variety of affirmative or negative vocalizations (e.g., "yeah," "uh-huh"), facial expressions, and body postures. Dittman (1972) shows that such devices are present in conversations involving 6-year-olds but are much less frequent than in those of older children and adults.

Another mechanism—cohesion—functions to sustain a topic and maintain the flow of meaning by systematically linking one utterance to another (Halliday & Hasan, 1976; Labov & Fanshel, 1977). Devices for establishing such intralinguistic (or endophoric) relations include deixis (discussed earlier), conjunction, ellipsis, reference, and substitution. Garvey and Geraud (1980) report that 3-year-old and 5-year-old children differentially use form reduction (e.g., "the boy ⟶ he") as a means of maintaining focus on an object. For example, when returning focus to a previously mentioned referent, after several intervening turns, the children tend to rename the referent ("the boy") rather than use the reduced form such as a pronoun ("he").

When topics are not maintained, children face communication breakdown. In effect, breakdowns may serve an important teaching function as children attempt to resolve the difficulty or misunderstanding. Awareness that a breakdown has occurred, of course, means that at least one member of the dyad is monitoring the interaction; successful repairs further require that the source of the difficulty be identified and then that an appropriate repair strategy be selected. These repair strategies may be viewed from the perspective either of the listener who has not received or understood the intended message or of the speaker who may amend it spontaneously or in response to listener confusion.

There are a variety of verbal and nonverbal means by which listeners can indicate confusion. No systematic attention has been given to children's use of nonverbal means (e.g., shrugged shoulders, perplexed facial expression) either alone or in combination with verbal expressions. However, investigators have studied the use of the contingent query, which is an unsolicited verbal request by a listener to gain additional information, confirmation, repetition, or clarification of some aspect of a previous message (Garvey, 1977). It appears that such repair initiatives are not used by children when conversing with adults until almost 3 years of age (Keenan & Schieffelin, 1976) but are increasingly apparent beyond that age (Garvey, 1977).

It is interesting to note, however, that in certain experimental situations even school-age listeners have failed to recognize or indicate their need for clarification (Markman, 1977, 1979; Spekman, 1978). This would appear to have important implications for instructional settings. For example, teachers need to understand that children are not always aware that they are not comprehending or know the source of their confusion or how to gather the needed clarification.

As for the speaker's role in the repair process, a number of accounts suggest that children as young as 2 at least attempt to respond in some fashion to contingent queries (Cherry, 1979, Keenan & Schieffelin, 1976; Miller & Ervin-Tripp, 1964). However, the success of repair attempts increases with age in both natural (Garvey, 1977) and experimental situations (Glucksberg & Krauss, 1967; Peterson, Danner, & Flavell, 1972).

The types of repair strategies utilized also may be analyzed from several perspectives. Clark and Andersen (1979) identify four types of structural repairs used spontaneously by 3-year-old speakers:

1. Phonological repairs involve a modification or change in the sound structure of words, resulting in clearer articulation.
2. Morphological repairs include corrections in the use of grammatical morphemes (e.g., "*Him* is ⟶ *He* is going home").
3. Lexical repairs are changes in word choice (e.g., "It's a *block* ⟶ a *square*") or the addition of modifiers (e.g., "*These blocks* ⟶ *These blue blocks* are big").
4. Syntactic repairs cover changes in the grammatical organization of words in phrases and sentences.

While all four are used by 3-year-olds, Clark and Andersen (1979) find that the appearance of lexical and syntactic strategies increases with age. In contrast to this taxonomy, Garvey (1977) suggests that speaker repairs be analyzed on the basis of the type of information provided (i.e., repetition, confirmation, specification, elaboration). Paralinguistic repair strategies such as changes in pitch, volume, tempo, and stress also may be used in conjunction with the various verbal strategies (Spekman & Roth, 1981).

*Environmental Context*

It has been noted that a number of levels of context may influence both the form and content of interactions. Speakers assess context so as to produce appropriate utterances; listeners use the context in their interpretation of received messages. Bloom's (1970) work, for example, plays a major role in demonstrating the importance of contextual information for understanding children's utterances. Speakers and listeners alike are responsible for the continuous monitoring of both linguistic and nonlinguistic contexts. This section addresses the impact of physical or environmental factors on discourse.

The physical environment appears to play several key roles in early language development. At the most basic level, it provides the content of communication, i.e., the subject matter, what is talked about. Children frequently use the physical context to determine the communicative intentions expressed by others and to develop the meaning of individual lexical items. Adults similarly use the context to determine children's meaning and the youngsters receive feedback to support or refute their interpretation of the environment.

Routines or experiences also may come to be associated with particular contexts that then may allow the children to make predictions regarding what others are likely to do and what is considered appropriate behavior. Halliday (1975), for example, argues that knowing an interaction has to do with a mother bathing a child makes it possible to predict that messages will refer to cleaning items and washing behaviors; it also can be predicted that the interaction will have a regulatory tone and thus will contain directions and instructions.

An important aspect of the physical environment at all levels of development involves the channels available for communication. The auditory channel conveys information expressed both verbally and nonverbally (tone, intensity, intonations). The visual channel conveys information expressed through such means as gestures, postures, facial expressions, and the like. Additional information is conveyed tactually in certain interactions through physical contact with the communication partner.

As the number of channels and means for communicating are reduced (such as during telephone conversations), an increasing burden is placed on the speaker to compensate by making the language used as clear and as explicit as possible. For example, young children typically combine their early linguistic attempts with gestural forms. Flavell et al. (1968), Spekman (1981), and others report that overall communication success is reduced significantly when the interlocutors do not share the same environment visually. The ability to deal with such environmental changes obviously is related to the notion of role-taking abilities discussed earlier; i.e., the speaker must be aware of the listener's perspective and adapt messages accordingly.

Another factor related to channels of communication is the availability of feedback. Feedback or adjustment mechanisms are posited as an important component of most models dealing with the processing of information. Without feedback—auditory or visual, verbal or nonverbal—the speaker remains unaware of the listener's interpretation. As a result, errors remain undetected and the communication process may be less accurate. Situations in which feedback is limited, such as talking on the telephone or to a large audience, are more difficult for many children and adults. Subjects in artificial situations where feedback is decreased or eliminated appear considerably distressed.

Physical context thus is a critical factor that may influence not only what is talked about but also the form of the communication. Environmental components affect the comprehension and production of messages at all stages of becoming a competent communicator, and part of that developmental process must involve an understanding of the context and learning how to control it or function within it.

### Section 2. Pragmatic Disorders in Learning Disabled Children

Unfortunately, the body of knowledge available on normal communicative development has not been applied extensively to the study of language impaired or learning disabled individuals of any age. While perhaps not surprising, given the relative recency of interest in normal pragmatic development, this paucity of data on disordered development severely limits assessment and remediation.

The limited research base that is available has grown in part from normal developmental data and in part from clinical reports that indicate many impaired children exhibit major communication deficits either transcending their problems with phonology, syntax, and/or semantics or existing even in the presence of normal language skill. Geller and Wollner (1976), for example, describe a boy who had received extensive training on question forms in a therapy situation. When given the opportunity to use these forms in a real world context, however, he said ''Who is it? What is it? Where is it?'' in rapid succession to the first person he encountered.

This section reviews the research in this area that focuses specifically on language impaired or learning disabled children. Like all children, those who are impaired are placed in a wide variety of school and social situations requiring interaction and communication with changing audiences, for different purposes, and under differing contextual constraints. It is important to try to understand how these children function under a given set of circumstances.

Relatively little is known about the communicative skills of preschool language impaired children. There is, however, an extensive body of literature that demonstrates quite consistently that by school age, the learning disabled are less popular and more socially rejected by their fellows than are their normally achieving peers and that they experience different interactions with their teachers (Bruininks, 1978a, 1978b; Bryan, 1974a, 1974b, 1976; Bryan, Wheeler, Felcan, & Henek, 1976; Chapman, Larsen, & Parker, 1979; Garrett & Crump, 1980; Scranton & Ryckman, 1979; Siperstein, Bopp & Bak, 1978). Given that these children also frequently experience specific linguistic deficits (Johnson & Myklebust, 1967; Wiig & Semel, 1980), examination of their communication abilities can provide insights into the rejection they experience as well as help to explore the relationships between their linguistic and social abilities.

The four-point schema described in the first section is the basis for an analysis of what is known about the communicative abilities of language learning disabled children. It should be noted that a certain amount of caution is appropriate when interpreting results of studies examining the pragmatic abilities of these children. Small sample sizes, theoretical and terminological inconsistencies, and divergent methodological procedures are common problems that limit the ability to generalize findings.

Major difficulties also arise from population definition and subject selection procedures. The learning disabled children selected for study typically constitute a heterogeneous, ill-defined group and vary from study to study. Evidence rarely is provided that indicates that they do have specific language disabilities. While many of them may, in fact, have overt or subtle language problems, this is not demonstrated in researchers' descriptions of their samples.

The procedures used to identify children, if specified at all, frequently are widely discrepant. For example, some of the work at the Chicago Institute for Learning Disabilities (Bryan, Donahue, & Pearl, 1981; Bryan, Donahue, Pearl, & Sturm, 1981) includes on the one hand children already identified as learning disabled by their school systems, and on the other, parochial school children the researchers have identified as learning disabled solely on the basis of the *Peabody Picture Vocabulary Test* (Dunn, 1965) and a reading achievement test such as the reading subtest on the *Woodcock-Johnson Psycho-Educational Battery*. That these groups of students might be considered equivalent is indeed questionable. It also might be asked whether either group truly has specific language problems or even whether either one represents the learning disabled population at all.

Thus, the extent of knowledge about the pragmatic abilities of learning disabled children is restricted by methodological problems even in the few studies that exist.

*Communicative Intentions*

No empirical reports are available that have investigated the range and form of prelinguistic and/or linguistic communicative intentions that are understood and expressed by children with specific language disorders in natural or spontaneous communication situations involving either adults or peers. The few studies that have used language impaired-language normal dyads unfortunately have focused almost exclusively on the communicative intentions and skills of the language of normal children (for example, Guralnick & Paul-Brown, 1977, 1980). Given the considerable clinical evidence indicating limited intentions and/or limited coding mechanisms and flexibility in language learning disabled children (see Blank, Gessner, & Esposito, 1979), this is indeed an area in critical need of research.

Laboratory studies in this area also are extremely limited. Snyder (1978) gives results of a study utilizing structured experimental tasks designed to elicit declarative (informing) and imperative (directing) utterances. Her subjects included both language delayed and normal children, matched for mean length of utterance (MLU), and all functioning at the beginning of the single-word stage of language development. Children's responses were ranked from global gestural performatives, to higher order gestures, to use of the word to accomplish the intent.

Snyder reports that the language delayed children relied more heavily on gestural performatives and less on words than did the normal children; further, the gestures used by the handicapped were more global and representative of earlier sensorimotor levels than those used by the normals. She suggests that the language delayed subjects, while able to acquire the needed vocabulary, are less able to use it in communicative situations. In other words, the children appear to be delayed pragmatically even more than linguistically. In contrast, developmentally disabled (or retarded) children have been found to have communicative skills commensurate with cognitive or mental age levels (Greenwald & Leonard, 1979; Miller, Chapman, & Bedrosian, 1977).

Two studies have investigated comprehension skills when the communicative intent is expressed in direct vs. indirect ways. Shatz, Shulman, and Bernstein (1980) tested the responses of five language disordered children (5 and 6 years old) to a variety of directive forms presented in a neutral context. The youngsters tend to interpret indirect forms (e.g., "Can you fit the ball in the truck?") as requiring an action and not information. These authors conclude that the language disordered children are comparable to the less sophisticated normal 2-year-olds studied by Shatz (1978b), who also demonstrated a primarily action-based response style. Working with older children, Pearl, Donahue, and Bryan (1979) find that their learning disabled children in grades three through eight are as likely as normal ones to respond appropriately to both direct and indirect requests for more information from an adult experimenter.

Given the limitations of these studies (e.g., limited number of intentions, small samples, narrow age ranges), it is evident that little actually is known about the production and comprehension of communicative intentions in these children. Studies, both naturalistic and experimental, are critically needed to investigate the full range of communicative intentions and means used for encoding them in language disordered children.

*Presupposition*

As noted previously, the ability to establish a shared perspective between communicative partners and then to utilize it in the creation of appropriate messages is an essential part of successful communication. Success requires the speaker to assess the characteristics of the listener (age, status, cognitive level) and the context that needs to be considered—the skill referred to as role taking. Once shared information has been established, it then can be presupposed or assumed, leaving the partners free to comment on new information.

The ability of children with language and learning problems to demonstrate role-taking abilities and appropriate linguistic coding mechanisms has been investigated from several perspectives.

One way of looking at presupposition is to determine how children code information that is new or changing and therefore cannot be presupposed. Snyder (1978) says her language delayed subjects at the one-word stage, in contrast to the chronologically younger normal children, not only use their existing vocabularies less frequently for communicative purposes but also that their verbal efforts are less efficient in that they frequently do not convey the most informative element. However, their gestural performatives do signal the most informative element the majority of the time.

The notion of coding essential information also has been investigated in the referential communication studies of Noel (1980) and Spekman (1981), both of whom compare 9- to 11-year-old learning disabled and normal children. Noel's (1980) subjects were asked to describe novel/ambiguous figures so that listeners would select the correct one from among several choices. When listeners heard the descriptions, they reported more identification errors from learning disabled speakers. Spekman's (1981) subjects were told to describe a pattern of attribute blocks so that the listener could produce the same pattern; this necessitated the exchange of both attribute and spatial information. A pretest had established that all subjects had the necessary vocabulary for coding the information needed. The learning disabled children provided significantly less of the information needed for successful task completion.

Another aspect of presupposition, the ability of children to make certain linguistic changes as a function of listener characteristics, also has been investigated. Fey, Leonard, and Wilcox (1981) report that language impaired preschool children use simpler language when addressing younger children, thus demonstrating sensitivity to listener age and adjustments similar to those made by normal children speaking with less advanced partners.

Studies by Bryan and Pflaum (1978) and Donahue (1980) investigate the ability of learning disabled boys and girls to modify syntactic complexity and the degree of politeness and persuasiveness of messages according to attributes of the listener. Both studies suggest there are important sex differences within samples of learning disabled children, with only the boys being less sensitive to their audience than the normal children. However, no satisfactory explanation for this difference has been offered. Further, given the small number of subjects in some cells during data analysis (e.g., two black nondisabled females), the results should be considered merely suggestive, with additional work indicated.

Looking at the use of deictic terms, Spekman (1978) finds that both the learning disabled and normally achieving children demonstrate inconsistent usage of these terms within the communicative context, indicating some continuing difficulty in the consistent maintenance of another's perspective. Typical errors include total failure to establish a referent, ambiguous reference, too great a time lapse between deictic references to the same object, use of deictics requiring shared visual environments when the partners are separated by a barrier, and failure to anchor spatial deictics (e.g., "Put the block on the left," vs. "Put the block about two inches to the left of the big, thick yellow square"). Spatial deictics cause the most difficulty for both groups, but the learning disabled children (boys only in this study) have a significantly higher percentage of errors than their normal peers.

In summary, there appears to be some evidence that learning disabled children demonstrate some deficits in role-taking abilities and their understanding of social variables. Whether or not these findings can be replicated in more natural spontaneous interactions remains to be determined. Furthermore, study of a wider variety of indicators of the ability to use presupposition appropriately among a wider age range of learning disabled children is needed.

## Social Organization of Discourse

As was true for communicative intentions and presuppositions, research really is just beginning into the ability of language impaired or learning disabled children to participate appropriately as partners in interactions. Early work in this area characterizes interactions involving learning disabled children as containing more hostility and less cooperation than those involving only normal children (Bryan & Bryan, 1978; Bryan, Wheeler, Felcan, & Henek, 1976). However, these analyses typically involve only counting the types of statements (e.g., rejection, competition, consideration, information source) emitted by, and directed to, learning disabled children. They do not attempt to analyze the dyad itself, that is, the sequencing of statement types and the appropriateness or inappropriateness of certain statement types in light of situational context or preceding remarks.

More recent work has focused on the interactions and the responsibilities for maintaining and repairing conversations of learning disabled children in interactions. The data appear to indicate that the learning disabled are somewhat less successful in assuming role responsibility in both speaker and listener positions. Spekman (1981) suggests, for example, that these children perform like their normally achieving peers when primary responsibility for structuring the task rests with the nondisabled, whereas there are significant differences when the learning disabled are expected to provide the structure and control.

Donahue, Bryan, and Pearl (1980) and Bryan, Donahue, Pearl, and Sturm (1981) investigate the conversational control demonstrated by second- and fourth-grade learning disabled and nondisabled children in a dyadic experimental task in which one child is given the responsibility for controlling the conversation. When placed in the role of host of a "TV talk show," the learning disabled children are less skilled in initiating and maintaining the interaction and in maintaining the dominant speaker role. Bryan, Donahue, and Pearl (1981) also find differences in the manner in which the learning disabled participate in a small-group problem-solving task: they are less persuasive and are more submissive to their peers.

Other investigators focus more specifically on the listener or receiver of information within a dyad and the former's ability to provide feedback, ask questions, and so on. Spekman (1981) reports that they ask as many questions as their normal peers but are less likely to request new information essential for task success. Donahue, Pearl, and Bryan (1980) report that their learning disabled subjects are less likely to request clarification and thus initiate the repair of communicative breakdowns when presented with less than adequate messages. Watson (1977) also finds less assertiveness in conversations involving young language impaired children as listeners. The differences appear to result not from linguistic differences or deficiencies but from the failure of the learning disabled to understand the social obligations required of listeners in such circumstances.

As many of these authors have noted with respect to interactions involving language disordered or learning disabled children, considerable responsibility for structuring and maintaining the conversation and for repairing communicative breakdowns rests with the normal communication partner, whether adult or normal peer (Bryan, Donahue, Pearl, & Sturm, 1981; Guralnick & Paul-Brown, 1980; Spekman, 1981; Stoel-Gammon & Coggins, 1977).

The educational value of the normal partner structuring the conversation, however, is open to debate. Some suggest that the normals, by accommodating their interaction styles to listener levels, provide valuable models for language impaired children. Bricker (1978), for example, believes that integrated preschool programs and classrooms can create a more demanding environment for the impaired pupils. It also has been proposed that the helpful, accommodating models may in fact be too controlling and too constraining, thereby permitting these youngsters to remain more passive participants in social interactions (Bates, 1976).

Sadler (1982) investigates the abilities of young language impaired children to initiate and maintain conversations successfully when interacting with other similarly disabled youngsters vs. nonhandicapped peers. As she hypothesized, she finds that the language impaired subjects assume greater responsibility for sustaining a conversation when communicating with disabled peers but demonstrate greater overall communicative capabilities when interacting with more responsive normal companions. Fey, Leonard, and Wilcox (1981) report greater assertiveness in their language impaired subjects when interacting with younger children of similar language levels than with their chronological age peers.

Again, considerably more work is needed in this area, focused specifically on linguistic and pragmatic modifications used by language impaired children in different social situations with different listeners.

*Environmental Context*

Although minimal data are available regarding the ability of language impaired/learning disabled children to function in certain social situations, there is even less information on systematic control of physical constraints. Spekman's (1981) learning disabled-normal and normal-normal dyads communicate under three conditions that vary the channels available for communication and the feedback between the group members. While the disabled subjects in general perform less successfully than their normally achieving peers, the two groups respond similarly to condition changes. Both are least successful when there is no shared visual input and no interaction permitted between the interlocutors.

**Section 3. Processing and Pragmatic Disorders**

Competence in discourse or pragmatics involves mastery of a rule system that necessitates the integration of linguistic, social, and cognitive skills. Pragmatic disorders thus may result from difficulties in any one or more of these component skills or to problems with the complex integration of all of them. Communicative problems apparently cannot be attributed to linguistic or cognitive differences alone. The increased performance demands of many communicative tasks seem to interfere with the use of information and skills the learning disabled children have been shown to possess in more isolated and less demanding tasks.

Conversely, it also should be noted that the presence of certain linguistic disabilities may or may not affect communication success. For example, Spekman (1978) says three of her learning disabled subjects appear to have retrieval difficulties yet are able to convey their messages via descriptions and circumlocutions. Normal partners also help compensate for these children's difficulties. Johnson and Myklebust (1967) describe several children with language disorders who compensate through the use of elaborate gestural systems, sound effects, or the like. While accurate articulation and intact semantic and syntactic systems may facilitate communication by permitting more explicit verbal messages on a wider variety of topics, it is possible to communicate successfully even in the presence of certain linguistic or processing deficiencies.

Previous chapters have discussed the relationships between processing problems and phonological, semantic, and syntactic development. That information should be kept in mind in the following discussion on processing and pragmatic disorders since deficits in other domains of oral language may interfere with adequate communication. It also should be noted that cognitive and social skills are required for communication. A disturbance at any level of information processing in any of these areas, either verbal or nonverbal, may interfere with communicative competence.

*Attention*

Attention is considered prerequisite to all areas of learning. Without attention directed to what is critical, for an appropriate span of time, important information is lost and learning is affected detrimentally. With respect to communication, children must selectively attend not only to a full range of linguistic variables, such as the form and content of what is being said, but also to a wide range of paralinguistic factors (intonation and gesture) and extralinguistic factors (physical context and communicative partner). Since so much information is occurring simultaneously, it may be difficult for the learning disabled (especially those considered distractible, perseverative, and/or disinhibited) to select what is critically important in each area.

It should be obvious that attention to all of the key factors is essential at a subsequent stage for the meaningful associations that must be made between and among the factors. For example, children who fail to attend to the intonation of an utterance will necessarily miss the information carried by the intonation that, in many instances, serves to convey a variety of emotional states or even to contradict the verbal and other nonverbal aspects of a message.

*Perception*

Also vital is the potential effect of deficits in perception on communication development. The concern here involves both auditory and visual perception because of the diverse nature of the information to be processed. As indicated earlier, some learning disabled children demonstrate auditory discrimination problems that may affect their ability to master both receptive and expressive aspects of the phonological, syntactic, and semantic systems of the language.

Beyond the need for auditory verbal discrimination, however, communicative competence also requires discrimination among a variety of nonverbal auditory stimuli such as intonation, pitch, stress, volume, tempo, and pause. Accurate visual discrimination also is required to process the wide range of visual stimuli conveying information essential for successful communication. Important visual distinctions include facial expressions, gestures, body postures, and social distances between communication partners. The distinctions in each of these areas frequently are quite subtle.

If discrimination of features that signal changes in meaning is accepted as essential for the subsequent step of attaching individual meanings to stimuli, it should be evident that perceptual deficits in any of these areas may affect the comprehension of communications from others, as well as their production. For example, children who do not see the difference between a frown and a sad facial expression will have difficulty associating them with their appropriate meanings. These youngsters would fail to see the significance of facial expressions and therefore might not attend to them at all. Those who do not perceive the difference between intonation patterns may fail to recognize that "I like your dress" may be an assertion or a sarcastic comment.

*Memory*

Problems of both auditory and visual imagery and short-term memory can influence the development of communication abilities. Since so much linguistic, paralinguistic, and extralinguistic information must be stored simultaneously so that pragmatic rules can be generated and then generalized, learning disabled children with deficits in short-term memory span may experience difficulty in this area. Rule generalization also requires long-term memory in that individuals must be able to compare a current situation with past experiences in order to determine similarities and differences.

For example, a boy who is learning something about a sense of audience will need to be able to compare two situations in which he said, "Give me that!" One involves his younger sister, from whom he is able to get the toy he wants; the other involves his father, from whom he receives a lecture on "respect for elders." Without the ability to recall such experiences, this child might not be able to determine that what made the difference in listener response was the age and status of the communicative partner. Memory problems also may interfere with children's ability to monitor conversations continuously as well as to retain information regarding referents and other material that, once established, may be (incorrectly) presupposed by the speaker to be available to the listener.

*Symbolization*

Symbolization involves attaching meanings to the variety of verbal and nonverbal symbols used to represent experience. As noted in previous chapters, learning disabled children frequently experience difficulty comprehending single words and/or strings of varying degree of syntactic complexity; this may interfere with comprehension of discourse or with subsequent production of appropriate conversations and the like.

In addition to the population of learning disabled students with verbal problems, however, researchers and clinicians have identified a subgroup with apparent nonverbal symbolization problems (Bryan, 1977; Johnson & Myklebust, 1967; Minskoff, 1980a, 1980b; Wiig & Harris, 1974). Although frequently grouped under the rubric of social "perception" problems, these difficulties can extend beyond the level of perception. As discussed in the previous section, some learning disabled children have problems in discrimination of nonverbal information; others can perceive the differences but fail to attach meaning to those perceptions. They demonstrate deficits in the understanding and/or appropriate use of both auditory and visual nonverbal symbols such as intonation, facial expressions, gestures, body postures, and social distances.

Problems in any of these areas may well have wide-ranging implications for the success or failure of social interactions. A person who unwittingly invades another's personal space, fails to recognize anger in another's intonation and volume, or commits a variety of other social faux pas will experience difficulty in establishing appropriate interpersonal relations.

The role of context is extremely important in determining meaning. The meaning of symbols often can be determined only by reference to the context in which they occur, i.e., only by inferring the communicative intention of the speaker. Since the same utterance can convey many different intentions, depending on the manner of presentation and/or the context of use, and since any one intention can be conveyed through many different verbal and nonverbal messages, it seems logical to suggest that learning disabled children with problems at the symbolization level might experience difficulty in determining the correct interpretation of messages.

The task becomes further compounded when it is considered that, in many instances, the various components of a message actually may convey conflicting or incongruent information. In such cases, it is necessary to determine just which part of the message should be given more attention. Mehrabian (1972), for example, finds that when verbal and nonverbal messages are incongruent, most people tend to rely on the meaning conveyed nonverbally. The learning disabled with problems in nonverbal symbolization might not have that option available and would be forced to rely only on the verbal message.

However, it must be remembered that communication systems, both verbal and nonverbal, have a tremendous amount of built-in redundancy. In instances when all components of the communication convey the same message, therefore, it may be possible for learning disabled children to miss one or more of the components and still manage to understand the whole.

A factor that makes communication so difficult in one sense is the necessity of attending to such a wide variety of verbal, nonverbal, and contextual elements, all of which may carry a range of meanings and have implications for the comprehension and production of messages. The fact that phonological, semantic, and syntactic accuracy are not sufficient, and that communication requires pragmatic accuracy as well, may create some of the problems that have been identified clinically in so many learning disabled children.

*Conceptualization*

Conceptualization involves higher level thinking skills such as inference and generalization. Successful communication requires the ability to infer information from both verbal and nonverbal components of a message as well as to take the perspective of the listener and infer what is shared knowledge, listener status, and so on. Difficulty with inference may affect communication in the areas of communicative intentions, presuppositions, and social organization of discourse.

Many learning disabled children have been found to be literal and concrete in their comprehension of information and have difficulty going beyond what actually is presented (see Chapter 6). Others have difficulty taking the perspective of another person, again perhaps because it requires them to infer information and characteristics about the other from the available context, both verbal and nonverbal. Children who are unable to take the listener's perspective and infer emotional status (e.g., "He is probably angry because I was rude to him yesterday") thus might be bewildered by subsequent interchanges.

In addition, inference is a conceptual skill with importance beyond oral communication. Chapter 7 suggests that children with problems inferring information in conversations also will have difficulty comprehending and producing appropriate written messages.

Successful communicators also must have the ability to (1) generalize the rules governing the social use of language, (2) use these rules in the comprehension and generation of messages, and (3) generalize their application in new settings or with new partners. Clearly, problems with rule generalization and application can interfere with comprehension and expression of communicative intent and presuppositions. While not addressed extensively in the learning disability literature, this difficulty also could include factors discussed earlier involving the social organization of discourse; rules of turn-taking; how and when to initiate, maintain, and terminate interactions; and how to repair communicative breakdowns.

As in the other areas, any distortions of the information entering the system will interfere with rule generalization. Thus, problems with attention, perception, memory, and/or symbolization will affect the quality of the data base from which rules are generalized; a faulty data base will result in faulty rules. Rule formulation and generalization also may be affected by a disturbance in the process of conceptualization or rule generation itself. It therefore is possible to conceive of instances in which the data base is intact and appropriate but the individual is unable to note or categorize the similarities and differences, i.e., the patterns—an essential step in the process of formulating rules. Given that pragmatic rules are dependent upon other rule-based systems (linguistic, social), children with problems in this area may be affected seriously.

The study of the development of pragmatic rules in disordered populations, has received little attention, although there is evidence that normal children follow certain rules (informativeness, speech changes with partner changes) from very early ages. However, given the clinical evidence of communicative difficulties at least among some language disordered and learning disabled children, some of these problems may result from failure to detect patterns and therefore to intuitively formulate the appropriate rule.

Torgesen (1979) suggests that learning disabled children are inactive learners and typically do not engage in the use of efficient strategies. While most of Torgesen's work focuses on a subgroup of learning disabled children with memory problems, his basic tenet may be applicable when looking at those who do not appear to apply rules. The question that must be asked, however, is whether problems are caused by (1) a basic inability to formulate rules in any area or (2) a failure to utilize rules or strategies that appear to be known or at least within the individuals' cognitive reach.

Flavell's (1970) distinction between mediation deficiencies and production deficiencies (or inefficiencies) appears to be relevant to this question. Such a distinction might be evident in instances in which learning disabled children cannot be differentiated from their normal peers during normal spontaneous interactions but are significantly different in more structured experimental communication tasks and situations. One role of the diagnostician obviously is to investigate the factors that may indicate the nature of the difficulty.

*Metapragmatic Abilities*

As in most areas of functioning (linguistic, cognitive, or whatever), communicators engage in appropriate behavior based on their implicit knowledge of the rule systems governing that conduct. In many instances it may be necessary, or at least helpful, to bring that rule system to the level of conscious awareness. A speaker asked to address two different audiences on the same topic will be more successful if able to use existing knowledge of the groups (background, interest, experience) in preparing the talks. Similarly, individuals may find themselves consciously deciding what to talk about and how to phrase it, based on their knowledge of the listener's mood or health. For example, ''Sue is acting particularly depressed today; therefore, I'll try to talk only about positive, happy things.'' The ability to detect and repair communication breakdowns likewise requires the skill to analyze objectively what has just occurred.

Conscious awareness of pragmatic rules in the learning disabled population has not been studied. However, some data are emerging to indicate that many of these children and adolescents do not seem to follow certain pragmatic rules intuitively (e.g., Bryan & Pflaum, 1978; Donahue, 1980; Spekman, 1981). Since these individuals also seem to have difficulty in other areas of metafunctioning (Hook, 1976), it seems logical to hypothesize that many of them would not be able to demonstrate an understanding of why certain messages would be considered appropriate or inappropriate, why certain message forms may be considered more polite, and so on.

## PART II.  DIAGNOSIS

Diagnostic assessment of pragmatic and communicative skills necessitate changes in or additions to many clinical procedures. No formal, well-standardized procedures exist in this area. More research obviously is needed on both normal and disordered development before such procedures can be organized and refined. Thus, it must be kept in mind that the suggestions here are just that—suggestions—and must be considered experimental at best. The discussion focuses first on general guidelines for assessment as well as some problems and constraints; specific assessment activities then are presented.

### Section 1.  General Guidelines and Problems

For many years, language skills have been assessed in an isolated setting with specific focus on singular components of the linguistic system. In other words, children have been expected to demonstrate their abilities in other than typical situations; the language has been decontextualized. In order to assess their functional use of language, however, meaningful contexts are absolutely essential. The children must be placed in environments that are as typical as possible. Ideally, the assessment process also should include a variety of different contexts by varying the communication partner(s), the constraints of the physical setting, the topic or task, and so on. Finally, the skills evaluated should include the range and form of communicative intentions expressed, the ability to take the perspective of an audience and to change language appropriately, and the capacity to play a meaningful and appropriate role in an interaction situation as both speaker and listener. In other words, the objective is integration of linguistic, cognitive, and social skills.

The collection of data in meaningful and natural contexts can be accomplished in different ways, each with advantages and disadvantages. Observations of interactions in naturalistic, familiar settings in either home or school environments are thought to provide the most typical context. These observations might include child-child, mother-child, and teacher-child interactions during free-play sessions, storytime, snacktime, specific lessons, or the like. Interactions usually are videotaped for 10 to 30 minutes. However, as with more traditional language sampling techniques, the analysis of such data always is limited by what the children choose to produce. The mere absence of a particular communicative intent, or failure to initiate new topics, or the like cannot be construed as an indication that such a skill is not part of the children's repertoire.

Sampling problems are reduced somewhat by using standardized elicitation procedures. Snyder (1978) and Dale (1980), for example, use very natural play tasks to elicit utterances with declarative or imperative functions. Such natural standardized settings are more desirable than many experimental ones that place children in unfamiliar environments performing new or atypical activities.

For example, Bryan, Donahue, Pearl, and Sturm (1981) report a study in which learning disabled and normally achieving children were paired to participate in a simulated television talk show with one playing the role of host and the other of guest. While this is a very interesting methodological procedure, clinicians should consider that performance could easily be affected by the degree of familiarity with typical talk shows, the ability to assume an unfamiliar role, the awareness of being "on camera," or a variety of other factors. Experimental procedures therefore need to be evaluated before being used as clinical assessment techniques. The more atypical the situation, the less possible it is to generalize findings to other contexts.

An additional problem may be common to both naturalistic observations and contrived experimental procedures: the preservation of data. Under ideal conditions, videotapes that provide a permanent record of both auditory and visual data appear to be the method of choice (Bloom & Lahey, 1978; Ochs, 1979). The permanent record permits multiple observations that are essential for the analyses that require simultaneous attention to linguistic, paralinguistic, and contextual factors, as well as to the different levels of functional analysis. However, videotaping is expensive and the transcription and coding processes may be extremely time consuming, thereby preventing its use in many clinical and school settings.

Another problem is the selection of the best or most appropriate coding system. While numerous taxonomies exist, selection decisions are hampered because the systems typically have been used with only small numbers of children and because support for reliability and validity is either nonexistent or minimal (Chapman, 1981; Dale, 1980).

Finally, and perhaps most importantly, it must be remembered that pragmatic analyses are analyses of intentions that, of necessity, must be inferred from the available data. While support for such inferences may come from a variety of sources other than just the language (e.g., intonation, stress, gestures, objects in the environment, the effect of an utterance on the listener), clinicians cannot be assured that their interpretation is in fact the same as the speaker's intent. Although this problem may be resolved somewhat by the use of several scorers, ultimately some amount of uncertainty will remain.

## Section 2. Activities and Coding Systems

In terms of general activities and settings that may be used to collect data, one of the most popular strategies is to videotape interaction sequences involving children and their mothers, same age or different age peers, teachers, or others in familiar environs. These observations may be conducted during free-play and other such relatively unstructured activities or in a variety of more structured situations such as specific games, tutoring, or referential communication tasks. The teacher/clinician must remember, however, that the nature of interactions may be a function of familiarity with the communicative partner, context, topic, and the like and that performances under one set of circumstances cannot necessarily be generalized to others.

It thus is important for a thorough assessment to observe the children in a variety of situations with a variety of partners and topics. Wiig and Semel (1976) find that learning disabled children may function adequately in familiar conversational settings with peers or parents but do less well under the stress of communicating with less familiar authority figures. At a minimum, diagnostic assessment of communicative competence should include interactions in these two settings. A further possibility is that some learning disabled children may manage to communicate adequately with one partner but have difficulty functioning in a group because of the added demands of relating in different ways to different people. Thus, a third useful setting may be to observe the children participating in a group project.

Once the data are collected, it is important to be clear about the kinds of pragmatic information to be assessed. As mentioned at the outset, a complete taxonomy of pragmatic skills has yet to be determined but a random selection of isolated pragmatic abilities obviously is not desirable. Use of an overall framework such as the one suggested in the first part of this chapter is therefore recommended. This section is divided into the four aspects of communicative skill that consider increasingly broader aspects of communication: communicative intentions, presupposition, social organization of discourse, and environmental context. Clinicians may want to screen skills in all four areas, then focus more specifically on those that appear to be most affected. In each area, activities that might elicit some of the specific behaviors of interest are considered. It should be stressed that the interaction sequences should be designed to yield data relevant to each skill area.

### Communicative Intentions

Numerous systems are available that permit analysis of the range of communicative intentions expressed. However, the systems are somewhat limited with respect to the developmental level to which they apply. Dore (1975, 1978), for example, recommends different systems for children at the one-word level vs. those beyond that point. There also are significant differences in terms of the intentions assessed among systems that claim to be appropriate at the same level. Finally, each of these systems should be considered only as a guideline in that there are not yet sufficient data to chart developmental sequences and the chronological or mental ages at which each skill should be accomplished.

There is widespread agreement that normal infants evidence communicative intent as early as stages IV and V of Piaget's sensorimotor stage of development. These intentions are expressed initially through nonverbal means that later are paired with early vocalizations. Initial verbal attempts to express various intentions may be accompanied by gestures but eventually verbal utterances are used alone.

Dunst (1978) has selected items from several developmental scales (e.g., Bayley, 1969; Uzgiris & Hunt, 1975) and organized them according to the model proposed by Bates et al. (1975) for perlocutionary, illocutionary, and locutionary acts of infancy. Among the nonverbal illocutionary behaviors noted are that the child: extends arms to be picked up, reacts negatively to having a toy taken away, waves bye-bye, shows objects to others to instigate interaction, points to call adult's attention, and pulls person to situation or new location. However, Dunst does not provide a taxonomy for organizing these behaviors according to the nature of the intent expressed.

Coggins and Carpenter (1981) have developed the *Communicative Intention Inventory* (CII), an observational scoring system for evaluating key early intentional communications. The CII is a criterion-referenced measure that focuses on the following eight types of communicative intentions selected from the work of Bates (1976a), Dore (1975), Greenfield and Smith (1976), and Halliday (1975): (1) comment on actions, (2) comment on objects, (3) request for action, (4) request of object, (5) request for information, (6) answering, (7) acknowledging, and (8) protesting. Once a message has been coded for type of intent, its form is analyzed as to whether it is gestural (e.g., pointing, gazing, touching), gestural-vocal (i.e., nonverbal actions plus nonverbal vocalizations), or verbal (i.e., lexical items).

Coggins and Carpenter are to be commended in that they provide at least some beginning statistical information to support the use of the CII. For example, they present standard errors of measurement for each category as well as high interrater reliability (.91). They also report similar patterns of usage among 16 children, ages 15 to 16 months, at the one-word stage of language development. However, the CII's appropriateness with those at other age levels, or its ability to differentiate between normal and communicatively impaired children, has not been demonstrated.

More coding systems are available that focus exclusively on communicative intentions expressed verbally. These measures investigate types of intentions but do not look specifically at the form. Dore (1975) defines the following behaviors, identified as primitive speech acts, that he finds used by children at the one-word stage of language development: labeling, repeating, answering, requesting action, requesting answer, calling, greeting, protesting, and practicing. Dore (1977, 1978) presents a more elaborate and highly defined system for use with preschool children. His major categories include the following:

- requests for information, action, or acknowledgment
- responses to requests
- descriptions of verifiable past and present facts
- statements of facts, rules, attitudes, feelings, and beliefs
- acknowledgments that recognize and evaluate responses and nonrequests
- organization devices that regulate contact and conversation
- performatives that accomplish facts by being said
- miscellaneous

It should be noted that these categories do not all represent the same area of pragmatic or discourse analysis. Chapman (1981) expresses concern that many coding systems mix levels of pragmatic analysis, thereby creating considerable confusion. For example, the first four categories in Dore's list appear to be related most closely to communicative intention while the sixth has more to do with social organization and the role of an utterance within discourse; the fifth could fall under either level. It is possible, therefore, that the same utterance could (and should) be coded under more than one category.

An additional problem is noted in examining Dore's (1978) subdivisions within each major category. To illustrate, in the first category, requests, an utterance is coded as either yes/no question, wh-question, clarification question, action request, permission request, or rhetorical question. Some confusion is generated by classifying some utterances according to syntactic structure (e.g., wh-question) and others according to the nature of what is being requested (e.g., permission).

Halliday's (1975) longitudinal study of his son Nigel results in several category systems of language functions that changed over time with the boy's development. Early uses of vocalizations and language, found between approximately 9 and 18 months, are classified as follows:

1. Instrumental: "I want" function—the expression of wants and desires
2. Regulatory: "Do as I tell you" function—the regulation of behavior of others
3. Interactional: "Me and you" function—the establishing of interactions with other people
4. Personal: "Here I come" function—the expression of personal feelings and attitudes

5. Heuristic: "Tell me why" function—the gaining of information and investigation of the world
6. Imaginative: "Let's pretend" function—the creation of an imaginary environment
7. Informative: "I've got something to tell you" function—the communication of new information about something.

The two functions identified by Halliday during the period from approximately 16 to 35 months—pragmatic and mathetic—represent a collapsing of earlier language functions. The pragmatic function, or the use of language to act on reality, combines the earlier instrumental, regulatory, and interactional functions. By contrast, the mathetic (pertaining to learning) function, which represents the child's use of language to comment on or to learn about reality, combines the interactional, personal, and heuristic functions.

Nigel entered a third or "adult" phase at about 36 months. The three functions Halliday identifies at this stage—ideational, interpersonal, and textual—actually incorporate the different levels of pragmatic analysis discussed earlier and indicate his sensitivity to the fact that any utterance may serve a variety of different functions within a unit of discourse. Each utterance may serve purposes relating to the expression of meaning (ideational), interaction with another person (interpersonal), and the forms of preceding and following utterances (textual).

The taxonomy of intentions thus varies from instrument to instrument, and experts do not agree as to the range of intentions that actually are expressed. Halliday's point that the intentions expressed by children change developmentally seems an important one to keep in mind.

Since none of these systems has been used extensively beyond the work of its author(s), their reliability and validity remain to be demonstrated empirically. As part of that process, it is necessary to examine their use with larger samples of normally developing children, their appropriateness in clinical and school settings, their ability to differentiate among children developing normally and those experiencing delays or disorders, and their ability to provide useful guidelines for instruction.

While these coding systems are intended primarily to be applied to natural, spontaneous language samples, it frequently may be necessary to design tasks or to structure the environment so as to elicit the particular communicative intent(s) of interest. A variety of experimental procedures are suggested in the literature and may be appropriate for use with preverbal and/or verbal children. For example:

• Requests for objects have been elicited by exposing children to enticing objects (Read & Cherry, 1978; Spekman & Roth, 1981; Sugarman, 1973).
• Requests for actions have been developed by giving children objects packaged in a manner that required assistance (Dale, 1980).

- Comments/declaratives have been obtained by engaging the children in a repetitive behavior (such as putting a block into a pail), and eventually introducing a new toy (Dale, 1980; Snyder, 1978).

Creative and imaginative clinicians will be able to develop a variety of similar activities in which use of a particular intention may be considered obligatory. Regardless of the system of choice, clinicians need to be sensitive to both the intention expressed and the manner or form(s) in which it is conveyed. They also should give attention to the effect of a particular utterance on the child's communicative partner, i.e., does it successfully accomplish the speaker's intent.

Thus far, all of the discussion has related to the production, rather than comprehension, of communicative intentions. This author was unable to locate any scale that specifically addresses understanding of the various intentions. The available empirical investigations of comprehension may provide some suggestions for assessment. Intentions that expect some kind of overt response from the children (e.g., requests for actions, requests for information) have received the most attention. Garvey (1975), Shatz (1978a, 1978b), and others have observed responses to direct and indirect requests from parents or peers in natural interaction situations. In such settings, however, clinicians must be aware that children's comprehension may be a function of both the linguistic request and a variety of contextual cues that can influence comprehension.

Carrell (1981) and Spekman and Roth (1981) focus on comprehension of the linguistic form of the directive by setting up familiar activities in which the children are expected to comply with the different types of directives. It must be noted, however, that not all instances of noncompliance can be interpreted as instances of misunderstanding. Garvey (1975), Spekman and Roth (1981), and others provide numerous examples of noncompliance that could be attributed to such factors as the children's interest in doing something else or their feeling that the request is unreasonable.

Others who have measured comprehension have required the children to make judgments regarding the appropriateness of someone else's response (Leonard, Wilcox, Fulmer, & Davis, 1978) or actually to produce different linguistic forms (Bock & Hornsby, 1981). Clearly, the metalinguistic level and difficulty of the response required may seriously confound the interpretation of children's behavior.

As is true in all areas of assessment, users of these systems or instruments are cautioned to examine the content of each carefully and not rely solely on its title. A case in point is the *Infant Scale of Communicative Intent* (Sacks & Young, 1980), purportedly designed to measure both receptive and expressive aspects of communicative intent. However, half of the items are appropriate for children from birth to 9 months, a time during which communicative intent usually is not thought to be present (Bates et al., 1975; Escalona, 1973; Sugarman, 1973). The remaining items, from 9 to 18 months, measure a wide range of linguistic, nonverbal, and communicative behaviors. For example, one at the 13- to 14-month level asks whether the child uses words of more than one syllable; another, from the 17- to 18-month level, asks whether the child has a vocabulary of 7 to 20 words. There would appear to be little relationship between items such as these and the notions of communication and communicative intent as defined in this chapter.

Another title, the *Clinical Evaluation of Language Functions* (CELF) (Semel & Wiig, 1980), may lead clinicians to expect an evaluation of the various functions (i.e., intentions) that language could accomplish. Analysis of the various subtests and a review of the manual, however, indicate that that is not its purpose and that the CELF actually is a test of semantics, linguistic structure, and memory rather than of communication and language functions per se.

Informally, in assessing communication intent, clinicians need some idea of (1) the types of intentions comprehended and expressed, (2) the linguistic forms involved (ranging from direct to indirect), (3) the nonverbal and paralinguistic means of communicating intent, and (4) the social conventions that govern interpretation and selection of particular nonverbal and linguistic forms of intention. The first part of this chapter provides a more detailed breakdown of the content of each area.

If children appear to have difficulty, a thorough assessment of each of these four areas of communicative intent must include analysis of attention, perception, and memory as well as linguistic (semantic and syntactic) and conceptual skills (inference and rule generalization) as they interact with comprehension and formulation of appropriate intent.

## *Presupposition*

Procedures in this area should focus on the ability of children to adopt the perspective of their communicative partners. The role-taking skills necessary for communicative success typically must be inferred from the linguistic, paralinguistic, and extralinguistic modifications that children make when communicating with different partners, for different purposes, and in different social situations.

Observation of typical spontaneous interactions provides one means for gathering such data. While no formalized coding systems are available that look at a variety of different aspects of role taking, clinicians informally should be sensitive to some of the following concerns:

**Informativeness:** What do children choose to talk about in a given situation? Do they encode what is novel or new or merely comment on what already is given or old? Do they code new information gesturally and/or linguistically? Situations in which new toys are introduced or activities or topics are changed provide excellent opportunities for observing their tendency to comment on novel elements. In older children, evaluations of a variety of descriptions can provide data on the degree of informativeness of their messages.

**Communication Partner Variables:** Do children talk or communicate differently to different communication partners? There is a wide variety of partner (audience) variables to which clinicians need to be sensitive: age, status, level of familiarity, cognitive level, linguistic level, and shared past experiences. Modifications indicative of children's sensitivity to these variables include the degree of politeness, the degree of intimacy, the linguistic form used to code a particular intent (e.g., a hint vs. a direct imperative), and the nature of the information that is presupposed vs. that commented upon explicitly. To illustrate the latter point, depending on whether a partner knew the speaker had gone to the zoo on the preceding day, the latter might say, "That sure was fun yesterday" rather than "The zoo sure was fun yesterday." Observations obviously must be conducted in situations allowing for interaction with different partners.

**Communication Purposes or Intentions:** Clinicians must go beyond evaluation of the variety of purposes for communicating (e.g., to share information, to seek information, to direct the behavior of another, to persuade) and examine whether children use different communication strategies according to the needs of their partner. To illustrate, one child's strategies for persuading another may be indicative of perspective taking, in that at young ages a child may argue egocentrically ("I want it") as compared to the more advanced strategies such as specifying the benefit to the partner ("If you let me have the ball, I'll let you borrow my mitt").

**Social Situation Variables:** Do children make modifications that reflect sensitivity to changes in communication situations or contexts? For example, while gestural and verbal means of communication may be appropriate in face-to-face conversations, are the children's verbal skills alone adequate in situations not permitting shared visual input? Do children talk differently about objects or events present in the environment as compared to those not present? Do they appear to recognize that rules governing behavior may change in different social environments such as home, playground, and classroom? Mehan (1976, 1979), for example, suggests that classrooms have unique systems of rules, frequently not stated explicitly, that govern many different aspects of behavior.

When evaluating these areas, clinicians/educators need to describe what the children talk about—their communicative intentions—in conjunction with a complete description of the communication environment. Specific analyses of linguistic devices that potentially provide information regarding presupposition and role taking should include instances of direct and indirect reference, of other forms of cohesion, and of deixis. Thus, it is important to look at the way in which referents are introduced as topics and then referred to later.

As discussed earlier, initial references to a topic of conversation typically involve indirect forms of reference (a girl); once introduced, the topic can be assumed to be shared by the interlocutors, and may then be referred to in a specific, direct fashion (the girl, she). It is not uncommon to hear conversations begin, "I didn't like *the* show . . . ," which is responded to immediately with, "What show?"

Referents may be established either exophorically (external to the discourse) or endophorically (within the discourse). An analysis of deictic terms and gestures may provide information primarily about the former. For example, Fillmore's (1975) framework allows for analysis of person/thing, spatial, and time deictics used either gesturally (referent must be present) or symbolically. The child who says "Put *this there*" (examples of a thing and a spatial deictic both being used gesturally) when the partner is behind an opaque barrier obviously is not establishing the referent clearly.

Halliday and Hasan (1976), in contrast, provide a system for evaluating relations, i.e., cohesive relations, that exist entirely in the text or discourse. The following types of cohesive relations may be present:

1. Reference: The boy went to the store. *He* bought some milk *there*.
2. Substitution: Do you have a red sweater? No, but I have a blue *one*.
3. Ellipsis: Are you going to the store? No, I'm not (going to the store).
4. Conjunction: It was snowing very hard. *Therefore,* classes were cancelled.

These cohesive relations link the various parts of any discourse. The clinician/educator needs to be sensitive to children's ability to understand and use these devices to establish such connections. It is not unusual to observe conversations involving children in which consecutive utterances (either two from the same child or consecutive ones from the partners) have no apparent relationship to each other.

A final point of analysis might relate to the distance between specific mention of the referent and later ties to it. While there is no rule, it would appear that the greater the distance, the more difficult it will be for the speaker to identify the referent. Garvey and Geraud (1980) find that 3- and 5-year olds are sensitive to distance; however, Spekman (1978) reports many fourth and fifth graders making confusing ties to referents first mentioned as many as 19 turns earlier.

While naturalistic observations provide an important component of the assessment process, it may be necessary or desirable to structure these analyses to allow more specific focus on certain variables of interest or to elicit behaviors not discerned in more natural contexts. A wide variety of structured dyadic activities is possible, including tutoring activities (teaching someone a game, how to play with a toy, or how to complete a puzzle) and referential communication tasks.

Referential communication tasks that have been used experimentally have one child (speaker) responsible for describing something (pictures, nonverbal designs, patterns of geometric shapes, map) in such a fashion that the partner (listener) can either select the object described or construct the pattern. The interlocutors typically are separated by an opaque barrier.

Such activities are useful in assessing role-taking ability and can be manipulated in countless ways so as to vary the partner, the type and amount of feedback available, the amount of interaction permitted, the purpose of the task, the nature of the materials communicated about, and so on.

Asking children to describe a movie, retell a story, or describe how to do something should provide additional units of extended discourse that can be analyzed for introduction of referents, as well as offer instances of cohesion and deixis.

### Social Organization of Discourse

An important aspect of an assessment of pragmatic skills involves children's ability to function in, and contribute to, the stream of discourse or conversation. Of necessity, this must involve their performing in both the speaker and listener roles and their ability to assume the responsibilities of each. Several researchers have addressed variables that should be evaluated (Blank & Franklin, 1980; Garvey, 1975, 1977; Sadler, 1982) but no one system of analysis is available that this author feels addresses all of the essential components. Therefore, the following list of variables is a composite and may serve to guide observations of clinicians/educators:

**Socialized vs. Nonsocialized Speech:** Sadler (1982) develops a coding system for looking at the social/nonsocial nature of speech that includes ideas taken from Garvey and Berninger (1981) and Keenan (1974). Sadler differentiates among four types of speech:

1. Speech not addressed to the partner, such as monologues, songs, rhymes, individual sound play, and narratives. Since not explicitly addressed to a listener, the partner is not obligated to respond.
2. Social speech addressed to a listener that thus imposes some sort of obligation on that individual. This includes comments, questions, directives, and so on. Such speech typically is clearly produced, adapted to the listener, and repaired quickly in instances of breakdown.
3. Ambiguously addressed speech in which the social/nonsocial distinction is difficult to make. Sadler describes such utterances as having a monologue quality yet being clearly produced and seemingly uttered at least partially for the listener's benefit. However, the speaker does not appear to expect a response and does not attempt a repair when a reply is not received.
4. Ritual verbal play in which there is turn alternation between partners and the speech of each partner is related. However, the content and form do not vary greatly within the exchanges as they would in a typical conversation.

The following, taken from Garvey and Berninger (1981), is illustrative of this final type of speech:

| *B.* | *K.* |
|---|---|
| 'Bye, Laddie. | |
| | 'Bye, Laddie. |
| Hi, Laddie. | |
| | Hi, Laddie. |
| Hi, 'bye, Laddie. | |
| | 'Bye, Laddie. |
| Hi, Laddie. | |
| | Hi, 'bye, Laddie. |

Attempts to quantify such measures may involve determining the proportion of total utterances falling into each category. At this point, it is not possible to specify the proportional use of each type of speech that would be considered normal or typical. It can be predicted that all types occur naturally and normally but that their use is determined, at least in part, by a child's age and other personal variables, as well as the communicative context (audience and physical environment) in which interactions occur.

**Turn-Taking and Talking Time:** Measures of the number of times each person talks and of the proportion of total time during which each child holds the verbal floor may provide some indication of whether a conversation is dominated by one of the participants or whether it can be characterized as more egalitarian in nature. Garvey and Berninger (1981) suggest that a pause of greater than one second signals the speaker's intent to transfer the speaking floor.

**Topic Initiation:** The interest here is in determining whether a child initiates conversational topics, the strategies used to initiate, and the outcome (success or failure) of initial attempts. Mueller (1972) identifies several variables thought to be related to the success or failure of a message: articulation clarity, grammatical completeness and form, social adaptation, use of attention-getting devices (e.g., "Hey," "Susan, . . . "), the degree to which content is relevant to continuing activities and listener interests, eye contact, and physical proximity. While some variables are better overall predictors of success or failure in receiving a reply, they all contribute to the outcome.

**Topic Maintenance:** What happens after a topic has been initiated? Does the child fail to respond, answer with an unrelated or noncontingent reply, or make a contingent response that is related in some fashion to the preceding utterance. Bloom et al. (1976) and Sadler (1982) suggest that contingent utterances may be examined further by differentiating between those that merely maintain the conversation (specific response to a question) and those that both maintain the topic and add new information. Sadler (1982, p. 61) provides the following examples:

1. *Maintains topic*

| *Mother* | *Child* |
|---|---|
| Now that's a beautiful one you have there. I think I like that better than mine. Can we trade? | |
| | No. |
| Well, who are you going to give it to? | |
| | My daddy. |

2. *Maintains topic and adds new information*

| | |
|---|---|
| Would you like to play with some dough while Mommy is cooking dinner? | |
| | Yes. I'll make some dough. |
| You can make some biscuits with your dough. | |
| | Can I eat some? |
| It'll make you sick if you eat it like that. We'll cook it when you're ready. | |
| | All right. I'll make five biscuits. |

(p. 47)

Contingent responses of the first type, while maintaining the topic of conversation, may do so only minimally, with the conversational responsibility returning very quickly to the other partner. Simultaneous speech in the form of "yeah," "uh-huh," and "okay," while someone else is talking, also keeps the conversation going but without transferring the conversational floor.

Topics may be maintained with responses other than simply answering questions or adding new information. Listeners also can ask questions of their own. A particular type of response, the contingent query, consists of a listener's unsolicited questions to indicate confusion or the need for previous messages to be elaborated, clarified, or repeated (Garvey, 1977). Examples include "Huh?" "What do you mean?" or "What color did you say?"

Thus, contingent queries play a crucial role in maintaining conversations by explicitly noting instances of potential communicative failure that may then be repaired. An examination of children's use of contingent queries may provide considerable information beyond their mastery of interrogative forms. It can provide insights with respect to their monitoring of the conversation, their sensitivity to ambiguous or confusing messages, the strategies available for signaling confusion, and the explicitness with which the request for clarification is made (e.g., "huh?" vs. "What time did you say you'd be home?").

**On-Topic Exchanges:** One unit of analysis is referred to by various names but numerous studies of dyadic interactions recommend that it be defined as a conversational sequence (typically involving an exchange of turns) on a shared topic (see, for example, Garvey & Baldwin, 1970; Sadler, 1982; Spekman, 1978). Once such units have been identified, it is interesting to determine the number of exchanges over which a topic may be maintained as well as to evaluate the roles played by the various utterances within this unit and the skills demonstrated by the children in both speaker and listener roles.

If learning disabled children have difficulty staying on topic, an analysis of off-topic remarks may indicate some pattern of error and suggest a possible processing disorder. For example, some of these children may consistently produce remarks that are only tangentially related to the partner's topic, indicating possible problems in language comprehension. Others may produce comments without regard for the topic under discussion or, conversely, may have difficulty switching to a new topic. Such behavior may indicate attentional problems of distractibility or perseveration. Of course, each hypothesis will need to be substantiated with additional evidence.

**Topic Termination:** While this author is unaware of any coding system that specifically addresses termination strategies, this would appear to be an area of potential interest. Everyone is aware of the frustration felt when a conversational partner changes the subject before closure has been reached on a particular topic. An analysis thus might involve looking at when and how topics are concluded.

**Conversational Repairs:** There are many points of communication breakdown, and thus of potential failure, within conversations. Communication breakdowns necessitate repair. Evaluations should be sensitive to which partner notes the breakdown, which one attempts to repair it, and the specific repair strategies utilized. A speaker may repair the breakdown spontaneously or may do so only following the listener's indication of the lapse through the use of contingent queries and other forms of feedback (e.g., perplexed facial expression, shrugged shoulders). The degree of specificity of the listener's feedback may influence the speaker's ability to provide the information needed.

Examples of repair strategies (adapted from Clark & Andersen, 1979; Garvey, 1977; Keenan & Schieffelin, 1976; and others) include phonological (e.g., increased articulatory precision), lexical (modification or change of word(s) used), morphological (modification of grammatical morphemes), syntactic (modification or change in syntactic structure), content (repetition, confirmation, specification, elaboration), and paralinguistic repairs (volume changes, contrastive stress, and pitch changes).

The success of any of these strategies in actually repairing breakdowns also must be considered. Some learning disabled children may have difficulty selecting appropriate strategies. For example, if they have made a lexical error, simply repeating the same message more loudly and with contrasting stress will not repair the breakdown. Correct interpretation of the contingent query also may be important for some of the learning disabled. Nonspecific contingent queries such as "Huh?" "What?" "What did you say?" What do you mean?" may not provide these children with enough information to determine where the error occurred, whereas normal children may need only a simple "What?" to recognize the source of the problem.

Blank and Franklin (1980) suggest it also is important to look at the conceptual complexity of utterances and the role that that might play in dialogues. In other words, if the conceptual demands of the language used are beyond the children's comprehension level, communication breakdown can be expected. Blank and Franklin utilize a system of analyzing utterances at four levels of abstraction that represent a continuum of increasing distance between immediate perceptions and the language used to deal with the material:

Level I (matching experience) utterances include those that identify and label objects, actions, and events in the environment, request objects or attention, imitate, or employ social routines.

Level II (selective analysis of experience) utterances indicate focus on selective aspects of experiences and include those that identify specific attributes of experiences (color, shape), note possession, location, or function, and compare experiences.

Level III (reordering experience) utterances restructure or reorder perceptions such as those that sequence things, define, establish conditional relationships and generalizations, and so on.

Level IV (reasoning about experience) is the most abstract level and is composed of utterances involving problem solutions, justification, identification of causes, prediction, and explanation of inferences.

Blank and Franklin (1980) suggest that it is important to look at the quality of children's response to messages with respect to the preceding utterance. They recommend a five-level scale: (1) adequate and appropriate, (2) inadequate, (3) no response, (4) request for clarification, and (5) ambiguous.

Blank and Franklin (1980) have used these scales to analyze the interactions of mother-child dyads in naturalistic settings. However, the same framework was also used in the development of a test, the *Preschool Language Assessment Instrument* (PLAI) (Blank, Rose, & Berlin, 1978a, 1978b). Its authors note that the four levels of complexity just defined tend to typify the language of instruction used by preschool teachers. Thus, the PLAI was developed for use with children 3 to 6 years old to (1) identify the appropriate language level for instruction, and (2) identify those considered at risk for school success.

The test is composed of 60 items, i.e., 15 questions or tasks at each level that are distributed throughout the instrument. Its authors contend that all levels may be used in any one classroom activity and therefore it is important to look at the children's ability to shift flexibly with these changes in task level. While normative data are not available, the authors do present some preliminary evidence to support the test's reliability and validity. By looking at interactions in a specific context, the PLAI appears to represent an important shift in testing that coincides with the emerging concern for discourse and the functions of language.

## Environmental Context

Each of the preceding sections has stressed that in order to obtain a representative sample of children's communicative behaviors, they must be given opportunities to communicate with different audiences and in different environments. Clinicians thus will want to manipulate the environment in a somewhat controlled or regular fashion and remain sensitive to the effects of such actions on both the form and the content of communication. Environmental or contextual factors that may be manipulated include: (1) objects present in the environment, (2) the nature of continuing activities, (3) the modality channels available for communication, and (4) the availability of feedback.

## Summary

It is premature to recommend any one technique or assessment procedure at this time. Diagnosis of problems in this area still is very much in the experimental stages particularly because knowledge of normal developmental sequences is far from complete. Decisions regarding procedure(s) for collecting and analyzing data must be based on a combination of the nature of the information of interest, the children's developmental level, and the communicative means available to them. Quite obviously, the quality of assessment will depend very much on the theoretical framework and clinical skills of the evaluator.

It is necessary to stress that evaluation of these skills will serve as only one level of analysis in the assessment process. Concerns raised about the functioning of learning disabled children in one or more areas must be followed by a series of probes that attempt to identify processing difficulties that may be contributing to the communicative problems observed.

For example, a boy who is observed to have problems interacting with peers (e.g., orders peers around, doesn't stop teasing when peers get upset) might be given a series of subtasks to evaluate:

- the child's linguistic skills (e.g., does he understand directives in other than direct imperative form?)
- the child's nonverbal skills (e.g., does the boy understand that a peer's crying indicates distress)
- the child's cognitive skills (e.g., can he select what is critical in a given situation and then formulate rules integrating linguistic, cognitive, and social skills?).

The goal of assessment must be to relate pragmatics to the other language skills addressed in previous chapters, to nonverbal and social areas of functioning, and to the different levels of information processing so as to determine patterns of strengths and weaknesses. For example, for a child who has difficulty interacting with peers, a thorough assessment may reveal:

- that the child has difficulty interacting primarily with peers in large groups
- that the problem appears to be primarily expressive, involving presupposition, and more specifically addressing the informational needs of the listener, especially of many listeners, at one time
- that a processing deficit at the level of conceptualization (inference) appears to be contributing to the problem
- that other pragmatic skills appear to be intact.

It also might be predicted that problems with inference could interfere with reading comprehension and that such a child undoubtedly would have considerable difficulty producing written communications. In any case, once the nature of the problem has been determined, then a reasonable plan for remediation can be established.

## PART III. REMEDIATION

### Section 1. Goals of Remediation

Bloom and Lahey (1978) declare that:

> Learning language is a process of inducing relationships among regularities the child has perceived in: the nonlinguistic world (the concepts that are the content of language); the linguistic signal (the arbitrary units that are the conventional forms of a language); and social interactions (the contexts that affect the use of language as a means of communication). (p. 571)

Most children induce the necessary relationships and regularities between and among the various components quite naturally and spontaneously. However, in instances of language and communication disorders, such regularities may remain undetected (for a variety of reasons) and therefore unavailable for use. The goal of remediation then should be to facilitate such learning, stressing the integration of skills, in order to enable the children to utilize their linguistic and nonlinguistic skills effectively for a variety of purposes, including communication.

Until the late 1970s, most language training programs and intervention approaches focused on the first two components discussed by Bloom and Lahey. These approaches have stressed learning isolated aspects of language structure or content. Instruction has been provided in isolated, frequently atypical or stilted contexts, with considerable emphasis on imitation and reinforcement. Although such emphasis may be necessary in some cases and isolated training does improve some aspects of specific language skills, such an approach is perhaps shortsighted and frequently results in rote abilities or splinter skills and the absence of rule induction.

A case in point is the young language disordered child described by Geller and Wollner (1976) who was able to correctly formulate interrogative forms but who did not appear to understand their purpose and thus did not know how and when to use them correctly to gain information. Thus, what has been overwhelmingly neglected is instruction in how to use language appropriately in different situations to achieve different purposes. It is not sufficient for children to know how to say something; they also must know what to say and when to say it.

While the overall goal should be to facilitate the acquisition of rules governing the uses of language in social contexts, specific remedial objectives in each area might include (but certainly not be limited to) the following:

1. Communicative intentions
   a. To increase the use of language for communicative or social purposes
   b. To increase the number of purposes or intentions for which language is used (e.g., requesting information, directing the behavior of others, participating in social rituals or routines)
   c. To increase the number of ways or forms in which a communicative intention may be expressed (e.g., gestural; single words; declarative, imperative, or interrogative; intonation and stress)
2. Presupposition
   a. To increase the number of utterances that code what is maximally informative
   b. To increase the use of utterances that reflect the sensitivity to different audiences and their unique needs (e.g., appropriate establishment of referents; changes in politeness; varied use of specific forms with audience changes; syntactic simplification with younger audiences)

3. Social organization of discourse
   a. To increase the number of utterances that follow those of others when a response is explicitly expected as well as when a response may be optional
   b. To increase the use of utterances that are linguistically contingent on those of others
   c. To increase the use of utterances that not only are contingent but also add information
   d. To increase the number of turns over which a topic is maintained
   e. To increase the use of utterances that successfully initiate conversations
   f. To increase the use of feedback strategies (e.g., contingent queries, head nods)
   g. To increase the use of a variety of repair strategies in instances of communicative breakdown
4. Environmental context
   a. To increase the use of appropriate communication skills in a variety of social situations
   b. To demonstrate appropriate communicative modifications that reflect sensitivity to changes in the channels available for communication and the availability of feedback.

While all of these goals relate specifically to expressive abilities, comparable objectives may be written for receptive skills. For example, to increase the number of correct responses to different forms that all express the same communicative intent (passing the salt when someone says "May I have the salt" or "The stew is very bland").

**Section 2.  Formal Programs**

No programs are available that either address all of the necessary components of pragmatic development or are specific enough to serve as curriculum guides. Bloom and Lahey (1978), Lucas (1980), and Simon (1979) do at least provide some suggestions and general guidelines for incorporating a pragmatic orientation into the more traditional linguistic framework that has determined therapy goals and approaches.

Since specific programs and recommendations have been discussed in phonology, syntax, and semantics, this section presents general principles and guidelines that clinicians should address either when planning to combine pragmatic instruction with other areas or when specifically addressing pragmatic difficulties. However, careful consideration must be given to methodology when pragmatic instruction is combined with other areas of language instruction such as syntax. It is important to note, in fact, that some of what occurs in typical or traditional language therapy sessions actually may be detrimental to the development of appropriate conversational skills.

Prutting, Bagshaw, Goldstein, Juskowitz, and Umen (1978) report that the most frequent instruction or response given by language clinicians is, "Say the whole thing," or "Use a complete sentence." While complete sentences may be necessary to demonstrate certain aspects of syntactic mastery, they actually are unnecessary and even inappropriate in many conversations. The mother who asks her child, "What do you want for breakfast this morning?" rarely would expect as an answer, "I want cereal for breakfast this morning." Instead, "cereal" or some other elliptical or abbreviated form would be expected and accepted.

## Section 3. Strategies for Remediation

Remedial instruction must be based on accurate assessment data that not only define the children's specific areas of weakness but also address specific patterns of strengths, learning style, processing abilities, receptive vs. expressive abilities, and so on. Obviously, priorities must be set, depending on any one child's profile. Instruction should make use of the skills the children already possess (e.g., those who know interrogative forms may be taught how to utilize them to gain more information or clarification and to direct the behavior of others) as well as introduce new skills (e.g., those who communicate only nonverbally may be taught how to accomplish the same purpose with linguistic signals).

In the absence of well-developed training programs, the clinician/educator obviously must have in mind a general framework around which to organize instruction. The framework presented in this chapter may be used since it addresses not only communicative intentions (the only aspect of pragmatics, for example, discussed by Lucas, 1980) and the means by which they may be expressed but also the ability to take the perspective of the audience and to participate appropriately in a variety of discourse situations in different contexts. Within each area, it also is necessary to keep abreast of research relating to normal developmental sequences because this may facilitate the sequencing of objectives as well as the pace of instruction.

In addition to the establishment of goals appropriate to the children's unique patterns of strengths and weaknesses, a number of other variables specifically related to pragmatics are important in the instruction of the learning disabled. Control of these variables is determined by the nature of their disability.

### *Location of Instruction*

One of the major problems with instruction that occurs exclusively in individual therapy sessions is that such an isolated context is atypical for the children. Attempts to provide more natural contexts frequently result in very stilted situations. Ideally, instruction in the areas of concern here should take place in settings that are natural and typical of children's real-life experiences. For this to occur, instruction must be provided in the classroom as well as in environments other than school (home, restaurant, store). Not only are such contexts natural and familiar, but by offering instruction in different situations, problems of carry-over and generalization (so common in more traditional approaches) may be avoided.

*Type of Activities*

The ideal situation, again, is to provide instruction in the context of activities that are interesting and motivating for the children. Free play or activities on the playground, mealtime, classroom instruction, group projects, and so on all are activities in which instruction may be provided.

Whenever possible, use should be made of children's ongoing activities. For example, in an art activity, the pupils should be encouraged to request the materials needed. When the intent of one child's spontaneous utterance to another is unclear and the interlocutors are unable to repair the breakdown, the teacher might intervene and help the speaker find another more appropriate way to express the intent. As simple as it may sound, the teacher should engage the children in conversations regarding current activities whenever possible.

However, just as during the assessment process, it frequently is necessary to structure materials and tasks in a manner that provides situations in which the use of a particular intention is obligatory or at least highly likely. Such activities should be made as natural as possible and must engage the children's interests in order to be effective.

For example, the teacher might misplace needed objects; present materials that cannot be obtained, opened, and/or operated without assistance; or fail to attend to a child. When working on repair strategies, the teacher might pretend that a child's utterance was not heard or understood. The teacher can provide such feedback in a variety of forms: verbally (''I don't understand'') or nonverbally (perplexed facial expression); explicitly (''Please repeat what you just said'') or generally (''What?''). By varying the form, the teacher highlights the different ways in which the need for repairs may be noted.

Role-playing activities and a variety of referential communication tasks also provide excellent opportunities for focusing on the full range of communicative skills.

*Communicative Partners*

A major criticism of traditional language therapy has been that skills demonstrated in the presence of the clinician frequently are not demonstrated in the presence of anyone else. Since part of pragmatic competence is the ability to communicate appropriately with different audiences, it is important to provide children with opportunities to interact with a variety of partners. Peers, younger (or older) children, school personnel, parents, and community individuals (e.g., waitresses, cashiers) all could be involved at some time. Opportunities also should be provided for dyadic as well as group interactions.

## Timing of Instruction

It may be necessary in many instances to set aside specific time periods for focusing on various aspects of pragmatic skill development. However, it must be remembered that social interactions occur as a natural part of most activities (e.g., snacktime, playground, passing out materials) so the teacher must remain alert to instructional opportunities that are available throughout the day.

For example, children's questions should be responded to appropriately. While the questions may be syntactically incorrect, the children will learn more about their function if the teacher answers rather than simply telling pupils to say them correctly. If the teacher wants to focus on the syntax error, that should be done after an appropriate response to the question. Thus, it is important, and likely to be more effective, to provide instruction at the time of an event rather than recreating the same situation later.

## Rule Induction vs. Rule Deduction

The discussion has focused on ways of using or manipulating the environment so as to highlight the presence of regularities and thus to facilitate the acquisition of the rules governing the social uses of language. The common assumption is that discovery learning is always the approach of choice. However, even though normally developing children induce such rules with little apparent effort, it seems unreasonable to assume that environmental manipulations (even with the important variables somehow highlighted) will always be sufficient for children with language and communication disorders to learn what is necessary. In fact, their difficulties may be related to a more generalized deficit in rule induction; that is, no matter how many opportunities are provided and no matter how well they are structured, the pupils do not generalize patterns from one situation to the next.

For such children, it may be more appropriate to teach at least some of the necessary rules in a more deductive fashion, i.e., explicit statement of the rule followed by sufficient opportunities for application and use. That approach also may be utilized at times even with children who can induce the rules. Gagné (1970), for example, notes that since man is a verbal being there really is no need for everything to be learned through discovery; in fact, explicit statement of rules may be a more efficient method. Thus, clinicians might formulate a variety of rules governing interactions (e.g., when requesting an unfamiliar adult to do something, a polite request form should be used) as well as classroom behavior (e.g., during large group discussion, pupils must raise their hand and be called upon before speaking; hand raising is not necessary during small-group activities) and conduct in other situations.

Some children who have struggled to figure out rules and generalizations frequently are observed to react to the explicit statement of the rule with "Aha!! So that's the way!!" Once learned, the rule may be applied easily and appropriately. However, clinicians must be cautioned that such understanding and application do not always occur. There is a danger that rules may be learned in a rote, mechanical manner in the absence of understanding when and how to use them. The provision of appropriate activities in which to practice what is learned therefore is essential.

### A Set for Regularity vs. a Set for Diversity

One potentially difficult aspect of providing instruction in pragmatics is that the rules and the meanings of utterances change so frequently. For example, it is not possible simply to teach that the purpose of questions is to gain information because they also may be used as a part of social routine (e.g., "Hi, how are you?"), to direct the behavior of another ("May I have the scissors?"), and to get someone to stop doing something ("Just what do you think you are doing?"). Thus, the same utterance form and, in many instances, even the same statement, can be used to accomplish a variety of intentions.

The communicative intention is determined on the basis of context, topic, interlocutors, paralinguistic factors, and so on. Any one communicative intention also may be accomplished in many ways. Therefore it is not feasible to teach children, for example, that when they want to direct the behavior of others they should use an imperative form. Obviously, imperatives are only appropriate with particular listener characteristics and situational factors.

Given the variety of possible exceptions and nuances, it is unlikely that all of them can be addressed specifically. However, the clinician/teacher must consider the best way in which to introduce such exceptions and must be sensitive to instructional alternatives. Is it better to teach children a basic rule first and only later introduce the variations (set for regularity)? Or is it better to teach them alternatives from the beginning so that if one interpretation or strategy fails, others are available (set for diversity)? There is no answer to these questions that will hold true for all children at all times; decisions must be based on the learning profiles of each individual one.

### Form of Instruction

When considering the form of instruction, two additional factors should be kept in mind: (1) the modalities used to provide both input and output may be varied and (2) the size of the message unit must be considered. On the first point, developmentally, children communicate initially through gestural means, then combine gestures with early vocalizations and verbalizations, and finally use linguistic means alone. Their developmental level and specific disabilities should determine the modalities to use.

While the ideal situation would be to develop oral verbal communication skills, predominantly visual systems of communication (e.g., American Sign Language, Signed English, Bliss symbols) are available and are being used increasingly with populations other than the deaf and hearing impaired. Verbal input from the clinician may be accompanied by gestures and by paralinguistic modifications (e.g., changes in stress, intonation, pause, duration, intensity) that can be used to highlight various aspects of the message. For older children, the printed words may serve to stabilize the auditory symbols.

On the second point, i.e., the size of the message unit, quite obviously receptive and expressive linguistic levels will determine whether single words, utterances of two or three words, well-formed complete sentences, or longer units of discourse are to be used.

In summary, this discussion has provided the clinician/educator with a framework, as well as general guidelines and recommendations, for working in the area of pragmatic skill development. Specific goals and instructional strategies are a function of the pupils' cognitive and linguistic levels of development as well as their learning style, processing abilities, and so on.

Training in communication skills must be done hand in hand with instruction in other language areas and in natural situations so that children will be able to communicate their intentions effectively as well as understand the intentions of others. Formal programs should be documented in some manner so as to demonstrate their effectiveness. As these programs are developed and marketed, consumers (clinicians/educators) must critically evaluate their theoretical soundness as well as expect empirical demonstration of their validity or effectiveness.

**REFERENCES**

Austin, J.L. *How to do things with words.* Oxford: Oxford University Press, 1962.

Bates, E. Peer relations and the acquisition of language. In M. Lewis & L. Rosenblum (Eds.), *Friendship and peer relations.* New York: John Wiley & Sons, Inc., 1975.

Bates, E. *Language and context: The acquisition of pragmatics.* New York: Academic Press, 1976.(a)

Bates, E. Pragmatics and sociolinguistics in child language. In D.M. Morehead & A.E. Morehead (Eds.), *Normal and deficient child language.* Baltimore: University Park Press, 1976.(b)

Bates, E., Camaioni, L., & Volterra, V. The acquisition of performatives prior to speech. *Merrill-Palmer Quarterly,* 1975, *21,* 205-226.

Bayley, H. *Bayley scales of infant development.* New York: The Psychological Corporation, 1969.

Blank, M., & Franklin, E. Dialogue with preschoolers: A cognitively-based system of assessment. *Applied Psycholinguistics,* 1980, *2,* 127-150.

Blank, M., Gessner, M., & Esposito, A. Language without communication: A case study. *Journal of Child Language,* 1979, *6,* 329-352.

Blank, M., Rose, S.A., & Berlin, L.J. *Preschool language assessment instrument: The language of learning in practice.* New York: Grune & Stratton, Inc., 1978.(a)

Blank, M., Rose, S.A., & Berlin, L.J. *The language of learning: The preschool years.* New York: Grune & Stratton, Inc., 1978.(b)

Bloom, L. *Language development: Form and function in emerging grammar.* Cambridge, Mass.: The MIT Press, 1970.

Bloom, L., & Lahey, M. *Language development and language disorders.* New York: John Wiley & Sons, Inc., 1978.

Bloom, L., Lightbown, P., & Hood, L. Structure and variation in child language. *Monographs of the Society for Research in Child Development,* 1975, *40*(2, Serial No. 160).

Bloom, L., Rocissano, L., & Hood, L. Adult-child discourse: Developmental interaction between information processing and linguistic interaction. *Cognitive Psychology,* 1976, *8,* 521-552.

Bock, J.K., & Hornsby, M.E. The development of directives: How children ask and tell. *Journal of Child Language,* 1981, *8,* 151-163.

Bricker, D. A rationale for the integration of handicapped and nonhandicapped preschool children. In M.J. Guralnick (Ed.), *Early intervention and the integration of handicapped and nonhandicapped children.* Baltimore: University Park Press, 1978.

Brown, R. *A first language.* Cambridge, Mass.: Harvard University Press, 1973.

Bruininks, Y.L. Actual and perceived peer status of learning disabled students in mainstream programs. *The Journal of Special Education,* 1978, *12,* 51-58. (a)

Bruininks, Y.L. Peer status and personality characteristics of learning disabled and nondisabled students. *Journal of Learning Disabilities,* 1978, *11,* 484-489. (b)

Bruner, J. The ontogenesis of speech arts. *Journal of Child Language,* 1975, *2,* 1-19.

Bruner, J. Early social interaction and language acquisition. In H.R. Schaffer (Ed.), *Studies in mother-infant interaction.* New York: Academic Press, 1977.

Bryan, T. An observational analysis of classroom behaviors of children with learning disabilities. *Journal of Learning Disabilities,* 1974, *7,* 26-34. (a)

Bryan, T. Peer popularity of learning disabled children. *Journal of Learning Disabilities,* 1974, *7,* 621-625. (b)

Bryan, T. Peer popularity of learning disabled children: A replication. *Journal of Learning Disabilities,* 1976, *9,* 307-311.

Bryan, T. Learning disabled children's comprehension of nonverbal communication. *Journal of Learning Disabilities,* 1977, *10,* 501-506.

Bryan, T., & Bryan, J. Social interactions of learning disabled children. *Learning Disability Quarterly,* 1978, *1,* 33-38.

Bryan, T., Donahue, M., & Pearl, R. Learning disabled children's peer interactions during a small-group problem-solving task. *Learning Disability Quarterly,* 1981, *4,* 13-22.

Bryan, T., Donahue, M., Pearl, R., & Sturm, C. Learning disabled children's conversational skills: The "TV talk show." *Learning Disability Quarterly,* 1981, *4,* 250-259.

Bryan, T., & Pflaum, S. Social interactions of learning disabled children: A linguistic, social and cognitive analysis. *Learning Disability Quarterly,* 1978, *1,* 70-79.

Bryan, T., Wheeler, R., Felcan, J., & Henek, T. "Come on dummy": An observational study of children's communications. *Journal of Learning Disabilities,* 1976, *9,* 661-669.

Camaioni, L. Child-adult and child-child conversations: An interactional approach. In E. Ochs & B.B. Schieffelin (Eds.), *Developmental pragmatics.* New York: Academic Press, 1979.

Carrell, P.L. Children's understanding of indirect requests: Comparing child and adult comprehension. *Journal of Child Language,* 1981, *8,* 329-345.

Carter, A.L. *The development of communication in the sensorimotor period: A case study.* Unpublished doctoral dissertation, University of California, Berkeley, 1974.

Carter, A.L. The disappearance schema: Case study of a second-year communicative behavior. In E. Ochs & B.B. Schieffelin (Eds.), *Developmental pragmatics.* New York: Academic Press, 1979.

Chapman, R.S. Exploring children's communicative intents. In J.F. Miller (Ed.), *Assessing language production in children: Experimental procedures.* Baltimore: University Park Press, 1981.

Chapman, R., Larsen, S., & Parker, R. Interaction of first-grade teachers with learning disordered children. *Journal of Learning Disabilities,* 1979, *12,* 225-230.

Charney, R. The comprehension of "here" and "there." *Journal of Child Language,* 1979, *6,* 69-80.

Cherry, L.J. The role of adults' requests for clarification in the language development of children. In R.O. Freedle (Ed.), *New directions in discourse processing,* Vol 2. Hillsdale, N.J.: ABLEX Publishing Co., 1979.

Chipman, H., & deDardel, C. Developmental study of the comprehension and production of the pronoun "it." *Journal of Psycholinguistic Research,* 1974, *3,* 91-99.

Clark, E.V. From gesture to word: On the natural history of deixis in language acquisition. In J.S. Bruner & A. Garton (Eds.), *Human growth and development: Wolfson College lectures, 1976.* Oxford, England: Clarendon Press, 1978.

Clark, E.V., & Andersen, E.S. Spontaneous repairs: Awareness in the process of acquiring language. *Papers and Reports on Child Language Development,* 1979, *16,* 1-12.

Clark, E.V., & Garnica, D. Is he coming or going? On the acquisition of deictic verbs. *Journal of Verbal Learning and Verbal Behavior,* 1974, *13,* 559-572.

Clark, E.V., & Sengul, C.J. Strategies in the acquisition of deixis. *Journal of Child Language,* 1978, *5,* 457-475.

Coggins, T.E., & Carpenter, R.L. *The communicative intention inventory: A system for observing and coding children's early intentional communication.* Unpublished manuscript, University of Washington, 1981.

Dale, P.S. Is early pragmatic development measurable? *Journal of Child Language,* 1980, *7,* 1-12.

deVilliers, J., & deVilliers, P. Competence and performance in child language: Are children really competent to judge? *Journal of Child Language,* 1974, *1,* 11-22.

Dickson, W. *The development of interpersonal referential communication skills in young children using an interactional game device.* Unpublished doctoral dissertation, Stanford University, 1974.

Dittman, A.T. Developmental factors in conversational behavior. *The Journal of Communication,* 1972, *22,* 404-423.

Donahue, M.L. *Conversational styles of mother-toddler dyads.* Paper presented at the American Speech and Hearing Association Convention, Chicago, November 1977.

Donahue, M.L. *Requesting strategies of learning disabled children.* Paper presented at the Fifth Annual Boston University Conference on Language Development, Boston, October 1980.

Donahue, M.L., Bryan, T., & Pearl, R. *Conversational strategies of learning disabled children.* Paper presented at the Fifth Annual Boston University Conference on Language Development, October 1980.

Donahue, M.L., Pearl, R., & Bryan, T. Learning disabled children's conversational competence: Responses to inadequate messages. *Applied Psycholinguistics,* 1980, *1,* 387-403.

Dore, J. *The development of speech acts.* Unpublished doctoral dissertation, City University of New York, 1973.

Dore, J. A pragmatic description of early language development. *Journal of Psycholinguistic Research*, 1974, *4*, 343-350.

Dore, J. Holophrases, speech acts and language universals. *Journal of Child Language*, 1975, *2*, 1-20.

Dore, J. "Oh them sherriff": A pragmatic analysis of children's responses to questions. In S. Ervin-Tripp & C. Mitchell-Kernan (Eds.), *Child discourse*. New York: Academic Press, 1977.

Dore, J. Requestive systems in nursery school conversations: Analysis of talk in social context. In R.N. Campbell & P.T. Smith (Eds.), *Recent advances in the psychology of language development and mother-child interaction*. New York: Plenum Press, 1978.

Dunn, L.M. *Peabody picture vocabulary test*. Circle Pines, Minn.: American Guidance Service, 1965.

Dunst, C.J. A cognitive-social approach for assessment of early nonverbal communicative behavior. *Journal of Childhood Communication Disorders*, 1978, *2*, 110-123.

Ervin-Tripp, S. Wait for me, Roller-skate. In S. Ervin-Tripp & C. Mitchell-Kernan (Eds.), *Child discourse*. New York: Academic Press, 1977.

Escalona, S. Basic modes of social interaction: Their emergence and patterning during the first two years of life. *Merrill-Palmer Quarterly*, 1973, *19*, 205-232.

Feffer, M. Developmental analysis in interpersonal behavior. *Psychological Review*, 1970, *77*, 197-214.

Fey, M.E., Leonard, L.B., & Wilcox, K.A. Speech style modifications of language impaired children. *Journal of Speech and Hearing Disorders*, 1981, *46*, 91-96.

Fillmore, C. *Santa Cruz lectures on deixis*. MS. Summer program in linguistics. Santa Cruz, Calif.: University of California, 1971. Reproduced by the Indiana University Linguistics Club, Bloomington, Ind., November, 1975.

Flavell, J. Developmental studies of mediated memory. In H.W. Reese & L.P. Lipsett (Eds.), *Advances in children development and behavior*, Vol. 5. New York: Academic Press, 1970.

Flavell, J. The development of inferences about others. In T. Mischel (Ed.), *Understanding other persons*. Totowa, N.J.: Rowan & Littlefield, 1974.

Flavell, J., Botkin, P., Fry, C., Wright, J., & Jarvis, P. *The development of role-taking and communication skills in children*. New York: John Wiley & Sons, Inc., 1968.

Gagné, R.M. *The conditions of learning*, 2nd ed. New York: Holt, Rinehart & Winston, Inc., 1970.

Garrett, M.K., & Crump, W.D. Peer acceptance, teacher preference, and self-appraisal of social status among learning disabled students. *Learning Disability Quarterly*, 1980, *1*, 40-48.

Garvey, C. Requests and responses in children's speech. *Journal of Child Language*, 1975, *2*, 41-64.

Garvey, C. The contingent query: A dependent act in conversation. In M. Lewis & L. Rosenblum (Eds.), *Interaction, conversation and the development of language: The origins of behavior*, Vol. 5. New York: John Wiley & Sons, Inc., 1977.

Garvey, C., & Baldwin, T. *Studies in convergent communication: I. An analysis of verbal interaction*. Baltimore: Johns Hopkins University, 1970. (ERIC Document Reproduction Service No. ED 045 647)

Garvey, C., & Baldwin, T. *Studies in convergent communication: III. Comparisons of child and adult performance*. Baltimore: Johns Hopkins University, 1971. (ERIC Document Reproduction Service No. ED 047 293)

Garvey, C., & Berninger, G. Timing and turn-taking in children's conversations. *Discourse Processes*, 1981, *4*, 25-57.

Garvey, C., & Geraud, V. *Factors influencing the form of continued nominal reference in children's talk.* Paper presented at the Fifth Annual Boston University Conference on Language Development, Boston, October 1980.

Garvey, C., & Hogan, R. Egocentrism revisited. *Child Development,* 1973, *44,* 562-568.

Geller, E.F., & Wollner, S.G. *A preliminary investigation of the communicative competence of three linguistically impaired children.* Paper presented at the New York Speech and Hearing Association, New York, 1976.

Gleason, J. Code switching in children's language. In T.E. Moore (Ed.), *Cognitive development and acquisition of language.* New York: Academic Press, 1973.

Glucksberg, S., & Krauss, R. What do people say after they have learned to talk? Studies of the development of referential communication. *Merrill-Palmer Quarterly,* 1967, *13,* 309-316.

Glucksberg, S., Krauss, R., & Weisberg, R. Referential communication in nursery school children: Method and some preliminary findings. *Journal of Experimental Child Psychology,* 1966, *3,* 333-342.

Greenfield, P., & Smith, J. *The structure of communication in early language development.* New York: Academic Press, 1976.

Greenfield, P., & Zukow, P. Why do children say what they say when they say it? *Papers and Reports on Child Language Development,* 1978, *15,* 57-67.

Greenwald, C., & Leonard, L. Communicative and sensorimotor development in Down's syndrome children. *American Journal of Mental Deficiency,* 1979, *84,* 296-303.

Grice, H.P. Logic and conversation. In P. Cole & J.L. Morgan (Eds.), *Syntax and semantics,* Vol. 3: *Speech acts.* New York: Academic Press, 1975.

Guralnick, M., & Paul-Brown, D. The nature of verbal interactions among handicapped and nonhandicapped preschool children. *Child Development,* 1977, *48,* 254-260.

Guralnick, M., & Paul-Brown, D. Functional and discourse analyses of nonhandicapped preschool children's speech to handicapped children. *American Journal of Mental Deficiency,* 1980, *84,* 444-454.

Halliday, M.A.K. *Explorations in the functions of language.* London: Edward Arnold, Ltd. 1973.

Halliday, M.A.K. *Learning how to mean: Exploration in the development of language.* London: Edward Arnold, Ltd., 1975.

Halliday, M.A.K., & Hasan, R. *Cohesion in English.* London: Longman, 1976.

Hickman, M. *Creating referents in discourse: A developmental analysis of linguistic cohesion.* Paper presented at the parasession of the Chicago Linguistic Society, Chicago, April 1980.

Hook, P. *A study of metalinguistic awareness and reading strategies in proficent and learning disabled readers.* Unpublished doctoral dissertation, Northwestern University, 1976.

Huxley, R. The development of the correct use of subject personal pronouns in two children. In G.B. d'Arcais and W.J.M. Levelt (Eds.), *Advances in psycholinguistics.* New York: Elsevier, 1970.

Hymes, D. Competence performance in linguistic theory. In R. Huxley & E. Ingram (Eds.), *Language acquisition: Models and methods.* New York: Academic Press, 1971.

Johnson, D.J., & Myklebust, H.R. *Learning disabilities: Educational principles and practices.* New York: Grune & Stratton, Inc., 1967.

Karmiloff-Smith, A. More about the same: Children's understanding of post articles. *Journal of Child Language,* 1977, *4,* 377-394.

Karmiloff-Smith, A. *A functional approach to child language: A study of determiners and reference.* Cambridge: Cambridge University Press, 1979.

Kaye, R. Toward the origin of dialogue. In H.R. Shaffer (Ed.), *Studies in mother-infant interaction.* New York: Academic Press, 1977.

Keenan, E.O. Conversational competence in children. *Journal of Child Language,* 1974, *1,* 163-183.

Keenan, E.O., & Klein, E. Coherency in children's discourse. *Journal of Psycholinguistic Research,* 1975, *4,* 365-380.

Keenan, E.O., & Schieffelin, B.B. Topic as a discourse notion: A study of topic in the conversations of children and adults. In C. Li (Ed.), *Subject and topic.* New York: Academic Press, 1976.

Krauss, R., & Glucksberg, S. The development of communication: Competence as a function of age. *Child Development,* 1969, *40,* 255-266.

Krauss, R., & Rotter, G. Communication abilities of children as a function of status and age. *Merrill-Palmer Quarterly,* 1968, *14,* 161-173.

Labov, W. The study of language in its social context. In W. Labov (Ed.), *Sociolinguistic patterns.* Philadelphia: University of Pennsylvania Press, 1972.

Labov, W., & Fanshel, D. *Therapeutic discourse: Psychotherapy as conversation.* New York: Academic Press, 1977.

Launer, P.B., & Lahey, M. Passages: From the fifties to the eighties in language assessment. *Topics in Language Disorders,* 1981, *1*(3), 11-30.

Leonard, L.B., Wilcox, M., Fulmer, K.C., & Davis, G.A. Understanding indirect requests: An investigation of children's comprehension of pragmatic meanings. *Journal of Speech and Hearing Research,* 1978, *21,* 528-537.

Lewis, M., & Freedle, R. Mother-infant dyad: The cradle of meaning. In P. Pliner, L. Krames, & T. Alloway (Eds.), *Communication and affect: Language and thought.* New York: Academic Press, 1973.

Looft, W. Egocentrism and social interaction across the life span. *Psychological Bulletin,* 1972, *78,* 73-92.

Lucas, E.V. *Semantic and pragmatic language disorders: Assessment and remediation.* Rockville, Md.: Aspen Systems Corporation, 1980.

Maratsos, M.P. Nonegocentric communication abilities in preschool children. *Child Development,* 1973, *44,* 697-700.

Maratsos, M.P. *The use of definite and indefinite reference in young children: An experimental study of semantic acquisition.* Cambridge, England: Cambridge University Press, 1976.

Marinkovitch, G., Newhoff, M., & MacKenzie, J. *"Why can't you talk?": Peer input to language disordered children.* Paper presented at the American Speech and Hearing Association convention, Detroit, November 1980.

Markman, E.M. Realizing that you don't understand: A preliminary investigation. *Child Development,* 1977, *48,* 986-992.

Markman, E.M. Realizing that you don't understand: Elementary school children's awareness of inconsistencies. *Child Development,* 1979, *50,* 643-655.

Masur, E. Preschool boys' speech modifications: The effect of listeners' linguistic levels and conversational responsiveness. *Child Development,* 1978, *49,* 924-927.

Mehan, H. *Learning lessons.* Cambridge, Mass.: Harvard University Press, 1979.

Mehan, H. Students' interactional competence in the classroom. *The Quarterly Newsletter of the Institute for Comparative Human Development,* 1976, *1,* 5-7.

Mehrabian, A. *Nonverbal communication.* Chicago: Aldine and Atherton Publishing Co., 1972.

Menig-Peterson, C. The modification of communicative behavior in preschool-aged children as a function of the listener's perspective. *Child Development,* 1975, *46,* 1015-1018.

Miller, J., Chapman, R., & Bedrosian, J. *Defining developmentally disabled subjects for research.* Paper presented at the Second Annual Boston University Conference on Language Development, Boston, October 1977.

Miller, W., & Ervin-Tripp, S. The development of grammar in child language. In R. Brown & U. Bellugi (Eds.), The acquisition of language. *Monographs of the Society for Research in Child Development,* 1964, (29, Serial No. 92) 9-34.

Minskoff, E.H. Teaching approach for developing nonverbal communication skills in students with social perception deficits. Part I: The basic approach and body language clues. *Journal of Learning Disabilities,* 1980, *13,* 118-124. (a)

Minskoff, E.H. Teaching approach for developing nonverbal communication skills in students with social perception deficits. Part II: Proxemic, vocalic, and artifactual clues. *Journal of Learning Disabilities,* 1980, *13,* 203-208. (b)

Mitchell-Kernan, C., & Kernan, K.T. Pragmatics of directive choice among children. In S. Ervin-Tripp & C. Mitchell-Kernan (Eds.), *Child discourse.* New York: Academic Press, 1977.

Mueller, E. The maintenance of verbal exchange between young children. *Child Development,* 1972, *43,* 930-938.

Noel, M.M. Referential communication abilities of learning disabled children. *Learning Disability Quarterly,* 1980, *3,* 70-75.

Ochs, E. Introduction: What child language can contribute to pragmatics. In E. Ochs & B.B. Schieffelin (Eds.), *Developmental pragmatics.* New York: Academic Press, 1979.

Parisi, D., & Antinucci, F. *Elementi di grammatica.* Turin, Italy: Boringhieri, 1973.

Pearl, R., Donahue, M., & Bryan, T. *Learning disabled and normal children's requests for clarification which vary in explicitness.* Paper presented at the Fourth Annual Boston University Conference on Language Development, Boston, September 1979.

Peterson, C., Danner, F., & Flavell, J. Developmental changes in children's response to three indications of communicative failure. *Child Development,* 1972, *43,* 1463-1468.

Piaget, J. *Language and thought of the child.* New York: Harcourt, Brace and Company, 1926.

Prutting, C.A. Process: The action of moving forward progressively from one point to another on the way to completion. *Journal of Speech and Hearing Disorders,* 1979, *44,* 3-30.

Prutting, C.A., Bagshaw, N., Goldstein, H., Juskowitz, S., & Umen, I. Clinician-child discourse: Some preliminary questions. *Journal of Speech and Hearing Disorders,* 1978, *43,* 123-139.

Read, B.K., & Cherry, L.J. Preschool children's production of directive forms. *Discourse Processes,* 1978, *1,* 233-245.

Rees, N.S. Pragmatics of language: Applications to normal and disordered language development. In R.L. Schiefelbusch (Ed.), *Bases of language intervention.* Baltimore: University Park Press, 1978.

Richards, M. Come and go reconsidered: Children's use of deictic verbs in contrived situations. *Journal of Verbal Learning and Verbal Behavior,* 1976, *15,* 655-665.

Rommetveit, R. *On message structure.* New York: John Wiley & Sons, Inc., 1974.

Rubin, K. Egocentrism in childhood: A unitary construct? *Child Development,* 1973, *44,* 102-110.

Sachs, J. Talking about there and that. *Papers and Reports on Child Language Development,* 1977, *3,* 56-63.

Sachs, J., & Devin, J. Young children's use of age-appropriate speech styles in social interaction and role-playing. *Journal of Child Language,* 1976, *3,* 81-98.

Sacks, G., & Young, E. *Infant scale of communicative intent.* Philadelphia: St. Christopher's Hospital for Children, 1980.

Sadler, R. *Variations in language impaired preschool children's participation in the maintenance of conversation with language impaired and language normal children.* Unpublished master's thesis, University of Maryland, 1982.

Sander, L.W. The regulation of exchange in the infant-caretaker system and some aspects of the context-content relationship. In M. Lewis & L.A. Rosenblum (Eds.), *Interaction, conversation and the development of language.* New York: John Wiley & Sons, Inc., 1977.

Schegloff, E. Sequencing in conversational openings. In J. Gumperz & D. Hymes (Eds.), *Directions in sociolinguistics: The ethnography of communication.* New York: Holt, Rinehart & Winston, Inc., 1972.

Schegloff, E., Jefferson, G., & Sacks, H. The preference for self-correction in the organization of repair in conversation. *Language,* 1977, *53,* 361-382.

Scranton, T., & Ryckman, D. Sociometric status of learning disabled children in an integrative program. *Journal of Learning Disabilities,* 1979, *12,* 402-407.

Searle, J.R. *Speech acts: An essay on the philosophy of language.* Cambridge: Cambridge University Press, 1969.

Semel, E.M., & Wiig, E.H. *Clinical evaluation of language functions.* Columbus, Ohio: The Charles E. Merrill Publishing Co., Inc., 1980.

Shaffer, H.R. (Ed.), *Studies in mother-infant interaction.* New York: Academic Press, 1977.

Shatz, M. Children's comprehension of their mother's directives. *Journal of Child Language,* 1978, *5,* 39-46 (a).

Shatz, M. On the development of communicative understandings: An early strategy for interpreting and responding to messages. *Cognitive Psychology,* 1978, *10,* 217-301 (b).

Shatz, M., & Gelman, R. The development of communication skills: Modifications in the speech of young children as a function of listener. *Monographs of the Society for Research in Child Development,* 1973, *38*(5, Serial No. 152).

Shatz, M., Shulman, M., & Bernstein, D. The responses of language disordered children to indirect directives in varying contexts. *Applied Psycholinguistics,* 1980, *1,* 295-306.

Simon, C.S. *Communicative competence: A functional-pragmatic approach to language therapy.* Tucson, Ariz.: Communication Skill Builders, Inc., 1979.

Siperstein, G.N., Bopp, M.J., & Bak, J.J. Social status of learning disabled children. *Journal of Learning Disabilities,* 1978, *10,* 98-102.

Snyder, L.S. Communicative and cognitive abilities and disabilities in the sensorimotor period. *Merrill-Palmer Quarterly,* 1978, *24,* 161-180.

Snyder, L.S. Assessing communicative abilities in the sensorimotor period: Content and context. *Topics in Language Disorders,* 1981, *1*(3), 31-46.

Spekman, N.J. *An investigation of the dyadic, verbal problem-solving communication abilities of learning disabled and normal children.* Unpublished doctoral dissertation, Northwestern University, 1978.

Spekman, N.J. Dyadic verbal communication abilities of learning disabled and normally achieving fourth- and fifth-grade boys. *Learning Disability Quarterly,* 1981, *4,* 139-151.

Spekman, N.J. Verbal communication and role-taking: An analysis of the use of deictics. In R. diPietro, W. Frawley, & A. Wedel (Eds.), *Proceedings of the First Delaware Symposium on Language Studies.* Newark, Del.: University of Delaware Press, 1982.

Spekman, N.J. & Roth, F.P. *Preschool children's comprehension and production of directive forms.* Paper presented at the Sixth Annual Boston University Conference on Language Development, Boston, October 1981.

Stoel-Gammon, C., & Coggins, T.E. *Making yourself understood: A study of self-correction strategies in the spontaneous speech of Down's syndrome children.* Paper presented at the Second Annual Boston University Conference on Language Development, Boston, October 1977.

Sugarman, S. *A description of communicative development in the prelanguage child.* Unpublished honors thesis, Hampshire College, Amherst, Mass., 1973.

Torgesen, J.K. Factors related to poor performance on memory tasks in reading disabled children. *Learning Disability Quarterly,* 1979, *2,* 17-23.

Uzgiris, I., & Hunt, J. McV. *Assessment in infancy: Ordinal scales of infant development.* Urbana, Ill.: University of Illinois Press, 1975.

Warden, D.A. The influence of context on children's use of identifying expressions and references. *British Journal of Psychology,* 1976, *67,* 102-112.

Watson, L.R. Conversational participation by language deficient and normal children. In J. Andrews & M. Burns (Eds.), *Selected papers in language and phonology II: Remediation of language disorders.* Evanston, Ill.: Institute for Continuing Professional Education, 1977, 104-109.

Webb, P., & Abrahamson, A. Stages of egocentrism in children's use of "this" and "that": A different point of view. *Journal of Child Language,* 1976, *3,* 349-367.

Wiig, E.H., & Harris, S.P. Perception and interpretation of nonverbally expressed emotions by adolescents with learning disabilities. *Perceptual and Motor Skills,* 1974, *38,* 239-245.

Wiig, E.H. & Semel, E.M. *Language disabilities in children and adolescents.* Columbus, Ohio: The Charles E. Merrill Publishing Co., Inc., 1976.

Wiig, E.H., & Semel, E.M. *Language assessment and intervention for the learning disabled.* Columbus, Ohio: The Charles E. Merrill Publishing Co., Inc., 1980.

Woodcock, R.W., & Johnson, M.B. *Woodcock-Johnson psycho-educational battery.* Boston, Mass.: Teaching Resources Corp., 1977.

# Chapter 6

# Conceptualization

*Gail P. Harris-Schmidt*

## PART I. CONCEPTUALIZATION AND LEARNING DISABILITIES

A major theme throughout this book is the interrelationship of language performance and cognitive processes. Discussions of children's knowledge of linguistic rules, metalinguistic ability, and pragmatic skills such as role taking suggest that language is learned within a larger framework of cognition. However, the exact nature of the relationship between language and thought still is an open question. This chapter first examines this issue, then focuses specifically on disorders of conceptualization and how they interact with dysfunctions in spoken language.

### Section 1. Approaches to Studying Conceptualization

*Language and Conceptualization: The Debate*

The relationships between language and conceptualization are intriguing for philosophers, linguists, and educators. The acquisition of meanings normally takes place through both experiences and language. Experiences, labels, objects, and ideas weave together in such a way that most individuals are able to organize, analyze, and discuss their worlds with relative ease. In working with language disordered children, however, knowledge of these relationships of experiences and language becomes even more crucial. Educators, therefore, must move from theoretical and philosophical questions to empirical tests and child-based research, examining not only the relation of semantics, or word meanings, to conceptualization but also how to explore these capacities in children.

Conceptualization may be viewed as a general term that includes categorization, classification, and concept formation, concept attainment, and (often) cognition or thinking in a global sense (Litowitz, 1979). Conceptualization involves the ability to abstract and to categorize; that is, to take a discrete series of objects or events and to group them according to some attribute common to all of them (Johnson & Myklebust, 1967). A concept, then, is all that an individual knows about a category of objects and events. A concept encompasses an extensive realm, which is the set of objects or examples that represents it. It also includes an intensive realm—the properties or attributes that define the concept.

For example, in the intensive realm, the concept "chair" has these attributes: seat for one person, a back, and usually four legs. Its extensive realm includes many examples such as rocking chairs, folding chairs, and easy chairs. The properties shared by "chair" with tables, couches, beds, and dressers are the intension of the category "furniture."

A concept also usually has a linguistic referent, a label. The learning of a concept thus returns to language: educators teach concepts with labels and compare concepts with words. How, then, does the language disordered child deal with nonverbal concepts?

The answer depends on the educator's (or clinician's) theoretical position on the development of cognition and language. The relative independence or interaction of these two areas is a topic of considerable debate. Rice (1980, pp. 9-11) outlines five major views:

1. Language and cognition are independent of each other; the innate linguistic processing mechanisms are unique and distinct from the general intellectual processes. Chomsky (1957) is cited as a proponent of this position because he believed that traditional theories of learning were inadequate to explain language acquisition. The *Language Acquisition Device* (LAD) of McNeill (1970) is designed to explain the idea that children use very particular strategies for acquiring language.
2. Language development depends on cognitive development. Two versions of this position, a "strong" and a "weak," have been proposed:
   a. In the "strong" version, the commonalities and universality across early utterances are linked by theorists to universal cognitive concepts. Piaget (1977) and Sinclair-de-Zwart (1973), adhere to this "strong cognition hypothesis." Piagetian theory (1977) assumes that basic categories of thought are developed during the sensorimotor period and that later language acquisition is dependent upon this early cognitive learning. It sees language as the "icing on the cake" rather than as an intrinsic and vital means for thought to develop.
   b. A "weak cognition hypothesis" grew out of some dissatisfaction with the strong view, especially because the latter could not explain how children who learned to talk about one meaning later acquired more complicated ways by which to express the same meaning (Bowerman,

1976). Thus, while cognition still is seen as primary, language also begins to be a source for continued growth in language and thinking.
3. Language and cognition share a common source. Bates (1976) and her colleagues propose that the interdependent areas of cognition and communication both develop from common, deep, underlying systems of cognitive operations that are not biased toward either one.
4. Language interacts with cognition. This hypothesis suggests that at an early point, children's experience with language may lead them to certain concepts. Vygotsky (1962) says the word plays the role of the means by which a concept is formed, later becoming the symbol of that concept.
5. Cognition depends upon language. In this view, concepts are formed as a result of learning words. This fifth view might be seen as the "strong" version of the fourth and corresponds to the "linguistic determinism" (language determines concept acquisition) espoused by Whorf (1956). More recently, Schlesinger (1981) has declared that for objects, actions, or properties to be permanent in children's minds, they must be anchored to invariant linguistic responses.

The theoretical premise upon which educators stand naturally has implications for the design of research and the model for diagnosis and remediation of disorders in language or conceptual development that they utilize. Research on conceptualization strongly reflects the debate. The following review of that research highlights what has been learned about the processes of conceptualization and the relative importance that language plays in this process.

Historically, in the field of psychology, the study of concepts proceeded without including a focus upon language, in keeping with the first two of the views just outlined. Traditional psychologically oriented concept formation studies often have involved classification tasks using stimuli that represent every possible combination of a number of sensory or perceptual attributes (e.g., sorting 27 items with three colors, three shapes, and three borders) (Anglin, 1977). A concept was defined as a conjunctive of some of the sensory (perceptual) invariants displayed by the stimuli. Subjects had to learn the defining attributes of objects in order to determine whether they were examples of a concept.

Piaget (1977) constructed classification tasks involving matrixes for which subjects were required to identify the intersecting attributes of their component items. Such concepts were well defined, neatly specified, and based on attributes of purportedly equal strength. Little concern was directed toward the meaningfulness of the task to the children, the meaningfulness or relevance of the objects, or the relevance of the task outside the testing situation.

However, concepts based solely on perceptual features increasingly were criticized as insufficient and often irrelevant to concept learning in real life. While some perceptual concepts such as color and shape are clear-cut, Lakoff (1973) adopts the term "fuzzy concepts" to describe the often shady boundaries between many real-life concepts. Objects can lie on the borders of concepts and not fit neatly into discrete conceptual spheres. For example, while tomatoes really are in the "fruit" category (botanically they are berries), they often are classified with vegetables because they are eaten with them. They are not good examples to use in teaching either category.

Rosch (1973, 1975) criticizes linguistic research for its treatment of categories as "internally unstructured," meaning that any item within the category is seen as being as good or familiar or typical as any other. Real categories, she says, consist of items that make up the core meaning of the category, the clearest instances, surrounded by other items with decreasing similarity to the core meaning. For example, a robin might be a very clear example of a bird to many people, while a chicken or an ostrich would be a more peripheral one in the conceptual structure of "birdiness." In this way, the traditional nonverbal approach to conceptualization becomes more linguistic.

At the other end of the spectrum, a purely linguistic method for studying conceptualization was that of asking individuals to define words. However, this opposing method has been criticized by Vygotsky (1962). He contends that this calls for concentrating on the word to the exclusion of any sensory materials and that such research yields information only about completely formed concepts. Further verbal explanations may not reveal all the individual's knowledge of a concept. However, word definitions (as in the *Wechsler Intelligence Scale for Children-Revised,* Definitions subtest, 1974) can elicit information regarding category elaboration (how many items and how they are organized for an individual with regard to a category), and many researchers do not agree with Vygotsky that definitions are finished products of concept formation (Anglin, 1977; Litowitz, 1977; Wolman & Barker, 1965). Litowitz (1977) describes in detail the growth of the definitional form as the children's access to the categories and the features that define various terms develop. Through definitions, it can be seen whether children can explain that an apple is a "fruit that's usually red and sweet," as opposed to, "you eat it" or "a thing in the store."

Word associations, another purely verbal task, also have been used in studying conceptualization. The shift from a syntagmatic response (a term that means the completion of a thought: "dog-run"; "apple-eat") to a paradigmatic, or category, response ("dog-cat"; "apple-orange") signifies a change in semantic organization of the children's concepts of the words.

Vygotsky's solution to the debate is to combine verbal and nonverbal elements in his classification tasks, which use both words and sensory items (1962). His methods for studying concept development include the use of nonsense words and artificial concepts in tasks in which children decide which items are "blicks" based upon their various perceptual features. More recently, other classification tasks have been devised that involve both the sorting of real objects (as opposed to nonsense objects) and verbal explanations about the categories used in the sorting task (Harris, 1979; Novy, 1981). In this kind of task, researchers have analyzed the undergeneralization and overlappings in studying the relationship between the classes or categories formed by the children (extension and intension) and their verbal explanations regarding those classes. Various presentation forms also may be used in such a task: real objects, pictures, or words may be sorted; questions may be phrased in a variety of ways; memory demands may be altered.

From this review, it appears that researchers' methods for studying conceptualization only tap the surface of an extremely complex psychological process. All of these tasks—sorting shapes, objects, pictures, or words, learning which nonsense labels signify a particular concept, definition making, similarity tasks, and word associations—can give clues about children's underlying semantic and conceptual organization but none of them presents a complete picture of conceptualization. A framework for viewing the organization of this semantic information is essential for understanding both normal and disordered conceptual and linguistic development.

## Models of Semantic-Conceptual Development

As discussed in Chapter 3 by Hoskins, models of semantic-conceptual growth emerge from several theoretical sources. The models devised in semantics tie in closely with the study of the manner in which concepts are acquired. Eve Clark's (1973) semantic feature hypothesis is useful in describing how children might overextend a word meaning because of a lack of sufficient features in their knowledge of that word (for small children, "dog" may possess only one feature [+ animal] and therefore is used to refer to many animals). As children mature, features are added so that the expanded terms more closely fit the objects being described. Clark's theory does not, however, address how children underextend labels (not recognizing a lollipop as "food" or a spider as a member of the category "animal"), nor the overlapping of adults' and children's categories.

Nelson (1974) emphasizes functions rather than percepts in the learning of words. Children's early actions with an object then determine their knowledge of the word. For example, the concept of a ball rolling would be learned before that of its roundness.

Theories of natural language concepts (Rosch, 1973, 1975) add the idea that the features making up a concept vary in typicality and saliency. Some are more typical than others in defining concepts (flight as typical of birds but not always an applicable feature). Rosch's notions are very important to the teaching and learning of concepts, their perceptual features, and their functions.

One of the most useful models for the study of children with language and conceptual disorders involves semantic relations theory. This model is based on a hierarchical network arrangement for conceptualization and memory. A concept is formed when meanings of objects are seen in relationships to other objects, ideas, or words (Miller & Johnson-Laird, 1977). A lexical or semantic network is viewed as a cross-referenced system (Evens, Litowitz, Markowitz, Smith, & Werner, 1979). The conceptual system is designed for efficient search through the associative network for a concept having certain specified characteristics. Miller and Johnson-Laird visualize a node with connectors (Figure 6-1). Each concept lists its perceptual and functional information, its label, all of its superordinate concepts, syntactic information, examples, and its subconcepts.

The description by Miller and Johnson-Laird is especially appropriate for the study of the development of concepts. They posit that words and percepts are not linked directly together but that both provide avenues to concept formation, as in Rice's fourth theory. The two kinds of learning, lexical and perceptual, must reinforce each other. Thus, lexical information can first be in a relatively unorganized state, represented by independent lexical entries. That is, a word can be learned in relative isolation at first. As information begins to accumulate, it organizes around simple conceptual cores. Psychological integration of the lexicon is dependent upon developments in the area of concepts that are reflected only indirectly in language. Thus, children at first may have to learn to recognize various kinds of birds as "birds" before they can move on to more linguistic specificity (e.g., robin, cardinal, bluejay) and more generality (birds vs. mammals vs. reptiles).

Very young children accumulate knowledge about the world and form primitive categories that they then use to acquire further information. Not only do they learn more about events, objects, and properties, they also learn how to organize the information already acquired more efficiently so they can use it most effectively in obtaining still more information and in utilizing it all in a variety of tasks (Litowitz, 1979). It is not, then, that the children are simply acquiring more information but that their manner of organization, storage, and access is constantly changing and maturing.

For example, infants learn about the world through their mouths and hands and may attempt to apply the nonverbal concepts of "suckable" and "bangable" to all objects. During their early years, children must discover that "eating" is an important property of apples but not of chairs, that "seating" is an important property of chairs that is shared by couches, for example, but that the relationship between "chairs" and "tables" is still different (Litowitz, 1979).

Children's early classification schemes reflect their inability to move about easily within the hierarchically organized conceptual framework. Piaget (1977) declares that children's concepts are in a state of disequilibrium because they move from particular to particular using transductive reasoning. Deduction also includes the ability to proceed from particular to particular but in addition from particular to universal and from universal to particular, all of which allow for generalization and logical rigor. New relations can be constructed because conscious realization of the linkages among objects, ideas, and words occurs.

**Figure 6-1** Model of Conceptualization

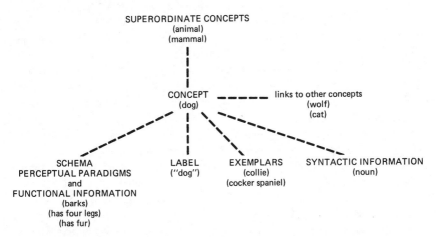

*Source:* Adapted from *Language and Perception,* by George Miller and Phillip Johnson-Laird, by permission of Harvard University Press, © 1977.

Young children are unable to bear in mind all of the dimensions involved so they move from part to part without integrating a hierarchically arranged whole (Gardner, 1972). Their attempts to move toward the structure are like those of the French *bricoleur,* a handyman who uses only the tools available when confronted with a repair problem. He begins with the event and goes to the structure rather than starting with the structure and working down to the event or solution (Gardner, 1972). In the same way, children are tied to their unique, individual experiences with objects in their early classification schemes.

Greenfield and Bruner (1973) and Litowitz and Harris (1976) suggest that egocentric reasoning is exemplified by children who group objects together based upon stories or themes marked by "you" or "I" (e.g., "I would eat with the spoon and then I'd wash the dishes"). As children develop they must move from a view of each entity as: (1) existing within itself, absolutely; toward (2) viewing relationships between objects and self; and, finally, toward (3) a fluid movement among conceptual relationships and superordinates.

*Problem Solving and Strategy Use in Conceptualization*

The ability to move about within this hierarchy involves an increasingly active and conscious search for structure and order. The efficient learner is an individual who has strategies and knows how to use them. Children differ in their possession of certain symbols, their recognition of them when given a strategy externally, and their ability to generate strategies and use symbols in a productive manner (Olson,

1966). Flavell (1970) distinguishes two different kinds of difficulties in using strategies productively. (1) Production difficulties are displayed when children can be urged to use a particular strategy, although they do not develop the strategy spontaneously. For example, when *told* to remember a list of items by category, the children's memory improves. (2) Mediational deficiencies are shown by children who can imitate a desired strategy in a given task but for whom it is ineffective in enhancing performance. For example, when children are given superordinate names to help organize a memory task, these names become merely more items to be remembered.

In young normal children, poor performance on classification tasks may involve production deficiencies. Lavatelli (1973) describes instances in which young children can sort or find the "one that doesn't belong" when supplied with the criterion for choice. However, when forced to abstract the common property themselves, and to extend the concept to other instances, they fail. A gap between what young children can do and what they actually do has been reported in many conceptual tasks (Bryant, 1974; Kail, 1976). Provision of relevant information to such children has led to better usage of helpful strategies for many of them (Gottfried, 1976; Harris, 1979; Miller, 1973; Neimark, 1974; Olson, 1966).

Miller's description of a "plan to form a plan" thus seems to be lacking in the developmentally young (Brown, 1974). If structure is provided, recognition tasks introduced, or external cues supplied, success in concept recognition tasks is possible. However, a production deficiency may inhibit the application of a concept learned in one instance to new material.

This internally regulated strategy deployment necessitates what Fodor (1975) calls a "language of thought." According to Fodor, people make choices relying on a possible state of affairs. They go beyond experiential data, forming hypotheses and testing them. This process of hypothesis testing parallels the classic theories of perceptual learning as well as perception as problem solving. However, the internally represented vocabulary of sensory data that confirm a given perceptual hypothesis is "impoverished" when compared to the vocabulary in which hypotheses regarding concepts are couched (Fodor, 1975, p. 4).

Thus, it is through language that conceptualization at the level of both conceptual organization and strategy deployment gains a depth and breadth of internal representations unknown to perceptual learning. The debate about the extent of the influence of language on cognitive development is crucial to the specific population considered in this book, i.e., language learning disabled children.

### Section 2. Conceptualization Disorders in Learning Disabled Children

To the extent that conceptualization is based on nonverbal perceptual learning, it may not be affected by a language disorder. However, the previous section argues for a close relationship between language and cognition, and it is not surprising that historically there has been interest in research on conceptualization among young persons with problems in understanding and expressing language. Early studies dealt mainly with adults.

Goldstein's (1948) classification experiments, used to distinguish brain injured from normal subjects, remain classic in the area. He asked subjects to sort a group of common objects into the ones they thought belonged together. He then had them sort the items another way, grouping articles with the one they had chosen and with the one the examiner had designated. Goldstein reports that normal subjects form distinct categories by selecting objects corresponding to an abstract concept. They could form abstractions and generalizations in order to pick out attributes and to subsume objects within a general category, shifting easily from one category to another.

He contrasts this flexible, abstract thinking with that of the brain injured, which he labelled concrete or situational thinking. The subjects become "stuck" on the visual thought, unable to switch to another principle of classification and highly involved in graphic-functional situations chosen from their real-life experiences and reproduced from memory. Their inability to shift focus or to break down perceptual wholes into parts, and their narrow conceptual limits all are aspects of Goldstein's description of "concrete."

McCaughran (1954) discusses the expansion of the term "concrete" as studies have revealed conceptual groupings based upon personal experience, narrative sequences, and private symbolic meanings. He delineates two main groups of definitions of concrete: (1) the inability to break wholes into parts or attributes, and (2) private, nonpublic principles of classification.

Bruner (1973) recognizes this second idea of concrete in his separation of "affective" categories, things grouped that evoke common, affective responses, as distinct from functional and formal groups. He also contrasts "concrete" with "abstract" in terms of ties to the immediate environment. Concrete in this case implies an inability to form complex, semantic interrelationships between words and experiences.

An interesting contrast to the usual striving for "abstractness" over "concreteness" is Wendell Johnson's (1946) description of "dead level abstracting." Persons responding at this level may never draw a general conclusion or may use words steeped in vagueness, ambiguity, and meaninglessness, as if the words were "cut loose from their moorings." Numerous adult aphasic patients function at such a level, moving transductively within one level but drawing neither inductive nor deductive conclusions.

Zuriff, Caramozza, Myerson, and Galvin (1974) attempt sorting tasks with adult aphasics. Their subjects choose which two of three words are the most similar in meaning because aphasics are incapable of sorting when the metalinguistic demands of the task are too unstructured. Zuriff et al. report that posterior (or Wernicke's) aphasics do not sort on the basis of any implicit hierarchical organization but on how easily two words can be used in a copular sentence (e.g., "wife" and "cook" were paired, not because both were persons but because an aphasic could say, "My wife is a good cook"). This type of response represents a syntagmatic response rather than a paradigmatic (more "adult," same-class) response. Reitan (n.d.) finds that a categorization test is a fairly valid indicator of persons with and without brain injury. The language and abstraction demands of the task are such that many brain-injured and aphasic adults find them very difficult.

*Concept Formation*

Unfortunately, in contrast to the work with adults, very little has been done on conceptualization with learning disabled children. Of the research available, some studies specifically investigate concept formation. Strauss and Werner (1942), pioneers in the field of minimal brain disorders in children, looked at classification tasks in order to analyze differences in groupings of children who were brain injured and those who were not. They found that the brain injured sorted 56 objects on the basis of inessential details, vague functional relationships, relationships in imaginary situations, and according to highly visual, perceptible aspects such as form and color, far more than the uninjured group. Thinking that their sorting tasks might be too restricted, perhaps curbing even more bizarre imaginings of the brain-injured, Strauss and Lehtinen (1947) devised picture-object tasks, allowing children to place any of a number of objects with a pictured scene. They found that the brain-injured children produced fantasy-based explanations and far-fetched choices.

This heightened sense of fantasy and imagination should not be confused with the development of creativity and play in children. While creative pretend and play may be indicative of a developing inner language and good conceptual growth, the flights of imagination shown by the brain-injured group express their inability to focus on the task and to inhibit irrelevant responses.

*Strategy Deficits*

Other studies delineate difficulties in strategy use by learning disabled children. Blalock (1977) discerns deficits in the abstraction of critical information and its application in a prediction task with preschool learning disabled children. She reports that many of the children have production deficiencies: they appear to have the concepts, rules, vocabulary, and experiences necessary for success on task but fail to apply them. If told to use the information or if allowed to participate in a "forced choice" task (which item does not belong), they perform as well as their normal counterparts. It may be that, receptively, they are beginning to fill in the information necessary for a useful network. However, expressively, their inability to problem solve hinders their application of the knowledge.

This also seems to be the case with the children seen by Harris (1979) and Novy (1981). In object-sorting tasks, both researchers find that the learning disabled children need more cues in order to be able to solve the tasks. Harris uses a variety of nonverbal cues (space restrictions, limiting the number of groups that can be formed) and verbal cues (helping the children locate one item for each group, supplying one superordinate term). Novy teaches them the definitional form—''an (item) is a kind of (superordinate)''—and says this is useful in fostering categorization. Many of the children in both of these studies might be seen as not without a basic semantic network but as lacking the ability to solve problems and apply the known words and relationships to a given task.

*Memory Concepts*

A third investigative interest in conceptualization has involved memory problems. A strong link between being able to organize information and being able to store it in memory has been found (Freston & Drew, 1974; Newman, 1980; Parker, Freston & Drew, 1975; Ring, 1976; Senf & Freundl, 1971). In these studies, learning disabled children are reported as not making use of the organization inherent in groups of words or pictures and as remembering fewer items than their normally achieving agemates. When the strategy is offered to them—to try to remember the items by groups—improvement is seen (Newman, 1980). Again, the inability to apply an available strategy unless the suggestion to do so is offered is suggested as a reason for task failure.

In summary, both classic and more recent research points to conceptualization disorders in this population. Although much more research is needed in the area, a number of reasons why language learning disabled children have difficulties in these tasks already are clear. These children may be (1) inflexible or concrete; (2) lacking strong recognition of the interrelationships of objects, ideas, and words; and/or (3) unable to use such knowledge. Both verbal and nonverbal disorders may interfere with conceptual development and strategy deployment. Underlying processing problems that contribute to such difficulties are explored briefly in the next section.

## Section 3. Conceptualization, Learning Disabilities, and Processing Disorders

Since there are many possible reasons for failure in a conceptual task, it is necessary to apply systematic analysis to determine the causes and to design appropriate remedial strategies. Conceptualization is essentially a connection between auditory verbal stimuli (words) and visual nonverbal stimuli (real world events); as a result disorders of either verbal or nonverbal, auditory or visual processing may interfere with adequate development.

As noted, problems may lie at the receptive level, i.e., in actually forming and understanding relationships among words, objects, and ideas, or at the expressive level, i.e., strategy use. Failures to form the conceptual network may stem from problems at any level of the "hierarchy of experience" (Johnson & Myklebust, 1967).

For example, problems of attention, with an inability to focus on relevant attributes or to sustain attention through a learning task, may interfere with conceptual development. As discussed in Chapter 1, attention disorders not only may cause difficulties at higher levels (i.e., symbolization, conceptualization) but also may be caused by top-down problems (e.g., attention not sustained because the child does not comprehend the task).

Perceptual problems can cause failure in the formation of meaningful relationships among concepts. Miller and Johnson-Laird's (1977) model is based on the joining of perceptual and lexical entries. Failure to differentiate words auditorily or to see parts and wholes visually may block normal access of perceptual input.

At the level of memory, children could fail a conceptualization task because of their inability to retain directions, to remember the meanings for words or pictures, or to recall categories. Difficulties at this level may result not only in the receptive inability to pull percepts and words together but in a breakdown of the expressive ability to solve problems or apply known information. Some memory problems may manifest themselves in that way; that is, children may recognize answers when given them but not recall or apply them. The cueing strategies discussed in the remediation section may trigger the ability to remember and then to use the known information.

Processing problems at the symbolic and conceptual levels may cause difficulty in the formation and generalization of rules that apply to morphological, syntactic, semantic, and pragmatic realms. A breakdown at the level of symbols may cause children to fail to understand such ideas as the plural "s" marker or the need for capital letters. Conceptual problems may add to a failure to understand the multiple meanings of words, the need to supply more information in a conversation, or the subtlety behind verbal humor. As also is discussed in the remediation section, the difficulties in conceptual understanding that affect the various language areas may be remediated at the level of conceptualization, with the intent that the results affect the lower levels of processing.

*Summary*

This section has reviewed the debate on the interrelationships of language and cognition, the influence of one on the other, and reasons why this argument is important in studying children with disorders in language or conceptualization.

The theoretical models range from those that state that language is not related to cognition at the source to those who argue for the strong influence of language on cognitive development, or vice versa.

Those believing that language does have a strong influence on cognition argue that language learning disabled children have a difficult time with conceptual tasks because they lack both the words to define the concepts to themselves and the vocabulary and syntax that are so useful for hypothesis testing and strategy deployment. Those who argue for the development of concepts without the guidance of language hold that these children do as well as normal youngsters, at least on tasks using nonverbal sorting or categorization.

Also presented have been theories on the development of word meanings and concepts, focusing on semantic relations theory (Evens et al., 1979; Miller & Johnson-Laird, 1977). This theory is believed to be relevant for looking at the organization of perception and language in a conceptual framework. It is argued that some learning disabled children simply have not made the connection among concepts in their view of the world so that they cannot recognize, recall, or store the similarities and differences among items and words because of various processing deficits. Others may have the network filled in at a recognition level but have little idea how to recall and use the recognized relationships to solve a given problem. There also may be a difference between children with actual semantic deficits and those who possess the vocabulary at some level but cannot use it effectively. All of these reasons for failure at conceptualization tasks must be explored in diagnosis and remediation.

## PART II. DIAGNOSIS

### Section 1. Available Standardized Tests

It is interesting that, in light of the great interest in classification, conceptualization, clustering in memory, and word associations, there are few formal tests that explore this important area adequately. In fact, while questions regarding conceptual development and strategy deployment in children with learning disabilities arise continually, existing diagnostic tests reflect insufficient and sporadic attention to concept attainment and categorization strategies.

Many intelligence tests do contain subtests that reflect children's verbal categorization abilities. The *Wechsler Intelligence Scale for Children-Revised* (WISC-R) (Wechsler, 1974), *Wechsler Preschool and Primary Scale of Intelligence* (WPPSI) (Wechsler, 1967), and the *Stanford-Binet Intelligence Test* (Terman & Merrill, 1960) contain subtests asking for verbal definitions and similarities or analogies between words, all of which reflect children's classification skills and their abilities to use superordinate, functional, and perceptual features to describe and define. Although scoring procedures reflect some attention to concept development (higher scores for the use of superordinates in the Similarities subtest on the WISC-R and WPPSI), the overall results produce a number measuring breadth of knowledge rather than an analysis of depth of response, so conceptual interpretations must be added by each examiner.

The nonverbal intelligence tests also consider and measure concept attainment. The *Columbia Mental Maturity Scale* (Burgemeister, Blum, & Lorge, 1972) uses a row of pictures in which one does not fit the category of the others. The children must decide on the basis for the grouping and eliminate the irrelevant item. The *Hiskey-Nebraska Test of Learning Aptitude* (Hiskey, 1966), which also uses pictures and an established group, requires the children to find another picture that will complete the given group. The *Leiter International Performance Scale* (Leiter, 1969) requires the pairing of pictures with others according to perceptually and conceptually based matchings. Raven's *Standardized Progressive Matrices* (1965) also are designed to assess nonverbal conceptual development through completion of matrixes. The *Development of Concepts Test* (Crager & Spriggs, 1972) emphasizes the recognition of similarity according to color, shape, function, and superordinate category and uses nonverbal stimuli as well as verbal explanations. Pairs of pictures are presented and the children are asked how they are alike. Answers can be analyzed according to the types of characteristics upon which the children are able to focus.

All of the nonverbal intelligence measures and the *Development of Concepts Test* rely on pictures as stimuli. They have preformed pairs or groups and the children are asked in some way to recognize the reason for the grouping. None of the tests allow the children to form their own grouping nor do any try to teach a grouping strategy through the use of some form of cueing.

Of the verbal tests, several of the newer language instruments, with their increased emphasis on semantics, contain sections that examine children's knowledge of categories of words. *The Word Test,* which is subtitled *A Test of Expressive Vocabulary and Semantics,* (Jorgensen, Barrett, Huisinga, & Zachman, 1981) includes subtests such as Associations, a task that assesses children's ability to select one word that does not belong in a group of four presented auditorily and to explain why it does not. Other subtests that examine categorization include Synonyms, Antonyms, and Definitions. All are expressive tasks that require the ability not only to name but also to explain answers as well. The *Test of Adolescent Language* (TOAL) (Hammill, Brown, Larsen, & Wiederholt, 1980) contains several subtests that involve processing of rather sophisticated multiple meanings of words and synonyms. The *Clinical Evaluation of Language Functions* (Semel & Wiig, 1980) has a number of conceptual subtests: Linguistic Concepts, Relationships and Ambiguities, and Word Associations. Memory and conceptualization are tested.

While many measures are valid for normal children, the needs of the learning disabled are not always met by a one trial, one mode of input and output design. That is, an instrument that gives these children only one chance from one test provides the examiner with little understanding of what they know, and they have little chance to show such knowledge. Children who become confused or distracted in a matrix task may fare very well on a structured word association measure. The true extent of handicapped children's knowledge might not be tapped by a measure that approaches that element from only one angle.

As Piaget (1977) discovered, simply using children's verbal rationales does not explore the extent of their knowledge of concepts. Their explanations often lag behind their ability to sort or complete matrixes or otherwise show their knowledge of various concepts. On the other hand, a categorization test that relies totally on nonverbal output leaves the tester wondering why the children made their choices and groups.

Some tests provide so much structure that the children's difficulties cannot be seen easily. Most tests do not call upon them to generate their own groups and organization with a number of diverse stimuli. Tests have been developed that explore their ability to recognize and explain similarities and differences and to recognize instances of items that do not belong in a category. However, as Lavatelli (1973) points out, the ability to find an object that does not belong in a given group of objects is not the same as being able to generate a group and extend a concept to new objects. Children may succeed at a task with the structure built into it (group formed by the examiner) but find more difficulty in a measure requiring the imposition of order on a group of disparate items.

## Section 2. Informal Tasks

Informal tasks that can be used to examine conceptual abilities can be derived from the experimental studies reviewed in the first section of this chapter. The tasks can be entirely verbal, primarily nonverbal, or combinations of these two. It is essential that all three of these types be carried out, so a systematic series of informal tasks must be designed.

*Nonverbal Tasks*

Primarily nonverbal tasks often involve some verbal directions but if it is desired to avoid language demands completely, gestural cues can be used. Nonverbal tasks should be given in an order from most receptive to most expressive. That is, an informal battery might start with a ''Which one does not belong?'' task involving percepts (colors, shapes), then proceed to a similar one using concepts (three items of furniture, one food). Wordings can be changed to simplify them. If children cannot understand, "Which one doesn't belong?", the clinician might use a gestured demonstration to be sure the task is comprehended (clinician covers up one, points to the three others, saying "Same" or nodding "Yes").

A nonverbal task that is expressive but quite structured calls on the children to complete a matrix with an item that fits in two categories: a column of yellow items intersecting a column of flowers is completed by a yellow flower.

Sorting tasks with perceptual items or real objects can be primarily nonverbal when studying children's expressive abilities. The nonverbal portion can be scored as to whether items are placed in a pattern or design (figural representation, Piaget, 1977), or by groupings that are perceptual (all wooden or all brown objects together) or categorical (all toys or all foods together).

However, until examiners add a verbal component, they do not really know why the children placed a certain group of items together. For example, were a toy, car, doll, and mouse placed together because the children knew they all were toys, or because they were all plastic, or all brown? Many times it is assumed erroneously that children possess a certain concept because of a final product, and this may not be so.

*Verbal Tasks*

Verbal tasks can be combined with nonverbal stimuli (pictures, objects) or used alone. Receptive tasks should be given first: children can be asked to "Show me the _____" at the levels of percepts (green ones, metal ones), functions (ones they play with, ones they eat), and superordinates (foods, toys, animals). A measure of flexibility might include asking the children to reclassify on another basis (e.g., "Can you do it by color now?" "How about by the way we use these?").

Receptive tasks can include multiple choice responses with word associations, synonyms, antonyms, similarities, or definitions. In allowing children to choose the correct response, educators also learn whether they "have" it at one level even if they cannot produce the answers expressively. For example, tasks might be designed such as: "Show me the one most like a *cat*: dog, radio, apple."

On the expressive verbal side, these same tasks can require the children to discuss or explain their answers. Word association tasks are among the most structured. In these, the clinician should measure whether the children have shifted from a syntagmatic response (finishing a phrase, as in "dog-barks") to paradigmatic, same-class responses ("dog-cat"). Some language impaired children may not recognize or use same-class responses.

Similarities tasks examine the usage of (1) attributes ("cat-dog: have fur"), (2) functions ("both run"), or (3) category knowledge ("both animals"), as well as look at children's responses that show lack of understanding of the concepts involved (youngsters who tell how the items are different rather than the same).

Definitions should be examined in more depth than do the WISC-R and WPPSI. Litowitz (1977) suggests that definitions develop from: (1) gestures or pointing; to (2) word associations ("shoe-sock"); to (3) completions of thoughts based upon personal experiences ("shoes-I have some sneakers"); to (4) functions ("shoes-you wear them"); to finally, (5) Aristotelian definitions ("shoes-clothing that you wear on your feet"), using superordinate terms and some descriptors. Thus, definitions tasks can evaluate the ability to use both categories and descriptors.

In contrast to entirely verbal tasks (similarities, definitions), those that combine both nonverbal sortings and verbal explanations are useful to compare perceptual and linguistic concepts and the extent to which language can be used as an explanation as well as a guide for conceptualization. Children's explanations may not be an entirely valid measure of the extent to which they use language internally to guide their sorting. There might be a difference if the clinician asked: (1) "Why did you sort them this way?" (i.e., asking for a justification or rationale), (2) "Now tell me how you did it," or "Tell me what you did," (i.e., asking for an "instant replay"), and (3) getting the children to verbalize as they go along.

Explanations should be compared to object, picture, and word card sortings so the clinician can establish whether the children are able to explain groups at various levels of abstraction. Bruner (1973) outlines levels for such explanations and Harris (1979) finds them useful for looking at learning disabled children's linguistic abilities. Bruner's levels from lowest to highest levels of abstraction include: (1) defeat ("I don't know"), (2) fiat equivalence (they are the same simply because the child says so), (3) themes (pretend stories linking items together), (4) perceptual responses (groupings based on color, size, shape, or material), (5) functional (uses of the objects as the explained basis for grouping), and (6) superordinates (group names such as foods, toys, animals, etc.). The knowledge of these levels of abstraction can provide information helpful in designing a remediation plan. A summary of all of these types of informal tasks is presented in Exhibit 6-1.

*Task Analysis*

When children fail on either a formal test or an informal task, the clinician must go back to examine the reasons why. The modes of input and output required, the level of processing demanded, and the stimuli used along with the verbal and nonverbal nature of the task must be taken into account. Using the frames of reference of Johnson and Myklebust (1967) discussed throughout this chapter, a series of questions can be asked related to the language level involved and the level of experience required.

Assuming that there is no evidence of hearing loss, it must be asked:

- Were there difficulties in discrimination; could the children perceive the differences in the words the clinician said?

**Exhibit 6-1** Summary of Types of Informal Tasks

| Nonverbal Receptive | Nonverbal Expressive |
|---|---|
| 1. Which one does not belong?<br><br>  a. perceptual<br>    (shapes, colors)<br><br>  b. conceptual<br>    (pictures, objects) | 1. Matrixes: fill in the missing item<br><br>2. Sorting tasks<br><br>  a. perceptual (shapes, colors)<br><br>  b. conceptual<br>    (pictures, objects) |
| **Verbal Receptive** | **Verbal Expressive** |
| 1. Show me the _____:<br><br>  a. perceptual<br><br>  b. functional<br><br>  c. superordinate<br><br>2. Multiple choice formats for any of the verbal expressive tasks | 1. Word associations<br><br>2. Similarities<br><br>3. Synonyms<br><br>4. Antonyms<br><br>5. Definitions<br><br>6. Explanations for sorting tasks<br><br>7. Sorting tasks using words printed on cards |

- Were there difficulties in comprehension?
- How complex were the instructions?
- Was memory a factor?
- Did the children forget the task requirements or items and, therefore, fail the task?
- Were the children's errors the result of word-finding problems, if they had to give explanations or answers in the test?
- Did formulation or syntax errors affect the ability to produce well-reasoned answers?
- Were the tasks perceptual or conceptual?

There also are questions with regard to the mediation and production deficiencies described in the earlier sections. Do the children know there is a problem to be solved? If so, can they respond to the requirements of the task only if enough structure and recognition responses are required? That is, some children are unable to solve the task when it is left somewhat open-ended and unstructured yet can show conceptual knowledge when some amount of structure is placed on the interaction. Such structuring is discussed in the section on remediation.

*Summary*

This discussion of diagnosis, both formal and informal, is designed to focus on the need for many kinds of tasks in a procedure for studying disorders in conceptualization. It is argued that a systematic study needs to be made of each child's knowledge and application of conceptual strategies. Tests and tasks are presented as verbal or nonverbal in nature, using perceptual or conceptual demands, focusing on receptive or expressive requirements, and involving various processes. By designing a systematic approach to diagnosis, remediation can be planned that focuses on the specific needs of the children tested.

## PART III. REMEDIATION

### Section 1. Goals of Remediation

The purpose of remediation is to foster generalization and problem solving in children and to promote their ability to go beyond a single instance. Remediation must be planned with that end in mind. Clinicians cannot teach single concepts in isolation, expecting them to be applied in other instances, unless they have designed procedures to help with that usage. With a complete battery of formal and informal diagnostic procedures, educators should be able to focus on the areas that need to be remediated and begin to understand the strategies that are most helpful.

### Section 2. Remediation for Nonverbal Conceptualization Disorders

If testing has revealed strengths in language, with most of the problems centering on nonverbal disorders, remediation should focus on the teaching of verbal strategies to cope with such weaknesses. Attention may be at the root of nonverbal conceptualization problems. Verbal cues as simple as, "Wait," "Listen," or "Stop" may help call attention to the features the children should be studying.

The children may have perceptual difficulties, failing to see the differences among stimuli. Remediation with those having problems at this level must necessarily focus on perceptual awareness; however, even here, clinicians should be aware of ways of fostering problem solving and task generalization. In getting children to focus on and attend to a particular stimulus, a clinician may teach them to verbalize and comment on various parts and to have a well-thought-out strategy for examining parts and wholes.

Receptive tasks can precede expressive ones if necessary. The informal diagnostic task utilizing, "Which one doesn't belong?" can be adapted to a remediation activity if children have difficulty at the recognition level. Ways of stating the directions can be varied as a cue. It also may be necessary to begin with real objects before moving to pictures, and from two of three objects being exactly alike to two of three being in the same category. It is clear that teaching must start with the level that reaches the children's need. One child may be trying to learn the concept "different" with vastly dissimilar items such as a chair vs. two dogs, while a more sophisticated youngster may be faced with mammals vs. birds, farm vs. wild animals, etc.

Expressive tasks can include sorting or matrixes, beginning with perceptually based items such as shapes or colors. These can be paired with verbal cues or kinesthetic ones in which the children trace the shape or size or feel the weight.

The use of cues to provide structure is a particularly important part of planning remedial strategies. Harris (1979) uses a sorting task that involves a series of both verbal and nonverbal cues designed to help foster more sophisticated sorts. The informal test involves having the children sort 20 common objects into groups of the ones they think belong together. Those who are not initially able to form groups of foods, toys, cooking utensils, and school supplies are given increasingly structured situations in which to respond.

Successful cues for the 7- and 9-year-old learning disabled children include limiting the number of groups they may make (just putting four boxes on the table forces many into "seeing" the four groups), providing one item for each of the four groups to get them started, and making one group with the verbal cues of naming each item and its superordinate term. The clinician says, "I'm putting the carrot here because it's food, and I'm putting the bread here because it's food," etc.

Novy (1981) also designed an informal task using picture sorts. His teaching method involves verbal cues designed to help better nonverbal sorts. He teaches the children to state that each item is "*a kind of* _____." Thus, the children practice saying the similarities among items by categorizing them in their definitions (an apple is a kind of food; an egg is a kind of food, etc.). The children improve their ability to sort by using this strategy. Newman (1980) designed a teaching strategy that uses the learning of categories to aid memory. Language and learning disabled students are able to remember more items from a group of pictures after they are taught to categorize those items. It thus can be seen that there are many verbal strategies that can aid in teaching the nonverbal concept of object sorting by category.

### Section 3. Remediation for Verbal Conceptualization Disorders

Remediation of verbal (or language-oriented) deficits can be designed to begin at lower, more perceptually based levels and move up the hierarchy toward development of verbal concepts fostering categorization of words, or it may begin with intact nonverbal conceptualization and use it to aid lower level deficits in symbolization.

With a bottom-up approach, the clinician must be sure that information is perceived correctly before associative memory tasks are attempted. The higher level processes of symbolic and conceptual thinking are added as the teacher is assured that items have been properly perceived and stored. However, as stated in Chapter 1, the hierarchy can be looked at from the top down and remediation designed accordingly.

It has been suggested in the section on nonverbal conceptual problems that learning concepts can aid memory. This also is true with verbal items to be stored in memory. Teaching by language units has often been used in language arts classes. It is an appropriate strategy for teaching language disordered children to store names and relationships in memory and for discussions of how community helpers are alike or different, how the four food groups vary, and what constitutes being a member of the furniture category. This method should be designed with the research of Rosch (1973, 1975) in mind. Items should be chosen that are "typical" and "central" members of the category before more peripheral examples are attempted.

At the symbolization level, children may have problems with word meanings, so working down the conceptual level may provide the added meaning to make the symbols more relevant. Using categories of stimuli and visual cues such as pointing out how certain groups of items are the same or different may provide the necessary aids.

Remediation can focus on categories of words, similarities and differences in meanings, multiple meanings, depth of understanding of words, and how networks are developed around concepts and words. The nonverbal cues mentioned in the section on nonverbal disorders may be helpful if the semantic problems stem from attentional or perceptual deficits. In addition, pictures, objects, demonstrations, and instances can help language disordered children understand the concept or meaning underlying words. Hoskins (see Chapter 3) discusses moving from the most central instances of a concept to more peripheral ones, those on the boundary. Thus, the relationship of how items are similar and different within and across categories are taught from the beginning. Children learn to examine, compare, and contrast concepts and to apply them to others. One of the most persistent problems in learning disabled children is that of rule generalization. Thus, clinicians cannot teach a single concept in isolation and expect children to apply it automatically.

For example, in a unit on foods, the teacher may begin not with naming a random group of food items or pictures but with identifying characteristics of various foods and then comparing them. Why are they alike and different? Is it their shape? Is it the taste? Where do the foods come from? Why are certain foods grouped together in the grocery store?

Questioning and examining relationships can be applied to many concepts, from those between simple and concrete groups such as fruits and vegetables to comparisons and contrasts of abstract concepts such as political systems or religious beliefs. Questioning and knowing when to cue and probe answers may offer one of the best ways to foster generalization.

For children with specific language deficits in other areas—phonologic, syntactic, pragmatic—teaching through conceptual units can be extremely useful. Phonological errors may never improve if articulation drills focus on mere sound production and imitation, with no concept presented of the meaning changes brought about by the change of a phoneme. Morphological and syntactic systems are filled with rules that must be understood in order to be applied. The meanings behind word order changes, sentences vs. questions, verb tenses, plurals, pronouns, prepositions, word endings, etc., can be explained from the level of the simple concepts involved in order to make the children aware of the differences.

### Section 4. Remediation for Problem Solving and Strategy Use

A growing concern in remediation for learning disabled children is that they fail to use and to generalize the knowledge that they hold. They do not spontaneously access information and apply it appropriately. Reid and Hresko (1981) discuss, from an information processing point of view, the failure of the "executive" function in these children's systems. They advocate a holistic approach to teaching, focusing on the children's active learning and elaboration of what they already know. In such remediation, goals can be developed with the children's cooperation. The purpose of tasks can be to work with generalization of strategies acquired, drawing inferences, monitoring for correctness, analysis of the sensibility of answers, and long-term memory storage. The final goal is to have active learners who control their own executive functions.

### Section 5. Summary

It has been argued throughout this chapter that the core of children's conceptual problems often is centered in either an underlying semantic deficit or in knowing how, when, and why to use basic knowledge. If it is the first case, then the clinician can focus on teaching words, features, and relationships among items and ideas—filling in the web of a deficient semantic network. It is not enough, however, to teach isolated words and ideas. Relationships among all of these must be the goal of remediation, with strategies for generalization fostered. If the problem lies in strategy deployment, then remediation should not focus on naming and semantic acquisition but on ways to make that knowledge "work" for the children.

It is difficult for many teachers to stand back and not give the answers when children make errors. However, to move beyond teaching simple concepts and isolated instances, educators must be willing to focus on the necessary verbal and nonverbal cues, those needed to move the children to the level of being able to understand conceptual relationships, to the level at which they can recognize and respond to the ideas, objects, words, and worlds about them.

## REFERENCES

Anglin, J.M. *Word, object and conceptual development*. New York: W.W. Norton & Company, Inc., 1977.

Bates, E. *Language and context: The acquisition of pragmatics*. New York: Academic Press, 1976.

Blalock, J. *A study of conceptualization and related abilities in learning disabled and normal preschool children*. Unpublished doctoral dissertation, Northwestern University, 1977.

Bowerman, M. Semantic factors in the acquisition of rules for word use and sentence construction. In D.M. Morehead & A.E. Morehead (Eds.), *Normal and deficient child language*. Baltimore: University Park Press, 1976.

Brown, R. The role of strategic behavior in retardate memory. In N.R. Ellis (Ed.) *International review of research in mental retardation* (Vol. 7). New York: Academic Press, 1974.

Bruner, J. Development of equivalence transformations in children. In J.M. Anglin (Ed.), *Beyond the information given*. New York: W.W. Norton & Company, Inc., 1973.

Bryant, P. *Perception and understanding in young children*. London: Methuen and Co., Ltd., 1974.

Burgemeister, B., Blum, L., & Lorge, I. *Columbia mental maturity scale*. New York: Harcourt Brace Jovanovich, Publishers, Inc., 1972.

Chomsky, N. *Syntactic structures*. The Hague: Mouton Publishers, 1957.

Clark, E. What's in a word? On the child's acquisition of semantics in his first language. In T.E. Moore (Ed.), *Cognitive development and the acquisition of language*. New York: Academic Press, 1973.

Crager, R., & Spriggs, A. *The development of concepts test*. Los Angeles: Western Psychological Services, 1972.

Evens, M., Litowitz, B., Markowitz, J., Smith, R., & Werner, O. *Lexical-semantic relations: A comparative survey*. Carbondale, Ill.: Linguistic Research, Inc., 1980.

Flavell, J. Developmental studies of mediated memory. In H.W. Reese & L.P. Lipsitt (Eds.), *Advances in child development and behavior* (Vol. 5). New York: Academic Press, 1970.

Fodor, J. *The language of thought*. New York: Thomas Y. Crowell Company, Inc., 1975.

Freston, C., & Drew, C. Verbal performance of learning disabled children as a function of input organization. *Journal of Learning Disabilities*, 1974, *7*, 24-28.

Gardner, H. *The quest for mind: Piaget, Levi-Strauss, and the structuralist movement*. New York: Vintage Books, Random House, 1972.

Goldstein, K. *Language and language disturbances*. New York: Grune & Stratton, Inc., 1948.

Gottfried, A. Effects of instructions and stimulus representation on selective learning in children. *Developmental Psychology*, 1976, *12*, 140-146.

Greenfield, P., & Bruner, J. Culture and cognitive growth. In J.M. Anglin (Ed.), *Beyond the information given*. New York: W.W. Norton & Company, Inc., 1973.

Hammill, D., Brown, V., Larsen, S., Wiederholt, J.L. *Test of adolescent language*. Austin, Texas: Pro-Ed, 1980.

Harris, G. *Classification skills in normally achieving and learning disabled 7- and 9-year-old boys: A study in conceptualization*. Unpublished doctoral dissertation, Northwestern University, 1979.

Hiskey, M. *Hiskey-Nebraska test of learning aptitude*. Lincoln, Neb.: Union College Press, 1966.

Johnson, D.R., & Myklebust, H.R. *Learning disabilities: Educational principles and practices*. New York: Grune & Stratton, Inc., 1967.

Johnson, W. *People in quandries: The semantics of personal adjustment*. New York: Harper & Row, 1946.

Jorgensen, R., Barrett, J., Huisinga, T., & Zachman, R. *The word test: A test of expressive vocabulary and semantics*. Moline, Ill.: LinguiSystems, Inc., 1981.

Kail, R. Children's encoding of taxonomic classes and subclasses. *Developmental Psychology*, 1976, *12*, 487-488.

Lakoff, G. *Hedges and meaning criteria*. In R. McDavid & A.R. Duckert (Eds.) *Lexicography in English*. New York: New York Academy of Sciences, 1973.

Lavatelli, C. *Piaget's theory applied to early childhood curriculum*. Cambridge, Mass.: American Science and Engineering, Inc., 1973.

Leiter, R. *Leiter international performance scale*. Chicago: C.H. Stoelting Co., 1969.

Litowitz, B. Learning to make definitions. *Journal of Child Language*, 1977, *4*, 289-304.

Litowitz, B., Harris, G., & Newman, D. *Conceptualization and memory problems in learning disabled children*. Paper presented at the International Association for Children with Learning Disabilities Conference, Milwaukee, 1979.

Litowitz, B., & Harris, G. *The development and uses of hypothetical speech: Evidence from definitions*. Paper presented at the American Speech and Hearing Association National Convention, Houston, Texas, November 1976.

Litowitz, B., Harris, G., & Newman, D. Studies of conceptualization and memory in learning-disabled children. *Learning Disabilities, an Audio Journal for Continuing Education*, 1981, *5*.

McGaughran, L.S. Predicting language behavior from object sorting. *Journal of Abnormal Social Psychology*, 1954, *49*, 183-195.

McNeill, D. *The acquisition of language: The study of developmental psycholinguistics*. New York: Harper & Row, Publishers, 1970.

Miller, G., & Johnson-Laird, P. *Language and perception*. Cambridge, Mass.: Harvard University Press, 1977.

Miller, R. The uses of concrete and abstract concepts by children and adults. *Cognition*, 1973, *2*, 49-58.

Neimark, E. Natural language concepts: Additional evidence. *Child Development*, 1974, *45*, 508-511.

Nelson, K. Concept, word and sentence: Interrelationships in acquisition and development. *Psychological Review*, 1974, *81*, 267-285.

Newman, D. *An investigation of learning disabled children's utilization of taxonomic organization to facilitate memory performance*. Unpublished doctoral dissertation, Northwestern University, 1980.

Novy, F. *Categorical reasoning and semantic organization in learning disabled and normal 7-year-old children*. Unpublished doctoral dissertation, Northwestern University, 1981.

Olson, D. On conceptual strategies. In J. Bruner, R. Olver, & P. Greenfield (Eds.), *Studies in cognitive growth*. New York: John Wiley & Sons, Inc., 1966.

Parker, T., Freston, C., & Drew, C. Comparison of verbal performance of normal and learning disabled children as a function of input organization. *Journal of Learning Disabilities*, 1975, *8*, 386-393.

Piaget, J. Judgment and reasoning in the child. In H.E. Gruber & J.J. Voneche (Eds.), *The essential Piaget*. New York: Basic Books, Inc., 1977.

Raven, J.C. *Standardized progressive matrices*. New York: The Psychological Corporation, 1965.

Reid, D.K., & Hresko, W.P. *A cognitive approach to learning disabilities*. New York: McGraw Hill Book Company, 1981.

Reitan, R. *The effects of brain lesions on adaptive abilities in human beings*. Unpublished manuscript. Indianapolis, Ind.: Indiana University Medical Center, Department of Surgery, n.d.

Rice, M. *Cognition to language: Categories, word meanings, and training*. Baltimore: University Park Press, 1980.

Ring, B. Effects of input organization on auditory short-term memory. *Journal of Learning Disabilities*, 1976, *9*, 591-595.

Rosch, E. On the internal structure of perceptual and semantic categories. In T.E. Moore (Ed.), *Cognitive development and the acquisition of language*. New York: Academic Press, 1973.

Rosch, E. Cognitive representation of semantic categories. *Journal of Experimental Psychology: General*, Vol. 104, 1975, *3*, 192-233.

Schlesinger, I. *Acquisition of words: The first steps*. Chapter in preparation (as cited in Rice).

Semel, E., & Wiig, S. *Clinical evaluation of language functions*. Columbus, Ohio: The Charles E. Merrill Publishing Co., Inc., 1980.

Senf, G., & Freundl, P. Memory and attention factors in specific learning disabilities. *Journal of Learning Disabilities*, 1971, *4*, 36-48.

Sinclair-de-Zwart, H. Language acquisition and cognitive development. In T.E. Moore (Ed.), *Cognitive development and the acquisition of language*. New York: Academic Press, 1973.

Strauss, A., & Lehtinen, L. *Psychopathology and education of the brain-injured child*. New York: Grune & Stratton, Inc., 1947.

Strauss, A., & Werner, H. Disorders of conceptual thinking in the brain-injured child. *Journal of Nervous and Mental Disorders*, 1942, *96*.

Terman, L., & Merrill, M. (Eds.). *The Stanford-Binet intelligence scale*, Form L-M. Boston: Houghton Mifflin Company, 1960.

Vygotsky, L. *Thought and language*. Cambridge, Mass.: The MIT Press, 1962.

Wechsler, D. *The Wechsler preschool and primary test of intelligence*. New York: The Psychological Corporation, 1967.

Wechsler, D. *Wechsler intelligence scale for children-Revised*. New York: The Psychological Corporation, 1974.

Whorf, B. Language, thought, and reality. Cambridge: Massachusetts Institute of Technology, 1956.

Wolman, R., & Barker, E. A developmental study of word definitions. *Journal of Genetic Psychology*, 1965, *107*, 159-166.

Zuriff, E., Caramozza, A., Myerson, R., & Galvin, J. Semantic feature representations for normal and aphasic language. *Brain and Language*, 1974, *1*, 167-187.

# Chapter 7

# Reading

*Elizabeth A. Noell*

Reading is a complex act that is integrally related to oral language in that the basis of written text is spoken language. However, reading in several senses is more than written speech. At the phonological level, the written code is superimposed on the spoken code in a complex manner and "decoding" requires cognitive skills beyond simple one-to-one matching. The language of written text also differs semantically, syntactically, and pragmatically from spoken language in significant ways; thus, reading comprehension also requires sophisticated cognitive and metacognitive skills. Previous chapters have considered comprehension and production of spoken language as well as the relationship of language to cognition. This chapter focuses on the area of comprehension of written language that builds upon both oral language and cognitive abilities.

## PART I. READING AND LEARNING DISABILITIES

Children growing up in a society that aspires to universal literacy face the need to learn to read and communicate through written language. During the past century, more and more people have been expected to achieve a certain standard of literacy—a standard that has become more stringent as society has become more complex. The criteria for literacy that were considered acceptable at the turn of the century no longer are relevant in today's world.

For example, a literate person at that time was one who could read simple and familiar texts such as religious catechisms (Weaver & Resnick, 1979). Given that standard, little emphasis was placed on comprehension. Instead, instruction focused on the development of fluent oral reading skill—the translation of visual, verbal symbols into speech. Now educators stress reading comprehension for the purpose of deriving meaning from written text and integrating the information in new contexts. With the advances in technology and increasing job demands for reading competency, this literacy expectation is much more realistic in contemporary society (Resnick & Resnick, 1977).

In some respects, the demands for universal literacy have gone beyond what is known as "functional literacy," which has come to mean the ability to read texts such as newspapers and magazines and to use the information to obtain employment (Resnick & Resnick, 1977). Society's demand for literacy puts heavy pressures on the pedagogical system. Furthermore, the ability to read is one of the most important determiners of success in school. For these reasons, reading research is one area that has commanded the most attention of investigators in the field of learning disabilities.

Learning to read entails complex psychological processes. In recent decades, theorists and practitioners have become increasingly concerned about the nature of the processes in learning to read and why certain individuals fail to read or do so slowly. Since the initiation of the concept of learning disabilities, with special emphasis on language disorders, researchers have generated numerous theories and investigated various assessment and remedial approaches to reading disabilities.

Although many individuals fail to learn to read for various reasons (e.g., emotional disturbance, mental retardation, lack of opportunity to learn, poor instruction, hearing loss, visual impairment), this chapter focuses on a specific population—learning disabled children, and their reading problems. The terms "reading disabled," "dyslexics," and "learning disabled readers" are used interchangeably to refer to a subgroup within the learning disabled population.

In this chapter, reading is viewed as a language-based process that requires decoding, comprehension, and thinking skills. Others have conceptualized reading in a similar manner (Carroll, 1977; Johnson & Myklebust, 1967; Myklebust, 1978; Risko, 1981; Stauffer, 1976; Strauss & Lehtinen, 1947). Dyslexia is regarded as a language disorder, a defect in the ability to translate the printed form of language into meaningful symbols (Myklebust, 1978).

The thesis here is that learning disabled readers do not constitute a homogeneous group. It is possible to distinguish those who encounter difficulties because of either poor decoding skills, generalized oral language, and/or thinking disorders. Many also have difficulty dealing with language at a metalinguistic level (Johnson & Hook, 1978; Vogel, 1972). Research supports the notion that there is not just a unitary dyslexia syndrome but that there are numerous subtypes and causes (Johnson & Myklebust, 1967; Lyon & Watson, 1981; Lyon, Reitta, Watson, Porch, & Rhodes, 1981; Lyon, in press; Myklebust, 1978; Rourke, 1978a, 1978b; Tallal, 1980).

However, extensive research remains to be done before any firm conclusions can be drawn regarding the nature of subtypes and the instruction that proves effective. Before discussing the assessment and remedial procedures, however, basic approaches to the study of reading and related disabilities are reviewed.

## Section 1. Studying Reading in Normal Children

Since the late 1800s when reading became the subject of scientific inquiry, it has been researched assiduously by investigators from many disciplines. The resulting voluminous literature has provided theories, theoretical models, and practical methods of instruction. This extensive body of literature is only highlighted here since an exhaustive review is beyond the scope of this chapter.

Over the past century, there have been two major lines of research on reading: (1) theory-based, focusing on basic reading processes, and (2) curriculum, comparing methods of teaching (Gibson & Levin, 1975). At the turn of the century, psychologists and educators were interested in understanding how individuals read. Controlled experiments were designed to offer support for carefully thought out theoretical positions. Much of this research was oriented toward the process involved in tachistoscopic word recognition (Cattell, 1886; Erdmann & Dodge, 1889, cited in Gibson & Levin, 1975; Godsheider & Muller, 1893, cited in Venezky, 1977).

The research also included studies of eye movement and eye-voice span that yielded information regarding how the eyes function during reading (Anderson, 1937; Buswell, 1920; Fairbanks, 1937; Hochberg, 1970; Quantz, 1897; Stone, 1941; Tinker, 1939, 1946; Walker, 1938; Woodworth, 1906). These investigations were guided by theories that applied not only to reading but also to perceptual learning and cognitive and linguistics development (Gibson & Levin, 1975).

The study of reading curricula also has a long history. Many current instructional practices had their beginnings many years ago. These approaches have differed over the years because the methods of teaching reading have been controversial and subject to many heated debates among psychologists and educators since the 1800s (Chall, 1967). The issues arise from different conceptions about the way children recognize words, the nature of the reading process, and the principles that should be stressed in reading programs (Harris, 1962). In education, shifting cycles can be observed throughout the years as one reading method was emphasized, then criticized and rejected, then revived either in its original form or with new semantics and trappings (Wilson & Hall, 1972).

Between 1920 and 1960, most of the research concentrated on methods of reading instruction: the sight or the analytic approach and the phonic or the synthetic. Proponents of the sight approach emphasize the whole word as the processing unit in reading. Children are taught first to read words as wholes. After they have learned a core list of words by sight, they begin to analyze them and the relationship between the letters and the sounds they make. In contrast to the analytic approach, instruction in phonics progresses from the smallest unit, the single letter, to the whole word. After learning letter sounds, the children are taught to synthesize or blend them into whole words.

Advocates of both the analytic and synthetic approaches have cited psychological theories of word perception to support their particular methods. As different periods in history have focused on either the synthetic or analytic methods of reading, parallel shifts or trends in theories of word perception in the psychological literature also can be observed.

After 40 years of concentrated research on reading curricula, the results are disappointing. Educators and researchers are in no better position to claim that one reading method is more efficacious than another. As one method has proved effective, an equal number of studies have produced results favoring some contrasting approach. While curriculum research and "the great debate" continue, there is an increasing reemphasis on the reading process rather than on teaching methods per se (Williams, 1979).

Since the 1960s, the focus has shifted again to theories of reading processes. Numerous implicit and explicit models have been formulated to explain and predict reading performance (Applebee, 1971; Carroll, 1964; Clymer, 1968; Goodman, 1965, 1967, 1976; Gough, 1972; Guthrie, 1973; Holmes, 1976; Holmes & Singer, 1964; LaBerge & Samuels, 1974; Massaro, 1975; Singer, 1971, 1976; Smith, 1971; Spache, 1964; Wiener & Cromer, 1967). In general, these models range from representing one aspect of the reading process such as perception or cognition to depicting the general organization of the essential cognitive and linguistic variables and processes in reading. Some models represent the requisite skills or processes for reading while others are based on any one or combination of three theories, the psycholinguistic, the information processing, or the neurological (Singer, 1976).

A particularly useful way to conceptualize these reading models is by noting whether they focus on top-down or bottom-up processes. Bottom-up models take, as the basic units of reading, lower level processes (e.g., letter and word recognition) that are believed to occur prior to and independent of higher order processes. Initially, letters or words are recognized, then syntactic information is processed, followed by a semantic interpretation based on the syntax of the sentence. This hierarchical processing is characterized by the notion that reading is controlled by the printed text and that reading comprehension occurs only after letters and/or words are recognized.

In contrast, top-down theories begin with higher level cognitive processes. Proponents of this theory characterize reading as an active process in which hypotheses and predictions regarding the meaning of the text are generated in the minds of the readers. Lower level processes are used only as needed. Information that is irrelevant or redundant is ignored.

*Selected Models of Normal Reading*

Two models, those of Goodman (1965, 1976) and LaBerge and Samuels (1974), are discussed next. They were chosen because Goodman's psycholinguistic model exemplifies a top-down approach while the LaBerge and Samuels theory of automatic information processing exemplifies a bottom-up strategy. These approaches are referred to in subsequent sections on diagnosis and remediation of reading problems in learning disabled children since they seem to be the most useful models of normal reading for understanding some aspects of the problems of these youngsters.

## The Goodman Model

Goodman (1965, 1976) presents three decoding systems in his psycholinguistic model that are used simultaneously during reading: (1) the graphophonic, (2) the syntactic, and (3) the semantic. The graphophonic system refers to graphic information (e.g., the letters, spelling patterns, words, phrases, and sentences that appear in print). It also includes phonological and phonic information. The phonological consists of sounds, sound patterns, phrases, and sentences created through pitch, stress and pause; the phonic involves a complex set of relationships between the phoneme and grapheme representations of language.

The syntactic system encompasses three types of information: sentence patterns, pattern markers, and transformational rules. Sentence patterns refer to grammatical sequences that occur in the language.

Article + N + V + ing + N

is an example of a common sentence pattern. Pattern markers involve function words, inflections, and punctuation intonation. Function words are those that occur frequently and have no referential meaning but that mark the grammatical function of the meaning bearing words in the sentence (e.g., "to," "the," "an"). Inflections are bound morphemes commonly referred to as affixes in reading. Common inflections are "s," "ing," "ed." Punctuation marks represent the paralinguistic information (e.g., pitch, stress, juncture) in speech. Transformational or grammatical rules are provided by the reader, not the text. These are the rules readers bring to the task to help them recognize and derive the deep structure meaning from the surface structure or printed text.

The last system, semantic, refers to the prior experience readers bring to the reading situation along with their concepts and vocabulary. These three aspects of semantic information work together to reconstruct the message as individuals read. Furthermore, they reorganize readers' experiences and concepts in relation to the words according to the context of what they are reading.

In general, normal readers:

• Scan along a line of print, picking up graphic cues guided by their language knowledge, cognitive styles, reading strategies they have learned, and the constraints they have set up based on previous textual information.

- Form a perceptual image of the word(s) based on the graphic cues and on expectations about the input.
- Check their memory for related phonological, syntactic, and semantic cues and make a tentative choice consistent with the graphic cues.

If the choice is acceptable, decoding is confirmed and meaning is assimilated with their prior knowledge base; if the choice proves unacceptable semantically, syntactically, or phonologically, readers regress and pick up additional graphic cues until they resolve the anomalous situation. Once meaning is attained, the cycle continues (Goodman, 1976).

### The LaBerge and Samuels Model

The LaBerge and Samuels (1976) model of reading acquisition is based on the assumption that visual information is transformed into meanings through a series of hierarchical processing stages. The processing of printed text involves distinctive features (e.g., angles, lines, curves, etc.), letters, spelling patterns, words, and groups of words that are related syntactically and semantically.

During reading, it is assumed that some or all of these levels are activated for direct processing from print to meaning:

- Outputs from the lower levels such as feature detectors, letters, and spelling patterns integrate to activate a word code.
- Information from the word level in turn is sent to higher levels.
- Meaning finally can be attained at those higher levels and a response is produced.
- Higher order systems (e.g., meaning) also can be activated on the basis of the information from any one lower level (e.g., individual letters).

For skills to become functional, they must be overlearned to the point where they are automatic, rapid, and independent of attention. This automaticity is achieved only after a high degree of accuracy is obtained, a process that takes place over several years.

In addition to this hierarchical model, LaBerge and Samuels (1974) present a three-stage theory of perceptual learning:

1. The first stage involves the selection of relevant features. Initially, the rate of learning in this process may be slow. With experience, however, individuals may develop strategies that allow them to move through the stage at an increasingly rapid rate.

2. The second stage finds these individuals organizing the feature into a higher order unit, a process that requires attention.
3. The third stage is characterized by automatic processing of the text. During this stage, the component subskills (e.g., chunking the information into higher order units) are coordinated within a very short time.

A criterion for determining whether a skill is automatic is that learners can complete its processing while directing their attention elsewhere. If each component process requires attention, then fluent reading is impossible because the attention capacity will be exceeded. Researchers have emphasized the necessity of automatic processing for the development of skilled reading (Gibson & Levin, 1975; LaBerge & Samuels, 1976; Mackworth, 1972; Schneider & Shiffrin, 1977; Smith, 1971).

Both the Goodman and LaBerge and Samuels models can be used to explain certain aspects of normal and atypical reading performance. Both bottom-up and top-down processes are necessary for fluent reading. Many learning disabled children have difficulty coordinating these processes in reading. Some rely too heavily on bottom-up methods and fail to use what they know about the language and/or subject matter to make sense of the text. Others rely on context and do not pick up sufficient graphophonic cues to decode words accurately. Still others may be able to utilize both processes but not at an automatic level.

The major weakness of these theories in terms of learning disabled children, however, is that both models focus primarily on word recognition and assume normal, automatic comprehension, an assumption that cannot always be made with these youngsters. Thus, models of normal reading are not able to explain all aspects of reading disorders.

## Section 2. Studying Reading Disorders in Learning Disabled Children

The theoretical impetus for the conception of reading disabilities evolved from the study of neuropsychological disturbances in brain-injured adults such as war wounded or stroke patients. In the late 1800s and early 1900s, a concerted effort was made to determine the causes of disorders in written language by localizing specific sensory, perceptual, and language functions to precise parts of the brain. Investigators were concerned with individuals who could not read because of dysfunction in the brain.

In 1892, Dejerine postulated the specific lesions underlying adult cases of pure word blindness without agraphia (Satz, 1976). Hinshelwood (1900) has been credited as the first to scientifically describe the condition of "word blindness" in a young boy. Terms such as word blindness and congenital word blindness

(Hinshelwood, 1900, 1917), strephosymbolia (Orton, 1937), developmental dyslexia (Critchley, 1964), and dyslexia (Johnson & Myklebust, 1967) have been used to designate reading disorders in learning disabled children.

Given these historical roots, much of the past and current research on reading in the field of learning disabilities is based on neurological theory (Bryant, 1964; Chalfant & Scheffelin, 1969; Clements, 1966; Denckla, 1972; Gordon, 1965; Hallahan & Cruickshank, 1973; Johnson & Myklebust, 1967; Mattis, French, & Rapin, 1975; Myklebust, 1978; Strauss & Lehtinen, 1947; Zangwill, 1962). Research often has involved an implicit or explicit concern for etiological factors associated with reading disabilities. In addition, the neuropsychological orientation has focused on the underlying dysfunction in learning disabled readers.

Many early neuropsychological theories (e.g., Orton, 1937; Zangwill, 1962) advanced a unidimensional concept of learning disabilities (Lyon, personal communication, 1981). Reading problems in learning disabled children typically were explained as a result of a single underlying cause. For example, Orton held that mixed dominance was the root of nearly all dyslexic symptoms.

Between 1930 and the late 1960s, efforts also were made to translate the early neuropsychological theories into remedial practices. Emphasis was on developing appropriate reading methods and educational intervention strategies rather than on investigating etiological factors. It was believed that the treatment of underlying psychological process deficits (as opposed to reading practice itself) would directly improve reading performance.

Most notable is the work of Barsch (1967), Cruickshank, Bentzen, Ratzebury, & Tannhauser (1961), Fernald (1943), Frostig (1965), Getman, Kane, Halgren, and McKee (1964), Gillingham and Stillman (1960), Kephart (1960), Strauss and Lehtinen (1947), and Strauss and Kephart (1955). Many of these remedial reading methods also partially reflect trends in psychology and education, representing extensions and modifications of previous positions. For instance, various remedial reading approaches have been influenced by the synthetic approach (Gillingham & Stillman, 1960) and the analytic approach (Fernald, 1943).

Since the 1960s, three trends in research have been evident. Some researchers continue to pursue neurological theories but, instead of the unidimensional point of view, now suggest that subgroups of learning disabled readers can result from several independent neurobehavioral deficits rather than from a single unitary deficit (Lyon, in press). Multiple syndrome paradigms in neurospychology have been formulated and used to explain the significant heterogeneity of reading problems in the learning disabled population (Benson, 1976; Luria, 1973; Lyon & Watson, 1981; Lyon, in press; Johnson & Myklebust, 1967). More recently, Lyon (in press) has provided theoretical and empirical support for the application of Luria's (1973) adult neuropsychological data to developmental reading problems characterized by differential diagnosis and prediction of instructional reading methods for learning disabled subgroups.

A second trend in research is described by Torgesen (1975). He points out that many approaches to the study of reading disabilities since the 1960s have focused on the identification of psychological characteristics correlated with reading failure, beginning with visual deficits and shifting later to auditory deficits. The psychological variables that have been investigated include processes such as visual and auditory attention, perception, and memory, as well as reasoning and verbal abilities and perceptual motor skills.

This line of research has not been concerned explicitly with etiological factors. While some researchers were investigating psychological processes, others (Bannatyne, 1966; Belmont, Flegenhermer, and Birch, 1973; Mann, 1971; Silberberg & Silberberg, 1969; Tarver & Dawson, 1978) were reviewing or testing the efficacy of the various instructional methods that focus on process deficits (e.g., Frostig's 1966 approach, Kirk & Kirk's 1971 psycholinguistic remedial approach).

In addition to neurological and process deficit conceptualizations of reading problems, there is a third line of research oriented exclusively toward instructional or educational variables. This approach emerged in the late 1960s and early 1970s because of conflicting empirical support regarding the efficacy of remediation of the underlying psychological process deficits (Hammill & Wiederholt, 1973; Mann, 1971; Salvia & Ysseldyke, 1978). At the same time, Bateman (1968), Englemann (1969), and Haring, Lovitt, Eaton, and Hansen (1978) excluded psychological process deficits in their remedial approaches. Instead, they recommended task analytic programming (i.e., the determination of which specific behavioral subskills must be taught) as a means of structuring remediation.

In spite of the apparent trend away from a process approach, considerable research continues to be directed toward process deficits related to reading disabilities. Starting in about 1978, however, there appears to have been a slight shift in the direction of this research. Influenced by the field of cognitive psychology, researchers (Blackman & Goldstein, 1982; Kogan, 1980; Lyon, in press; Newman, 1980; Readence & Baldwin, 1978; Torgesen, 1978, 1980) have focused more heavily on cognitive strategies and styles. Their work maintains the view that learning disabled readers (and learning disabled children in general) do not perform well because they fail to adapt to tasks through the use of efficient and organized strategies such as verbal rehearsal and categorization to aid memory. Empirical support for this view is derived from studies on:

- selective attention (Hallahan, Gajar, Cohen, & Tarver, 1978; Hallahan, Tarver, Kauffman, and Graybeal, 1978; Ross, 1976; Tarver, Hallahan, Kauffman, & Ball, 1976; Tarver, Hallahan, Cohen, & Kauffman, 1977; Vrana & Pihl, 1980)
- memory skills (Newman, 1980; Torgesen, 1977a, 1977b, 1978, 1980)

- problem solving (Maker, 1981; Stone, 1980)
- conceptual tempo (Coburn, in preparation; Denney, 1974).

### Section 3. Reading Disability and Processing Deficits

Learning to read requires a unique combination of skills. Learning disabled individuals may fail to read, or read inefficiently, for a number of reasons even though they exhibit the same level of impairment or the same reading behavior. A multidimensional model of reading disabilities is essential to encompass the complexity of this act. It can be seen from the historical review presented in the two preceding sections that theorists in both normal and disordered reading are compelled to return to concepts that describe and explain underlying processes in reading.

Research on methods and curricula have not yielded any convincing evidence to validate methods of instruction per se. The most fruitful approach to understanding reading disability must have at least two essential characteristics: (1) it must focus on processes involved in learning to read (and processing deficits that appear to influence learning to read), and (2) it must be multidimensional to encompass the unique combination of skills required in reading.

The theoretical framework advanced by Johnson and Myklebust (1967) meets these criteria and is useful in analyzing individuals' reading performances. They use multiple frames of reference to describe the nature of specific disturbances in reading and provide a dynamic hierarchy of the cognitive processes involved in learning: attention, perception, memory, symbolization, and conceptualization. They assert that a processing deficit can occur at any one of these levels, resulting in atypical reading behavior. Lower level processes also may affect the functioning of the remaining levels, and vice versa.

Within the broad framework of language, reading can be viewed as a visual symbol system superimposed on an auditory symbol system. Within this visual symbol system, input, integration, and output are important to conceptualizing disabilities. This theoretical frame of reference considers reading disabilities in terms of breakdowns at different points during information processing: the reception of information (the intake of information), its integration (the association of meaning with experience), and its expression (the output). Learning disabilities in reading thus can be conceptualized in terms of the levels and stages at which information processing is most impaired.

To describe and clarify the multiple possible reasons why learning disabled children may have difficulty learning to read, it is useful to focus directly on levels of both auditory and visual processing. However, in line with the focus of this book, the emphasis here is on the effects of auditory deficits. Specifically, it is crucial to understand the effect that deficits in oral language, metalinguistic awareness, and thinking skills may have on learning to read.

*Oral Language and Reading*

Learning to read is more than acquiring a skill; it is an integral part of total language development. Reading is a visual verbal system through which individuals receive, integrate, and organize experience (Myklebust & Johnson, 1962). Reading is intimately related to oral language, the two together constituting language. Reading and oral and written language are understood only in relation to each other (Myklebust & Johnson, 1962). Researchers have expressed this relationship in a variety of ways. Mattingly (1972), for instance, reports that "reading is parasitic on language" (p. 145). Venezky (1968) states that "reading is translating from written symbols to a form of language to which the person can already attach meaning" (p. 17). Johnson and Myklebust (1967) posit that reading is a visual symbol system superimposed on a preestablished oral language system. Goodman (1965, 1976) describes reading as a psycholinguistic process in which there is an interaction between thought and language.

Reading is viewed as a form different from but parallel to oral language. Both reading and listening involve sampling, predicting and sequencing processes. Individuals draw upon their oral language skills as they develop control over the written language. To understand the reading process, Goodman states that it is necessary to comprehend how oral language works and how readers use language. Individuals' ability to read depends in large part on their prior learning and experience with oral language. By the time normal children enter school, they have developed considerable competence in the use of language for communication.

Since linguistic deficiencies have been commonly associated with reading disabilities (Cohn, 1961; Ingram, 1960; Johnson & Myklebust, 1967; Vernon, 1971), it can be concluded that it is important to know how well reading disabled children can handle both symbol systems—the spoken and the read. Moreover, it is useful to know whether the deficit is specific to oral language, to reading, or to both since the direction of remediation will vary accordingly (Weaver & Dickenson, 1979).

Deficiences in auditory receptive language and/or auditory expressive language interfere with bottom-up processes in learning to read, i.e., those that synthesize letters into words, words into sentences, and so on involving word recognition and syntactic processing and semantic interpretation. Language deficits also may interfere with top-down processes (those that make use of readers' specific semantic and syntactic knowledge, and also their store of general knowledge for predicting unfamiliar words.)

Auditory receptive language involves three component processes: (1) auditory verbal discrimination, (2) auditory comprehension for single words and connected language, and (3) auditory verbal memory (Johnson & Myklebust, 1967). Each of these subareas is critical for the development of fluent reading behavior.

Dyslexic individuals may exhibit any combination of deficits in this area. (Although auditory verbal memory is included under the rubric of auditory receptive language, in this chapter it is discussed separately in the section on that topic. This allows for a more cohesive discussion since there are numerous memory tasks that include both auditory receptive and auditory expressive processes.)

**Auditory Verbal Discrimination:** Clinically, it has been recognized that auditory verbal discrimination deficiencies are related to reading problems (Chalfant & Scheffelin, 1969; Ingram, 1960; Johnson & Myklebust, 1967; Vellutino, 1977; Vernon, 1971; Wepman, 1960, 1973, 1975). Auditory verbal discrimination or perception requires the ability to hear differences between minimally contrasted words such as "shack-sack," "pin-pen" (Johnson & Myklebust, 1967). Some reading disabled children do not receive information accurately at the input level, which in turn can affect processing at the integration (meaning) and output stages (oral reading). As a result, they may have difficulty associating sounds and letters. A perceptual problem such as this can affect processing at subsequent levels such as memory (remembering the sounds the letters make).

Behaviorally, learning disabled readers may make similar sounding word substitution errors during oral reading (as well as spelling), reflecting an underlying processing deficit in auditory verbal discrimination (e.g., "ban-band"; "festfist"; "pin-bin"). Of course, it cannot be assumed, based on these substitutions in oral reading or spelling, that the problems lie entirely at the level of perception. In some cases, children "misperceive" words because they comprehend one word but not the other, (e.g., "fest-fist"). Hence, individuals' auditory perceptual skills must be tested either formally or informally.

**Comprehension:** Intact auditory verbal comprehension also is necessary for good reading performance. If children do not comprehend the spoken word(s), they will not understand the vocabulary, sentences, and/or paragraphs they read. This is because reading skills are acquired by learning visual verbal symbols for previously acquired auditory receptive and expressive language (Johnson & Myklebust, 1967; Risko, 1981). Thus, individuals with deficits in oral language comprehension are likely to have similar problems in reading comprehension.

On occasion, clinicians observe learning disabled readers who are able to decode the printed text rather quickly but without comprehension. These individuals are referred to as hyperlexics or word callers (Danks & Fears, 1979; Huttenlocher & Huttenlocher, 1973; Johnson & Myklebust, 1967). According to Johnson and Myklebust's input-integration-output frame of reference, hyperlexics can process information at the input and output stages. They can detect all the distinctive features and spelling patterns and can translate written information into the auditory code (Goodman, 1976; LaBerge & Samuels, 1974). However, since these dysfunctional individuals fail to comprehend what they read, the breakdown can be pinpointed at the integration stage. Johnson & Myklebust (1967) note that these hyperlexic children often manifest a similar behavior (e.g., echolalia) in spoken language. In such instances, they repeat words and sentences they hear but are unable to attach meaning to them. Echolalic behavior usually occurs when the children fail to comprehend what they hear.

Researchers and practitioners (Bloom & Lahey, 1978; Carrow, 1973; Cecci, 1978; Epstein, 1977; Johnson & Myklebust, 1967; Wiig & Semel, 1980) note that it is necessary to distinguish between the comprehension of single words (including morphology) and longer units of language such as sentences and narratives. Knowing a word and knowing grammar represent different mental capacities, and deficits in each may have differential effects on both decoding and comprehension in reading.

Depending on the nature and scope of their language disorders, discrepancies in auditory comprehension of single words, morphological endings, sentences, and conversations (see Chapters 3, 4, and 5) may be revealed within and across learning disabled readers. Some of these children may have difficulty at only one level while others experience comprehension deficiencies in some or all of these areas in varying degrees. In any event, such language disorders can affect decoding and reading comprehension.

If children have a receptive vocabulary deficiency, they will not be able to make efficient use of context cues to reconstruct the passage and reorganize their experiences according to the words in the message. Clinically, it has been observed that some dyslexics have difficulty reading and comprehending directions because they have a poor understanding of multiple meanings of words. One 8-year-old boy, for example, failed to understand the word "check" as a verb in the following direction, "Check your answer on the answer sheet to see if you are correct." He understood "check" only as a noun (e.g., a mark).

In her study, Groshong (1980) notes that learning disabled children have difficulty comprehending multiple meanings of words. For example, they are asked to explain the meanings of certain target words in the following types of sentences:

"The girls gave peanuts to the elephant. They put them in the *trunk*" (p. 176).
"The girls packed some old clothes. They put them in the *trunk*" (p. 178).

On reading tasks, older school-age children with auditory comprehension deficits invariably fail to understand metaphors, similes, and figures of speech that require an understanding of multiple word meanings and inferences. These children tend to be concrete and literal in their interpretations.

As for morphology, in terms of Goodman's model (1965, 1976), if children have difficulty with word endings such as the past verb tense "ed" or the possessive "s" in spoken language, then they are likely to have problems using morphological and syntactic cues in printed text to predict and read words with these suffixes. Similarly, some individuals have difficulty decoding (predicting words in context) and comprehending text because of syntactic disorders.

As children get older, they become exposed to increasingly complex sentences in their textbooks. As a result, they may experience more difficulty in later grades than they had in earlier ones. A failure to understand complex sentences in auditory language also can interfere with reading and fluency. Remedial efforts can help some children to the point where they no longer exhibit these morphosyntactic problems in auditory receptive or expressive language. However, such problems can surface when they have to deal with another symbol system such as reading.

It has been this author's clinical experience that disabled readers who have basic underlying comprehension deficits for connected spoken language (i.e., groups of sentences) also have reading comprehension problems for stories. However, there have been a few instances in which dyslexics actually perform better on reading comprehension tasks because they have poor auditory memory spans that limit the amount of information they can retain. During reading, they have the opportunity to review the parts they did not remember. Unless the speaker repeats the information, this opportunity is not possible during listening tasks.

Researchers also have been investigating the comprehension of larger structural units such as stories and the relations between paragraph listening and reading comprehension (deHirsch, Jansky, & Langford, 1965; Fry, Johnson, & Muehl, 1970; Nahmias, 1982; Weaver, 1978; Weaver & Dickenson, 1979). The literature is suggesting that children with reading comprehension problems will experience similar difficulties in listening.

In auditory expressive language, subcomponent processes are organized around expression of longer units of language, including the following: articulation, sequencing sounds in words, word retrieval, syntax, and oral formulation (sentences for stories) (Johnson & Myklebust, 1967). Some learning disabled children may have good auditory comprehension but exhibit a primary deficit in one or more of these expressive areas; others also may have accompanying auditory receptive language deficits. Therefore, it is essential to determine whether a reading disability is caused by an underlying auditory expressive language problem or by both auditory receptive and expressive language deficiencies.

The more severe reading disabled cases are most likely to exhibit a primary deficit in auditory receptive language, particularly comprehension. Auditory expressive language deficits generally interfere with performance on reading tasks that demand a spoken response (Johnson & Myklebust, 1967). In the author's clinical experience, learning disabled readers with a deficit in auditory expressive language often perform poorly on oral reading tasks but better on silent reading activities. Each of these expressive language disorders is discussed in terms of its effect on reading performance.

**Articulation:** Deficits in articulation have been associated with poor reading (Cohn, 1961), although it appears that inadequacy of more complex and highly developed linguistic functions are more significant (deHirsch, Jansky, & Langford, 1964; Vernon, 1971). There are, however, certain articulation problems—apraxia—that can interfere with reading performance. Apraxic individuals are unable to pronounce words because of a failure to execute the motor patterns of speech, although the strength for movement is intact (Chalfant & Scheffelin, 1969; Chappell, 1973; Darley, Aronson, & Brown, 1975; Johnson & Myklebust, 1967; Nielsen, 1946, Yoss & Darley, 1974).

With apraxic cases, oral reading is disrupted the most. For example, one severely apraxic 7-year-old girl's oral reading was completely unintelligible. She also was unsuccessful in learning to read through a phonics approach. However, she could read silently using a whole word method and could demonstrate her comprehension by answering multiple choice questions or by locating answers in the text.

Another type of expressive deficiency, sequencing sounds in words, may cause difficulty in oral reading. Individuals exhibiting problems in this area have trouble ordering sounds and syllables correctly in spoken words. This may be caused by auditory sequential memory problems (Johnson, 1979). For example, in oral language learning disabled readers may say "spfisically" for "specifically," "aminal" for "animal," "perolator" for "percolator." When these same individuals encounter these words in oral reading, they often make similar errors.

However, a few will read them better because the printed word can serve as a visual cue for the proper auditory verbal sequence. Multisyllabic words generally are the most difficult for them to read orally. Clinicians often hear dyslexics say when they come across a multisyllabic word, "I know that word but I cannot say it," but they usually can read the words silently.

**Word Retrieval:** An inability to recall words often is observed in dyslexic populations (Denckla & Rudel, 1976; Johnson & Myklebust, 1967; Lyon, in press; Mattis, French, & Rapin, 1975). Individuals with word retrieval difficulties usually comprehend a word when it is spoken out cannot recall it. Terms that have been used to describe this disorder include verbal amnesia (Broca, 1861, cited in Cohn, 1970; Nielsen, 1946); nominal aphasia (Head, 1926); semantic aphasia (Luria, 1966); anomia (Berry & Eisenson, 1956; Critchley, 1964; Geschwind, 1967).

Manifestations of word-finding difficulties include any one or more of the following behaviors: gestures, pantomime, delayed responses, circumlocutions, semantic word substitutions, and an overuse of semantically empty words such as "thing" or "stuff." Many hesitations, repetitions, and nonfluencies also can be observed. Learning disabled readers with dysnomia experience difficulty with oral reading tasks. For instance, a dysnomic 6-year-old boy could not read the word "hop" orally but when asked if he knew what the word meant, he said, "yes, like a bunny." Others make word substitutions that have no graphic similarity with the target word (e.g., "hill" for "mountain," "man" for "boy," "go" for "come") but that are associated semantically in some way. Similar behaviors have been observed by others (Johnson & Myklebust, 1967; Johnson, 1979).

This atypical reading behavior can be explained in terms of the LaBerge and Samuels (1974) model of normal reading. In the example of the dysnomic boy, he is going straight from print to meaning, apparently bypassing a phonological code since he is unable to reauditorize. It is interesting to note that this is a case in which an inefficient reader is engaging in a behavior (going straight from print to meaning) that is typical of highly skilled readers (LaBerge & Samuels, 1974; Smith, 1971).

In addition to performing poorly on oral reading tasks, dysnomic individuals often are not proficient on cloze reading tests that require them to generate an appropriate word to complete a sentence (e.g., Woodcock, 1973). Their performance is better on multiple choice tests (e.g., Gates & MacGinitie, 1972; Karlsen, Madden, & Gardner, 1976).

**Syntax and Formulation:** Goodman (1967) states that intact oral syntactic abilities are important for reading. Children can draw upon their syntactic abilities in oral language to predict words in sentences as they read. A number of researchers have investigated the syntactic skills of learning disabled readers (Andolina, 1980; Fry, Johnson, & Muehl, 1970; Johnson & Myklebust, 1967; Vellutino, 1977; Vogel, 1972; Wiig & Semel, 1975, 1976).

In general, they have found that many dyslexics have difficulty applying syntactic cues to decode sentences because they do not have the requisite oral linguistic skills. Research (Wren, 1980) and clinical observation suggest that, on the one hand, there are some learning disabled readers who make grammatical errors in simple, declarative sentences; on the other hand, there are individuals who are able to formulate simple sentences but cannot speak in grammatically complex sentences.

The level of the development in oral syntax may directly affect the children's ability to use syntax as an aid to decoding as well as comprehension of what they read. It is likely that children will be able to comprehend sentences only at a level commensurate with oral language ability. Interestingly, however, there are a few language disordered children who respond better to visual verbal information (printed text) than to auditory verbal information. Although they still make grammatical errors in oral reading, their oral reading of sentences is slightly better than their syntax in daily spoken language. This diagnostic finding can be useful in designing a remedial program (i.e., written language could serve to facilitate and stabilize oral language skills).

Children with oral formulation deficits (problems combining sentences to relate an idea) may have difficulty with reading comprehension per se. Others may have difficulty answering open-ended recall reading comprehension questions that require more than a word or phrase response, e.g., the *Durrell Analysis of Reading Difficulty* (Durrell, 1955).

Researchers such as Hickman, 1979; Podhajski, 1980; and Stone, 1980 have been interested in the ability of learning disabled individuals to use discourse devices to organize oral narratives. Halliday and Hasan (1976) define "discourse" or "text-forming" devices as the elements in language that supply cohesion to a narrative discourse. These devices include referential expressions such as pronouns and indefinite and definite articles. The research is beginning to demonstrate that particular groups of learning disabled children have poor organizational skills on narrative tasks. Podhajski (1980) reports that her learning disabled subjects are deficient in the use of specific forms of oral narrative language, i.e., indefinite, introductory expressions, and nouns that serve as transitions between story clauses.

It may be speculated that problems in the use or comprehension of such narrative discourse devices could interfere with readers' awareness of these linguistic forms in written text; in turn, that could affect reading comprehension of stories. For example, some learning disabled children have difficulty understanding sentences that contain anaphoric and cataphoric reference, terms denoting information preceding or following the immediate text, respectively (Halliday & Hasan, 1976).

Other readers may understand the passage but be unable to organize their responses to tell what they know. In their study, Fry, Johnson, and Muehl (1970) report that poor readers are less adept at organizing and integrating their ideas to form a coherent story. Moreover, they tend to provide unrelated details. Some learning disabled readers may have a basic listening comprehension deficit, others may have only oral formulation problems, while still others have a deficit specific to the area of reading.

**Auditory Memory Processes:** Auditory memory processes, mainly short term, have been investigated extensively in the reading disabled population (Burns, 1975; Chalfant & Scheffelin, 1969; Elbert, 1979; German, 1977; Johnson & Myklebust, 1965; Johnson, 1957; Katz & Deutsch, 1967; Kluever, 1971; Newman, 1980; Senf & Freundl, 1971; Vernon, 1971). Tasks used to measure memory skills include recalling a list of digits, random words, and sentences. In general, learning disabled readers have been found to perform consistently poorly on these tasks when compared to normal readers. Based on the research data, it can be concluded that many dyslexics have auditory short-term memory deficits.

Auditory memory problems may affect reading ability in a variety of ways. At the decoding level, children with short-term memory problems may not be able to hold the individual sounds of an unfamiliar word in mind long enough to synthesize the word. Others may not be able to recall the letter sounds or letter names.

Short-term memory also may affect reading comprehension. Children who are unable to hold sentence-length units in mind may have difficulty comprehending entire sentences when reading. Information gained at the beginning of a paragraph may not be retained long enough to be integrated with that obtained at the end of a paragraph.

Other children with short-term memory deficits may be able to comprehend what they read but may not retain it long enough to answer questions about it or retell the story. However, those with short-term memory problems should not be confused with children with auditory comprehension problems. The former perform adequately on multiple-choice questions or can find the answer in the text, suggesting that comprehension is adequate but that poor memory does not allow them to indicate what they understand. Children with poor comprehension, on the other hand, have difficulty even locating the answer in the text since they have not understood it adequately.

## Metalinguistic Awareness and Reading

Language is a rule-governed system. When children learn to speak they are learning the phonological, morphemic, syntactic, and discourse rules of the language. However, they follow these rules intuitively and do not have explicit knowledge of them, as does a linguist.

Metalinguistic awareness refers to the ability to reflect upon language as-an-object as well as comprehend and produce it (Cazden, 1972). It is individuals' conscious awareness of the prosodic, phonological, semantic, and syntactical features that comprise their language. Metalinguistic awareness is manifested in the ability to analyze, manipulate, and apply these features in abstract situations where semantic cues are absent (Hook, 1976).

Language in this case is taken out of the communicative context (e.g., asking children to isolate sounds in words, determine the grammatic correctness of sentences, or judge whether a sentence is a question or statement based on intonation). Although by school entrance most children have mastered the important elements of their oral language, they continue to refine their metalinguistic skills. Their awareness of language continues to develop throughout the school years.

Gibson and Levin (1975) indicate that children are able to produce language before they have an analytic understanding of its internal structure. Although very early in life children begin to show an awareness of their language (e.g., verbal play with words), most metalinguistic skills relevant for reading (such as analyzing words into their component sounds) develop around age 5½.

It is generally agreed that metalinguistic awareness is important in the acquisition of literacy skills (Cazden, 1972; Ehri, 1979; Elkonin, 1973; Gibson & Levin, 1975; Glutman & Rozin, 1977; Hook, 1976; Johnson & Hook, 1978; Leong,

1979; Liberman, Shankweiler, Liberman, Fowler, & Fischer, 1977; Liberman, Liberman, Mattingly & Shankweiler, 1980; Mattingly, 1972; Miller, 1976).

Children who have primary deficits in the comprehension and production of spoken language (as noted in the previous section) also encounter problems at a conscious metalinguistic level. They do not have sufficient linguistic skills to apply rules adequately in novel situations and to use language to talk about the structure of spoken words or sentences. However, many learning disabled readers do not have major problems in auditory language comprehension or expression but do have difficulty detaching language from its meaning and analyzing its form. These individuals are deficient in the awareness of the rule system of their language and in the application of this knowledge to reading.

The study of metalinguistic skills in normal and learning disabled readers has focused mainly on three aspects of language: intonation, phonology, and syntax. Little work has been done with learning disabled readers in semantics or the relation between awareness of text structure and comprehension, although there has been some speculation (Miller, 1976). This section focuses on the significance and implications of metalinguistic awareness of intonation, phonology, and syntax on reading performance.

**Intonation:** The perception of stress patterns or intonation develops very early in life, before real speech. Initially, children depend on intonation to some extent to comprehend language. Similarly, they use intonation first to mark grammatical structures such as questions. Lefevre (1964) emphasizes the importance of internalizing intonation patterns of the language for the development of syntax and reading comprehension. Gibson (1972) says children must learn to analyze intonation patterns in words and phrases and this learning is not complete until they are 5 or 6 years old.

Hook (1976) and Vogel (1972) examine the relation between metalinguistic awareness of intonation (melody) patterns, syntax, and reading in dyslexic children. Vogel devised a test of recognition of melody pattern for declarative and interrogative sentences, asking her learning disabled readers to judge whether or not a statement composed of nonsense words is asking or telling something. Sentences are transformed into yes/no questions by using a marked rising breath contour at the end. For example, "mim you po to droll seeway?" vs. "coys make to low ees plotting" (p. 132).

Hook (1976) uses Vogel's test in addition to her own, which contains real words; for example, "The cat is sitting down" or "The black dog is eating food?" (p. 44). Hook extends Vogel's study by asking her subjects to apply melody pattern to change sentences into questions (e.g., "I ate dinner," "I ate dinner?"). Dyslexic children in both studies have difficulty recognizing melody patterns.

Lieberman (1967) suggests that children's knowledge of grammar influences their perception of intonation. Many dyslexics often have poor syntactical skills

(Vogel, 1972). Apparently, there are interacting cues from both systems that influence metalinguistic awareness. Hook (1976) finds that the application of intonation to generate questions from statements is more difficult for the learning disabled than the recognition of melody pattern. They also perform better on the recognition test containing real-word sentences than on the one with nonsense words.

What do these results mean in terms of reading? While keeping in mind that syntactic and semantic features are important and interrelated, clinicians may speculate that the awareness of intonation patterns will come into play during oral reading. Since by its very nature written language has no recourse to shared prosodic features, as does oral language, readers must apply their knowledge of these features to the printed text. Teachers often comment that poor readers do not read with expression. It may be that the conscious awareness of intonation could influence their ability to attend to the diacritical marks (question and exclamation marks) in the text, read in phrase or clause units, and/or note attitudes and emotions displayed by the characters, especially in dialogues. Clinical experience suggests that some learning disabled children have greater difficulty reading dialogues than narratives or prose.

**Phonology:** Linguistic awareness involving the isolation and manipulation of phonological elements is important in learning to read. To read analytically, children must be able to treat speech sounds as individual units and discriminate and manipulate them (for example, segment words into their constituent phonemes and blend them together). The awareness of the phonetic structure of speech is related to the acquisition of phonics skills (e.g., sounding out words) as a work-attack strategy (Downing, 1973; Elkonin, 1973; Hook, 1976; Liberman & Shankweiler, 1979; Shankweiler & Liberman, 1979; Vellutino, 1977).

With respect to perception of phonemes, Wepman (1960) reports that auditory discrimination is correlated with reading ability. Although most children have developed adequate auditory discrimination by 8 years of age, Hook (1976) says her learning disabled readers continue to have difficulty when they are required to discriminate sounds in nonsense words.

A number of investigators have affirmed that poor readers are deficient in phoneme segmentation—the isolation and manipulation of sounds in words. (Helfgott, 1976; Hook, 1976; Liberman, Liberman, Mattingly & Shankweiler, 1980; Myklebust, Bannochie, & Killen, 1971; Shankweiler & Liberman, 1972). A test developed by Hook (1976) entails learning a language code similar to pig Latin. She describes this task as the best predictor of group membership. None of her learning disabled readers could perform the task or apply the rules with proficiency, whereas the normal readers could. Liberman et al., (1979) also find that poor readers have difficulty recoding visual information in auditory short-term memory for efficient storage. Elbert's (1979) study with learning disabled readers also supports these empirical findings.

Metalinguistic analysis of auditory information may be divided developmentally into the following levels: segmenting sentences into words, words into syllables, and, finally, words into phonemes. Karpova (1966) asks children to repeat sentences and then respond to questions: "How many words are here?" and "Which is the first . . . second . . . third . . . word?"

Three developmental stages are observed in this task. The youngest children are unable to break up the sentence on the basis of individual words but can do so on the basis of meaning or semantic units. For example, "The boy is laughing." A 7-year-old says there is only one word in the sentence because "only one boy is laughing." Somewhat older children can isolate nouns in the sentence. In response to the sentence, "Galya and Vova went walking," a child replies, "There are two words. Vova is one, and Galya is the other." The final stage is reached by the oldest children, who can break sentences into all of their separate words.

Liberman, Shankweiler, Fischer, and Carter (1974) ask their subjects to isolate syllables and phonemes in words. The procedure is in the form of a game in which the children tap a wooden dowel on the table a certain number of times to indicate the number of sounds or syllables. The result: syllables are easier to isolate than individual sounds.

**Syntax:** Goodman (1976) states that efficient readers use morphological and syntactical constraints to predict words in sentences. Studies comparing oral reading errors of normal and poor readers show that poor readers do not use structural cues inherent in grammatical morphemes and syntax to aid sentence processing (Goodman, 1970; Levin & Kaplan, 1970; Steiner, Weiner, & Cromer, 1971; Weber, 1970). Numerous studies also have investigated the metalinguistic abilities of learning disabled readers to recognize and apply morphological and syntactical rules (Hook, 1976; Kass, 1966; McClure, Kalk, & Keenan, 1980; Semel & Wiig, 1975; Vogel, 1972; Wiig, Semel, & Crouse, 1973).

In general, it has been found that the learning disabled are deficient in their metalinguistic awareness of syntax. This deficit seems to interfere with their ability to decode words based on the syntax of the sentence and to self-correct when errors are syntactical in nature. These children tend to do worse on metalinguistic nonsense words than on similar tasks using real words.

Hook (1976) says some of her subjects did better on the grammatic closure of the *Illinois Test of Psycholinguistic Abilities* (Kirk, McCarthy, & Kirk, 1968) than on the *Berry-Talbott Language Tests 1* (Berry, 1966). The former test involves applying morphological endings to real words, the latter contains nonsense words.

Vogel (1972) finds that her learning disabled readers can recognize correct grammatical sentences (e.g., "Does this sound correct?" "Was you there last week?"). However, they do not perform as well as the normals on the Berry-

Talbott Test. Based on the Vogel and Hook findings, Johnson and Hook (1978) hypothesize that there is a "developmental progression from skill in recognizing grammatically, to applying it in a structured, nonspontaneous situation, to finally being able to apply this knowledge to nonsense words" (p. 217).

*Thinking Disorders and Reading*

In addition to reading problems stemming from a variety of linguistic and metalinguistic deficits, thinking and conceptual disorders can seriously affect reading ability. In their clinical work, Strauss and Lehtinen (1947) observe disorders of thinking in children who demonstrate normal intelligence when measured in terms of standardized intelligence tests. They report that thinking disorders are reflected by peculiarities in reasoning and concept formation (see Chapter 6).

Since reading entails cognitive processes of knowing, reasoning, and inferring (Carroll, 1977), children with disturbances in thinking and concept formation are handicapped in interpreting reading material in addition to understanding the more complex demands of life in general (Strauss & Lehtinen, 1947). Reading, therefore, is a thinking act. Others also support this notion. Stauffer (1977) states that the ability to think critically (i.e., to problem solve, hypothesize, conceptualize, generalize, and make logical assumptions) is crucial to reading comprehension. Vernon (1971) postulates that learning to read involves conceptual reasoning, "in particular in abstracting the essential characteristics of printed and spoken words and in generalizing these to cover a wide range of minor variations" (p. 78). Myklebust (1978) describes a dyslexic subgroup, mainly "inner language dyslexia," in which individuals have difficulty with cognitive processes involving meaning, abstraction, and concept formation. Inner language, which can be verbal or nonverbal, is fundamental to auditory expressive language, reading, and written language.

Thinking and thinking disorders have not been well defined in psychology and education. As Myklebust (1978) comments, the evaluation and identification of inner language disorders are complex and equivocal. Moreover, it is the author's belief that it often is difficult to separate reading disorders caused by poor verbal thinking skills from reading disabilities that result from poor auditory comprehension. Based on Myklebust's (1964) language hierarchy, many dyslexics who have thinking disorders naturally exhibit auditory comprehension disorders.

In terms of the model of normal reading discussed in the first part of this chapter, children with thinking disorders will have difficulty with top-down processes, i.e., those that include hypotheses and predictions about the meaning of the text. Moreover, learning disabled readers who are deficient in auditory comprehension processes more than likely will experience difficulty in abstract reasoning and making inferences on verbal tasks.

On reading comprehension tests, reading disabled children who have primary thinking disorders often fail to answer questions based on inferences, conclusions, and generalizations. Many have problems in abstracting the main idea (a conceptual whole) from a group of individual sentences. Clinical experience suggests that many of these individuals can answer fact questions and often retain what they comprehend in a rote manner. Rarely going beyond the linguistic information, some dyslexics are concrete and literal in their interpretation of the text.

Vernon (1971) cites studies that suggest that reading achievement may be related to the ability to form concepts. Goins (cited in Vernon, 1971), for instance, reports that poor readers have difficulty with classifying and noting differences between similar objects. Harris (1979), in investigating the classification skills of learning disabled children, many of them dyslexic, says they are inferior to their normal counterparts.

Stone's (1980) study determined that a subgroup of learning disabled adolescents who have generalized conceptual and reasoning difficulties also have poor auditory language and reading comprehension skills. Individuals in Stone's subgroup have difficulty using a ''control-of-variables'' strategy on a Piagetian problem solving task, The Bending Rods. The learning disabled subjects could not make unconfounded tests of at least three variables to determine what factors caused the rods to bend: length, material, diameter, place of weight attachment. This subgroup is similar to Myklebust's (1978) ''inner language dyslexic'' population.

Strauss and Lehtinen (1947) note that their thinking disordered subjects often give ''far-fetched'' and unusual explanations for their solutions to problems. The following is a case example that illustrates their description of thinking disorders.

A 20-year-old man of average intelligence had a severe thinking and reading disorder. He was an excellent decoder in reading and, for the most part, could answer rote, factual questions on reading comprehension tests. However, he had difficulty distinguishing fact from opinion as well as abstracting main ideas, inferences, and conclusions from written material. He often gave correct answers for which he did not know the reason, and said, ''Just because I told the right answer doesn't mean that I know why.''

This man also had difficulty classifying, generating superordinate labels for his categories, isolating variables, and testing hypotheses. His poor reading skills greatly affected his daily life experiences. For example, not understanding cause-and-effect relationships, he told his clinician one day that he did not understand why Irish Republican Army hunger strikers were dying from starvation. To explain the cause/effect relationship between not eating and dying of starvation, the clinician used an analogy. The following dialogue illustrates his [the client's] thinking disorder, and failure to understand the analogy:

Clinician: What happens if you do not water a plant?
Student:   It dies.
Clinician: Well, do you think the same thing will happen if you don't eat or drink?
Student:   No, I'm not a plant. I'm not green.

These thinking problems affected other daily life experiences such as understanding how to use a checking account, how to go about determining flight arrival times for a given airline, how to use the Yellow Pages, etc.

This individual also had difficulty with hypothetical thinking. For example, on many occasions, he could not make up a story about a picture because he was not there at the time when it was taken. He did not know what happened and, therefore, could "not tell the truth." On another occasion, he claimed that he did not have to buy or consider buying health insurance because he had never gotten sick. He further indicated that health insurance was not an important variable to consider when evaluating job offers. Health insurance did not concern him because he reasoned that since he never got sick, he never would. According to this man, what has never happened in the past could never possibly occur in the future.

In this example, it is apparent that the problems lie at the level of conceptualization and occur at the integration (meaning) stage. Such problems affect the output (e.g., verbal reasons or explanations). His auditory language and written language reflect his basic problems in thinking skills.

## Visual Processing & Reading

Although the major emphasis in this chapter is on auditory processing deficits and their relation to reading, visual verbal processing deficiencies cannot be overlooked as possible contributing factors in reading disability. While such deficits can interfere with the acquisition of fluent reading skills (Elbert, 1979), their significance remains controversial among professionals (Vellutino, 1977). The author's clinical experience with school-age and adult learning disabled readers suggests that problems of visual discrimination and memory for words can affect the acquisition and stabilization of word attack skills.

As for visual perceptual deficits, some individuals continue to have difficulty detecting visual similarities and differences among words. However, it should be pointed out that similar manifestations of reading errors can occur for quite different reasons. For example, problems at the symbolization level can account for decoding errors that appear to be perceptual but that in fact are not. To illustrate, individuals may substitute the word "trail" for "trial" not because they have a visual perceptual problem involving letter reversals or missequencing but because the word "trial" may not be in their receptive vocabulary.

Visual short-term memory deficits may interfere with stabilization of sight vocabulary. Learning disabled children with poor short-term visual memory often cannot recognize a word previously read although they may have encountered it only a few sentences earlier. They read as if they are encountering each word for the first time and often overuse phonetic analysis, attempting to sound out every letter.

In sum, the view here is that visual perceptual and memory deficits can contribute to reading disorders. However, problems in oral language and/or metalinguistic awareness often coexist.

## PART II. DIAGNOSIS

### Section 1. A Framework for Assessment

Reading is an extremely complex skill based, as noted, on processing both auditory and visual information. While visual perceptual and memory skills are crucial for processing printed symbols, a wide variety of auditory and cognitive skills are involved in translating those symbols into meaningful messages. Children with reading disabilities may have difficulty both decoding and comprehending printed text because of a variety of disorders.

A comprehensive diagnostic evaluation of children with reading disorders must consider reading from two perspectives:

1. The variety of underlying deficits that may interfere with reading must be taken into account, as discussed in the first part of this chapter. This in itself is not enough, however.
2. A direct investigation of reading behavior also is necessary to assess the skills that may be lacking in an individual child. Reading skills generally are broken down into decoding (or word recognition) and comprehension; a number of subskills are important in these major components of the reading act.

Neither of these perspectives is sufficient by itself for an adequate diagnosis of reading disorders. Researchers have questioned the effectiveness of an entirely process-oriented approach (Hammill & Larsen, 1974), suggesting that focusing only on underlying processes fails to bring about much progress in actual reading. However, an entirely skill-oriented approach also is questionable. Simply assessing skills or strategies possessed by or lacking in a particular child fails to give teachers much indication as to either how or what to teach that youngster.

Since children with reading disorders often exhibit similar behaviors but for different underlying reasons, simply describing the behaviors (or skills) is not enough to determine how to begin teaching. For example, children may manifest similar difficulty finding the main idea on a test of silent reading of paragraphs. However, one may do so because of inadequate auditory memory, another because of poor thinking skills, and a third because of poor comprehension of oral syntax that makes comprehending passages containing complex structures extremely difficult.

In these cases, adequate diagnostic information as to the source of the problem is crucial. While each of these children may lack the same specific comprehension skill in reading, the clinician would go about teaching that deficient skill (e.g., finding the main idea) in very different ways. Thus, breakdown of skills, while important, does not address the problem of how to teach these children.

In many cases simply indexing reading skills does not even provide educators with adequate information as to what to teach. In decoding, for example, numerous word-attack strategies are available and none are necessary in all cases for learning to read. Phonics, while an extremely useful skill, is not necessary and many auditory dyslexics have learned without recourse to it. The fact that children do not know or use phonics does not imply that phonics must be taught.

A comprehensive approach to diagnosis that incorporates both approaches may provide a rationale for deciding which skills and strategies to emphasize with particular children as well as for choosing the best methods for presenting instruction in carefully selected skills (for example, whether and in what order decoding skills such as phonics, structural analysis, etc., should be taught). An adequate framework for reading diagnosis therefore must include a thorough assessment of both auditory and cognitive processes (including oral language, metalinguistic, and thinking skills) as well as direct testing of the complex act of reading itself and the subskills identified in the major components of decoding and comprehension.

The assessment of oral language and relevant metalinguistic skills has been discussed in the sections on diagnosis in Chapters 2, 3, 4, and 5, and of thinking skills in Chapter 6 so these are not repeated here. It is important to point out, however, that it is not enough to assess these areas in isolation. The dynamic relationship between spoken and written language and cognitive processes must be kept in mind. Information about oral language becomes meaningful as it is related to the various skills necessary for decoding printed text and comprehending its meaning (see the previous part of this chapter). The assessment of decoding and comprehension is the topic of the next two sections.

The act of reading is extremely complex, and testing children's ability as well as diagnosing their disorders, is equally complex. Clinicians must have a good knowledge of the available diagnostic tests for, as this discussion has suggested, reading is not a single type of conduct but an interrelated group of behaviors ranging from reading lists of isolated words, to reading poetry, to reading a dictionary or telephone book (Gibson & Levin, 1975). Similarly, not all tests measure the same reading behaviors, and the variety of such instruments can be overwhelming. The following two sections provide frameworks for designing comprehensive reading assessments in the major areas of decoding and comprehension, keeping in mind that any adequate diagnosis must:

- assess reading in a variety of situations
- take into consideration and control for such variables as the nature, length, and difficulty of the text
- permit the diagnostician to discern patterns of strengths and weaknesses in reading skills
- allow the integration of pertinent information with respect to deficits in auditory, visual, and cognitive abilities.

Numerous authors (Hansen & Lovitt, 1977; Harris & Sipay, 1975; Johnson & Myklebust, 1967; Roth & Perfetti, 1980; Salvia & Ysseldyke, 1978) highlight the importance of using tests to isolate individual variables or contrasts in understanding the variety of problems in learning disabled children (for example, oral vs. silent reading or reading lists of words vs. reading in context). Johnson (personal communication) takes this important notion a significant step further by suggesting that a comprehensive diagnosis must include multiple tests to investigate decoding vs. comprehension, oral vs. silent reading, and single words vs. context, and must determine how these variables relate to deficits in processing abilities. This chapter suggests that an even finer analysis of a variety of reading tests can contribute significantly to determining childrens' error patterns that then can be related to strengths and weaknesses.

## Section 2. Decoding

There are numerous reading tests but not one assesses all aspects of decoding completely. For instance, reading single words on the *Wide Range Achievement Test* (Jastak & Jastak, revised 1978) is very different from reading in context on the *Gilmore Oral Reading Test* (Gilmore & Gilmore, 1968). Some individuals do not perform equally well on these tests because they tap different reading processes. A variety of tests, therefore, are needed to cover a range of behaviors for adequate diagnosis.

However, after having given a comprehensive test battery, it is not always easy to formulate a cohesive profile; numerical test scores alone yield little information regarding the types of errors the readers make. This information is necessary so that hypotheses can be generated about the nature of the problem and the conditions under which the errors occur. Clinicians need to be able to put numerous pieces of information into a meaningful whole in order to understand why an individual is performing in a particular way or making certain patterns of errors.

To aid the clinician in diagnostic decisions and remedial planning, this section and the next offer a framework for organizing tests according to what they examine as well as analyzing their results and patterns of errors. This framework encompasses Johnson and Myklebust's (1967) task analysis as well as conceptual frameworks developed by Hansen and Lovitt (1977), Harris and Sipay (1975), Roth and Perfetti (1980), and Salvia and Ysseldyke (1978). These sections do not review validity, reliability, and other data of available diagnostic and criterion-referenced tests. This information can be found in Anastasi (1968), Salvia and Ysseldyke (1978), and Spache (1976).

*Analysis of Test Characteristics*

Reading tests traditionally have been grouped into two main categories, oral and silent. Educators (Ekwall, 1977; Hansen & Lovitt, 1977; Johnson, 1979; and Johnson & Myklebust, 1967) note the importance of distinguishing between oral and silent reading. In terms of learning disabled children, this dichotomy is particularly important because many exhibit discrepancies in their performance on these two types of measures. Those with auditory expressive language disorders often perform poorly on oral reading tests. For example, children with word retrieval problems, apraxia, or morphosyntactic language problems tend to read better silently. There may be at least a two-year discrepancy between oral and silent reading. Other educators report similar clinical findings (Johnson, Blalock, & Nesbitt, 1978). By viewing children's unique problems in light of these differences, diagnosticians can resolve seemingly conflicting test results.

Diagnostic tests also can be categorized as to whether they assess decoding skills at a single-word or discourse level (Spache, 1972). In addition, Roth and Perfetti (1980) and Krieger (1981) indicate that word identification depends on two sources: context-free information within a word and contextual information provided by discourse. Diagnostic tests often reflect this dichotomy as well; for example, the reading subtest of the *Wide Range Achievement Test* is an oral measure of single words whereas the *Gilmore Oral Reading Test* assesses decoding skills in context.

This classification scheme is useful for interpreting test results in learning disabled readers. For instance, some children with auditory comprehension or oral syntax problems do better on vocabulary than on contextual reading tests. The nature of their problems can prevent them from efficiently predicting words and using context clues to aid decoding. If they do not understand sentences (even at a metalinguistic level), they will have difficulty anticipating words as they read sentences. On the other hand, those with fairly good oral language skills may rely more heavily on context to decode words. These children may have auditory verbal or visual verbal processing deficits that hinder their ability to read single words on oral or silent vocabulary tests.

However, it is not enough simply to note whether the tests assess oral or silent reading, single word identification, or contextual decoding. The framework must be expanded to include at least five other variables, whether:

1. the words are meaningful or nonsense (Johnson & Myklebust, 1967)
2. the words are phonetically regular, sight, or rule-based
3. the tests contain pictures
4. the rate of presentation is a factor
5. the nature of the reading selection affects results.

Some learning disabled readers have particular difficulty with nonsense words (Myklebust, Bannockie, & Killen, 1971; Hook, 1976). Others can read all the phonetically regular words but not the sight words. Still others perform better when they have pictures to which to refer. The nature of the material itself also is important when the children are reading in context; the difficulty level, type of text (expository, narrative, etc.), and subject matter are all vital characteristics that may affect performance.

The reading on the *Wide Range Achievement Test* and the word recognition subtest on the *Peabody Individual Achievement Test* (Dunn & Markwardt, 1970) contain both phonetically regular and sight words, whereas the identification subtest on the *Woodcock Reading Mastery Test* (Woodcock, 1973) involves nonsense words. Silent reading vocabulary tests may include pictures, as on the vocabulary subtest on the *Gates-MacGinitie Reading Tests* (Gates & MacGinitie, 1972). The rate of presentation of words also can be an important variable; some word identification instruments (e.g., the *Gates-McKillop Reading Diagnostic Tests,* Gates & McKillop, 1962) require a flash showing of words as well as an untimed presentation. A discrepancy in performance in the timed and untimed versions may suggest a lack of automaticity in decoding.

## Analysis of Errors and Strategies

The discussion thus far has developed a framework for analyzing important dichotomies or variables in reading tests that reflect the pluralistic character of the decoding process. These variables can be extremely helpful in analyzing reading performance in learning disabled children. However, in addition to the evaluation of tests themselves, two other types of analyses are important for understanding decoding difficulties: (1) of reading errors and (2) of decoding strategies.

Most oral contextual reading tests categorize errors according to the following: substitutions, omissions, additions, mispronunciations, repetitions, hesitations, and examiner pronunciations. This is useful since it illuminates different patterns of errors among individuals: a child who substitutes and/or omits words is committing more serious mistakes than one who hesitates and repeats, since the former often changes the meaning of the text.

Using this classification scheme, diagnosticians also may observe a change in the error patterns over a period of time, even though the level of performance may not change. A given individual, for example, may make primarily substitutions. Upon a reevaluation of reading skills, the errors may be found to consist mainly of repetitions, hesitations, and/or self-corrections. When comparing reading performance across tests, diagnosticians also should be cognizant of the types of errors for which children are penalized. For instance, hesitations are considered errors on the *Gilmore Oral Reading Test* but on the *Gates-McKillop Diagnostic Reading Tests* or the *Gray Oral Reading Test* (Gray & Robinson, 1967) they are not.

The Goodman and Burke (1971) *Reading Miscue Inventory* is a tool for determining patterns of errors in terms of graphophonics, syntax, and semantics. It provides additional categories that are not included on the error analysis sections of standardized tests. Moreover, this inventory can be used to describe the nature of the substitutions, omissions, mispronunciations, reversals, and additions that are simply counted by other measures. For example, it is one thing to note that children substitute words and another to realize that most of their substitutions reflect an underlying auditory receptive or expressive language problem in syntax. This information is important for remedial planning.

It also is necessary to know whether the children have a variety of strategies available. These include phonics, sight words, structural analysis, and context (Gray, 1960) or graphophonemic, semantic, and syntactic cues (Goodman, 1970). Reliance on any one of these methods to the relative exclusion of others results in inefficient reading. Determining whether children apply strategies requires analysis of patterns of their errors on the various formal and informal tests. The diagnostician also needs to know whether the children use these strategies automatically and can apply them flexibly in all reading situations (LaBerge & Samuels, 1974). The ability to use various decoding strategies often depends on many of the variables discussed earlier as well as readers' interest and motivation.

*Informal Analysis*

To make reasonable hypotheses regarding the nature of individuals' problems with decoding, or word recognition, a final type of analysis can be extremely helpful: informal testing and/or diagnostic teaching follow-ups to the formal diagnostic tests (Johnson & Myklebust, 1967). During informal testing, the examiner controls for the types of word lists or reading material in order to confirm patterns of errors that were observed in the diagnostic evaluation. For instance, if the examiner feels that the child has difficulty reading phonetically regular CCVC (consonant-consonant-vowel-consonant) words, then structured word lists containing these types should be prepared. Clinicians then can ascertain whether a decoding error is isolated and random error or whether the individual has not mastered the phonic rules.

Following informal testing, clinicians can provide some diagnostic teaching in which they systematically control technique(s) that facilitate learning. For example, controlling for vowel sounds often is an effective teaching strategy. Some learning disabled readers improve their performance if they have to remember only one vowel sound. This technique allows them to direct their attention toward sounding out the consonants.

### Underlying Processes Related to Decoding

During formal or informal testing and/or diagnostic teaching, it is important to assess the underlying processes (auditory and visual) at each step of the Johnson and Myklebust (1967) hierarchy of experience. This analysis yields information regarding the level(s) at which reading performance breaks down: attention, perception, memory, symbolization, and conceptualization. In addition, different modes of input and output should be considered when assessing the level(s) of impaired processing in order to determine under what conditions the deficits occur. This information, in turn, can be related to the error analyses on standardized tests and reading inventories. The nature of letter and word substitutions, omissions, etc., for example, often can be accounted for by the processing strengths and weaknesses.

The following includes examples of how clinicians may go about constructing informal tasks to assess each level of the hierarchy of experience:

- At the level of attention, the examiner may cue the individual in some way to attend to all the letters of words and on that basis can note any improvement in reading performance.
- At the level of perceptual processing, the individual can be asked to discriminate words auditorily and visually (e.g., "fist-fest," do they sound the same? Do they look the same?).
- At the level of memory, the child may be asked to: read the words orally (visual-verbal input, visual-motor output, or marking response), repeat words after the examiner (auditory-verbal input, auditory-verbal output), or analyze words into their component sounds and syllables (also auditory-verbal input, auditory-verbal output).
- At the level of symbolization, the examiner can determine whether the individual knows the meanings of the words or sentences.

- At the level of conceptualization, the child's understanding of the word meanings and/or sentences in relation to other words and sentences (e.g., categories, main ideas) can be assessed. Also included at this level are metalinguistic tasks requiring the reader to detect and organize patterns of words (e.g., a group of words containing the past verb tense "ed," short vowel "a," etc.).

Although the assessment of skills at each level of the hierarchy of experience provides information regarding the underlying process deficits interfering with fluent reading, clinicians should be cautioned against making absolute conclusions as to the causes of poor decoding skills. The state of the art is such that practitioners are not certain that the tests in fact assess the psychological processes they purport to evaluate. Moreover, it is not clear exactly how the psychological processes are related to the reading act.

Rather, the approach to diagnosis should be to relate patterns of errors (within and across reading tasks) to the underlying processing deficits in addition to reporting test scores. A diagnostic evaluation should include a summary of which processes are deficient and which are relatively intact. For example, one adolescent boy had difficulty comprehending how morphological endings were used in words (e.g., "depends," "depended," "depending," "dependent"). Consequently, he misread morphological endings. He also had problems with morphology in his speaking and written language.

Based on these patterns of errors across all symbol systems, the direction of remediation for one child is designed differently from other individuals who make similar decoding mistakes in reading but not in oral language. In the former case, it was apparent that this youth did not have an adequate oral language base to bring to the reading task. Remedial efforts therefore focus on the improvement of morphological systems in his receptive language (auditory comprehension), spoken language, reading, and written language. The work on auditory comprehension provides a foundation for remediation in auditory expressive language, reading, and written language.

Thus, it is important in diagnosis to relate test information (patterns of errors) to underlying psychological processes. It is not enough to examine behavioral subskills or to report scores.

*Summary*

To obtain an adequate assessment of decoding ability in disabled readers, it is necessary to consider a wide variety of characteristics of the material selected and structure a diagnostic battery around them. By controlling these variables, clinicians can detect patterns of strengths and weaknesses that may give significant clues as to the nature of the children's problems and the best way to handle the problem in remediation.

Learning disabled children rarely do equally well (or equally poorly) on a variety of reading tests, although the instruments purportedly measure the same thing. This apparent confusion can be turned to the diagnosticians' advantage if they conduct a systematic analysis of the nature of the requirements of the task as well as the characteristics of the stimulus material. By contrasting performance on oral and silent reading, for example, clinicians may interpret any discrepancy as an indication of possible interference from processing deficits and in this way develop a profile of strengths and weaknesses for each child.

Clinicians must select a variety of tests that provide information about the following variables important in decoding (word identification): silent reading/oral reading, isolation/context, meaningful words/nonsense words, pictures/no pictures, timed/untimed presentation.

Observation of type of errors made in these different contexts as well as the variety of decoding strategies used adds another dimension to the diagnosis that aids in pinpointing problems. Such observations also allow diagnosticians to assess automaticity of strategies as well as changes in mistake patterns over time.

Informal reading tests can supplement formal ones to provide additional variables that are equally important in reading diagnosis. It is essential to vary the characteristics of the stimulus systematically, both in and out of context, including: types of words read (phonetic, sight, rule), type of material (explanation, dialogue, story), semantic complexity, subject matter, and syntactic complexity.

The interest and motivation of the child are critical to a valid assessment of reading as in any area of evaluation.

Discrepancies within and among these variables—that is, patterns of strengths and weaknesses in reading itself—can then be related to previous assessments of oral language, metalinguistic and thinking skills, and visual processing so that the most appropriate form of remedial instruction may be planned.

Finally, it should be noted that the order of areas tested in diagnosis may vary from one evaluation to the next. If the major problem appears to involve oral language, and it is suspected that these deficits affect learning to read, a comprehensive reading diagnosis may follow a thorough analysis of language and thinking abilities. However, if reading is the presenting problem, it may be desirable to assess decoding and comprehension first. After determining the pattern of strengths and weaknesses, hypotheses as to specific areas of oral language deficit may be confirmed or refuted. In any event, a thorough evaluation of auditory and cognitive skills must be a major component of a reading diagnosis.

## Section 3. Comprehension

It is generally accepted that the primary goal in reading is to derive meaning from the printed text. Reading comprehension requires the ability to understand the "ideas, concepts, propositions, facts, injunctions, arguments, inferences, qualifications, conditions, attitudes, emotions, and anything else that might be expressed'' (Carroll, 1977, pp. 1-2). As indicated previously, in order to comprehend, individuals must bring their background knowledge and experiences to bear on the reading task. Children with oral language comprehension and/or thinking problems have deficient reading comprehension. As emphasized in the first section of this chapter, the diagnostician should assess children's functioning in these areas as well as in reading comprehension itself.

Furthermore, it is important to distinguish children who have reading comprehension problems because of poor decoding skills from those who have general oral language comprehension deficits. Many learning disabled children with poor decoding skills have difficulty comprehending since they spend so much effort and time in word identification that they lose the meaning. Therefore, in order to get an accurate measure of comprehension, it is essential to assess that skill using passages in which the children can decode every word.

In contrast, those with reading comprehension problems but good decoding skills invariably exhibit deficits in auditory receptive language or thinking skills. These problems are more fundamental than a specific reading disability. It is not very likely that clinicians will find a child with poor reading comprehension, good decoding skills, and good listening comprehension. Nahmias (1982) reports that her learning disabled readers' listening comprehension is significantly inferior to normally achieving readers. Her data suggest reading comprehension problems reflect a more basic deficit in auditory language comprehension.

*Analysis of Test Characteristics*

Reading comprehension tests also can be categorized according to whether they assess oral or silent reading understanding of single words or connected language (Ekwall, 1977; Hansen & Lovitt, 1976; Harris & Sipay, 1975). Ekwall emphasizes the importance of contrasting comprehension of vocabulary with larger units of language on both oral and silent reading measures.

Some learning disabled readers with attention problems comprehend better on oral reading measures because the nature of the task forces them to attend to and read each word. The auditory feedback serves to stabilize their comprehension. Others, however, comprehend less well on oral reading tests because the auditory feedback proves distracting. Those with severe oral formulation or apraxia may exhibit poor oral reading comprehension because it takes so much effort and time to produce words verbally that they forget the meaning of the passage by the time they have said the words.

When evaluating reading comprehension, diagnosticians also should analyze the skills that are being assessed. Skills identified as important for reading comprehension include: the ability to read for main ideas, recall details, draw inferences and conclusions, make generalizations, follow a sequence of events, grasp the author's purpose, and evaluate what is read (Ekwall, 1977; Harris & Sipay, 1975).

However, not all tests include these types of questions. For example, the *Gilmore Oral Reading Test* and the *Durrell Analysis of Reading Difficulty* contain mainly factual questions whereas the *Metropolitan Achievement Tests* (Durost, Bixler, Wrightstone, Prescott, & Balow, 1970) includes main idea and inferential questions. The *Stanford Diagnostic Reading Test* (Karlsen, Madden, & Gardner, 1976) at the upper levels provides separate scores of literal comprehension (information printed in the text) and inferential comprehension (information that must be inferred from the text). It is important for diagnosticians to analyze errors to determine whether individuals have particular difficulty with certain kinds of questions. Some children with thinking disorders are superior in answering rote, factual questions because they require little integration and conceptualization of the material so the readers are not forced to move beyond the printed page.

Different modes of response also are required on various reading tests. Some *(Durrell Analysis of Reading Difficulty)* demand a spoken response while others *(Metropolitan Achievement Tests)* provide multiple-choice questions. Readers with word retrieval and formulation difficulties tend to perform better on a multiple-choice format. Other tests entail matching sentences to pictures *(Peabody Individual Achievement Test, Gates-MacGinitie Reading Tests)*. Some learning disabled individuals have difficulty interpreting pictures and consequently perform poorly, not because of a reading comprehension problem but because of nonverbal difficulties. Hence, it is important for clinicians to vary the response format to obtain clues as to the children's strengths and weaknesses.

A further response problem involves the role of memory. Many comprehension tests, both silent and oral, assess comprehension by requiring children to recall answers to questions. Those with memory problems may do poorly on such tests not because of poor comprehension but because of an inability to remember what they read. It is incorrect to assume that the problem is in comprehension per se. Rather, a comparison of performance on a variety of tests—one that allows the children to find the answer in the passage and another that requires them to recall the answer—can highlight the existence of memory as opposed to comprehension difficulties.

*Informal Analysis*

It also is important to determine informally the level(s) (word, sentence, or paragraph) at which comprehension breaks down. Some learning disabled children perform differently on vocabulary tests in contrast to contextual reading measures.

On the one hand, some do well on vocabulary comprehension but, because of oral comprehension problems for connected language, have difficulty understanding printed sentences, particularly when they become increasingly complex.

Others may have more difficulty integrating a group of written sentences and/or paragraphs. As the units get longer, comprehension decreases. Some actually may perform better on contextual reading than on vocabulary tests because of the additional clues provided in the passage.

In this context, two additional variables must be considered: (1) the length of the passage and (2) the linguistic complexity of the sentence. The length of the passage can be analyzed in terms of the number of sentences or paragraphs present. Diagnosticians should note whether comprehension improves or deteriorates depending on the passage length. Reading performance can be compared on different stories having different lengths but the same topics and writing style.

Semantic complexity must be analyzed to determine whether children fail to comprehend passages because they do not understand the meaning (literal, figurative, multiple meanings) of individual words. Passages may be rewritten informally to simplify vocabulary demands to determine whether comprehension improves.

Syntactic complexity is another important factor. Written syntax is considerably more difficult than spoken syntax, certain syntactic forms being reserved almost exclusively for written language. For example, as early as fourth grade, the syntax in a typical social studies book exceeds the spoken capacity of many language disordered children.

Those who appear to function adequately in typical conversations may have significant difficulty with the more advanced syntax in written language, thereby lowering their comprehension of the material. For example, clauses and sentences such as "How much precipitation a place gets in a year is important" or "Because Leonardo has such great talent in each of the many things that he did, he was unlike anyone else" may cause difficulty for children with syntax comprehension problems. Diagnosticians should analyze the syntax of text material and may need to devise simplified informal paragraphs to determine whether problems at this level interfere with comprehension.

Certain discourse features of the reading material are important variables that can affect reading comprehension. Children with problems in pragmatic aspects of oral language (see Chapter 5) also tend to have difficulty comprehending written language. Some have particular problems understanding dialogues. To comprehend dialogue, individuals must be able to understand pronoun referents, the meaning of quotation marks and commas in relation to the speaker, and the speaker-listener relationship. While some learning disabled children can comprehend spoken dialogues because of the many nonverbal aspects of communication, they have difficulty understanding the sparser written form.

*Summary*

A process of test selection and error analysis of results is proposed for comprehension similar to that suggested for decoding. It is important to select tests that contrast comprehension skills themselves as well as characteristics of the material to be read and the various response formats used to assess comprehension. By using a variety of formal and informal measures, a profile can be developed that highlights learning disabled children's strengths and weaknesses and illuminates possible contributing factors to the comprehension problem as well as appropriate content and strategies for remediation.

It is necessary to determine whether comprehension problems appear to result primarily from decoding difficulty or from more generalized oral language or thinking deficits. Oral language problems may interfere with reading comprehension in numerous ways. These may be isolated and identified by varying (formally or informally) the nature of the task in terms of oral or silent reading, single words or context, length of the passage, vocabulary level (semantic complexity), and syntactic complexity, as well as discourse and communicative aspects of the text.

It is as important to vary the mode of response as it is the nature of the material to be read. Comprehension generally is assessed by asking questions of readers. By varying the way the children respond (recognition/recall, oral/written), clinicians may gain useful diagnostic information. They also must vary the types of comprehension questions presented.

Inferential comprehension problems may be identified by analyzing specific types of questions on formal measures. It is useful to follow up inferential reading questions with similar passages and questions presented orally. Children with thinking problems often cannot draw inferences, grasp main ideas, see cause/effect relationships, and so on in any context, spoken or written. It is important to identify strategies the children use (if any) to aid comprehension.

Thus it can be seen that problems in oral language (semantics, syntax, pragmatics) and in decoding can interfere with reading comprehension. Problems at virtually every level of the hierarchy, pupil attention and memory, and higher level conceptualization and thinking skills also may interfere. It is the diagnosticians' task to develop a profile of language disordered children by selecting formal and informal tests that vary the requirements of reading comprehension tasks, then integrating that information with knowledge of the youngsters' language and thinking skills.

## PART III. REMEDIATION

### Section 1. Goals of Remediation

It is generally agreed that in today's society (where the demands of literacy are high) the appropriate goal of reading instruction should be adequate silent comprehension of a variety of written materials ranging from job applications and cookbooks to newspapers and novels. The ultimate goal for reading disabled individuals does not deviate from this standard.

There are, fortunately, many different instructional paths that eventually may lead to this goal. Hence, the more specific objective of remediation of reading disabilities must be to design the most appropriate instructional program to meet the needs of these children.

It is important to recognize the need to integrate reading goals in a total approach to improving auditory language and cognitive functioning. As described in Chapter 1, attention must be given, on the one hand, to specific reading skills and objectives and to integrating this instruction into larger content areas such as science, social studies, literature, and practical life skills. On the other hand, however, similar emphasis must be placed on instruction that focuses on individuals' particular strengths and deficits in discrimination, memory, oral language, and metalinguistic and thinking skills.

The view in this chapter on the diagnosis and remediation of underlying psychological processes is similar to the one espoused by Johnson and Myklebust (1967). As clinicians work on a specific subskill or content area, they should try at the same time to improve the processing deficits. It is rarely appropriate to attempt to remediate a psychological process in isolation and it often is helpful to improve psychological processes through instruction in content areas. By noting the level(s) of processing and modality(ies) that are most impaired, clinicians can organize the teaching materials in such a way as to capitalize on areas of strength to improve the deficits. For example, if individuals substitute auditorily similar words (e.g., "gap" for "cap") because of underlying processing deficits in auditory verbal discrimination and auditory verbal memory, the teacher may utilize their visual verbal strengths to remediate the deficits (e.g., "gap-cap," do they look the same? or point to "gap, cap").

### Section 2. Strategies for Remediation

Since the goals of integrated remediation must be to increase reading skills in decoding and comprehension in a variety of contexts as well as to improve perception, language, memory, and the thinking skills as they relate to reading, remedial strategies must focus on the systematic control of variables that have been identified in the diagnostic evaluation as important to the children's performance. Once the reading problem has been located as one of decoding or comprehension (or both), clinicians must select reading materials and use instructional strategies that are appropriate in terms of various characteristics of the text:

1. oral or silent reading
2. isolated words or context
3. meaningful or nonsense words

4. pictures or print
5. semantic complexity (vocabulary level)
6. syntactic complexity
7. discourse features of the text
8. subject matter
9. passage length

as well as decoding strategies to be taught (Goodman, 1977):

10. semantic cues
11. syntactic cues
12. graphophonic cues (including phonics, linguistic patterns, structural analysis)

and the type of comprehension response to be required:

13. recognition or recall
14. oral or written
15. literal or inferential
16. facts or ideas and events (concepts, feelings, characterization, etc).

General guidelines are available from the fields of normal reading and reading disorders. Models of normal reading such as those of Goodman (1965, 1976) and LaBerge and Samuels (1974, 1976) give an overview of important processes, particularly in decoding. Goodman, for example, details aspects of oral language (syntactic and semantic) that can be utilized to teach children to predict unknown words, a process that can be confirmed with minimal graphophonic information. The LaBerge and Samuels model is important for its explanation of visual perceptual processes and its emphasis on coordination of multiple processes to the point of automaticity.

The value of these models in planning remediation is their focus on the integration of decoding and comprehension, helping clinicians to avoid teaching isolated skills and providing broad guidelines for work on both top-down and bottom-up processes in reading. However, more specific guidelines are needed to make decisions such as, whether or not to begin with top-down processes and, if so, whether they should be semantic or syntactic. These models also provide little guidance on selecting the type of reading material that is best for a particular learning disabled child, or in knowing how to teach.

The principle of teaching to both strengths and weaknesses of the learning disabled (Johnson & Myklebust, 1967) offers more specific guidelines. Clinicians begin by selecting the variables that best utilize the children's strengths. For example, those with visual perceptual and memory problems but adequate language skills initially are best taught oral reading in context with an approach to word attack that emphasizes semantic, syntactic, and phonetic cues. Other graphophonic cues such as linguistic patterns ("rat," "cat," "bat," "hat"), may be chosen at first because of auditory similarity.

As progress is made in reading using the children's strengths, work may be introduced to improve deficit areas as they relate to reading. If clinicians want to teach sight words to readers who have visual verbal memory problems, they can have the individuals visually discriminate words and discuss the similarities and differences among them (e.g., "walk: wak, wakl, walk, wlak"). Intact perceptual processes can be used to facilitate memory.

Higher level processes (e.g., classification) also can help lower level ones. For example, the teacher or individual may categorize the words on some basis (e.g., all words with "ed," or "ough," or, "these items" are all transportation items). With categorization, less information needs to be retained in visual verbal memory. Moreover, the pattern among the words is highlighted and made explicit, which in turn can aid memory.

For children with comprehension problems because of poor auditory short-term memory and thinking skills, remediation may need to begin with silent reading in context where passages are controlled for vocabulary and syntax, passage length (beginning with one or two sentences), and pictures, as well as the type of comprehension response required (pointing to the picture that best illustrates the answer). However, it also is important to use strong visual skills to improve comprehension and memory. If the children are weak in comprehending, remembering, and recounting sequence of events, they may be taught to arrange pictures of the events in order, match them to strips with printed descriptions of the events, read the strips orally, repeat the sequence using one-word printed cues, and finally repeat the sequence from memory. In this way, they may eventually both comprehend and remember sequences more easily and be able to answer more typical comprehension questions such as, "What happened after _____."

## Section 3. Formal Reading Programs

Children with language learning disabilities, because they are not a homogeneous group, do not all benefit from the same remedial approach to reading. Since they include numerous subgroups, it is neither possible nor appropriate to recommend one remedial program or reading series. However, this does not mean that learning disabilities specialists should not use published reading series or formal programs. In fact, the framework presented earlier is designed to help clinicians make sense of the myriad of materials available, to make some logical selections from among these tools, and to supplement them with teacher-designed activities to suit the individual learning profile of each disabled reader.

Kaluger and Kolsen (1978) classify published materials and reading programs into two main groups: normal approaches and special approaches. Normal approaches include look-say, language experience, and linguistic readers. Special remedial approaches include Gillingham and Stillman (1960), Fernald (1943), Spalding and Spalding (1962), MWM (Minskoff, Wiseman, and Minskoff, 1972) (based on the *Illinois Test of Psycholinguistic Abilities,* ITPA, Kirk, McCarthy, & Kirk, 1968), and Distar (Engelmann & Bruner, 1973, 1974, 1975). Both normal and remedial programs are available to teachers of the learning disabled and must be analyzed carefully to determine which, if any, is an appropriate method for a specific child.

It is beyond the scope of this chapter to present a detailed analysis of each reading approach. However, using the framework described here and in Johnson and Myklebust (1967), a careful analysis of the input and output as well as the variables controlled by each program will enable clinicians to select and if necessary modify published material to suit the needs of specific children. For example, for children with good visual skills but difficulty with semantic and syntactic aspects of oral language, the clinician may select a published series using a sight approach that avoids oral reading. However, since the children will have difficulty using semantic and syntactic context cues (top-down process), the clinician will want to focus initially on visual bottom-up strategies for word recognition.

For others with poor visual skills but adequate auditory verbal processes, a Gillingham and Stillman approach (i.e., a multisensory, synthetic phonics approach) may be appropriate, or the visual-motor steps may need to be modified (e.g., arranging anagrams instead of writing words) if visual-motor deficits appear to interfere. Fortunately, there are many possible variations and combinations of formal and informal materials, thus enabling clinicians to design individualized programs.

To demonstrate more specifically how an individualized reading program can be used to meet the needs of a language learning disabled child, a case study follows.

## Section 4.  Case Study

C.F. was a 7-year-old girl of low average intelligence with moderate auditory receptive language and severe auditory expressive language problems. Her oral language deficits interfered with her ability to acquire decoding and comprehension skills in reading. In the area of auditory receptive language, she had auditory verbal discrimination and auditory comprehension problems.

Auditory verbal memory was not a problem as long as the tasks contained sentences within her auditory comprehension and required nonverbal responses such as carrying out a series of commands. Because of her severe auditory expressive language problems—oral apraxia and syntax and formulation difficulties—she could not perform auditory memory tasks that required her to repeat sentences, a series of words, or digits. Visual verbal processes such as visual discrimination were relatively intact.

To summarize her problems in terms of the input-integration output frame of reference, this student had moderate input problems (e.g., auditory verbal discrimination, auditory verbal memory), moderate integration problems (auditory comprehension) and severe output problems (apraxia, syntax, and formulation). Her nonverbal abilities were superior to her verbal abilities. She had deficits at every level of the hierarchy of experience: perception (auditory verbal discrimination), memory (auditory verbal material requiring spoken responses), and symbolization and conceptualization (auditory comprehension, syntax, and oral formulation). With these auditory processing deficits, C.F. failed to learn to read for two years through a phonics approach.

Taking into account her strengths and weaknesses, the following remedial reading program was implemented. Because of her auditory receptive vocabulary and articulation problems, the nature of the reading vocabulary was controlled; that is, the reading vocabulary (meaningful nouns and verbs) was kept within her auditory comprehension. Nonsense words were never used. She was taught to read words that she could pronounce fairly easily. The syntax of the sentences was controlled so that they were within her auditory comprehension and oral syntax; that is, the sentences were similar to the ones she used in her spoken language. Sentences such as "Dan can fan a man" were considered inappropriate; instead, sentences such as "The girl is jumping" were chosen.

Because of her severe oral apraxia, it was necessary to control for the response mode of output. Reading tasks that did not require a spoken (or auditory-verbal) response were used. C.F. demonstrated her knowledge by matching words and sentences to pictures or by pointing to them when they were spoken by the teacher. She demonstrated her comprehension of stories by pointing to words and sentences in the text that answered the question, pointing to pictures, gesturing, or by arranging a series of sentences so that they were in the proper sequence, etc. As she learned to spell a few words, written language was used as an avenue (visual-motor response) to indicate what she knew. (During the diagnostic evaluation, it was observed that she could write some of the words that she could not articulate intelligibly.)

In terms of the hierarchy of experience, activities at the perception, symbolization, and conceptualization levels were used to aid memory or the retention of the words. For example, at the level of perception, C.F. noted visual similarities and differences among words and sentences (e.g., "girl" vs. "glir"; "the girl jumping" vs. "the girl is jumping"). When working on phonics, the teacher first had her visually discriminate them (e.g., "cap-cab," do they look the same?), then do so auditorally ("cap-cab," do they sound the same?).

It should be pointed out that the visual verbal discrimination task facilitated her ability to hear sound differences in words. At the symbolization level, the student matched words or sentences to pictures. Conceptualization tasks such as categorizing words according to their structural or graphic similarities were used (all the words have "at," "ing," "b" in the initial position). These kinds of tasks helped her to learn (remember) the words taught in the reading lessons. Thus, the teacher utilized her strengths to improve her weaknesses.

With regard to the decoding skills, remediation focused initially on teaching her sight words, structural analysis, context clues, and phonics, in that order. Because of her auditory processing deficits and repeated failure to learn through a phonics approach, the initial reading instruction emphasized a whole-word approach. The sight words consisted of meaningful nouns and verbs to which affixes could be added (e.g., "boy, boys," "jump, jumping"). Johnson and Myklebust (1967) stress the importance of teaching meaningful words to children with auditory disorders.

In each lesson, four words (many of which were taken from her basic reader) were taught, one at a time, by matching them to pictures. Then, usually during the same lesson, work on structural analysis was introduced. This was done by adding affixes (e.g., "ing," "s") to the root words. This allowed the teacher to embed the words into simple sentences (and, later, into stories) for work on context (e.g., "the boy is jumping"). Sight words such as "the," and "is" were learned easily in the context of the sentence. Activities such as pointing to the words in sentences (which words say "the"), cutting up sentences into words and arranging them to form sentences, pointing to sight words in scrambled sentences (e.g., "the boy jumping the") proved useful.

Phonics was introduced shortly after the instruction began in the other areas. Because of the student's auditory processing deficits in auditory verbal discrimination, auditory analysis, and synthesis, phonics was taught using a whole-word or analytic approach. Word families (e.g., "at: cat, fat, hat") were used initially. However, as soon as possible, CVC words with varying consonants in the initial and final positions (e.g., "cat, cap, pan") were introduced. (The vowel sound was kept constant across all words.)

Clinical experience with teaching word families suggests that these students often learn to focus on the ends of words and do not scan systematically from left to right. However, phonics instruction with word families does reduce the load on visual and auditory verbal memory, which is important to keep in mind when teaching children with memory problems.

C.F. first learned to match the phonics words ("bat," "hat," "fat") to pictures and identified them by pointing to the words when named by the clinician. Visual and auditory verbal discrimination tasks were implemented using these words. Since C.F. did not have problems with nonverbal material (pictures, environmental sounds, tones), these were considered inappropriate for discrimination exercises. C.F. also categorized words based on word families and later by vowel sounds or consonants. Then she spelled words with anagrams "b-at" to match a model and later without the model present. This procedure facilitated her auditory analysis skills. As she saw letters being manipulated and moved around, she was better able to detect sounds in words.

To teach letter sounds, the clinician, showing the whole word spelled with anagrams, "b-at," asked, "What letter says 'b,' 'f,' 'h'?" etc. Later, only the individual letters were presented ("b," "f," "h"). The phonics words were chosen carefully so that following these recognition tasks, she could fairly easily articulate (or learn to articulate) the sound and words on recall tasks (e.g., what sounds does this letter make?). Following this procedure, C.F. wrote the words on paper. After she learned to read a few phonetically regular words, they were incorporated into the work on structural analysis and into sentence and story comprehension.

Reading instruction was integrated with speech and language therapy. The learning disabilities specialist and speech pathologist worked closely to develop an integrated program in reading, writing, speech, and language development. The results of this approach were very encouraging. In addition to a dramatic advance in reading, this child's articulation and syntax development improved markedly through the instruction in reading. For example, reading tasks that required her to arrange printed words to formulate sentences proved more effective in improving syntax than repeating sentences after the clinician about a stimulus picture. Similarly, reading the printed letters during the speech therapy exercises aided articulation.

*Summary*

The theme of this chapter has been that learning disabled readers do not constitute a homogeneous population. Broadly speaking, it is possible to distinguish subgroups of learning disabled individuals who encounter reading problems because of inadequate decoding, oral language, or thinking skills. To diagnose and remediate reading disabilities, it has been stressed that it is necessary to consider the underlying cognitive, linguistic, and metalinguistic processes, all of which interact to affect reading performance.

A person may fail to read, or may read inefficiently, for any number of reasons. The direction of remediation will vary depending upon the unique combination of integrities and deficits in these areas. Therefore, a thorough evaluation should be undertaken not only of the skills specific to reading but also of the skills related to cognition and reasoning as well as auditory receptive and expressive language and metalinguistic awareness. Reading performance should be assessed in the total context of cognitive and language development. Until this is done, the educator lacks true understanding of the nature and scope of an individual's reading disability.

## REFERENCES

Anastasi, A. *Psychological testing*. New York: The Macmillan Company, 1968.

Anderson, I.H. Eye-movements of good and poor readers. *Psychological Monographs*, 1937, *48*, 1-35.

Andolina, C. Syntactic maturity and vocabulary richness of LD children. *Journal of Learning Disabilities*, 1980, *13*, 372-377.

Applebee, A.N. Research in reading retardation: Two critical problems. *Journal of Child Psychology and Psychiatry*, 1971, *12*, 91-113.

Bannatyne, A.D. The color phonics system. In J. Money (Ed.), *The Disabled Reader*. Baltimore: The Johns Hopkins Press, 1966.

Barsch, R. *Achieving perceptual-motor efficiency: A space-oriented approach to learning*. Seattle: Special Child Publications, 1967.

Bateman, B. The efficacy of an auditory and visual method of first grade reading instruction with auditory and visual learners. In H.K. Smith (Ed.), *Perception and reading*. Newark, Del.: International Reading Association, 1968.

Belmont, I., Flegenheimer, H., & Birch, H.G. Comparison of perceptual training and remedial instruction for poor beginning readers. *Journal of Learning Disabilities*, 1973, *6*, 230-235.

Benson, D.F. Alexia. In J.T. Guthrie (Ed.), *Aspects of reading acquisition*. Baltimore: The Johns Hopkins Press, 1976.

Berry, M.F. *Berry-Talbott language tests 1. Comprehension of grammar*. Rockford, Ill.: M.F. Berry, 1966.

Berry, M.F. & Eisenson, J. *Speech disorders: Principles and practices of therapy*. New York: Appleton-Century-Crofts, 1956.

Blackman, S., & Goldstein, K.M. Cognitive styles and learning disabilities. *Journal of Learning Disabilities*, 1982, *15*, 106-115.

Bloom, L., & Lahey, M. *Language development and language disorders*. New York: John Wiley & Sons, Inc., 1978.

Bryant, N.D. Characteristics of dyslexia and their remedial implications. *Exceptional Children*, 1964, *31*, 195-200.

Burns, S. *An investigation of the relationship between sequential memory and oral reading skills in normal and learning disabled children*. Unpublished doctoral dissertation, Northwestern University, 1975.

Buswell, G.T. An experimental study of eye-voice span in reading. *Supplementary Educational Monographs*, No. 17. Chicago: University of Chicago, Department of Education, 1920.

Carroll, J.B. *Language and thought*. Englewood Cliffs, N.J.: Prentice-Hall, Inc., 1964.

Carroll, J.B. Developmental parameters of reading comprehension. In J.T. Guthrie (Ed.), *Cognition, curriculum and comprehension*. Newark, Del.: International Reading Association, 1977.

Carrow, E. *Test of auditory comprehension of language*. Austin, Texas: Urban Research Group, 1973.

Cattell, J.M. The time it takes to see and name objects. *Mind*, 1886, *11*, 63-65.

Cazden, C.B. *Child language and education*. New York: Holt, Rinehart & Winston, Inc., 1972.

Cecci, R. Evaluation of oral language disorders in children. *Bulletin of the Orton Society*, 1978, *28*, 194-207.

Chalfant, J.C., & Scheffelin, M.A. *Central processing dysfunctions in children: A review of research*. NINDS Monograph No. 9, Bethesda, Md.: U.S. Department of Health, Education, and Welfare, 1969.

Chall, J.S. *Learning to read: The great debate*. New York: McGraw-Hill Book Company, 1967.

Chall, J.S. The great debate: Ten years later, with a modest proposal for reading stages. In L.B. Resnick & P.A. Weaver (Eds.), *Theory and practice of early reading*. Vol. I. Hillsdale, N.J.: Lawrence Erlbaum Associates, Publishers, 1979.

Chappell, G.E. Childhood verbal apraxia and its treatment. *Journal of Speech and Hearing Disorders*, 1973, *3*, 362-368.

Clements, S.D. *Minimal brain dysfunction in children*. Washington, D.C.: U.S. Department of Health, Education, and Welfare, 1966.

Clymer, T. What is reading? Some current concepts. In H.M. Robinson (Ed.), *Innovation and change in reading instruction*, The 67th Yearbook of the National Society for the Study of Education, Part 2. Chicago: The University of Chicago Press, 1968, 7-29.

Coburn, D.L. *An investigation of conceptual tempo and visual search strategies in learning disabled and normally achieving children*. Unpublished doctoral dissertation, Northwestern University, in preparation.

Cohn, R. Delayed acquisition of reading and writing abilities in children. *Archives of Neurology*, 1961, *4*, 153.

Cohn, R. Amnestic aphasia and other disturbances in naming. *Archives of Neurology*, 1970, *22*, 515-520.

Critchley, M. *Developmental dyslexia*. Springfield, Ill.: Charles C. Thomas, Publisher, 1964.

Cruickshank, W.M., Bentzen, F., Ratzebury, F.H., & Tannhauser, M. *A teaching method for brain injured and hyperactive children*. Syracuse, N.Y.: Syracuse University Press, 1961.

Danks, J.H., & Fears, R. Oral reading. In L.B. Resnick & P.A. Weaver (Eds.), *Theory and practice of early reading* (Vol. 3). Hillsdale, N.J.: Lawrence Erlbaum Associates, Inc., 1979.

Darley, F.L., Aronson, A.E., & Brown, J.R. *Motor speech disorders*. Philadelphia: W.B. Saunders Company, 1975.

deHirsch, K., Jansky, J.J., & Langford, W.S. *Predicting reading failure*. New York: Harper & Row, 1966.

Denckla, M.B. Color naming: Defects in dyslexic boys. *Cortex*, 1972, *8*, 164-176.

Denckla, M., & Rudel, R. Rapid "automized" naming (R.A.N.): Dyslexia differentiated from other learning disabilities. *Neuropsychologia*, 1976, *14*, 471-479.

Denney, D.R. Relationships of three cognitive style dimensions to elementary reading abilities. *Journal of Educational Psychology*, 1974, *66*, 702-709.

Downing, J. *Comparative reading: Cross-national studies of behavior and processes in reading and writing*. New York: The Macmillan Publishing Co., Inc., 1973.

Dunn, L.M., & Markwardt, F.C. *Peabody individual achievement test*. Circle Pines, Minn.: American Guidance Service, 1970.

Durost, W.N., Bixler, H.H., Wrightstone, J.W., Prescott, G.A., & Balow, I.H. *Metropolitan achievement tests*. New York: Harcourt Brace Jovanovich Publishers, 1970.

Durrell, D.D. *Durrell analysis of reading difficulty*. New York: Harcourt Brace Jovanovich and World, Inc., 1955.

Ehri, L.C. Linguistic insight: Threshold of reading acquisition. In T.G. Waller & G.E. MacKinison (Eds.), *Reading research: Advances in theory and practice*. New York: Academic Press, 1979.

Ekwall, E.E. *Diagnosis and remediation of the disabled reader*. Boston: Allyn & Bacon, Inc., 1977.

Elbert, J.C. *An investigation of the representation and access of information in short-term memory of learning disabled and normal children*. Unpublished doctoral dissertation, Northwestern University, 1979.

Elkonin, D.B. USSR. In J. Downing (Ed.), *Comparative reading: Cross-national studies of behavior and processes in reading and writing*. New York: The Macmillan Publishing Co., Inc., 1973.

Englemann, S. *Conceptual learning*. San Rafael, Calif.: Dimensions Publishing Co., 1969.

Engelmann, S., & Bruner, E.C. *Distar Reading I*. Chicago: Science Research Associates, 1973.

Engelmann, S., & Bruner, E.C. *Distar Reading II*. Chicago: Science Research Associates, 1974.

Engelmann, S., & Bruner, E.C. *Distar Reading III*. Chicago: Science Research Associates, 1975.

Epstein, A.G. Tests for assessment of language development. *Bulletin of the Orton Society, 1977, 27*, 54-71.

Fairbanks, G. The relation between eye movements and voice in oral reading of good and poor readers. *Psychological Monographs, 1937, 48* (Whole No. 215) 78-107.

Fernald, G.M. *Remedial techniques in basic school subjects*. New York: McGraw-Hill Book Company, 1943.

Frostig, M. Education of children with learning disabilities. In E.C. Frierson & W.B. Barbe (Eds.), *Educating children with learning disabilities*. New York: Appleton-Century-Crofts, Inc., 1966.

Fry, M.A., Johnson, C.S., & Muehl, S. Oral language in relation to reading achievement among select second graders. In D.J. Bakker & P. Satz (Eds.), *Specific reading disability* (Vol. 3). Rotterdam: Rotterdam University Press, 1970.

Gates, A.I., & MacGinitie, W.H. *Gates-MacGinitie reading tests*. New York: Teachers College Press, 1972.

Gates, A.I., & McKillop, A.S. *Gates-McKillop reading diagnostic tests*. New York: Teachers College Press, 1962.

German, D. *Investigation of word-finding skills in children with learning disabilities and normal children*. Unpublished doctoral dissertation, Northwestern University, 1977.

Geschwind, N. The varieties of naming errors. *Cortex, 1967, 3*, 97-112.

Getman, G.N., Kane, E.R., Halgren, M.R., & McKee, G.W. *The physiology of readiness: An action program for the development of perception for children*. Minneapolis: Programs to Accelerate School Success, 1964.

Gibson, E.J. Reading for some purpose: Keynote address for the conference on "Relationships between speech and learning to read." In J.F. Kavanagh & I.G. Mattingly (Eds.), *Language by ear and by eye*. Cambridge, Mass.: The MIT Press, 1972.

Gibson, E.J., & Levin, H. *The psychology of reading*. Cambridge, Mass.: The MIT Press, 1975.

Gillingham, A., & Stillman, B. *Remedial training for children with specific disability in reading, spelling and penmanship*. Cambridge, Mass.: Educators Publishing Services, Inc., 1960.

Gilmore, J.V., & Gilmore, E.C. *Gilmore oral reading test*. New York: Harcourt Brace Jovanovich, 1968.

Glutman, L.R., & Rozin, P. The structure and acquisition of reading I: Relations between orthographies and the structure of language. In A.S. Reber & D.L. Scarborough (Eds.), *Toward a psychology of reading: The proceedings of the CUNY conferences*. Hillsdale, N.J.: Lawrence Erlbaum Associates, Publishers, 1977.

Goodman, K.S. Analysis of oral reading miscues: Applied psycholinguistics. *Reading Research Quarterly, 1965, 5*, 9-30.

Goodman, K.S. Reading: A psycholinguistic guessing game. *Journal of the Reading Research Specialist, 1967, 6*, 126-135.

Goodman, K.S. Behind the eye: What happens in reading? In H. Singer & R.B. Ruddell (Eds.), *Theoretical models and processes of reading*. Newark, Del.: International Reading Association, Inc., 1976.

Goodman, Y.M. Using children's reading miscues for new teaching strategies. *The Reading Teacher,* 1970, *23,* 455-459.

Goodman, Y.M., & Burke, C.L. *Reading miscue inventory: Procedure for diagnosis and evaluation.* New York: The Macmillan Company, 1971.

Gordon, N.S. Minimal cerebral dysfunction. *Spastics Quarterly,* 1965, *14,* 4-11.

Gough, P.B. One second of reading. In J.F. Kavanaugh & I.G. Mattingly (Eds.), *Language by ear and by eye.* Cambridge, Mass.: The MIT Press, 1972.

Gray, W. *On their own in reading.* Glenview, Ill.: Scott Foresman and Co., 1960.

Gray, W.S., & Robinson, H.M. *Gray oral reading test.* Indianapolis: The Bobbs-Merrill Co., Inc., 1967.

Groshong, C.C. *Ambiguity detection and the use of verbal context for disambiguation by language disabled and normal learning children.* Unpublished doctoral dissertation, Northwestern University, 1980.

Guthrie, J.T. Models of reading and reading disability. *Journal of Educational Psychology,* 1973, *65,* 9-18.

Hallahan, D.P., & Cruickshank, W.M. *Psychoeducational foundations of learning disabilities.* Englewood Cliffs, N.J.: Prentice-Hall, Inc., 1973.

Hallahan, D.P., & Kauffman, J.M. *Introduction to learning disabilities: A psychobehavioral approach.* Englewood Cliffs, N.J.: Prentice-Hall, Inc., 1976.

Hallahan, D.P., Gajar, A.H., Cohen, S.B., & Tarver, S.G. Selective attention and locus of control in learning disabled and normal children. *Journal of Learning Disabilities,* 1978, *11,* 231-236.

Hallahan, D.P., Tarver, S.G., Kauffman, J.M., & Graybeal, N.L. Selective attention abilities of learning disabled children under reinforcement and response cost. *Journal of Learning Disabilities,* 1978, *11,* 42-51.

Halliday, M.A.K., & Hasan, R. *Cohesion in English.* London: Longmans, 1976.

Hammill, D.D., & Larsen, S.D. The effectiveness of psycholinguistic training. *Exceptional Children,* 1974, *41,* 3-15.

Hammill, D.D., & Wiederholt, J.L. Review of the Frostig visual perception test and the related training program. In L. Mann & D. Sabatino (Eds.), *The first review of special education,* Vol. 1, Philadelphia: Journal of Special Education Press, 1973.

Hansen, C.L., & Lovitt, T.C. The relationship between question type and mode of reading on the ability to comprehend. *The Journal of Special Education,* 1976, *10,* 53-60.

Hansen, C.L., & Lovitt, T.C. An applied behavior analysis approach to reading comprehension. In J.T. Guthrie (Ed.), *Cognition, curriculum and comprehension.* Newark, Del.: International Reading Association, 1977.

Haring, H.G., Lovitt, T.C., Eaton, M.D., & Hansen, C.L. *The fourth R: Research in the classroom.* Columbus, Ohio: The Charles E. Merrill Publishing Co., Inc., 1978.

Harris, A., & Sipay, E. *How to increase reading ability.* New York: Basic Books, 1975.

Harris, G. Classification skills in normally achieving and learning disabled seven and nine year old boys: A study in conceptualization. Unpublished doctoral dissertation, Northwestern University, 1979.

Harris, T.L. Some issues in beginning reading instruction. *The Journal of Educational Research,* 1962, *56,* 5-19.

Head, H. *Aphasia and kindred disorders of speech,* Vol. 1. New York: The Macmillan Company, 1926.

Helfgott, J. Phonemic segmentation and blending skills of kindergarten children: Implications for beginning reading acquisition. *Contemporary Educational Psychology,* 1976, *1,* 157-169.

Hickmann, M. *The development of narrative skills and learning disabilities.* Paper presented at the Annual Northwestern Learning Disabilities Conference, Evanston, Ill., 1979.

Hinshelwood, J. Cognitive word-blindness. *Lancet,* 1900, *1,* 1506-1508.

Hinshelwood, J. *Congenital word-blindness.* London: H.K. Lewis, 1917.

Hochberg, J. Components of literacy: Speculations and exploratory research. In H. Levin & J.P. Williams (Eds.), *Basic studies on reading.* New York: Basic Books, Inc., 1970.

Holmes, J.A. Basic assumptions underlying the substrata-factor theory. In H. Singer & R.B. Ruddell (Eds.), *Theoretical models and processes of reading.* Newark, Del.: International Reading Association, Inc., 1976.

Holmes, J.A., & Singer, H. Theoretical models and trends toward more basic research in reading. *Review of Educational Research,* 1964, *34,* 127-155.

Hook, P.E. *A study of metalinguistic awareness and reading strategies in proficient and learning disabled readers.* Unpublished doctoral dissertation, Northwestern University, 1976.

Huttenlocher, P., & Huttenlocher, J. A study of children with hyperlexia. *Neurology,* 1973, *26,* 1107-1116.

Ingram, T.T.S. Pediatric aspects of specific developmental dysphasia, dyslexia, and dysgraphia. *Cerebral Palsy Bulletin,* 1960, *2,* 254-267.

Jastak, J.F., & Jastak, S.R. *Manual: The wide range achievement test.* Wilmington, Del.: Guidance Associates, 1978.

Johnson, D.J. Remedial approaches to dyslexia. In A.L. Benton & D. Pearl (Eds.), *Dyslexia: An appraisal of current knowledge.* New York: Oxford University Press, 1978.

Johnson, D.J., Blalock, J.W., & Nesbitt, J.A. Adolescents with learning disabilities: Perspectives from an educational clinic. *Learning Disability Quarterly,* 1978, *1,* 24-36.

Johnson, D.J., & Hook, P.E. Reading disabilities: Problems of rule acquisition and linguistic awareness. In H.R. Myklebust (Ed.), *Progress in learning disabilities* (Vol. 4). New York: Grune & Stratton, Inc., 1978.

Johnson, D.J., & Myklebust, H.R. Dyslexia in childhood. In J. Hellmuth (Ed.), *Learning disorders* (Vol. 1). Seattle: Special Child Publications, 1965.

Johnson, D.J., & Myklebust, H.R. *Learning disabilities: Educational principles and practices.* New York: Grune & Stratton, Inc., 1967.

Johnson, D. Process deficits in learning disabled children and implications for reading. In L. Resnick and P. Weaver (Eds.), *Theory and Practice of Early Reading,* (Vol. 2). Hillsdale, N.J.: Lawrence Erlbaum Associates, Publishers, 1979.

Johnson, M.S. Factors related to reading disability. *Journal of Experimental Education,* 1957, *26,* 1-26.

Kaluger, G., & Kolsen, C. *Reading and learning disabilities.* Columbus, Ohio: The Charles E. Merrill Publishing Co., Inc., 1978.

Karlsen, B., Madden, R., & Gardner, E.F. *Stanford diagnostic reading test.* New York: Harcourt Brace Jovanovich, Publishers, 1976.

Karpova, S.N. [The preschooler's realization of the lexical structure of speech.] In D.I. Slobin (Ed. and trans.), *Abstracts of Soviet studies of child language*; in F. Smith & G.A. Miller (Eds.), *The genesis of language.* Cambridge, Mass.: The MIT Press, 1966.

Kass, C.E. Psycholinguistic disabilities of children with reading problems. *Exceptional Children,* 1966, *32,* 533-539.

Katz, P.A., & Deutsch, M. Auditory and visual functioning and reading achievement. In M. Deutsch (Ed.), *The disadvantaged child*. New York: Basic Books, Inc., 1967.

Kephart, N.C. *The slow learner in the classroom*. Columbus, Ohio: The Charles E. Merrill Publishing Co., Inc., 1960.

Kirk, S.A., & Kirk, W.D. *Psycholinguistic learning disabilities*. Urbana, Ill.: University of Illinois Press, 1971.

Kirk, S.A., McCarthy, J.J., & Kirk, W.D. *Illinois test of psycholinguistic abilities*. Urbana, Ill.: University of Illinois Press, 1968.

Kluever, R. Mental abilities and disorders of learning. In H.R. Myklebust (Ed.), *Progress in learning disabilities* (Vol. 2). New York: Grune & Stratton, Inc., 1971.

Kogan, N. Cognitive styles and reading performance. *Bulletin of the Orton Society*, 1980, *30*, 63-78.

Krieger, V. A hierarchy of "confusable" high-frequency words in isolation and context. *Learning Disability Quarterly*, 1981, *4*, 131-138.

LaBerge, D., & Samuels, S.J. Toward a theory of automatic information processing in reading. *Cognitive Psychology*, 1974, *6*, 293-323.

LaBerge, D., & Samuels, S.J. Toward a theory of automatic information processing in reading. In H. Singer & R. Ruddell (Eds.) *Theoretical models and processes of reading*. Newark, Del.: International Reading Association, 1976.

Lefevre, C.A. *Linguistics and the teaching of reading*. New York: McGraw-Hill Book Company, 1964.

Leong, C.K. Children's concepts of language in learning to read. *Bulletin of the Orton Society*, 1979, *29*, 115-128.

Levin, H., & Kaplan, E.L. Grammatical structure and reading. In H. Levin & J.P. Williams (Eds.), *Basic studies on reading*. New York: Basic Books, Inc., 1970.

Liberman, I.Y., & Shankweiler, D. Speech, the alphabet and teaching to read. In L.B. Resnick & P.A. Weaver (Eds.), *Theory and practice of early reading* (Vol. 2). Hillsdale, N.J.: Lawrence Erlbaum Associates, Publishers, 1979.

Liberman, I.Y., Liberman, A.M., Mattingly, I., & Shankweiler, D. Orthography and the beginning reader. In J.F. Kavanagh & R.L. Venezky (Eds.), *Orthography, reading and dyslexia*. Baltimore: University Park Press, 1980.

Liberman, I.Y., Shankweiler, D., Fischer, F.W., & Carter, B. Explicit syllable and phoneme segmentation in the young child. *Journal of Experimental Child Psychology*, 1974, *18*, 201-212.

Liberman, I.Y., Shankweiler, D., Liberman, A.M., Fowler, C., & Fischer, F.W. Phonetic segmentation and recoding in the beginning reader. In A.S. Reber & D.L. Scarborough (Eds.), *Toward a psychology of reading: The proceeding of the CUNY conferences*. Hillsdale, N.J.: Lawrence Erlbaum Associates, Publishers, 1977.

Lieberman, P. *Intonation, perception and language*. Cambridge, Mass.: The MIT Press, 1967.

Lindamood, C.H., & Lindamood, P.C. *L.A.C. test: Lindamood auditory conceptualization test*. Boston: Teaching Resources Corporation, 1971.

Luria, A.R. *Higher cortical functions in man*. New York: Basic Books, Inc., 1966.

Luria, A.R. *The working brain: An introduction to neuropsychology*. New York: Basic Books, Inc., 1973.

Lyon, R. Subgroups of learning disabled readers: Clinical and empirical identification. In H.R. Myklebust (Ed.), *Progress in learning disabilities* (Vol. 5). New York: Grune & Stratton, Inc., in press.

Lyon, R., & Watson, B. Empirically derived subgroups of learning disabled readers: Diagnostic characteristics. *Journal of Learning Disabilities*, 1981, *14*, 256-261.

Lyon, R., Reitta, S., Watson, B., Porch, B., & Rhodes, J. Selected linguistic and perceptual abilities of empirically derived subgroups of learning disabled readers. *Journal of School Psychology*, 1981, *19*, 152-166.

Mackworth, J.R. Some models of the reading process: Learners and skilled readers. *Reading Research Quarterly*, 1972, *7*, 701-733.

Maker, C.J. Problem solving: A general approach to remediation. In D.D. Smith (Ed.), *Teaching the learning disabled*. Englewood Cliffs, N.J.: Prentice-Hall, Inc., 1981.

Mann, L. Psychometric phrenology and the new faculty psychology: The case against ability assessment and training. *The Journal of Special Education*, 1971, *5*, 3-14.

Massaro, D.W. *Understanding language: An information processing analysis of speech, reading and psycholinguistics*. New York: Academic Press, 1975.

Mattingly, I.G. Reading, the linguistic process, and linguistic awareness. In J.F. Kavanagh & I.G. Mattingly (Eds.), *Language by ear and by eye*. Cambridge, Mass.: The MIT Press, 1972.

Mattis, S., French, J.H., & Rapin, I. Dyslexia in children and young adults: Three independent neuropsychological syndromes. *Developmental Medicine and Child Neurology*, 1975, *17*, 150-163.

McClure, J., Kalk, M., & Keenan, V. Use of grammatical morphemes by beginning readers. *Journal of Learning Disabilities*, 1980, *13*, 262-267.

Miller, G.A. Text comprehension skills and process models of text comprehension. In H. Singer & R.B. Ruddell (Eds.), *Theoretical models and processes of reading*. Newark, Del.: International Reading Association, 1976.

Minskoff, E., Wiseman, D., & Minskoff, J. *The MWM Program for developing language abilities*. Ridgefield, N.J.: Educational Performance Associates, 1972.

Myklebust, H.R. *The psychology of deafness*. New York: Grune & Stratton, Inc., 1964.

Myklebust, H.R. Toward a science of dyslexiology. In H.R. Myklebust (Ed.), *Progress in learning disabilities* (Vol. 4). New York: Grune & Stratton, Inc., 1978.

Myklebust, H., & Johnson, D. Dyslexia in children. *Exceptional Children*, 1962, *29*, (1), 14-25.

Myklebust, H.R., Bannochie, M., & Killen, J. Learning disabilities and cognitive processes. In H.R. Myklebust (Ed.), *Progress in learning disabilities* (Vol. 2), New York: Grune & Stratton, Inc., 1971.

Nahmias, M.L.V. *Inferential listening and reading comprehension of discourse in normal and reading disabled children*. Unpublished doctoral dissertation, Northwestern University, 1982.

Newman, D.G. *An investigation of learning disabled children's utilization of taxonomic organization to facilitate memory performance*. Unpublished doctoral dissertation, Northwestern University, 1980.

Nielsen, J.M. *Agnosia, apraxia, aphasia*. New York: Paul B. Hoeber, 1946.

Orton, S. *Reading, writing and speech problems in children*. New York: W.W. Norton & Company, Inc., 1937.

Podhajski, B.R. *Picture arrangement and selected narrative language skills in learning disabled and normal seven-year-old children*. Unpublished doctoral dissertation, Northwestern University, 1980.

Quantz, J.O. *Problems in the psychology of reading*. New York: The Macmillan Company, 1897.

Readence, J.E., & Baldwin, R.S. The relationship of cognitive style and phonics instruction. *The Journal of Educational Research*, 1978, *72*, 44-52.

Resnick, D.P., & Resnick, L.B. The nature of literacy: An historical exploration. *Harvard Educational Review*, 1977, *47*, 370-385.

Risko, V.J. Reading. In D.D. Smith (Ed.), *Teaching the learning disabled*. Englewood Cliffs, N.J.: Prentice-Hall, Inc., 1981.

Ross, A.O. *Psychological aspects of learning disabilities and reading disorders*. New York: McGraw-Hill Book Company, 1976.

Roth, S.F., & Perfetti, C.A. A framework for reading, language comprehension, and language disability. *Topics in Language Disorders*, 1980, *1*, 15-28.

Rourke, B.P. Reading, spelling, arithmetic disabilities: A neuropsychological perspective. In H.R. Myklebust (Ed.), *Progress in learning disabilities* (Vol. 4). New York: Grune & Stratton, Inc., 1978. (a)

Rourke, B.P. Neuropsychological research in reading retardation: A review. In A.L. Benton & D. Pearl (Eds.), *Dyslexia, An appraisal of current knowledge*. New York: Oxford University Press, 1978. (b)

Salvia, J., & Ysseldyke, J.E. *Assessment in special and remedial education*. Boston: Houghton Mifflin Company, 1978.

Satz, P. Cerebral dominance and reading disability: An old problem revisited. In R.M. Knights & D.J. Bakker (Eds.), *The neuropsychology of learning disorders: Theoretical approaches*. Baltimore: University Park Press, 1976.

Schneider, W., & Shiffrin, R.M. Controlled and automatic human information processing: I. Detection search and attention. *Psychological Review*, 1977, *84*, 1-66.

Semel, E., & Wiig, E. Comprehension of syntactic structures and critical verbal elements by children with learning disabilities. *Journal of Learning Disabilities*, 1975, *8*, 53-58.

Senf, G.M., & Freundl, P.C. Memory and attention factors in specific learning disabilities. *Journal of Learning Disabilities*, 1971, *4*, 94-106.

Shankweiler, D., & Liberman, I.Y. Misreading: A search for causes. In J.F. Kavanagh & I.G. Mattingly (Eds.), *Language by ear and by eye*. Cambridge, Mass.: The MIT Press, 1972.

Shankweiler, D., & Liberman, I.Y. Exploring the relations between reading and speech. In R.M. Knights & D.J. Bakker (Eds.), *The neuropsychology of learning disorders: Theoretical approaches*. Baltimore: University Park Press, 1979.

Silberberg, N.E., & Silberberg, M.C. Myths in remedial education. *Journal of Learning Disabilities*, 1969, *2*, 209-217.

Singer, H. Theoretical models of reading: Implications for teaching reading. In H. Singer & R.B. Ruddell (Eds.), *Theoretical models and processes of reading*. Newark, Del.: International Reading Association, Inc., 1976.

Singer, H. Theories, models and strategies for learning to read. In F.B. Davis (Ed.), *The literature of research in reading with emphasis on models*. New Brunswick, N.J.: Iris Corporation, 1971.

Singer, H. Conceptualization in learning to read. In H. Singer & R.B. Ruddell (Eds.), *Theoretical models and processes of reading*. Newark, Del.: International Reading Association, Inc., 1976.

Slingerland, B.H. *Slingerland screening tests for identifying children with specific language disability*. Cambridge, Mass.: Educators Publishing Services, Inc., 1970.

Smith, F. *Understanding reading*. New York: Holt, Rinehart & Winston, Inc., 1971.

Spache, G.D. *Examiners manual: Diagnostic reading scales* (Rev. ed.). Monterey, Calif.: CTB-McGraw Hill, Inc., 1972.

Spache, G.D. *Diagnosing and correcting reading disabilities*. Boston: Allyn & Bacon, Inc., 1976.

Spache, G.B. & Spache, E. *Reading in the elementary school*. Boston: Allyn & Bacon, Inc., 1964.

Spalding, R.B., & Spalding, W.T. *The writing road to reading: A modern method of phonics for teaching children to read*. New York: William Morrow & Co., Inc., 1962.

Stauffer, R.G. Reading as cognitive functioning. In H. Singer & R.B. Ruddell (Eds.), *Theoretical models and processes of reading*. Newark, Del.: International Reading Association, 1976.

Stauffer, R.G. Cognitive processes fundamental to reading instruction. In J.T. Guthrie (Ed.), *Cognition curriculum and comprehension*. Newark, Del.: International Reading Association, 1977.

Steiner, R., Weiner, M., & Cromer, W. Comprehension and syntactic responses in good and poor readers. *Journal of Educational Psychology*, 1971, *62*, 506-513.

Stone, A.C. Adolescent cognitive development: Implications for learning disabilities. *Bulletin of the Orton Society*, 1980, *30*, 79-93.

Stone, L.C. Reading reactions for varied types of subject matter: An analytical study of eye movements of college freshmen. *Journal of Experimental Education*, 1941, *10*, 64-77.

Strauss, A., & Kephart, N.C. *Psychopathology and education of the brain-injured child*. (Vol. 2) New York: Grune & Stratton, Inc., 1955.

Strauss, A.A., & Lehtinen, L.E. *Psychopathology and education of the brain-injured child* (Vol. 1). New York: Grune & Stratton, Inc., 1947.

Tallal, P. Language and reading: Some perceptual prerequisites. *Bulletin of the Orton Society*, 1980, *30*, 170-178.

Tarver, S.G., & Dawson, M.M. Modality preference and the teaching of reading: A review. *Journal of Learning Disabilities*, 1978, *11*, 5-17.

Tarver, S.G., Hallahan, D.P., Cohen, S.B., & Kauffman, J.M. The development of visual selective attention and verbal rehearsal in learning disabled boys. *Journal of Learning Disabilities*, 1977, *10*, 491-500.

Tarver, S.G., Hallahan, D.P., Kauffman, J.M., & Ball, D.W. Verbal rehearsal and selective attention in children with learning disabilities: A developmental lag. *Journal of Experimental Child Psychology*, 1976, *22*, 375-385.

Tinker, M.A. Reliability and validity of eye movement measures of reading. *Journal of Experimental Psychology*, 1939, *19*, 732-746.

Tinker, M.A. The study of eye movements in reading. *Psychological Bulletin*, 1946, *43*, 93-120.

Torgesen, J. *Problems and prospects in the study of learning disabilities*. Chicago: University of Chicago Press, 1975.

Torgesen, J.K. The role of nonspecific factors in the task performance of learning disabled children: A theoretical assessment. *Journal of Learning Disabilities*, 1977, *10*, 24-34. (a)

Torgesen, J.K. Memorization processes in reading disabled children. *Journal of Educational Psychology*, 1977, *69*, 571-578. (b)

Torgesen, J.K. Performance of reading disabled children on serial memory tasks: A review. *Reading Research Quarterly*, 1978, *19*, 57-87.

Torgesen, J.K. Implications of the LD child's use of efficient task strategies. *Journal of Learning Disabilities*, 1980, *13*, 364-371.

Vellutino, F.R. Alternative conceptualizations of dyslexia: Evidence in support of a verbal deficit hypothesis. *Harvard Educational Review*, 1977, *47*, 334-354.

Venezky, R. In J.F. Kavanagh (Ed.), *Communicating by language: The reading process*. Bethesda, Md.: U.S. Public Health Service, U.S. Department of Health, Education, and Welfare, 1968.

Venezky, R. Research on reading processes: A historical perspective. *American Psychologist*, May 1977, 339-345.

Vernon, M.D. *Reading and its difficulties*. Cambridge: Cambridge University Press, 1971.

Vogel, S.A. *An investigation of syntactic abilities in normal and dyslexic children*. Unpublished doctoral dissertation, Northwestern University, 1972.

Vrana, F., & Pihl, R.O. Selective attention deficit in learning disabled children: A cognitive interpretation. *Journal of Learning Disabilities,* 1980, *13,* 364-371.

Walker, R.Y. A qualitative study of eye movements of good readers. *American Journal of Psychology,* 1938, *51,* 472-481.

Weaver, P.A. Comprehension, recall and dyslexia: A proposal for the application of schema theory. *Bulletin of the Orton Society,* 1978, *28,* 92-113.

Weaver, P.A., & Dickinson, D.K. Story comprehension and recall in dyslexic students. *Bulletin of the Orton Society,* 1979, *29,* 157-171.

Weaver, P.A., & Resnick, L.B. The theory and practice of early reading: An introduction. In L.B. Resnick & P.A. Weaver (Eds.), *Theory and practice of early reading.* Hillsdale, N.J.: Lawrence Erlbaum Associates, Publishers, 1979.

Weber, R.M. A linguistic analysis of first grade reading errors. *Reading Research Quarterly,* 1970, *5,* 427-452.

Wepman, J.M. Auditory discrimination, speech and reading. *Elementary School Journal,* 1960, *60,* 325-333.

Wepman, J.M. *Auditory discrimination test.* Chicago: Language Research Associates, 1973.

Wiener, M., & Cromer, W. Reading and reading difficulty: A conceptual analysis. *Harvard Educational Review,* 1967, *37,* 620-643.

Wiig, E.J., & Semel, E.M. Productive language abilities in learning disabled adolescents. *Journal of Learning Disabilities,* 1975, *8,* 578-586.

Wiig, E.H., & Semel, E.M. *Language disabilities of children and adolescents.* Columbus, Ohio: The Charles E. Merrill Publishing Co., Inc., 1976.

Wiig, E.H., & Semel, E.M. *Language assessment and intervention for the learning disabled.* Columbus, Ohio: The Charles E. Merrill Publishing Co., Inc., 1980.

Wiig, E.H., Semel, E.M., & Crouse, M.A. The use of English morphology by high-risk and learning disabled children. *Journal of Learning Disabilities,* 1973, *6,* 457-465.

Williams, J. Reading instruction today. *American Psychologist,* 1979, *34,* 917-922.

Wilson, R.M., & Hall, M. *Reading and the elementary school child.* New York: Van Nostrand Reinhold Company, 1972.

Woodcock, R. *Woodcock reading mastery test.* Circle Pines, Minn.: American Guidance Service, 1973.

Woodworth, R.S. Vision and localization during eye movements. *Psychological Bulletin,* 1906, *3,* 68-70.

Wren, C. The relationship of auditory and cognitive processes to syntactic patterns in learning disabled and normal children. Unpublished doctoral dissertation, Northwestern University, 1980.

Yoss, K.A., & Darley, F.L. Developmental apraxia of speech in children with defective articulation. *Journal of Speech and Hearing Research,* 1974, *17,* 399-416.

Zangwill, O.C. Dyslexia in relation to cerebral dominance. In J. Money (Ed.), *Reading disability: Progress and research needs in dyslexia.* Baltimore: Johns Hopkins Press, 1962.

# Chapter 8

# Written Language

*Suzanne Timble Major*

## PART I. WRITTEN LANGUAGE & LEARNING DISABILITIES

Language may be defined as the ability to attach meaning to words and to employ words as symbols for thought. In that respect, written language may be considered as the element of the process that uses symbols for thought so that the result is a visual, readable representation.

Written language frequently has been described as the "last acquired language skill." In fact, it normally is developed only after oral language has been nearly mastered and the written symbol system used in reading has been introduced. Where oral language most typically is learned in an unstructured setting, written language is taught in a comparatively structured manner. Written language skills represent a culmination, a summative type of learning in which the auditory symbol system basic to oral language is translated to the visual, using an intricate combination of auditory, visual, and motor skills.

Based on that view of written language, the complexity of this level of performance is evident. Litowitz (1981, p. 74) states that writing "subsumes previous skills and processes" and requires an "indirect, abstract way of relating between the writer and his or her world," i.e., using the visual rather than the auditory symbol system. This indirect use of symbols is referred to as the "second order" of symbolization by Vygotsky (1962), with the visual symbol superimposed on the auditory verbal symbol, which in turn represents an actual experience or concept, twice removed. This superimposition of the visual process on the auditory verbal symbol results in a complex language process that is extremely difficult for many learning disabled students to master.

### Section 1. Approaches to Studying Written Language

Although written language is a basic and essential means of communication, it has received comparatively little attention from either theorists or practitioners. A review of the research in language development clearly indicates that the major focus long has been on oral rather than written language. There is a tendency to assume that the explanations and theories governing the development and use of oral language can be applied readily to written language. Yet, although there are multiple parallels in the development of the two, there is significant question as to whether conclusions about oral language progress and disorder can be applied to written language behaviors.

Approaches to written language come from three sources: (1) language pathologists, (2) English educators and psycholinguists, and (3) developmental descriptions. The following sections describe each of these in more detail.

*Language Pathology Approach*

Language pathologists have focused on the investigation of models of normal development and deviations from them. Their approach to diagnosis and remediation of disability is based largely on discrepancy from and approximation to normal language. For example, the work by Lee (1966, 1974) and others traces the development of certain syntactic forms in the oral language of normally developing children. Using that information as a basis for a scope and sequence type of analysis, Lee identifies disorders in the development of oral language and approaches a corrective program based on those deficiencies so that remediation proceeds according to the pattern of normal acquisition of syntactic forms.

The main thrust of early investigations of written language per se, as of oral language, was to identify a single measure that could be used to evaluate written language development. Mean sentence length, or inventories of syntactic forms used or used in error, received the most attention and were found to demonstrate increased maturity at least in terms of production.

*Psycholinguistic Approaches*

Investigation into written language has come mainly from the directions of English education and of psychology and linguistics. The psycholinguists, in their blending of the disciplines of psychology and linguistics, also have considered the application of psycholinguistic theory to written language. Psycholinguists generally are concerned not with the basic processing skills related to visual-motor production, spelling, or mechanics but only with those that are fundamental in the development of transformational grammar. Chomsky's (1965) transformational model has been used in their analysis of both oral and written language.

Much of the emphasis in psycholinguistic research is on the use of subordination in written language as a measure of syntactic maturity. LaBrant (1933) was one of the earliest language specialists to investigate sentence structure by using the clause as the unit of analysis. LaBrant reports that the average number of clauses per sentence, as well as the ratio of the number of dependent clauses to the total number of clauses, increases with age. Together with Anderson, in the 1933 study, she developed a subordination index to measure grammatic complexity, finding that clause length was a better measure of syntactic maturity than sentence length.

The study of subordination as a measure of syntactic maturity progressed from LaBrant's early work and now is associated most widely with Hunt's work with ''T-units'' (1966). T-units are terminal units, or word groupings, that can be started with a capital letter and ended with some form of terminal punctuation (period, question mark, exclamation point), usually consisting of a main clause and any subordinate clause attached to it.

A clause is defined by Hunt as one subject or one set of coordinate subjects with one finite verb or one finite set of coordinate verbs. Hunt's studies demonstrate that from the very early grades, students' use of adjective clauses within sentences increases in number. Further, as syntax matures, he notes more single-word adjectives used before nouns and more prepositional phrases modifying nouns. These findings led Hunt to measure syntactic maturity through subordination.

Hunt's T-units are categorized by length. In his research he compares written samples of 1,000-word ''skilled adult'' samples from nonfiction magazine articles (*Harper's* and *The Atlantic Monthly*). Length is measured by dividing the total number of words by the total number of clauses. Hunt provides the example: ''She said he ought to try harder,'' which with seven words and two clauses has a clause length of 3.5 words. His data indicate that normal fourth graders write clauses averaging 6.6 words in length; eighth graders' clauses are 20 percent longer and twelfth graders' 30 percent longer.

The clauses from the skilled adult samples are 175 percent longer than those of the fourth graders, suggesting that growth in syntactic maturity continues steadily into adulthood. Hunt concludes that ''the reduction and consolidation of many clauses into one is intimately related to syntactic growth'' (1966, p. 739).

The basic concept in the study of T-units as an index of syntax is that mature writers are able to communicate more information in a more compact format and can combine increased numbers of such units in a meaningful manner. As students increasingly use subordinate clauses, more information about the main sentence nouns is embedded at increasingly more difficult levels. Hunt's T-unit concept has been reexamined by numerous other theorists and applied to reading and readability as well as to written language.

Endicott (1973) explores the T-unit as a measure of children's syntactic organizational ability. He defines a T-unit as the extent to which children combine units of complexity in language involving suspension of thought and mental manipulation of syntactic structures before they break off and begin again. Endicott proposes a scale that further refines the basic T-unit to account for morphemic analysis as well, including the definition of four comemes or units of complexity.

The comemes allow for weighting of the words that are embedded or subordinated.

His evaluation provides a greater weighting to represent the mental act of "accomplishing the compression" and develops a complexity ratio to represent the increased intricacy achieved through subordination. The addition of the comeme appears to add more information as to how efficiently the students are using language but has the disadvantage of increased complexity and subjectivity in scoring, particularly as to how the weighted values are determined.

Several criticisms can be levelled at these methods of analysis. First, except for Hunt's (1965, 1966) approach (T-units), none of the methods has been applied extensively. The lack of research or practical application of theory in written language is a continuing problem that, in spite of increased attention to the subject, is far from a solution. Anderson (1937), Endicott, Hunt, and LaBrant are examples of theorists who have attempted to better understand written language processing by investigating performance in terms of subordination. This approach is psycholinguistic in nature in that it takes into consideration the cognitive processes of embedding, also considered by these specialists in their discussions of deep structure. Still, the correlation between the development of written syntactic structures and cognition is largely unexplained; only the development of the performance is being studied.

A second but lesser criticism is that all of the methods are of considerable complexity and require that the practitioner engage in extensive training; significant time also must be spent in using and tabulating the various formulas for evaluation purposes. The training/complexity criticism is not, however, a serious one. The very nature of language is complex; a simplified tutored approach does not provide the information necessary for progress in research, diagnosis, or remediation.

The third concern involves the multimodal application of the major language theories. It may very well be that a transformational approach, applicable to the development of oral grammar, is equally useful for written language, and that a syntactic density formula that explains growth in written language has equivalent application in reading. These assumptions are untested, however. They are being applied to cognitive production, which involves significant changes in the types of processing required. Application of established theory to written language provides a necessary and useful starting point but requires intensive and more comprehensive research to ascertain whether the rationale is valid.

An approach that bridges the language pathology and psycholinguistic methods of measuring the maturity of written syntax is the consideration of syntactic complexity by Botel and Granowsky (1972). They also base their approach on the theory of transformational-generative grammar but investigate development by assigning point scores (0 to 3) to various syntactic structures. The point scores are derived from theory as well as from studies of frequency of usage, review of experimental findings, and "intuitions of the authors" where experimental data are inconclusive. These criteria for assigning values to the identified structure allow significant subjectivity to enter the scoring system. Botel and Granowsky recommend their formula for use in assessing readability but it is unclear how accurate it is. It does have the advantage of accounting for syntactic forms, an element not included in most readability formulas.

However, just as research data on oral language have questionable application to written language, the meager findings on written language must be examined carefully before being superimposed on another language function. This approach, though applied more easily than that of Endicott, still is cumbersome as to tabulation and training. In most ways, it is a return to the pathologists' frequency approach that uses categorization of language structures rather than analysis of how grammatic forms are generated and used. The result permits evaluation of levels of written language and error analysis but does not provide an explanation of underlying structures or development.

There is little theory that could be identified as a corpus of literature that could be applied solely to the development of written language. However, there is much that can be gained from understanding the language pathology and psycholinguistic approaches to oral language as related to the development or generation of language forms and combinations. As investigators produce more refined means measuring written language, there will evolve a more sophisticated theory of the development and disorders of written language that will go beyond merely focusing on the syntax of written samples.

*Developmental Approach*

Developmentally, written language is dependent on the ability to process and use oral language and to read. In addition, children must be able to perceive the visual stimulus, recall and interpret it, then use it in a written formulation. Johnson and Myklebust (1967) suggest that by approximately age 6, children have developed the visual and auditory discrimination as well as the visual-motor integration and cognitive and language functioning that are prerequisites for conveying ideas through simple written sentences, so that by that age they are ready to begin to write.

Both oral and written language depend upon the students' experiential background. A youngster who has had limited opportunities will have fewer expressive abilities and will have more difficulty understanding and learning relationships between verbal symbols and the relevant experiences. Oral language or speaking skills are a prerequisite to writing. Written language uses a system of visual symbols or graphemes to represent auditory symbols or phonemes already learned. The visual system is superimposed upon the auditory. Therefore, the auditory or oral system must be functioning efficiently before writing can be learned.

The students, having mastered oral language, must learn to recognize consistent phoneme-grapheme relationships and distinguish those that are inconsistent. In addition, the nonverbal elements of oral language, including tempo, pause, inflection, and stress must be translated as appropriate into their written counterparts by means of spacing and punctuation. Where speakers can emphasize individual meaning units, words, or concepts by varied intonation, writers must communicate those nonverbal feeling aspects through choice of words and use of punctuation.

Litowitz (1981) characterizes the difference in the two modes by using Lopate's (1977) descriptions of oral language—improvisational, relatively unpremeditated, impulsive—and contrasting those with the nature of written language: "premeditated, intentional, and willed" (p. 80). Students must be able to perceive, retain, and attach meaning to the auditory formulation in a consistent and instantaneous manner before transforming it to visual, written form.

The development of basic visual processing skills also is prerequisite to written language. In the visual processing channel, perception and motor skills begin to develop from birth. Researchers have carefully documented the development of a child's pencil grasp, and subsequent ability to imitate and copy figures, from the simplest scribble response. Beery (1967) draws upon the earlier and frequently noted research of Cattell (1960), Gesell (1956), and Griffiths (1954) to establish norms for the *Developmental Test of Visual-Motor Integration*. There is no question that efficient visual-motor skills are prerequisite to legible written language. Basic copying and printing skills are introduced as early as preschool or kindergarten although developmentally normal children may not be ready to form some letters until age 6 or 7. Intact visual-motor skills along with structured teaching and practice enable students to form figures, letters, and numbers correctly and to understand and use spacing and size relationships so that the written product is easily recognized by others.

At a slightly higher level of development, spelling requires that the auditory-visual correspondence be recognized, recalled, and then transformed into a visual-motor product. Spelling is the aspect of the written language process by which letter patterns are retrieved and selected from long-term memory storage and encoded into a visual written form. This visual reformulation, or revisualization, is required for the reproduction of individual figures, for words in spelling, and for other aspects of the mechanics involved in written language.

Once children begin to use written language, three developmental patterns are obvious:

1. As children mature, their productivity—the number of words they write—increases at a regular rate. Productivity, or the quantity of verbal

output, has been found by Meckel (1963) and others to correlate with age. The mean sentence length (dividing the total number of words written in the story by the total number of sentences) generally is used to measure productivity. Mean sentence length provides an estimate of written language development and in that sense may be useful as an initial indicator or screening device. Measures of productivity are not useful diagnostically, however, because such a simple quantitative score provides no information as to the quality or complexity of the words or syntax used or their correctness.

2. As students mature, they write longer sentences.
3. A larger proportion of their clauses are subordinated, as noted by McCarthy (1954). As students develop written language, they must internalize the rules that govern the structural and mechanical aspects of language. Studies of rule-based behavior by Kohlberg (1968) and Piaget (1970) demonstrate that all incremental changes in language ability are qualitative, reflecting a specific level of development. The understanding and use of rules of punctuation, morphology, and syntax are needed for adequate written expression; errors in the use of these rules may indicate a disorder in the understanding of language or its structure, and as such may be interruptive of the communication objective.

The interaction of theories of cognitive and language development has been studied from various perspectives, but as McNeill (1970) notes, not in a comprehensive way. McNeill suggests that a reformulation of the cognitive theory could lead to a stronger grip on language. Review of the available theory from developmental, Piagetian, or psycholinguistic research provides a more complete understanding of the role cognition plays in the acquisition of language (see Chapter 6). Still, there has been little investigation into the application of that research to written language.

Models used to explain the acquisition of oral language consider the children's innate capacity for language and investigate the means by which they generate language. Chomsky (1965) discusses a "language acquisition device" (LAD) by which children process language, sorting out the regular formations, then developing a means of using and adapting them for communicative purposes. It is possible that the pupils deal with written language in similar fashion, either sorting out the oral syntax they hear, and encoding it into written form as needed, or sorting out the written words as read, again later encoding them into written form.

It is not yet clear how the models by Chomsky or of other theorists apply to written language learning. At this point, written language acquisition is explained only by its own developmental progression or by application of oral language theories to the written form.

### Section 2. Written Language Disorders in Learning Disabled Children

There is a significant lack of research into the development of written language in learning disabled children. As noted by Moran (1981), "empirical investigations of spontaneous or elicited writing samples of learning disabled subjects have been few" (p. 271). The available research typically compares normal with deficient written language development using more of a quantitative than a qualitative approach.

Boder (1971), in a study of dyslexic students, identifies three distinctive types of spelling patterns:

1. a dysphonetic pattern that is characterized by a primary deficit in symbol-sound integration so that the youngsters are unable to develop phonetic analysis skills
2. a dyseidetic pattern that is demonstrated by an inability to perceive visually letters and whole words as configurations
3. a mixed pattern that leads to difficulty with both phonetic analysis and visual perception of the configuration.

Consideration of spelling as a visual expressive skill, dependent upon the prerequisite visual receptive skill of reading, suggests that it is not surprising that Boder finds these patterns also reflected in reading error patterns of dyslexic students.

A replication of Boder's work by Whiting and Jarrico (1980) shows that the spelling errors of normal learners do not coincide with these three patterns but rather are largely phonetically equivalent to the dictated spelling words. This research indicates that there are significant differences in the learning processes of learning disabled students that are qualitative, not just quantitative. These studies also provide further confirmation of Johnson & Myklebust's (1967) hierarchical approach in that errors in the input process of reading are reflected in the correlative output process of spelling, confirming the hypothesis that good expressive skills depend on integrity of reception.

In a comparison of written production of normal and learning disabled students, Myklebust (1973) reports that the latter score significantly lower in syntax, ideation, and production (total number of words and words per sentence, but not number of sentences). Using the same *Picture Story Language Test* (PSLT) (Myklebust, 1965), Poteet (1978) says the learning disabled students in his study wrote only half as many words and sentences as the normal ones. They made more punctuation errors and omitted words more frequently but did not differ significantly from the normal group in syntax or ideation.

Research by Poplin, Gray, Larsen, Banikowski, & Mehring (1980) uses the *Test of Written Language* (TOWL) (Hammill & Larsen, 1978) rather than the

PSLT to compare written language performance of the two groups in grades three through eight. The results indicate that the learning disabled are significantly lower on three of the five subtests and on total score at grades three and four; on four of the five subtests and total score at grades five and six; and on all subtests and the total score at grades seven and eight. Their scores on the spelling, word usage, and style subtests are significantly lower at all grade levels, indicating less effective performance "in the more mechanical, conventional aspects of written expression" (p. 52).

The study's authors also note that those three tests use a "contrived" format, i.e., one that measures written language in an objective manner rather than being derived from the written language sample. Scores on vocabulary and thematic maturity are low but never more than one standard deviation below the norm. This finding, taken with the scores on the contrived subtests, suggest to Poplin et al. that learning disabled students should be encouraged in their creative writing efforts but less emphasis should be placed on mechanics, at least initially.

Moran (1981) uses a paragraph writing task, scored by her own analytic system, the *Diagnostic Evaluation of Expository Paragraphs* (DEEP). This system evaluates syntactic maturity, use of conventions or language rules, spelling, and mechanics. She reports that in subjects in grades seven to ten, the only significant differences are in the lower spelling scores of the learning disabled subjects, a finding somewhat consistent with the results of Poplin et al. (1980), Poteet (1978), and Whiting and Jarrico (1980) (noting that Myklebust's (1965, 1973) studies do not investigate spelling differences).

Overall, however, little commonality is found when these studies are viewed together. The potential multiple causes and characteristics of learning disabled students, in combination with the many elements that are integral to written expression, probably explain the different results. Any type of learning disability is accompanied by written language difficulties, since writing is considered the highest level of language processing.

## Section 3. Disorders of Written Language & Processing Deficits

It is evident that even with adequate development in other areas of language processing, students may have a deficit that particularly affects written language ability. Because of the multifaceted nature of written language, and the complex interdependence of the component skills involved, there are numerous possible explanations for a breakdown in the system that results in a disorder in this field. Such a disorder is called dysgraphia, a specific learning difficulty or inability related to visual expressive ability.

If it is assumed that written language represents the highest level of language performance, it follows that that level will not be achieved unless the lower levels of language processing are intact. There has been incredibly little research focused on written language disorders, most likely because of the very subjective nature of this skill and the difficulty found in attempts to quantify the spontaneous form. Myklebust (Johnson & Myklebust, 1967) has made the greatest effort in this area, and application of his hierarchy of experience adds significantly to the understanding of written language problems. Myklebust suggests that ostensibly all the preceding levels of language development in the hierarchy are established before written language is achieved. As that model assumes that output will follow input, children first must learn to read and to develop a facility with the visual symbol system—letters, words, and sentences—that can be recalled when needed for writing. Further, according to Myklebust, the children must be able to learn each aspect of language, both auditorially and visually, and be able to transduce or make associations between modalities, then converting those aspects into motor patterns.

*Visual Processing*

Specifically, at a very basic level, once the students have sufficiently attended to a visual stimulus, whether literal or pictorial, they need to acquire some efficiency in visual perceptual and visual-motor skills. They must be able to scan a visual stimulus, perceive its distinctive characteristics, and discriminate how it is similar to or different from other stimuli. Visual-motor skills depend upon sufficient visual perception. Students must have fine motor skills in order to comfortably grasp, manipulate, and direct the writing instrument. Visual-motor skills enable them to use eye and hand together to visually direct the pencil and produce the desired legible result.

Results of the research on the role of visual-motor functioning vary greatly. Studies by Frostig (1966) indicate that visual-motor performance correlates at a low level with the reading achievement of normal students from first through third grade; is not predictive of reading achievement in the higher grades; and the results of her test are not a useful tool in the diagnosis of brain damage. However, other investigations suggest that visual-motor ability is highly correlated with achievement as well as with brain damage. Bender's work (1938) investigates the visual-motor functioning involved in copying designs and its relationship to brain damage and emotional disturbance. She concludes the fundamental visual-motor function in children is "associated with language ability . . . and . . . various functions of intelligence such as visual perception, manual motor ability, memory, temporal and spatial concepts, and organization or representation" (p. 112).

The visual-motor approach to learning is expanded by theorists Getman (1965) and Kephart (1971). Kephart suggests that children first learn through motor and perceptual motor experiences and that these provide the foundation for all later, higher level learning. In terms of the visual-motor skills needed for writing, Kephart puts particular emphasis on perceptual motor matching skills and has designed diagnostic and remedial procedures to aid in the development of such skills. Getman's model, although also perceptual motor, puts primary emphasis on vision, which he defines as a primary learning skill (not equivalent to sensory acuity). He considers basic visual perceptual skill a prerequisite to higher level skill development.

Many theorists have explored perception and perceptual motor development. However, few, including Getman and Kephart, provide programs that integrate the training of perceptual skills with other aspects of learning, resulting in the most significant weakness in these perception-oriented approaches. Research has regularly found that training perceptual skills alone does not result in improved learning (Goodman & Hammill, 1973).

In the educational sphere, the work of Birch and Belmont (1965) and deHirsch (1963) support the correlation between visual-motor integration and resultant reading scores. Research generally suggests that visual-motor skills most likely affect achievement only in indirect ways. Poor handwriting legibility, including uneven or inconsistently formed figures, may be caused by difficulties in either visual or motor abilities, so differential diagnosis is required. A deficit at this level of functioning is identified as visual-motor apraxia, a disorder similar in nature to oral apraxia. In such a case, the deficit is related to an inability to recall the motor pattern required to produce the output. Although visual perception is intact and the students may be able to copy the stimulus or describe it orally, spontaneous written production is difficult or impossible.

At the imagery level of the hierarchy, visual memory skills are integral to written production, particularly spelling. Students must be able to revisualize the word, the letters needed, and their sequence. The need is for a distinct image of the word that can be recalled for reproduction—spelling the word. A deficit in this area may be a key factor distinguishing the written language production of normal and learning disabled students.

*Visual-Auditory Interaction*

To communicate successfully in a written format, in addition to integrity in visual-motor, perception, and memory skills, students must be able to relate the visual symbol or word with its auditory and experiential counterparts and reproduce that symbol in a comprehensible form. Pupils with a learning disability in symbolization will have difficulty in selecting and using the correct, appropriate word in a written composition.

At the level of conceptualization in the hierarchy, students must be able to use these symbols in meaningful combinations. To use written language effectively, the conceptual sum of the symbol combinations must exceed the value of its individually enumerated parts. As Bruner (1973) suggests, the students must go beyond the limits of the literal information given. For Myklebust, this is the hierarchical level where conceptualization skills are needed to generate the rules used for combining words, so that linguistic structures are carefully regulated for correct production. Conceptualization skills enable the pupils to use the visual symbol system to solve problems and to express creative ideas and abstract thought.

Studies of oral language of both normal and language impaired children indicate that the latter are using a system that is different (qualitatively) and/or less efficient than that of normal students. These differences are demonstrated using both a psycholinguistic model, as in Menyuk's studies (1964, 1971) and a language pathology model (Lee, 1974).

An assumption is made that the rules that students generate and apply to the learning and use of oral language are equally applicable to written language and that the cognitive theory applied to learning oral language fits equally well with the written. There is little research to either confirm or deny such an assumption.

## PART II.  DIAGNOSIS

Written language is considered one of the more difficult to measure forms of symbolic behavior and, as a result, frequently has been left unevaluated. Only since the mid-1970s have diagnostic techniques gone beyond evaluation of the mechanics of writing. The newer contributions have come from both language pathologists and psycholinguists. Myklebust's (1965) information processing perspective provides a useful means for study and improvement of written language evaluation.

In some ways, the measurement of written language is less complex than that of other symbolic behavior in that the students' production is in the form of a permanent, visual record (as contrasted with oral or social behaviors). At the same time, as the "last acquired" of these skills, the evaluation of written language is proportionately more complex in that all of its component processes—auditory, visual, and motor—must be considered when a disorder is identified.

The concerns over evaluation of written language are increased by the fact that disorders in that area are not considered problematic until age nine or ten. Visual-motor problems, particularly reversals or spelling difficulties, may draw some attention during the primary years but relatively little meaningful or cohesive production is expected. Once students are expected to write reports, summaries, and creative works, the problem may become more obvious. However, because of the difficulty of pinpointing or testing, a written language problem still may exist without remediation.

## Section 1.  Holistic Scoring

When evaluation does occur in the regular classroom, it is based most frequently on an informal, subjective review of the students' work. This may result in only a gross estimate of the pupils' abilities, usually identifying significant problems in penmanship, spelling, syntax, or organization. However, that evaluation may be used as the basis for a remedial program and for additional in-depth and more objective analysis. Teachers who take the time to require students to write, and who then analyze those samples even informally, can at a minimum begin to teach the deficit skills and refer pupils for more specialized evaluation and remedial help.

A slightly more formal approach to the evaluation of written language samples is found in the holistic approach used by the Educational Testing Service (1978) and others. A holistic scoring system is based on the concept that the reader reacts to a written composition as a whole or gestalt so that the composition is judged on the basis of a comparative, rather than an absolute, standard. Using this method, scorers are trained by reading sample papers that are considered typical of the identified standards.

Generally three or four ratings are involved, although a holistic system may use a scale with as many as ten. Once trained, two or three scorers read each paper quickly and without deliberation, generally making no corrections or comments; the scores they give are compared and a majority decision reached. As noted by Mullis (1976), this system works well to separate the better papers from the poor but provides little analysis as to what is involved in the score. Mullis presents a modification of the holistic scoring system that takes into account "primary traits" of the composition. The score is dependent upon the likelihood the writing will achieve the desired effect so that, for example, work that has persuasion as its purpose is scored differently from an explanatory composition. Using this method with students aged 9, 13, and 17 years, Mullis finds significant "slippage in overall coherency" from 13 to 17 and concludes that the average writer is "uneasy with the conventions of written language" (p. 6).

Still more specificity is added to a holistic scoring system in the *Paul Diederich System* (1974), as described by Suhor (1977). Rather than providing one score for the composition, this system involves a holistic rating in each of the areas of ideas, organization, wording, flavor, usage, punctuation, spelling, and handwriting. Suhor suggests that the holistic approach is useful for teachers or inservice purposes but is not practical for mass testing. (This latter conclusion is subject to question because the Educational Testing Service uses a holistic system to score the writing sample portion of the College Board Examination.)

Holistic scoring provides a more objective and more efficient method for teachers who otherwise would be unwilling to make writing assignments at all or be unable to review them. It is not a substitute for detailed critique and correction, nor can it be considered at all diagnostic in nature. Holistic scoring may be a useful approach for screening written language problems but it cannot be used even in a more detailed form to identify disorders of written language or to provide the basis for remedial teaching.

## Section 2.  Diagnostic Analysis

Comprehensive efforts to evaluate written language must take into consideration the broad areas of production noted earlier (penmanship, spelling, syntax, and organization) but in addition must carefully analyze the students' previous education and experience as well as their component processing skills and ability to integrate them.

Ideally, analysis of written language would be included as one part of a comprehensive diagnostic evaluation. Of particular importance to understanding a disorder of written language are the component skills involved in basic fine motor and visual-motor ability and visual as well as cross-modal processing. Students' receptive processing skills should be evaluated carefully in both auditory and visual channels. If receptive processing is intact, visual expressive processes must be assessed, with particular emphasis on the skills required for visual-motor spelling and written language performance.

As Myklebust (1973) emphasizes, "A disorder may occur at any . . . or at more than one level" (p. 23). It is necessary diagnostically to determine the degree of intactness at all levels and not to infer deviations simply on the basis of the presenting symptomatology. Diagnostically the need is to appraise each level of function to the extent possible because written language disorders may derive from a number of receptive and expressive conditions. In addition, students' ability to use the component skills in an integrated manner in mechanics and in written formulation must be analyzed.

### Visual Perceptual and Motor Abilities

At a basic level, correlative with Myklebust's hierarchy of experience, students need efficient visual perceptual and motor skills. A multitude of tests measure those skills, including the frequently used *Developmental Test of Visual-Motor Integration* (Beery, 1967), the *Developmental Test of Visual Perception* (Frostig, 1966) and the *Bender Gestalt Test for Young Children* (Koppitz Scoring System, 1963).

Such tests typically measure basic visual processing skills by requiring the students to copy or trace geometric figures or to complete some other paper-and-pencil task. As a result, the pupils may do poorly because of visual perceptual problems or visual or fine motor dysfunctions. Some students may not be able to copy or trace the figure because of an inability to perceive its distinctive characteristics or the way the parts or lines of the figure are joined, others may have difficulty controlling or directing the pencil. Both types of students may score poorly but the total alone will not distinguish the cause of the deficit.

Diagnosticians must take care to evaluate visual perception skills in isolation as well as in combination with the directed motor performance since both types of skill are requisite to writing. Numerous measures that isolate visual perceptual skills require only a minimal motor response, usually marking. The task usually asks the students to identify and mark figures that are alike or different, or find a part or shape that would make an incomplete stimulus whole. Instruments that test this "purer" form of visual perception include the *Motor-Free Visual Perception Test* (Colarusso & Hammill, 1972) and the *Primary Mental Abilities Test* (PMA) (Thurstone, 1963) subtests of spatial relations and perceptual speed. Most reading readiness tools include subtests for visual perception, although the material is likely to be too immature for older students.

If the visual perceptual skills are intact, then poor performance on a copying/drawing test may be caused by poor fine motor skills or an inability to coordinate eye and hand, a visual-motor problem. Students' fine motor skills are evaluated most easily through informal observation of pencil grasp or of tasks involving buttoning or zipping, or of manipulation of small puzzle pieces, blocks, or other objects. If fine motor skills are accomplished with ease and efficiency, the problem is likely to involve using eye and hand together. It is only by carefully differentiating these basic skills that an accurate diagnosis can be made and an appropriate remedial plan implemented. Students with visual perceptual difficulties are not ready for, and will benefit little from, a visual-motor training program.

*Visual Memory*

Visual memory skills are basic to the reformulation required for spelling and the rules and mechanics of written language. Visual memory may be measured formally by requiring students to view a stimulus and, once it is removed, to identify or reproduce it. For example, the *Detroit Tests of Learning Aptitude* (Baker & Leland, 1967) present sequences of pictures or letters that the student must recall and name orally (introducing a possible confounding auditory element). The *Illinois Test of Psycholinguistic Abilities* (Kirk, McCarthy, & Kirk, 1968) presents a sequence of figures on tiles. Upon removal of the sequence, the students arrange the tiles to replicate the original order, introducing fine motor skills as a possible confounding element.

The ideal format for measuring short-term visual memory skills is one in which a stimulus is viewed and, upon removal, is identified by the subject from multiple choices, as in the Visual Memory Subtest of the *Hinskey-Nebraska Test of Learning Aptitude* (Hinskey, 1966). In addition, objective spelling tests that use a multiple-choice format are a good means of measuring longer term revisualization skills. Students must be able to recall and revisualize the correct sequence of letters in order to respond correctly.

Informally, observation of reading and spelling behaviors may provide the first indication of a visual memory problem. Students who do not develop sight vocabulary at a normal rate or who do poorly in written spelling may be evidencing a visual memory problem. They frequently may be able to recognize the proper formulation, selecting the correct word from multiple choices, but be unable to recall it from memory storage without some help. Evaluation of visual memory skills must be comprehensive enough to include both recognition and recall as well as memory for both verbal and nonverbal stimuli.

*Spelling*

In evaluation of spelling skills, responses to different formats provide an indication of strengths and weaknesses; the learning disabled frequently demonstrate a particular pattern of errors, as noted by Boder's research (1971). A comprehensive review of spelling must include a variety of response opportunities (dictation, multiple choice, oral testing). Rather than only requiring the students to identify or write the correct spelling in isolation, the procedures used should implement a variety of contextual formats, including the use of cloze techniques, as well as spontaneous writing and proofreading. Typically, however, a single format is used.

Myklebust's *Picture Story Language Test* (PSLT) (1965) does not evaluate spelling at all. Many group tests measure spelling using an objective, multiple-choice format, evaluating recognition only. This format also is found on such individually administered tests as the *Peabody Individual Achievement Test* (PIAT) (Dunn & Markwardt, 1970). The *Test of Written Language* (TOWL) (Hammill & Larsen, 1978) uses a traditional dictation format, measuring recall, as does the *Wide Range Achievement Test* (WRAT) (Jastak, Bijou, & Jastak, 1978). Use of these formats in isolation does not provide information as to: (1) the types of errors made or the students' approach to spelling or (2) their ability to maintain spelling efficiency when the task also requires meaningful communication. A more comprehensive, diagnostic approach is needed.

*Mechanics*

A variety of standards may be used to evaluate punctuation. Although there is a fairly general consensus as to correct beginning and ending punctuation, there frequently is much disagreement as to intermediate punctuation. In effect, however, it is not the minor variations in punctuation that disrupt the communication effort, so they should be of little concern. Errors in capitalization and use of terminal punctuation (period, question marks, exclamation points) may be indicative of a significant disorder in the understanding or use of language.

At this point, a general caution as to the evaluation of mechanical aspects of written language (spelling, punctuation, and usage) is in order. While writing is an expressive or output skill, attempts to measure written language ability frequently have used a receptive format in which students are required only to recognize an error in spelling, punctuation, or syntax. This in effect reduces the task to one of recognizing rules, or of reading rather than acquiring written language. Such a receptive format does allow for group testing and, as a result, produces highly standardized scoring. At the same time, however, it has changed completely the nature of the task from one that is expressive, creative, and subjective, to one that is highly stratified and capable of being scored.

For example, as a prototype of group achievement instruments, the *Iowa Tests of Basic Skills* (Hieronymous & Lindquist, 1971) use exercises that may or may not contain a misspelled word and the students must identify which, if any, of the words contain errors. The mechanical skills of capitalization, punctuation, and usage are tested on the Iowa with a similar format. These tests provide highly standardized objective scores as well as guidelines for item analysis and suggestions for improving instruction in each of the areas assessed.

In similar fashion, the *Stanford Achievement Test* (Kelley, Madden, Gardner, & Rudman, 1964) uses a multiple-choice format to measure spelling and language (including usage, punctuation, capitalization, and sentence sense). The editors of the Stanford emphasize the important concept that the most valid test of a person's ability to use language correctly is the extent to which the individual demonstrates those mechanics in writing. In spite of some loss of validity, those editors recommend this "somewhat artificial fashion" (p. 5) of testing as a simplified means of measurement and scoring.

Overall, there is little evidence that the ability to recognize errors in written language is related to the ability to produce written language free of such mistakes. In agreement with the editors of the *Stanford Achievement Test* (Kelley et al., 1964) Lloyd-Jones (1977), in discussing primary trait scoring, emphasizes that the language subtest results of group achievement tests generally are too lacking in validity to be considered conclusive estimates of writing ability.

Diagnosticians may use results of standardized tests such as the Iowa and Stanford to advantage as indicative of the students' receptive understanding of the mechanical skills measured. Clinicians should consider, in addition to experiential or nonlanguage handicaps that might explain a low score, that students who do poorly on such receptive measures of these skills:

1. may have a deficit at a lower level of processing visual information and therefore need additional testing
2. may have a visual perceptual or visual-motor problem that has made their accurate marking of the machine-scored answer sheet difficult or impossible

3. may have a visual memory deficit that is made evident by multiple-choice measures of spelling and usage, so that the score is an accurate reflection of a learning disability.

As to individualized, diagnostic measures of mechanics in written language, the PSLT (Myklebust, 1965) and the TOWL (Hammill & Larsen, 1978) provide the norm among what is available. The PSLT includes a "syntax quotient" based on various error types found in word usage, word endings, and punctuation. Errors of addition, omission, substitution, and word order are categorized, then tallied, resulting in a score that is found frequently in measures using a language pathology approach to diagnosis. While the PSLT gathers the data from the spontaneous language sample, the TOWL uses a slightly more structured approach, measuring word usage in a cloze format and style (punctuation) in a framework that has the students rewrite incorrect sentences. Both of these tests produce information far beyond that available through the multiple-choice format. Still, they provide little information on the quality or complexity of the usage except for the diagnosticians' own informal interpretation.

### Formulation: Ideation, Syntax, Organization

In spite of advances in understanding of the written language process and its diagnosis, there are few evaluative instruments that are both diagnostically comprehensive and well standardized. In fact, there are very few instruments that can be considered diagnostic in nature, and those that are available measure varying elements of written production. Several instruments measure the mechanics of writing and spelling but few also include evaluation of syntax and organization. However, there are tests designed to evaluate written language that provide more detailed information than the informal screening or the receptive objective measure otherwise available. Diagnostic tests are revised continually and new tests are published. The following are representative of the few available tests of written language, but not as an exhaustive sample. Diagnosticians must review any test carefully before use, considering its purpose and how a particular instrument will help achieve that purpose.

Myklebust (1965), with his PSLT, was perhaps the first to devise a diagnostic test of written language that had a theoretically sound basis and some degree of standardization, and also was available commercially. The major objective of the PSLT is the study of language diagnosis and development. The test uses a photograph as a stimulus for students to produce a written language sample. The scoring is based on productivity (number of words, number of sentences, words per sentence), syntax (word order, punctuation, and use of morphemes), and meaning (measured by an "abstract-concrete" rating scale) as attributes of effective communication.

The original PSLT standardization sample included 747 students aged 7 to 17 years, in six age groups. Myklebust reports that the most stable and continuous growth over that 10-year span occurs in the productivity score. The syntax score, which he describes as measuring correctness in terms of its influence on meaning, grows rapidly to age 9, slows to age 11, and shows little increase after that to age 17. Meaning, as measured by the abstract-concrete scale, shows gradual growth through age 15.

It is interesting to compare Myklebust's findings with those of Mullis (1976), who uses the primary trait method of holistic scoring. The studies, though using drastically different methods of scoring, both indicate decreasing growth in meaning (or coherency, as Mullis calls it) before age 17. Although this may be related to the development of increased independence at this age, it does not relate to other measures of language or intellectual ability that suggest higher levels of performance beyond age 15. Further research in this area is needed.

Myklebust's contribution to more objective diagnosis of written language disorders has been significant and the PSLT remains a useful instrument for certain applications. Several considerations are important, however. The photograph used (portraying a young boy playing with dollhouse toys) is infantile and outdated, particularly for older students. Since written language is rarely a concern with young students, the poor photograph greatly limits the utility of the test. It also is cumbersome to score and provides minimal information at the symbolic or conceptual levels. Examiners must become familiar with a scoring system that entails 51 pages of detailed explanations and examples and results in scores that Myklebust concludes are incomplete as to both validity and reliability. Standardization data also are incomplete at certain age levels. The PSLT results provide no clear directions for a remedial program. It should be used with discretion in selected situations where diagnosticians are certain as to how useful the resultant information will be.

After Myklebust, little progress was made toward more efficient written language diagnosis until 1978, when Hammill and Larsen developed a significant new measure, their *Test of Written Language* (TOWL). This is designed to aid educators:

1. to identify students whose written expression is below average and who as a result need special help
2. to identify students' strengths and weaknesses in various writing abilities
3. to document students' progress in writing
4. to conduct research in writing.

Its authors describe the TOWL as a measure "designed to be easily administered, highly reliable and valid and instructionally relevant . . . suitable for testing both individuals and groups . . . in grades three through eight" (p. 10). The test uses both a spontaneous written language sample and more objective "contrived" items to evaluate student performance in vocabulary, thematic maturity, thought units, handwriting, spelling, word usage, and style. The test has been found to be highly reliable but the results of the validity studies are less clear.

The difficulties involved in establishing criterion-related validity can be appreciated in that well-standardized measures of written language are not available. Hammill and Larsen use the PSLT and teacher ratings, measures that have questionable reliability and validity, as the external criteria to provide some evidence of validity. Construct validity is based on age differentiation on subtest scores and subtest intercorrelations. In addition, significant correlations with another Hammill test, the *Test of Language Development* (TOLD) (Newcomer & Hammill, 1977) are high.

The format of the *Test of Written Language* is good; it provides a more comprehensive analysis of written language than the PSLT and is much less burdensome to score. Its only apparent limitations relate to its small range (grades three through eight) and the need for more complete studies of validity. In light of the changes in written expressive ability identified by these studies, it is important to continue to evaluate performance through adolescence in order to fully understand the changes that occur.

As an alternative approach to standardized testing, Weiner (1980) developed the *Diagnostic Evaluation of Writing Skills* (DEWS) to identify students who require remedial instruction and to provide a basis for directing remediation. Weiner's 41 evaluation criteria are designed to measure skills ranging from visual-motor to syntax and conceptualization. The criteria are distributed in six categories: graphic, orthographic, phonologic, syntactic, semantic, and self-monitoring. The DEWS criteria can be applied to any sample of student writing, regardless of topic. (Weiner suggests a school autobiography for older students and a topic such as "My Favorite Activity" for younger ones.)

Weiner's approach is not standardized and there is no information available on its validity and reliability. Significant deficits are not easily differentiated from minor ones and real gains are not easily measured because of the qualitative nature of the scale. She reports that Kagan (1979) used DEWS to obtain a comparison of writing skills and reading levels in a study of the cause of reading disability. In a comparison of normal and reading disabled boys, Kagan finds significant differences in performance on the first five categories of the DEWS scale. Weiner reports that this therefore confirms Kagan's hypothesis that students with reading disability can be identified by their writing and, as a result, the need for expensive, time-consuming batteries of standardized diagnostic tests is eliminated.

These conclusions are overly broad, however. The sample used in the research is small (n = 31); further, it is unrealistic to use a nonstandardized subjective measure of writing as a substitute for a diagnostic battery yielding standardized results. In considering Myklebust's hierarchy, it is understood that students with reading disabilities—problems with input—are most likely to have difficulty with the related output—writing. It is inappropriate, then, to use an informal evaluation to identify reading problems, particularly since the measure provides no information as to types of reading and/or related processing errors. However, DEWS does provide teachers with a comprehensive, easily used means of critiquing students' written production; included as part of an informal review, it can help clinicians focus on specific problems and plan a remedial approach.

## Pragmatic Aspects

Although there is evidence of progress in written language evaluation, the emphasis still is being placed on basic structure and basic elements of production, with little attention to the pragmatic or higher level cognitive processes involved. For example, in her discussion of developmental issues, Litowitz (1981) considers the concept of audience in terms of how the student writer must select words and place them in a context so that they are fully intelligible to the potential reader. Referring to work by Vygotsky (1962) on "textualization," i.e., the need to explain meaning more fully in written as contrasted to oral language, Litowitz characterizes this as a need for "deliberate semantics" or "deliberate structuring of the web of meaning" (p. 82). Such selection and structuring also is present in good oral language but communication in writing allows more careful choices to be made.

The tests reviewed here do evaluate word and structure choice as to correctness and, to some degree, complexity by categorizing and counting the forms. However, the quality of those choices is not measured and is difficult to quantify for assessment purposes.

## Elicitation of Written Samples

There is consensus among language specialists that to evaluate expressive oral or written language validly, a language sample must be elicited. This is particularly important and practical with written language as it is the students' actual performance, rather than a transcription, that serves as the permanent record. It is important to consider, however, that a variety of factors may determine the degree to which the sample is representative.

Certainly, the student writer's motivation and perception of the purpose of the writing task, and of the target audience, will have some effect on the ultimate product. The great variety of stimuli used to elicit the writing also should be considered since there is no basis to conclude students' written performance remains constant in response to different types of stimuli. Where the photograph in Myklebust's test (1965) is inappropriate in its depiction of a young boy, the TOWL (1978) uses a pictorial stimulus (a cartoon sequence depicting a trip to another planet) that some respondents find to be confusing and silly. Such nonverbal pictorial stimuli are useful in that they do not require reading ability but they can cause confusion because of students' problems with visual perception or social awareness; these pictures also become outdated.

These various confusions may be minimized by using a verbal stimulus but presenting it both orally and visually to minimize the effect of a reading problem. The use of a written school autobiography is one possible approach, as suggested by Weiner (1980), but this can be confounded by the students' self-perceptions and views of school. Several short topic sentences, presented both orally and visually, offer a good alternative. Researchers have used a variety of sentences, a popular choice being, "If I had a million dollars, I would . . . ," or Weiner's "My favority activity." Such verbal stimuli can be structured to have universal appeal across a wider age range and are less easily outdated.

## PART III.  REMEDIATION

Just as there are no entirely satisfactory evaluative measures of written language development, there are few well-designed remedial approaches. After surveying remediation texts and studies on time allocation in learning disabilities class-rooms, Silverman, Zigmond, Zimmerman, and Vallecorsa (1981) note that "the teaching of written language remains a virtually ignored area" (p. 92). The diagnosis/remediation gap in language and learning disorders has received a great deal of attention. That gap has been minimized in many areas of learning by improvement in teacher training programs and the attention of materials/program publishers. However, there still is a dearth of well-designed materials or programs available to remediate written language disorders.

For many years, great effort was placed on the remediation of visual-motor skills, with emphasis on training eye and hand together. Few remedial programs were available for improvement of the other skills involved in written language such as visual perception (apart from the motor component) or visual memory. Materials to improve the mechanics of spelling or syntax also were few in number, and little if anything was available that could aid in remediation of the symboliza-tion or conceptualization skills.

Oral language, as a skill, develops from birth through a combination of factors: children's innate ability, experiences, structured and unstructured practice, feed-back, and teaching. Written language, as a skill, though also related to children's ability and experience, depends to a much greater degree on structured (rather than unstructured) practice, feedback, and teaching.

Many schools now place little emphasis on the actual teaching of written language. As noted by Weiner (1980), the qualitative similarities of errors made by normal and reading disabled boys suggest the need for greater teaching emphasis in writing skills for all students. In most cases the basic mechanics are taught in spelling or language periods but little time is spent in development of the symbolic and conceptual aspects of written expression as the daily curriculum has become more and more overloaded with extra subject matter (e.g., sex and consumer education) and teachers have become more burdened with extra responsibilities (modular schedules, individual education plans).

An objective format (true/false, multiple-choice, or cloze) has become increasingly predominant in both testing and teaching. Many publishers provide objective units or summative tests to accompany the teaching materials. This reduces the burden on teachers in terms of both test construction and time spent in grading. The disastrous side effect is that a premium is put on selecting the one correct response and the students have significantly fewer opportunities to produce a creative written response. Students may progress to the college or even graduate level without ever having to write an essay test.

A remedial program, therefore, must take into consideration the students' background and experience. It may be that they suffer not from a written language disorder but rather from a lack of education or experience with written language. In that case, although general remedial principles are useful, a developmental writing program with great emphasis on practice is likely to be all that is needed.

## Section 1.  Goals of Remediation

Careful evaluation of the learners' processing strengths and deficits provides the basic principles for constructing a remedial plan. The importance of working on the component areas of visual, auditory, and motor processing, then integrating them into the structured output required for spelling and written language, cannot be overly stressed.

The basic goal in remediation of written language skills is that the students be able to (1) retrieve the necessary visual symbols (units, words, sequences) and (2) recall the necessary motor sequence for production. They should be able to write with efficiency: quickly and easily, with a high degree of correctness, so that clear communication is accomplished. Responses must become habitual.

In planning remediation, the prerequisite skills to writing play an important role. Chalfant and Scheffelin (1969) suggest a basic six-step developmental approach to the writing task: (1) scribbling; (2) tracing, (3) copying, (4) completing tasks where a portion of the stimulus is missing, (5) writing from dictation, and (6) writing propositions. There is a tendency to ignore those early stages of development when teaching older students. However, it may be appropriate to include scribbling or tracing exercises to remediate those skills. The interdependence of written and other language forms also must be utilized in planning the remediation program. Teachers should integrate reading and oral language experiences with the writing program.

A most important element in planning is that of developing positive attitudes toward writing. Many learning disabled students receive so much negative feedback on their papers that they are unwilling to write at all. Some teachers also use writing assignments as punishment, resulting in increased hostility toward written production. Teachers must emphasize the importance and utility of legible handwriting and written communication and convince the students that the goals presented are attainable.

In addition, several studies have found that student participation in the choice of teaching strategy results in improved performance. In a study of strategies to teach handwriting, Kosiewicz, Hallahan, and Lloyd (1981) report that when teacher-imposed treatments are contrasted with those chosen by students, the latter produce far superior handwriting performance. In determining goals and strategies for the written language program, it is just as important to consider the students' interests and style of learning as their processing and language strengths and weaknesses.

## Section 2.  Teaching Strategies

*Handwriting*

Since many learning disabled students have poor handwriting skills, remediation in that area may be the first step in improving written language. It must be determined first whether visual perception and visual motor skills are intact (or otherwise made part of the remediation program). At that point, teachers should become familiar with basic components of good handwriting, often forgotten or unknown to learning disabilities clinicians, particularly those working with older students. Good writing posture, efficient pencil grasp, correct paper position, and an appropriate writing instrument are important considerations before corrective programs are implemented.

Many techniques, though useful, are difficult to implement with older students. For example, chalkboard exercises, tracing, or using templates may be appealing to younger pupils but may appear too elementary at junior high or high school levels. Practitioners also must always consider whether the teaching technique is closely enough related to the deficit skill to be transferred, e.g., writing on a chalkboard involves more gross motor movement, on a vertical plane, quite different from the usual handwriting task. Similarly, tracing exercises may provide little or no visual feedback, so that upon completion, neither teachers nor students can identify whether there has been improvement.

There are many commercially available handwriting programs that use a developmental approach. However, when teaching handwriting to the learning disabled, practitioners should consider whether additional auditory or tactile reinforcement will be helpful and whether the students, regardless of age, should be taught manuscript or cursive.

*Spelling*

As students with spelling problems frequently have underlying memory problems, a method of remediation is needed that puts less rather than more emphasis on memory skills (while remediation also proceeds with that underlying processing deficit). One approach, emphasizing discovery rather that memorization of rules, is the *Childs Spelling System* (1973).

The conceptual framework for this system suggests that learning not only is more rapid but also more permanent when the students take an active rather than a passive role in the process. Therefore, rather than presenting lists of words and rules to learn as the typical spelling program would, the Childs system presents words that are relevant to the desired learning, requiring the students to analyze the material and discern or discover the pattern or rule. This approach maximizes the learning disabled students' strength, which could be normal or above-average intelligence and interests, and puts minimal emphasis on the particular weakness that generally affects spelling—visual memory. Meanwhile, remediation of the visual memory deficit can proceed toward minimizing that deficient ability eventually.

Fernald (1971) also recommends an interest-based vocabulary as the basis for remediation of spelling problems. Her multisensory approach includes word pronunciation, visualization, tracing, and writing in carefully sequenced steps, with appropriate modifications for older students. Such multisensory approaches are useful for students who can handle that variety of stimuli; they also provide a unique clinical, individualized teaching approach with intensive review that is useful for the learning disabled.

Teachers must contrast these interest-based approaches to spelling with commercially available programs that typically use a rule-based approach, presenting new words by families or spelling generalizations. Each approach has some advantages; the strategy chosen must be determined on the basis of student need and characteristics.

*Punctuation, Syntax, Formulation*

Remediation programs designed to develop or stimulate growth in mechanics and formulation must be based on patterns of normal development because of the lack of any other research-based rationale. There has been continual debate in the educational field as to how written language usage should be taught. Grammar traditionally was taught through a rule-based approach, with emphasis on parts of speech, sentence diagrams, and drills. In recent years, evaluations of writing skills that have emphasized the quality of writing, the investigation of subordination, and modification of words have led to teaching students to write by developing sentence expansion or combining techniques. Another approach puts greatest emphasis on student motivation.

In a prototypical sentence expansion or sentence-combining approach, the teacher provides structured practice, first presenting multiple, related simple sentences, then reducing them to subordinate clauses, and finally embedding the reduced clauses in sentences. The opposite approach also is used, starting with a complex sentence and breaking it into simple sentences. Either method teaches students the psycholinguistic principles of embedding or subordination.

DiStefano and Marzano (1979) advocate "base clause expansion," an approach that they consider less mechanical and less demanding of time and expense to the teacher. Their method presents students with a base clause and a set of instructions for its expansion. The instructions are based on research findings determinative of written language behaviors or skills developed at different age levels. For example, DiStefano and Marzano report that the factor of clauses per T-unit is predictive of quality in 9-year-old pupils' compositions, suggesting that written language exercises for that age group should require increasing ability to subordinate. This approach permits greater student creativity than either a rule-based or a sentence-combining system. It is grounded in sequential skills development that has important implications for students with written language disorders.

Approaches that focus on writer motivation emphasize creating an environment that will promote students' desire to write. Oral language is used as a stimulus for written expression, as suggested by Silverman et al. (1981) and, initially, standards for spelling, punctuation, and grammar are not considered. As production increases, with writing becoming more fluent, rules for correct production can be introduced. Silverman et al. recommend a discussion period in which teacher and students generate questions about a given topic such as an advertisement for a make-believe product. Students then organize their written answers to those questions. This method of encouraging output from students whose written production is low has been found to be successful.

As noted in various studies, students with language disorders do not simply demonstrate a lower level of performance but use a different system for acquisition of language. They do not necessarily generate rules in the usual way. Careful examination is needed to determine which rules they have generated and which structures they can produce correctly. With a foundation established by that information, an approach utilizing base clause expansion has the advantages noted in the discussion of spelling methods (i.e., high interest). Rather than requiring extensive memorization, a discovery approach is utilized, requiring the students to experiment with structures and to discern patterns as part of the learning process. The use of oral language as a stimulus may prove helpful.

There is no one particular approach that will prove successful for all students with written language disorders. Because written language represents a highly complex level of performance, depending on an adequate foundation of auditory, visual, and motor processing skills at all levels of the hierarchy, thorough diagnosis is imperative. Given the variety of component skills that may cause poor written language, the goals and strategies for remediation must be chosen with care. The complexity of written language requires that those various subskills not only be mastered in isolation but also be integrated for communicative purposes.

The study of written language diagnosis and remediation is ripe for investigation. Myklebust's work (1965, 1973) has provided a useful model for the analysis of the skill; application of the findings of other language pathologists, psycholinguists, and English educators has further enhanced this effort. However, the end result is that there still is no well-developed corpus of information to explain written language, its development, and its related disorders.

## REFERENCES

Anderson, J.E. An evaluation of various indices of linguistic development. *Child Development*, 1937, *8*, 62-68.

Baker, H., & Leland, B. *Detroit tests of learning aptitude*. Indianapolis: The Bobbs-Merrill Co., Inc. 1967.

Beery, K.D. *Developmental test of visual-motor integration*. Chicago: Follett Educational Corporation, 1967.

Bender, L. *A visual-motor gestalt test and its clinical use*. New York: The American Orthopsychiatric Association, 1938.

Birch, H.G., & Belmont, L. Auditory-visual integration, intelligence and reading ability in school children. *Perceptual and Motor Skills*, 1965, *20*, 295-303.

Boder, E. Developmental dyslexia: A diagnostic screening procedure based on three characteristic patterns of reading and spelling. In B.D. Bateman (Ed.), *Learning Disorders* (Vol. 4). Seattle: Special Child Publications, 1971.

Botel, M., & Granowsky, A. A formula for measuring syntactic complexity: A directional effort. *Elementary English*, 1972, *49*, 513-516.

Bruner, J.S. *Beyond the information given*. New York: W.W. Norton & Company, Inc., 1973.

Cattell, T. *The measurement of intelligence of infants and young children*. New York: The Psychological Corporation, 1960.

Chalfant, J.C., & Scheffelin, M.A. *Central processing dysfunctions in children*. NINDS Monograph No. 9. Bethesda, Md.: Department of Health, Education, and Welfare, 1969.

Childs, S.B., & Childs, R. *The Childs spelling system: The rules*. Cambridge, Mass: Educators Publishing Services, Inc., 1973.

Chomsky, N.A. *Aspects of the theory of syntax*. Cambridge: The MIT Press, 1965.

Colarusso, R.P., & Hammill, D.D. *Motor-free visual perception test*. San Rafael, Calif.: Academic Therapy Publications, 1972.

deHirsch, K. Concepts related to normal reading processes and their application to reading pathology. *Journal of Genetic Psychology*, 1963, *102*, 277-185.

Diederich, P. Measuring growth in English. Urbana, Ill.: National Council of Teachers of English, 1974.

DiStefano, P., & Marzano, R. Basic skills in composition: A new approach. *English Education*, 1979, *9*, 117-121.

Dunn, L., & Markwardt, F. *Peabody individual achievement test* (PIAT). Circle Pines, Minn.: American Guidance Service, Inc., 1970.

Educational Testing Service. The concern for writing. *Focus 5*. Princeton, N.J.: Author, 1978.

Endicott, A.L. A proposed scale for syntactic complexity. *Research in the Teaching of English*, 1973, *7*, 5-12.

Fernald, G. *Remedial techniques in basic school subjects*. New York: McGraw-Hill Book Company, 1971.

Frostig, M. *Developmental test of visual perception*. Palo Alto, Calif.: Consulting Psychologists Press, 1966.

Gesell, A. *Developmental schedules*. New York: The Psychological Corporation, 1956.

Getman, G. The visuomotor complex in the acquisition of learning skills. In J. Hellmuth (Ed.), *Learning Disorders* (Vol. I). Seattle: Special Child Publications, 1965.

Goodman, L., & Hammill, D.D. The effectiveness of the Kephart-Getman activities in developing perceptual-motor and cognitive skills. *Focus on Exceptional Children*, 1973, *4*, 1-9.

Griffiths, R. *The abilities of babies*. New York: McGraw-Hill Book Company, 1934.

Hammill, D.D., & Larsen, S.C. *Test of written language*. Austin, Texas: PRO-ED, 1978.

Hieronymous, A.N., & Lindquist, E.F. *Iowa tests of basic skills*. Iowa City, Iowa: Houghton Mifflin Company, 1971.

Hinskey, M.S. *Hinskey-Nebraska test of learning aptitude*. Lincoln, Nebraska: University of Nebraska, 1966.

Hunt, K.W. Grammatical structures written at three grade levels. *Research Report #3*. Urbana, Ill.: National Council of Teachers of English, 1965.

Hunt, K.W. Recent measures in syntactic development. *Elementary English*, 1966, *43*, 732-739.

Jastak, J., Bijou, S., & Jastak, S. *Wide range achievement test* (WRAT). Wilmington, Del.: Jastak Associates, Inc., 1978.

Johnson, D.J., & Myklebust, H.R. *Learning disabilities: Educational principles and practices*. New York: Grune & Stratton, Inc., 1967.

Kagan, J.A. Study on the causes of reading disability. Unpublished manuscript, Harvard University, 1979.

Kelley, T.L., Madden, R., Gardner, E.F., & Rudman, H.C. *Stanford achievement test*. New York: Harcourt Brace & World, Inc., 1964.

Kephart, N. *The slow learner in the classroom*. Columbus, Ohio: The Charles E. Merrill Publishing Co., Inc., 1971.

Kirk, S.A., McCarthy, J.J., & Kirk, W.D. *Illinois test of psycholinguistic abilities*. Urbana, Ill.: University of Illinois Press, 1968.

Kohlberg, L. Early education: A cognitive developmental view. *Child Development*, 1968, *39*, 1013-1062.

Koppitz, E.M. *The Bender gestalt test for young children*. New York: Grune & Stratton, Inc., 1963.

Kosiewicz, M.M., Hallahan, D.P., & Lloyd, J. The effects of an L.D. student's treatment choice on handwriting performance. *Learning Disability Quarterly*, 1981, *4*, 281-286.

LaBrant, L. Studies of certain language developments of children in grades four to twelve inclusive. *Genetic Psychology Monographs* No. 4, 1933.

Lee, L. Developmental sentence types: A method for comparing normal and deviant syntactic development. *Journal of Speech and Hearing Disorders*, 1966, *31*, 311-330.

Lee, L. *Developmental sentence analysis*, Evanston, Ill.: Northwestern University Press, 1974.

Litowitz, B. Developmental issues in written language. *Topics in Language Disorders*, 1981, *1*, 73-89.

Lloyd-Jones, R. Primary trait scoring. In C.R. Cooper & L. Odell (Eds.), *Evaluating writing*. Urbana, Ill.: National Council of Teachers of English, 1977.

Lopate, P. The transition from speech to writing. In B. Zavatsky & R. Padgett (Eds.), *The whole world catalogue 2*. New York: McGraw-Hill, 1977.

McCarthy, D. Language development in children. In L. Carmichael (Ed.), *Manual of child psychology*. New York: John Wiley & Sons, Inc., 1954.

McNeill, D. The development of language. In P.H. Mussen (Ed.), *Manual of child psychology* (Vol. 1). New York: John Wiley & Sons, Inc., 1970.

Meckel, H.C. Research on teaching composition and literature. In N. Gage (Ed.), *Handbook of research on teaching*. Chicago: Rand McNally Co., 1963.

Menyuk, P. Comparison of grammar of children with functionally deviant and normal speech. *Journal of Speech & Hearing Research*, 1964, *7*, 109-121.

Menyuk, P. *The acquisition and development of language*. Englewood Cliffs, N.J.: Prentice-Hall, Inc., 1971.

Mullis, I. *Highlights and trends from national assessment: Writing and change in writing skills*. Denver: Education Commission of the States, 1976. (ERIC Document Reproduction Service No. ED 128 814)

Myklebust, H.R. *Development and disorders of written language* (Vol. 1): *Picture story language test*. New York: Grune & Stratton, Inc., 1965.

Myklebust, H.R. *Development and disorders of written language* (Vol. 2): *Studies of normal and exceptional children*. New York: Grune & Stratton, Inc., 1973.

Newcomer, P., & Hammill, D.D. *Test of language development*. Austin, Texas: Empiric Press, 1977.

Piaget, J. Piaget's theory. In P.H. Mussen (Ed.), *Manual of child psychology* (Vol. 1). New York: John Wiley & Sons, Inc., 1970.

Poplin, M.S., Gray, R., Larsen, S., Banikowski, A., & Mehring, T. A comparison of components of written expression abilities in learning disabled and nonlearning disabled students at three grade levels. *Learning Disabilities Quarterly*, 1980, *3*, 46-53.

Poteet, J.A. *Characteristics of written expression of learning disabled and nonlearning disabled elementary school students*. Muncie, Ind.: Ball State University, 1978. (ERIC Document Reproduction Service No. ED 159 830)

Silverman, R., Zigmond, N., Zimmerman, J., & Vallecorsa, A. Improving written expression in learning disabled students. *Topics in Language Disorders*, 1981, *1*, 91-99.

Suhor, Charles. *Mass testing in composition: Is it worth doing badly?* New Orleans: New Orleans Public Schools, Louisiana Division of Instruction (sponsored by HEW), 1977. (ERIC Document Reproduction Service No. ED 147 807)

Thurstone, T.G. *Primary mental abilities test*. Chicago: Scientific Research Associates, Inc., 1963.

Vygotsky, L.S. *Thought and language*. Cambridge, Mass: The MIT Press, 1962.

Weiner, E. The diagnostic evaluation of writing skills (DEWS): Application of DEWS criteria to writing samples. *Learning Disability Quarterly*, 1980, *3*, 54-59.

Whiting, S.A., & Jarrico, S. Spelling patterns of normal readers. *Journal of Learning Disabilities*, 1980, *13*, 45-47.

# Index

## A

Acoustic speech signal, 40-41
Additions, 61
Adjectives, semantic assessment and, 100
Adverbs, semantic assessment and, 100
Affrication, 44
American Sign Language, 207
Anastasi, A., 270
Andersen, E. S., 170
Anderson, J. E., 299, 300
Anglin, J. M., 87, 89, 91
Aphasia, 10, 116, 226
  syntax problems and, 135-36, 144
Apraxia, 284
  analysis of, 51-52
  articulation problems and, 257
  diagnosis of, 69-71
  remediation and, 76-78
  syntactic production and, 135
  tests and, 30
Articulation, 178
  elicitation procedures and, 67, 68
  errors in, 45, 49-50, 61
  perception and, 48-49
  problems with, 52-53
  reading and, 256-57
  syntactic problems and, 135
  testing, 62-66
  therapy, 71-76

Assessment. *See* Diagnosis
*Assessment of Children's Language Comprehension* (ACLC, Foster, Giddan, & Stark, 1972), 138
Assimilation processes, 44
Attention
  disorders in, 53
  language development and, 9
  learning disability model and, 19
  pragmatic disorders and, 179
  reading and, 251, 273
  syntactic problems and, 131
*Auditory Association Subtest (Illinois Test of Psycholinguistic Abilities,* Kirk et al., 1968), 101
Auditory discrimination. *See* Speech sound discrimination
*Auditory Discrimination Test,* 59
Auditory synthesis (blending), 55
Austin, J. L., 159

## B

Babbling, 41
Bagshaw, N., 203
Banikowski, A., 304
Bankson, N., 75
Barron, C., 45
Bateman, B., 251
Bates, E., 158, 168-69, 187, 219
Baughman, G., 69

Beery, K. D., 302
Belmont, L., 307
*Bender Gestalt Test for Young
    Children,* 310
Bender, L., 306
Bentzen, F., 250
Berkley, R., 143
Berninger, G., 194, 195
Bernstein, D., 174
Berry, M., 72-73
*Berry-Talbott Test of Grammar* (1966),
    140, 263-64
Birch, H. G., 307
Blache, S., 75
Blalock, J., 226
Blank, M., 157, 198
Blending (auditory synthesis), 55
Bloom, L., 9, 19, 104, 141, 142, 168,
    171, 195, 200-201, 202
Blue, C. M., 94
Boder, E., 304, 312
*Boehm Test of Basic Concepts* (1971),
    97, 100-101
Bolders, J., 124
Botel, M., 300-301
Braille, 19
Bricker, D., 177
Brown, R., 86, 117, 120, 124, 141
Bruner, J., 223, 225, 233, 308
Bryan, T., 174, 175, 177, 185
Bryen, D., 17, 24, 32, 143, 147
Bunce, B., 73, 76
Burke, C. L., 272


C


Caramozza, A., 225
Carpenter, R., 124, 187
Carrell, P. L., 190
Carrow, E., 137
*Carrow Elicited Language Inventory*
    (CELI, 1974), 140
    *Producing Formulated Sentences
        Subtest* of, 141

Carrow-Woolfolk, E., 11, 13, 24, 25
Carter, B., 263
Category structure
    semantic assessment and, 97
    semantic remediation and, 106
Cattell, T., 302
Chalfant, J., 20, 319
Chapman, R., 160, 168, 188
Chappell, G., 69, 77
Chicago Institute for Learning
    Disabilities, 173
Children
    classification schemes of, 222-23
    communicative intentions and, 160,
        163-64, 168-69
    conceptualization disorders in,
        224-29
    conversational assertiveness in, 177
    conversational utterances to avoid
        using with, 94
    defining learning disability and,
        14-17
    egocentric nature of, 164, 168
    hostility of learning disabled, 176
    language development in, 8-9
    phonological disorders in, 47-53
    phonology in normal, 40-46
    pragmatic disorders in, 172-78
    preschool training and, 177
    reading and
        learning disabled, 249-52
        normal, 245-49
    receptive and expressive problems
        and, 18-19
    semantic disorders in, 92-95
    semantic research and, 85-92
    syntactic disorders in, 121-30
        processing and, 131-36
    syntax and, 113-16
    written language problems and,
        305-308
*Childs Spelling System,* 321
Chomsky, Carol, 30, 116
Chomsky, N., 61-62, 63, 117, 123,
    218, 298, 303

Choral speaking, 148-49
Clark, E. V., 87, 91, 170, 220
Clark, M., 66
Classification
  of communicative intentions, 160
  conceptualization
    remediation and, 237
    and tasks of, 224
  experiments (concepts), 225-26
  schemes of children, 222-23
  syntactic problems and, 115
  of word categories, 93
Clauses
  syntactic analysis and structure of,
    119-20, 125, 126-27, 129, 139
  written language and, 299
*Clinical Evaluation of Language
  Functions* (CELF, Semel & Wiig,
  1980), 139, 191, 230
Coalescence, 45
Coding procedures
  *Natural Process Analysis* and, 64
  pragmatic assessment and, 185,
    186-200
Coggins, T. E., 187
Cognitive processes
  child's word meanings and, 90
  language and, 218-19
  language development and, 6-7
  language learning model and, 12-13,
    17, 21
    revised, 25-26
  phonological development and, 39
  reading and, 264
  syntax remediation and, 147-48
  written language and, 300
Cohesion, 169
Collins, A., 90
*Columbia Mental Maturity Scale
  Burgemeister, Blum, & Lorge,
  1972), 230
Communication. *See also* Communicative intentions
  as function of language, 4-5
  interpersonal, 25

partner variable and, 169, 177, 192,
    204-205
  pragmatic disorder assessment and,
    186-200
  presupposition and, 162-64, 175-76,
    191-94
  reading and, 253
  referential, 175, 204
  semantic remediation and, 103, 104
  syntactic forms and, 132
  written language and, 307
Communication failure
  examples of, 162-63
  inadequate information exchange
    and, 4-5
  repair and, 177, 197-99
  topic maintenance and, 169
*Communicative Intention Inventory*
  (CII, Coggins & Carpenter, 1981),
  187
Communicative intentions. *See also*
  Communication
  defining, 158
  deictics and, 164-66
  direct and indirect reference and,
    166-72
  environment and, 171
  forms of, 161-62
  overview of, 159-60
  pragmatic disorders and, 173-74
    diagnosis of, 186-91
    presupposition and, 192
    remediation and, 201-206
  range of, 160-61
  rule generalization and, 182
  social conventions covering, 162-64
Comprehension, 12, 26, 132, 180, 182
  apraxia and auditory, 70
  children's word, 92, 93, 94, 108
  communicative intent and, 174
  deficit in listening, 259
  learning disability model and, 19
  morphology assessment and, 137-38
  pragmatic assessment and, 190
  problems of language, 1-3

reading, 254-56, 260, 275-79
  educators and, 243-44
  remediation and, 280-81, 282
  semantic assessment and reading,
    102
  syntactic, 138-39, 150
  syntactic structure and, 116, 125,
    133-34
  inflectional endings and, 131-32
  testing, 30
  of words, 255
Compton, A., 73
Conceptualization
  definition of concept and, 219-20
  diagnosis and, 229-35
  disorders in learning disabled
    children and, 224-29
  early word use and, 88-89, 90, 91
  hierarchy of experience and, 20
  learning disability model and, 21, 24
  learning process and, 23
  perception and, 22
  phonological disorders and, 55
  pragmatics and, 158-59
  problem solving and, 223-24, 238
  processing and
    disorders of, 227-29
    pragmatic disorders and, 182-83
  reading and, 264, 274
  remediation and, 235
    verbal and nonverbal disorders of,
      235-38
  semantic disorders and, 95-96
    assessment and, 96, 99
    remediation and, 105, 106, 107
  studying, 217-24
  syntax and, 134-35
  written language and, 307-308
Consonants
  apraxia remediation and, 76
  assimilation processes and, 44
Conversational control, 177
Conversational repairs, 170, 177,
  197-99
Conversational topics, pragmatic

assessment and, 195-97
Costello, J., 75
Crouse, M., 126
Cruickshank, W. M., 250
Crystal, D., 46, 47, 117, 118, 119-20,
  123, 124, 126-27, 136, 139, 143,
  144, 145, 146

**D**

Dale, P. S., 185
Darley, F., 59-60, 62, 69, 70, 77
Deafness, 27, 207
Decoding
  reading
    assessment and, 269-75, 276
    Goodman model and, 247, 255
    remediation and, 280-81
Definitional forms
  organization of, 94-95
  semantics and, 90-91
    assessment and, 98-99, 101
deHirsch, K., 307
Deictics, 164-66, 167, 176
Dejerine, Joseph Jules, 249
*Detroit Tests of Learning Aptitude*
  (DTLA, Baker & Leland, 1967),
  140, 311
*Developmental Sentence Scoring* (DSS,
  Lee, 1974), 142
*Developmental Sentence Types* (DST,
  Lee, 1966), 142
*Developmental Test of Visual-Motor
  Integration*, 302, 310
*Developmental Test of Visual Percep-
  tion* (Frostig, 1966), 310
*Development of Concepts Test* (Crager
  & Spriggs, 1972), 230
Dever, R. B., 145, 148-49, 150-51
deVilliers, J., 42
deVilliers, P., 42
Diagnosis
  apraxia, 69-71
  conceptual disorders, 235-38

learning disabilities model and, 28-31
phonemic production disorders, 61-69
pragmatic disorders, 184-200
reading problems and, 267-79
semantic disorders, 96-101
speech sound discrimination, 56-60
syntactic disorders, 119, 136-44
written language disorders, 304-305, 308-318
*Diagnostic Evaluation of Expository Paragraphs* (DEEP, Moran, 1981), 305
*Diagnostic Evaluation of Writing Skills* (DEWS, Weiner, 1980), 316, 317
Dialectal differences, 47
*Dictionary of Idioms* (Boatner & Gates, 1966), 97
Diederich, Paul, holistic scoring system of, 309
Discourse
　coding system and, 188
　competence in, 178
　defining social organization of, 158
　deictic forms and, 165
　direct and indirect referents and social organization of, 167-71
　pragmatic disorders and, 176-78
　　assessment of, 194-200
　　remediation and, 202
　symbolization and comprehension of, 180
　syntax comprehension and, 133-34
Discrimination. *See also* Speech sound discrimination
　apraxia remediation and speech sound, 76-78
　assessment of speech sound, 56-60
　pragmatics and auditory, 179-80
　problems, 2
　　speech sound, 48-49, 53-54
　reading and auditory verbal, 254
　syntax and auditory, 131-32
　therapy and speech sound, 71-72

Distar remedial program, 283
DiStefano, P., 322
Distinctive feature analysis
　articulation remediation and, 74-75
　phonological analysis and, 49, 61-62, 63, 73
Distortions, 61
Dittman, A. T., 169
Donahue, M., 169, 174, 175, 177, 185
Dore, J., 186-88
Dukes, P., 8
Dunn, C., 45
Dunst, C. A., 187
*Durrell Listening-Reading Series* (1970), 102
Dysarthria, 46, 51-52
Dysgraphia, 51, 305
Dyslexia, 127, 250, 254, 255, 256, 257 258, 259, 261-62, 264, 265, 304
Dysnomia, 135, 257-58
Dyspraxia, 70

**E**

Eaton, M. D., 251
Echolalia, 255
Education Testing Service, 309
Elbert, J. C., 263
Elbert, M., 50, 73
Elicitation procedures
　articulation testing and, 66-69
　pragmatic assessment and, 185
　syntactic assessment and, 142
　written language and, 317-18
Embedding, 285
　syntax and, 126, 132, 133
Endicott, A. L., 299-300, 301
Englemann, S., 251
Engler, L. F., 120
Engmann, D., 63, 74
Environment
　defining context of, 158
　defining learning disability and, 14
　impaired children and, 177

language learning model and, 11
language and social, 7
pragmatic disorders and, 178
   assessment of, 199
   instruction and, 202, 203
   referents and context of, 171-72
   semantic remediation and, 104
   syntactic remediation and, 149-50
Errors
   apraxia and auditory, 70-71
   articulation, 45, 49-50, 68, 70,
      74-75
   capitalization, 312
   children's word usage, 87, 89-90,
      93-94, 100, 101, 108
   phonemic problems and, 55
   phonological, 238
   process, 50, 61
   production, 53
   reading, 270, 271-73, 274
      substitution and, 254
   spelling, 304, 313
   spontaneous word usage, 98
   syntactic, 126-29
   written language assessment and,
      313
Ervin-Tripp, S., 161
Esposito, A., 157
Evaluation. *See* Diagnosis
Experience, hierarchy of, 19-21, 22
Expressive language, 32, 207, 253
   apraxia assessment and, 70
   comprehension problems and, 3
   conceptualization tasks and, 232,
      236
   development, 43
   disorders, 46, 47, 51
   learning disabilities as dysfunction
      in, 25
   learning disabled children, 18-19
   phonological problems and, 52-53
   reading and language disorders and,
      256-60
   reading problems and, 5
   semantic assessment and, 98-99

syntactic assessment and, 139-44
syntax and, 115-16, 122, 125, 126,
   135, 136
Eye movement, reading and, 245


# F

Facial expressions, 170, 180
Facilitation, 149
Fant, C., 41
*Federal Regulations,* learning
   disabilities definition in, 14
Feedback, 33, 157, 169, 172, 177,
   197, 276
Fernald, G. M., 250, 283, 321
Fey, M. E., 175, 178
Fillmore, C., 124, 165-66
Fischer, F., 54, 55, 263
Fisher, H., 63
*Fisher-Logemann Test of Articulation
   Competence* (1971), 63
*Fitzgerald Key* (1963), 151
Flavell, J., 163, 171, 183, 224
Fletcher, P., 119, 124, 143
Fodor, J., 224
*Fokes Sentence Builder* (1976), 151
Fowler, C., 54, 55
Franklin, E., 198
Freedman, P., 124
Fronting (word substitution process),
   43
Frostig, M., 250, 306
Fry, M. A., 259


# G

Gagné, R. M., 205
Galvin, J., 225
Garman, M., 119, 124, 143
Garvey, C., 169, 170, 190, 193, 194,
   195
*Gates-MacGinitie Reading Tests*
   (1972), 271

Geller, E. F., 172, 201
Geraud, V., 169, 193
Gerber, A., 17, 24, 32, 143, 147
Gesell, A., 302
Gessner, M., 157
Gestures
  communicative intentions and, 161,
    162
  defining terms and, 98
  deictics and, 166
  language disorders and, 178
  nonverbal communication and, 170
  pragmatic disorders and, 174
Getmen, G., 250, 306-307
Gibson, E., 55, 260, 261
Gillingham, A., 250, 283
*Gilmore Oral Reading Test* (1968),
  269, 270, 271
Gliding (word substitution process), 43
Glottal replacement, 45
*Goldman-Fristoe-Woodcock Test of
  Auditory Discrimination* (GFW), 59
Goldstein, H., 203
Goldstein, K., 225
Goodman, K. S., 253, 258, 263
  reading model of, 246, 247-48, 281
Goodman, Y. M., 272
Gottsleben, R., 145
Grammar, 255
  language and, 7
  oral, 300
  oral reading and, 258
  syntax and, 113, 146
    case, 118, 124
    comprehension of function of, 125
    formulation of, 135-36
    transformation, 117-18, 119,
      123-24, 125
  written language and, 299, 321
*Grammatic Closure Subtest (Illinois
  Test of Psycholinguistic Abilities*
  Kirk et al., 1968), 140
Granowsky, A., 300-301
Grapheme-phonemes relationships,
  301-302

Graphophonic decoding system, 247,
  248
Gray, R., 304
Greenfield, P., 187, 223
Griffith, P., 31
Griffiths, R., 302
Groshong, C. C., 255
*The Growth of Word Meaning* (Anglin),
  87

**H**

Halgren, M. R., 250
Hallahan, D., 53, 320
Halle, M., 41, 61-62, 63
Halliday, M. A. K., 160, 187, 188-89,
  193, 259
Hammill, D. D., 315-16
Handicapped individuals
  defining, 14
  language disorders and, 27
Handwriting, 307, 320
Hansen, C. L., 251, 270
Hansen, R., 69
Haring, H. G., 251
Harris, A., 270
Harris, G. P., 93, 223, 227, 233, 236,
  265
Hasan, R., 193, 259
Hayden, M., 49
Hearing impairment, 27, 207
Hickman, M., 167, 259
Hierarchy of experience, 19-21, 22
Hinshelwood, J., 249
*Hinsky-Nebraska Test of Learning
  Aptitude* (1966), 230, 311
Holistic scoring, 309-310, 315
Holland, A., 103-104
Homonymy, 65, 76
Hook, P., 22, 57, 261-62, 263-64
Hoskins, Barbara B., 221, 237
Hresko, W. P., 238
Humphreys, J., 75
Hunt, K. W., 299-300
Hyperlexics, 254-55

**I**

Ideation, 314
*Illinois Test of Psycholinguistic Abili-
ties* (Kirk et al., 1968), 263, 311
  *Auditory Association Subtest* of, 101
  *Grammatic Closure Subtest* of, 140
Immediate Constituent Analysis,
  118-21
Infants, 168, 222
  communicative intentions of,
  159-60, 187
*Infant Scale of Communicative Intent*
  (Sacks & Young, 1980), 190
Inference, 182
Inflection
  morphological, 114, 125
  syntax and, 131-32
Information processing
  communicative intent and, 182
  learning disability models and, 18,
  19
  semantic
    assessment and, 102
    disorders and, 95
Information sharing, 163
Information theory, 16, 17
Informativeness (communicative
  context), 191-92
Ingram, D., 42-44, 50, 64-65, 73,
  75-76, 119, 123, 124
Input stimuli, 56-57
Instruction. *See* Teaching strategies
Intelligibility assessment, 66
Intervention. *See* Remediation
Intonation, reading and, 261-62
*Iowa Tests of Basic Skills*
  (Hieronymous & Lindquist, 1971),
  313

**J**

Jakobson, R., 41, 76
Jarrico, S., 304, 305

Johnson, C. S., 259
Johnson, D. J., 18, 19, 20, 21, 22, 25,
  46, 57, 69, 102, 107, 131, 132, 134,
  136, 138, 151, 178, 233, 252, 253,
  254, 264, 270, 273, 280, 283, 285,
  301, 304
Johnson-Laird, P., 222, 228
Johnson, Wendell, 225
Johnston, J. R., 126
Juskowitz, S., 203

**K**

Kagan, J. A., 316
Kahmi, A., 126
Kaluger, G., 283
Kane, E. R., 250
Karpova, S. N., 263
Kavale, K., 53
Keenan, E. O., 168, 169, 194
Kephart, N. C., 250, 306-307
Khan, L. M., 44
Kneedler, R., 53
Koeningsknecht, R., 148, 150
Kohlberg, L., 303
Kolsen, C., 283
Kosiewicz, M. A., 320
Koury-Parker, D. I., 54
Krieger, V., 270
Kwiatkowski, J., 68

**L**

LaBerge, D., reading model of, 246,
  248-49, 258
LaBrant, L., 298-99, 300
Lahey, M., 9, 104, 142, 200-201, 202
Lakoff, G., 88, 219-20
Language. *See also* Expressive
  language; Language learning
  disabilities; Oral language;
  Receptive language; Written
  language

articulation therapy and, 72
assessment of abstract, 97
cognition and, 218-19, 229
concepts of natural, 221
conceptualization and, 217-21
defined, 6-8
development, 218
of normal, 6-10
developmental approach to, 301-303
disorders, 46-47
early use of, 188
language pathology approach to, 298
learning, 200
model of, 11-13
psycholinguistic approach to,
298-301
remedial planning and, 33
semantic remediation and relevant,
104
social use of, 182
spontaneous, 98, 136
pragmatic disorder remediation
and, 204
syntax
and pragmatic features of, 133-34
remediation and, 146
sample collection and, 141-42,
146
Language acquisition, 303
*Language Acquisition Device* (LAD,
McNeill, 1970), 218
*Language Assessment, Remediation,
and Screening Procedure* (LARSP)
Crystal et al., 1976), 119-20, 139,
143, 145
Language comprehension. *See*
Comprehension
Language delay, 47, 174
Language deviance, 47
Language learning disabilities
analysis of, 1-6
clinical, 28
conceptualization disorders and,
224-29
conversational utterances to be

avoided and, 94
defining, 13-17
diagnostic implications and, 28-31
models of, 17-24
revised, 25-28
normal language development and,
6-10
pathology, 10-13
phonology and, 47-55
pragmatic disorders and, 172-78
reading and, 249-52, 264-66
remedial implications and, 31-35
semantics and, 92-95
syntactic disorders and, 121-30
written language and, 297-308
Language performance, 26-27
Language processing. *See* Processing
Larsen, S., 304, 315-16
Lavatelli, C., 224, 231
Learning
conceptualizing, 23
perceptual, 248-49
syntax remediation and areas of,
146-47
verbal and nonverbal, 18, 19
Learning disability
conceptualization and, 224-29
conversational utterances to be
avoided and, 94
language
analysis of, 1-6
clinical, 28
defining, 13-17
diagnostic implications and, 28-31
models of, 17-24
revised, 25-28
normal language and, 6-10
pathology, 10-13
remedial implications and, 31-35
phonology and, 47-53
processing disorders and, 53-55
pragmatic disorders and, 172-78
preschool training and, 177
reading and, 249-52, 264-66
semantics and, 92-95

sex differences and, 175-76
syntactic disorders and, 113-36
written language and, 297-308
Lee, L., 148, 150, 151, 298
LeFevre, C. A., 261
Lehtinen, L., 226, 250, 264, 265
*Leiter International Performance Scale*
(1969), 230
Lemme, M., 69
Leonard, L., 119, 123, 124, 126, 143,
175, 178
Levin, H., 55, 260
Lexicon
acquisition, 87
conceptualization and, 222
semantic
assessment and, 97-98
remediation and core, 103-105,
109
syntactic problems and, 119
Liberman, I., 54, 55, 261-62, 263
Lindsay, P., 90
Linguistic approach to articulation
problems, 72-73
Linguistic deficiencies, 253
Linguistic knowledge, 7
Linguistic rule systems, 12
Literacy, 243-44, 279
Litowitz, B., 90-91, 220, 223, 233,
297, 302, 317
Lloyd, J., 320
Lloyd-Jones, R., 312
Lock, J., 57
Logemann, J., 63
Longhurst, T., 119, 143
Loparte, P., 302
Lorentz, J., 72
Lovitt, T. C., 251, 270
Lubert, N., 48
Lucas, E. V., 202, 203
Lynch, J., 11, 13, 24, 25

**M**

McCarthy, D., 86, 116, 303
McCaughran, L. S., 225

McDonald, E., 68
McKee, G. W., 250
McNeill, D., 218, 303
McReynolds, L., 50, 63, 73, 74
Mark, L., 54
Marzano, R., 322
Mathematics, 96, 102-103
Matthews, D. A., 48
Mattingly, I. G., 253
Meckel, H. C., 303
Mehan, H., 192
Mehrabian, A., 181
Mehring, T., 304
Melody recognition, 261
Memory
attention disorders and, 53
conceptualization disorders and,
227, 228
remediation and, 237
language development and, 9
learning disability model and, 20
phonological disorders and, 54
pragmatic disorders and, 180
reading and, 252, 260, 267, 273, 282
auditory, 259-60
remediation and, 33
semantics and, 90
assessment and, 102
disorders and, 95, 107
sequential problems and, 257
syntactic problems and, 132, 135
tests and problems with, 30
written language and visual, 307,
311-12
Menn, L., 44
Menyuk, P., 44, 119, 123, 308
Metalinguistic skills, 190
learning disability model and, 21-22
phonological disorders and, 55
reading and, 260-64
speech sound assessment and, 58, 60
Metapragmatic abilities, 182-83
Metathesis, 45
Miller, G., 224
Miller, J., 124, 141, 142, 143, 144,
145

Miller, R., 222, 228
*The Miller-Yoder (M-Y) Test of
  Grammatical Comprehension*
  (1975), 122, 137
Models
  articulation disorder, 41-42
  of conceptualization, 221-22
  language learning four-dimensional,
    11-13
  of learning disabilities, 17-24
    diagnosis and, 28-31
    remediation and, 31-35
    revision of, 24-28
  of normal language development,
    9-10, 131
  phonological development, 42-43
  reading, 246-49, 255, 281
  semantic, 90
  of semantic-conceptual development,
    221-23
  speech and language pathology, 46
  written language, 303
Moran
  writing samples and, 304
  writing task of, 305
Morehead, D., 119, 123, 124
Morphology, 68-69, 132, 238
  conceptualization and, 134
  defined, 114
  problems with, 136
  reading and, 255
  syntactic assessment and, 136-38,
    139-44
*Motor-Free Visual Perception Test*
  (Calarusso & Hammill, 1972), 311
Motor skills, written language and,
  306, 310-11
Muehl, S., 259
Mueller, E., 169, 195
Mulhern, S., 148, 150
Mullis, I., 309, 315
Muma, J. R., 149, 150
MWM remedial program, 283
Myerson, R., 225
Myklebust, Helmer R., 16, 18, 19, 20,
  21, 22, 46, 69, 102, 107, 131,
  132, 134, 136, 138, 178, 233,
  252, 253, 254, 264, 265, 270,
  273, 280, 283, 285, 301, 304,
  306, 308, 310, 312, 314-15, 316,
  317, 323

**N**

Nahmias, M. L. V., 276
*Natural Process Analysis* (NPA,
  Shriberg & Kwiatkowski, 1980),
  63, 64
Nelson, K., 88, 91, 106, 221
Newman, D., 236
Noel, M. M., 175
Norlin, P. A., 90
Norman, D., 90
*The Northwestern Syntax Screening
  Test* (NSST, Rev. ed., Lee, 1971),
  122, 137, 139
Nouns, learning common, 89
Novy, F., 227, 236

**O**

O'Donnell, L., 142
Omissions, 61
Onstine, J., 75
Oral language, 115. *See also*
  Language; Speech
  assessment of, 268
  language performance and, 26-27
  problems with, 4
  reading and, 5, 253-60, 278, 279
  semantic assessment and, 102
  written language and, 297-98,
    301-302, 308, 318, 322
Organization
  of definitions and explanations,
    94-95
  semantic
    assessment and, 99, 102
    disorders and, 95
  written language assessment and,
    314

Orton, Samuel T., 16, 250
Otitis media, 57

**P**

Panagos, J., 31
Parsons, C., 75
Parts of speech
  syntax and, 116-17, 122
  assessment of, 142
*Paul Diederich System* (holistic
  scoring), 309
*Peabody Individual Achievement Test*
  (Dunn & Markwardt, 1970), 271,
  312
*Peabody Picture Vocabulary Test*
  (Dunn, 1965), 97, 99, 100, 173
Pearl, R., 174, 177, 185
Perception
  articulation and, 48-49, 53-54
  articulation therapy and speech
    sound, 71-72
  conceptualization and, 22
    disorders and, 228, 235
  early word use and, 87-88
  language development and, 9
  learning disability model and, 20
  phonetic and phonemic assessment
    and, 56
  pragmatic disorders and, 179-80
  problems of social, 181
  reading and, 273, 282
  speech, 40-41
  of words, 246
  written language
    and motor, 306-307
    and visual, 302, 310-11
Perfetti, C. A., 270
Performance approach (syntax),
  115-16
Perozzi, J., 143
Pflaum, S., 175
Phonemes
  acoustic speech signals and, 40-41

apraxic assessment and errors of, 70
articulation
  assessment and, 68-69
  disorders and, 50
  remediation and, 72
  distinctive features analysis and, 74
  features of, 61-62
  graphemes and, 301-302
  reading and, 262
  speech sound production and, 41-42
  vowel shifts and, 42
Phonemic production disorders
  analysis of, 49-51
  diagnosis, 61-69
  remediation, 71-76
Phonology
  apraxia and, 51-52
  classifying disorders of, 46-47
  defined, 39
  diagnosis and, 56-71
  dysarthria and, 51-52
  goals in analysis of, 64-66
  learning disabled children and,
    47-53
  misarticulation and, 52-53
  in normal children, 40-45
  phonemic production disorders and,
    49-51
  processing disorders and, 53-55
  reading and, 262-63
  remediation and, 71-78
  review of basic terms and, 39-40
  speech sound discrimination
    problems and, 48-49
Phrase structure, syntax and, 126, 128
Piaget, J., 168, 218, 219, 222, 231,
  303
Pictures
  articulation therapy and nonsense, 75
  elicitation techniques and, 66-67
  identification task and, 56-57, 62
  morphological assessment and,
    137-38
  picture-object tests (concept
    formation) and, 226

reading tests and, 271
semantic
    assessment test and, 96-97, 99-100
    remediation and, 106, 107-108
*Picture Story Language Test* (PSLT,
    Myklebust, 1973), 304, 305, 312,
    314-15, 316
Pierce, D., 149
Piercy, M., 54
Play
    pragmatic assessment and, 186
    semantic remediation and, 106
Podhajski, B. R., 259
Poplin, M. S., 304, 305
Poteet, J. A., 304, 305
Pragmatics, 8
    conceptual framework for, 158-72
    defining, 158
    diagnosis of disorders in, 184-200
    disorders in learning disabled
        children and, 172-78
    processing and disorders in, 178-83
    reading and, 278
    remediation and, 200-207
    rules of, 183-84
    written language and, 317
*Preschool Language Assessment
    Instrument* (Blank, Rose, &
    Berlin, 1978a, 1978b), 198-99
Presupposition (communicative
    context)
    communicative intentions and,
        163-64
    defined, 158
    development of, 163
    pragmatic disorders and, 175-76
        assessment and, 191-94
        remediation and, 201
*Primary Mental Abilities Test* (PMA,
    Thurstone, 1963), 311
Problem solving, 22, 33, 177, 252
    conceptualization and, 223-24, 238
*Procedures for the Phonological
    Analysis of Children's Language*
    (Ingram, 1981), 63

Process
    adult word simplification and, 42
    articulation therapy and
        phonological, 75-76
    decoding (reading), 273-74
    Ingram's model of, 42-43
    language comprehension and, 12
    learning problems and, 23-24
Processing
    conceptualization disorders and,
        227-29
    deficits in, 14-17
        written language and, 305-308
    deviant phonological development
        and analysis of, 50
    hierarchy of experience and, 19-21,
        22
    information, 18, 19
    interpersonal communication and, 25
    modality, 23
    phonology and disorders of, 53-55
    pragmatic disorders and, 178-83
    reading disability and, 251, 252-67,
        280
    semantic disorders and, 95-96
    syntactic disorders and, 131-36, 147
*Producing Formulated Sentences
    Subtest (Carrow Elicited Language
    Inventory* CELI, 1974), 141
Pronunciation problems, 52
Pronunciation, written language
    and, 313, 321-22
Prosody, apraxia and deviant, 70
Prutting, C., 143, 203
Psychological processes
    language disorders and, 10-11
    language rules and, 25
    learning disabilities models and, 17
    reading and, 244
        remediation and, 280

**Q**

Quillian, M. R., 90

# R

Ratzebury, F. H., 250
Raven, J. C., 230
Reading
   auditory perception deficit and, 54
   curriculum, 245, 246, 252
   diagnosis and, 267-79
   language comprehension problems
      and, 2-3
   language disabilities and, 27
   learning disabled children and,
      249-52
   metalinguistic awareness and,
      260-64
   in normal children, 245-49
   oral language and, 5
   processing deficits and, 252-67
   remediation and, 279-83
   semantic disorders and, 96
      assessment and, 102
   syntactic errors and, 127
   visual memory problem and, 312
*Reading Miscue Inventory* (Goodman &
   Burke, 1971), 272
Receptive language, 32. 207, 253, 256
   apraxia assessment and, 70
   conceptualization tasks and, 232,
      235-36
   disorders, 46
   learning disabilities as dysfunction
      in, 25
   learning disabled children and, 18-19
   phonological problems and, 52
   reading problems and, 5
   semantic assessment and, 97-98
   syntactic assessment and, 136-39
   syntax and, 115-16, 122, 125, 135
Redundancy, 181
Rees, N., 8
Referential communication, 175, 204
Referents
   direct and indirect, 166-72
   linguistic, 218

   social situation variables and,
      192-94
Reid, D. K., 238
Reitan, R., 226
Remediation
   auditory (speech sound), 54
   conceptualization disorders and,
      235-38
   content planning and, 8
   elicitation techniques and, 67-68
   language deviance and delay and, 47
   language theory and, 31-32
   learning disability models and, 31-35
   phonemic disorders and, 71-78
   pragmatic disorders and, 200-207
   semantic disorders and, 102,
      103-108
   syntactic disorders and, 119, 120,
      127, 144-51
   reading, 251, 253, 256, 279-86
   written language disorders and,
      318-23
Research
   conceptualization, 219-21
   language, 157
   pragmatic disorder, 172-78, 184
   reading, 244, 245-46, 249-51, 255
   semantics, 86-92, 109
   syntactic, 113-21, 124-25
   written language, 297-303, 304, 306
Retardation, 27
   defining, 14
Retrieval
   reading and word, 257-58
   semantic assessment and, 98, 107
   syntactic problems and, 135
   tests and problems with, 30
Rice, M., 218, 222
Riegel, K. F., 90
Role-taking
   assessing ability for, 194
   communicative intentions and, 163
   pragmatic disorder remediation and,
      204
   presupposition and, 175

social variables and, 176
Rommetveit, R., 162
Rosch, E., 88, 89, 91, 106, 220, 221, 237
Rosenbek, J., 69
Roth, F. P., 190
Roth, S. F., 270
Ruder, K., 73, 76
Rule generalization, 33
  communication and, 182
  learning disability model and, 21
  memory and, 180
  syntax and, 134
Rule induction vs. rule deduction (pragmatic disorder remediation), 205-206
Rule learning
  language development and, 9
  language disability model and, 21
  syntax and, 114-15, 147
Rule systems
  language and, 9
  language learning model and, 12, 25
  phonology, 45, 63
Rummelhart, D., 90

**S**

Sadler, R., 177, 194, 195-96
Salvia, J., 270
Samuels, I. J., reading model of, 246, 248-49, 258, 281
Scheffelin, M., 20, 319
Schieffelin, B. B., 168, 169
Schlesinger, I., 124, 219
Schrandt, T., 119, 143
Selective commentary (syntax), 117, 123
*Semantic Feature Hypothesis* (Clark), 87
Semantics
  communication and, 178
  conceptualization and, 221-23, 229

defined, 85-86
diagnosis and
  areas to assess and, 97-99
  assessment battery rationale and, 96-97
  other areas of learning and, 102-103
  testing procedures and, 99-101
processing and disorders of, 95-96
reading and, 247, 278, 283
remediation and, 103-108
semantic disorders in children and, 92-95
study conclusions and, 108-109
studying, 86-92
syntactic problems and, 119
syntax and, 133, 134, 146
Semel, E., 12, 18, 24, 48, 99, 101, 113, 122, 125, 126, 133, 186
Sensory system, 19
Sentences, 255
  auditory discrimination assessment and, 58
  auditory language comprehension and reading and, 256
  communication failure and, 4-5
  reading model and, 247
  syntactic problems and, 120-21, 126, 128, 134, 138, 140, 141-42
  syntax and length of, 117, 122, 142
  word meanings and problems with, 3-4
  written language and, 303
Sequencing, 99, 176, 197, 257
Sex differences (learning disability), 175-76
Seymour, C. M., 48
Shankweiler, D., 54, 55, 263
Shatz, M., 174, 190
Shriberg, L., 68
Shulman, M., 174
Signing, 207
Silverman, R., 318, 322
Simon, C. S., 202

Sinclair-de-Zwart, H., 218
Singh, S., 49, 50
Sipay, E., 270
*Slingerland Screening Tests for Identifying Children with Specific Language Disability* (1970), 52
Smith, J., 187
Snyder, L. S., 163-64, 174, 175, 185
Social situations
  communicative intentions and, 162-64
  comprehension of word meanings and, 94
  language disabilities and, 6
  language learning model and, 11
  pragmatic disorder assessment and, 192-200
  pragmatic disorders and discourse and, 176-78
  referents and discourse and, 167-71
*Sound Discrimination Test* (Templin), 59
Spache, G. D., 270
Spalding, R. B., 283
Spalding, W. T., 283
Speech. *See also* Oral language
  apraxia and connected, 70
  disorders, 46-47
  language pathology and, 27
  language performance and, 26-27
  pathology, 10-13
  perceiving, 56
  socialized vs. nonsocialized, 194-95
  subtle problems with, 52-53
  symbolic nature of, 47
Speech acts, 159
  primitive, 188
Speech sound discrimination. *See also* Discrimination
  apraxia remediation and, 76-78
  assessment of, 56-60
  problems with, 48-49, 53-54
  syntactic problems and, 131-32
  therapy and, 71-72
Speech sounds
  language and, 7

phonology and production of, 41-46
remediation (apraxia) and, 76-78
therapy and perception of, 71-72
Spekman, N. J., 31, 146, 165, 171, 175, 176, 177, 178, 190, 193
Spelling, 27
  written language and, 302, 304, 307, 311, 314
  assessment and, 312
  remediation and, 321
Stampe, D., 42
*Standardized Progressive Matrices* (Raven, 1965), 230
*Stanford Achievement Test* (Kelley et al., 1964), 313
*Stanford-Binet Intelligence Test*, 229
Stark, J., 9
Stauffer, R. G., 264
Stillman, B., 250, 283
Stimulability assessment, 66
Stone, A. C., 259, 265
Stopping (word substitution process), 43
Strategy use in conceptualization, 223-24
  deficits, 226-27
Strauss, A., 16, 226, 250, 264, 265
Strephosymbolia, 250
Structural analysis (syntax), 118-21, 124-30, 142-45
Sturm, C., 177, 185
Subordination index, 299, 300
Substitution
  dysnomia and, 257-58
  phonological analysis and, 65-66
  process of word, 43-45
  reading and, 254
  of speech sounds, 41, 61
Suhor, Charles, 309
Syllables
  apraxia remediation and nonsense, 77
  articulation errors and, 71
  phonological analysis and, 44-45
  speech sound therapy and, 77

Symbolization
  conceptualization and, 237
  learning disability model and, 20
  phonological disorders and, 54-55
  pragmatic disorders and, 180-82
  reading and, 253, 273
  syntactic problems and, 132-34
  written language and, 297, 307,
    308
Symbols
  deictics and, 166
  processing and, 228
  reading
    and verbal, 254
    and visual, 252
  speech and, 47
  use of, 223-24
Syntactic usage, deviant patterns of,
  120-21
Syntax
  communication and, 178
  communicative intentions and, 161
  defined, 114-15
  diagnosis
    expressive morphology measures
      and, 139-44
    receptive morphology measures
      and, 136-38
    receptive syntax measures and,
      138-39
  investigating disorders of, 32
  learning disabled children and
    disorders of, 121-30
  learning problems and oral, 5-6
  modifying, 175
  processing and disorders of, 131-36
  reading and, 247-48, 255, 258-59,
    263-64, 278, 283
  remediation and, 144-51
  studying, 113-21
  written language and, 299-300
    assessment and, 313, 314
    remediation and, 321
*Syntax One* (Ausberger, 1976), 145
*Syntax Two* (Ausberger, 1976), 145

**T**

Talking and turn-taking, 195
Tallal, P., 54
Tannhauser, M., 250
Teaching strategies. *See also*
  Remediation
  phonemic disorders (apraxia) and,
    77-78
  pragmatic disorders and, 202-207
  reading, 245, 252
  semantic disorders and, 103-108
  syntactic disorders and, 148-51
  written language, 318, 319, 320-23
*The Templin-Darley Tests of
  Articulation* (1969), 67
Terminal units, 299, 300, 322
*Test of Adolescent Language* (TOAL,
  Hammill et al., 1980), 230
*Test for Auditory Comprehension of
  Language* (TACL, Carrow, 1973),
  137, 139
*Test of Language Development*
  (TOLD, Newcomer & Hammill,
  1977), 139, 316
Tests
  analysis of uses of, 29-31
  apraxia and, 69-71
  conceptualization disorders and,
    229-31, 235
  conceptualization tasks as, 231-35
  intelligence, 229-30
  phonemic production, 61-69
  pragmatic disorder, 187, 190, 191,
    194-99
  reading, 265, 269, 270-71, 275,
    276-77
  semantic disorder assessment,
    96-101, 108
  speech sound discrimination, 56-60
  syntactic disorders and, 137-44
  written language, 309-318, 319
*Test of Syntactic Abilities* (*TSA Syntax
  Program*, Quigley & Power,
  1979), 145
*Test of Written Language* (TOWL,

Hammill & Larsen, 1978), 304, 312, 314, 315-16, 317
Theory
  articulation therapy and, 72-73
  phonological, 41-43
  reading and neurological, 250
  remediation and language, 31-32
  speech act, 159
Therapy. *See* Remediation
Thinking problems, 2
  reading and, 264-66
  tests and, 277
Toombs, M., 49
Topics of conversation, 195-97
Torgesen, J. K., 54, 183, 251
*TSA Syntax Program*, 145
T-units, 299, 300, 322
Turn-taking (talking), 195
Turton, L., 66
Tyack, D., 145

U

Umen, I., 203
Underachievers, 14, 15
*A University Grammar of Contemporary English* (Quick et al., 1973), 120

V

Vallecorsa, A., 318
Van Riper, C., 71
Venezky, R., 253
Vernon, M. D., 264, 265
Videotaping, 185, 186
Visual-auditory interaction, 307-308
Visual processing, 306-307
Visual skills, 283
Vocabulary
  auditory discrimination problems and, 58
  conceptualization and, 229

language
  assessment and, 96, 97, 99, 100
  disordered individuals and, 93
  remediation and, 103, 105
  reading assessment and, 277, 279
  receptive deficiency in, 255
  semantics and, 86
  written language scores and, 305
Vocabulary Subtest (*Wechsler Intelligence Scale for Children—Revised* WISC-R, 1974), 101
Vocalization, 43, 188
Vogel, S., 122, 261, 263-64
Voicing (assimilation process), 44
Volitional control, apraxia therapy and, 76, 78
Vowels
  apraxia remediation and, 76
  assimilation processes and, 44
  neutralization of, 44
  shifts in, 42
Vygotsky, L., 219, 220, 297, 317

W

Watson, L. R., 177
*Wechsler Intelligence Scale for Children—Revised* (WISC-R, 1974), 101, 229, 233
*Wechsler Preschool and Primary Scale of Intelligence* (WPPSI, 1967), 229, 233
Weiner, E., 316, 318
Weiner, F., 73, 75
Weir, R., 141
Weiss, C., 56, 62, 66
*Weiss Comprehensive Articulation Test* (1978), 66
Wepman, J. M., 116, 262
Werner, H., 16, 226
Wertz, R., 69
Whiting, S. A., 304, 305
Whorf, B., 219
*Wide Range Achievement Test* (Jastak

& Jastak, revised, 1978), 269, 270, 271, 312
Wiig, E., 12, 18, 24, 48, 99, 101, 113, 122, 125, 126, 133, 186
Wilcox, K. A., 175, 178
Wing, C., 12
Winitz, H., 49, 73
Wollner, S. G., 172, 201
*Woodcock-Johnson Psycho Educational Battery*, 173
*Woodcock Reading Mastery Test* (1973), 271
Word associations, 220, 232
Word blindness, 249-50
Words
  comprehension
    of meaning of, 2, 3
    of single, 255
  conceptualization
    and categories of, 237
    and defining, 220
  definition of language and, 6
  differences between, 56
  "frozen forms" of, 45
  homonymy and, 65, 76
  metalinguistic ability and, 55, 58
  nonsense, 57, 59, 75, 114
  phonological testing and, 56, 57, 58, 59
  pronouncing polysyllabic, 52
  reading models and, 249
  reading and retrieval of, 257-58
  recognition of tachistoscopic, 245
  semantic disorders and, 92-95, 96
  semantics
    and meaning of, 85-92, 99, 101
    remediation and, 103-108
  sentence construction and, 3-4
  simplification of adult, 42
  speech sound therapy and, 77
  syntax and structure of, 120, 121, 125, 128
    abstract, 132-33

substitution process (Ingram) and, 43-45
substitution of speech sounds and, 41
teaching reading and, 245, 246
visual processing and, 266
word-finding difficulties and, 257
*The Word Test* (Jorgensen et al., 1981), 230
Wren, C. T., 32, 122, 124, 126, 127, 132, 136, 142
Writing. *See* Written language
Written language, 249, 262
  defined, 297
  diagnosis and, 308-18
  dysgraphia and, 51
  language performance and, 26-27
  learning problems and, 5-6, 297-308
  mechanical aspects of, 312-14
  perception and, 53
  processing deficits and disorders of, 305-308
  remediation and, 318-23
  semantic
    assessment and, 102
    disorders and, 96
  studying, 297-303
*Wug Test* (in Bergo, 1958), 126, 140

**Y**

Yoder, D., 145
Yoss, K., 69, 70, 77
Ysseldyke, J. E., 270

**Z**

Zigmond, N., 318
Zimmerman, J., 318
Zuriff, E., 225

## Author

**Carol T. Wren** is Assistant Professor in the Program in Reading and Learning Disabilities at DePaul University, Chicago.

## Contributors

**Gail P. Harris-Schmidt** is Assistant Professor in the Program in Learning Disabilities at St. Xavier College, Chicago.

**Elizabeth A. Noell** is Learning Disabilities Specialist at Boys Town Institute, Omaha.

**Barbara B. Hoskins** is Coordinator of Language Programs at Almansor Education Center, Alhambra, California, and Instructor in Special Education at Whittier College in Whittier, California.

**Nancy J. Spekman** is Assistant Professor in Special Education at the University of Maryland.

**Suzanne Timble Major** is a practicing attorney and formerly was Associate Professor in Reading and Learning Disabilities at DePaul University.

All of the authors received their doctorates in Learning Disabilities from Northwestern University.